WHY HUMANAE VITAE WAS RIGHT:
A READER

Why Humanae Vitae Was Right:
A Reader

Edited by
Janet E. Smith

Foreword by John Cardinal O'Connor

IGNATIUS PRESS   SAN FRANCISCO

Cover by Riz Boncan Marsella

ISBN 0-89870-433-2
Library of Congress catalogue number 93-77449
Printed in the United States of America

CONTENTS

FOREWORD

If Janet E. Smith continues thinking and writing in accordance with her current standards and competency, the Church in the United States is going to be very deeply in her debt. Her editing of, introduction to and essays in *Why Humanae Vitae Was Right: A Reader* strongly suggests that she *will* continue such thinking and writing.

Indeed, her earlier work, *Humanae Vitae: A Generation Later,* has already put the Church in her debt, with its masterful elucidation of and support for magisterial teaching. Now she goes beyond. Her latest work does many things well, at least two things extraordinarily well.

First, no honest, open reader of Janet E. Smith's work can fail to see the beneficial effects for all humanity in accepting *Humanae Vitae,* first published in 1968, misunderstood, spurned, ridiculed by so many. Nor can an honest, open reader fail to see the tragic consequences of the rejection of this encyclical.

Secondly, the *Reader* explores the anthropology that informs *Humanae Vitae,* doing precisely what Pope John Paul II has urged theologians to do: to illuminate more clearly "the biblical foundations, the ethical grounds and the personalistic reasons" behind the doctrine of the encyclical.

I am personally grateful for Janet E. Smith. *Why Humanae Vitae Was Right: A Reader,* does more than answer superficial arguments against the encyclical; it provides superlative affirmation of an encyclical too long treated childishly and a challenge to the very best of theologians to press on with what our Holy Father has invited them to do.

+ John Cardinal O'Connor
Archdiocese of New York

INTRODUCTION

In the sixties, most were terrified at what might be the devastations and fallout of a nuclear holocaust. Few realized that the pill, a key element of the sexual revolution, would have detonated another kind of holocaust, the sexual holocaust. One of the prophecies made in *Humanae Vitae* was that the widespread use of contraception would lead to a "general decline in morality". Who can deny that such has happened, especially in the sexual realm? Premarital sex is now the norm, pregnancy outside of marriage is at epidemic proportions, in some cities the number of abortions is higher than the number of births, divorce is a common experience, pornography is not isolated to seedy parts of the city but has entered our living rooms through prime-time television, the lyrics of many rock songs would constitute actionable sexual harassment if uttered in the workplace, and AIDS and other sexual diseases are rampant. The fallout of the sexual holocaust is pervasive; society houses an incalculable number of the walking wounded who suffer the psychological and spiritual aftereffects and bear the scars of sexual irresponsibility. That their wounds are invisible perhaps makes them all the worse.

The futuristic science fiction novel the *Canticle of Leibowitz* described a post–nuclear holocaust age in which a small band of monks attempted to preserve the wisdom that had been lost with the conflagrations of the atom bomb and to recover such inventions as electricity. The Church is in a somewhat similar position, as she attempts to preserve the wisdom of the ages about what constitutes sexual morality and tries to recover what makes for wholesome family life. We have exploded ourselves back into or even beyond the Stone Age (one suspects those in the Stone Age were not as perverse in their sexual behavior as people in our age) in respect to our understanding of human sexuality. Nearly the sole voice crying out in this wilderness has been the Catholic Church.

The Magisterium of the Church, in opposition to the secular realm and to the widespread dissent among her own theologians, has not ceased to proclaim that contraception is a moral evil. While this teaching has seemed to most a sure sign that the Church refuses to enter the modern age, many are beginning to suspect that there is at least some wisdom in the Church's teaching. *Humanae Vitae* may have been the most countercultural document ever written. It was not well received at the time it was issued, and it has been largely neglected since. Few then, and few now, are capable of seeing that the view of man, sexuality, and marriage that leads to the use of the pill is not one that is compatible with human dignity, sexual responsibility, and spousal love. Nevertheless, some individuals have been gifted with such insight; they have answered the plea of Pope Paul VI and Pope John Paul II to probe more deeply the anthropology that informs the Church's teaching. Indeed, some of the authors in this volume anticipated the teachings of *Humanae Vitae*.

This collection of essays on *Humanae Vitae* attempts to bring together some of the best explanations and defenses of the Church's teaching. Few are aware that there have been energetic and worthy defenses of this teaching. This is not surprising, since they tend to appear in journals and publications that are not widely available. The general reader should find much here to stimulate his thinking on this issue; the student may find a good beginning to research here and some roadmaps to further research. Yet, some of the essays were chosen in spite of the fact that they may be somewhat inaccessible to the general reader; I wanted to include some essays that were in out-of-the-way places but that would be useful to ethicists and moral theologians interested in this issue as well as more popular articles that should be of interest and accessible to all.

Each essay is preceded by a brief introduction of the author and his or her essay; each is followed by references to suggested further reading. Where appropriate, I have also included references to portions of my book *Humanae Vitae: A Generation Later* (Washington, D.C.: The Catholic University of America Press, 1991), in which I treat the topics in each essay. Further bibliographical assistance can be found in the footnotes and bibliography of that book.

PART ONE

Essays Prior to Humanae Vitae and Early Defenses

I

CONTRACEPTION AND CONJUGAL LOVE

by
Paul M. Quay, S.J.

Father Quay's essay is all the more remarkable for having been published some seven years before *Humanae Vitae* was issued. In some ways it surpasses even the arguments of *Humanae Vitae* in its defense of the Church's teaching, in its shift from talk of natural-law principles to its concern with the meaning of conjugal love. It is prescient for its use of concepts and terms that have been incorporated into the defense of *Humanae Vitae* by John Paul II. Quay speaks of sexual intercourse being like a language and thus as having a meaning that must be respected. When he speaks of this symbolic meaning being one of total self-giving of the partners to one another, he anticipates the line of argument developed by John Paul II by some twenty years. Indeed, he even calls the contraceptive act of sexual intercourse a "lie", a description that entered the Church's discourse only with *Familiaris Consortio,* though it appeared in Karol Wojtyla's *Love and Responsibility* before that. Quay is particularly lucid on the meaning of the language of sexual intercourse as he shows how the procreative meaning is a "transcendental meaning" that assists spouses to some extent in overcoming their inescapable existential loneliness. After he completes his more philosophical explanation of the evil of contraception, he relates this evil to other forms of malice against God.

17

Before he develops his innovative description of the meaning of sexual intercourse, Quay skillfully identifies many of the inadequacies of earlier formulations of natural-law arguments against contraception. Dissenters from *Humanae Vitae* typically accuse the Church of "physicalism", that is, of putting too much weight on the physical or animal purpose of sexual intercourse, that of propagating the species, and of neglecting the more specifically human purpose of spousal intimacy. Quay grants that some early defenses were guilty of such misrepresentation of the human act of sexual intercourse. He seeks to render more explicit the elements of natural-law reasoning that require taking into account the distinctively human purposes of sexual intercourse.

Quay's essay remains a superb defense of the Church's teaching on contraception. It illustrates that even in the days before Vatican II, those who reflected deeply upon the meaning of marriage and sexuality recognized that contraception violates not only the physiological meaning of sexual intercourse but also its human and spiritual meaning.

This essay appeared in *Theological Studies* 22 (1961): 18–40.

CONTRACEPTION AND CONJUGAL LOVE

by
Paul M. Quay, S.J.

Few arguments in the domain of morality seem as unpersuasive to the great majority of Americans as the customary natural-law arguments against contraception as a "frustration of the generative act". Even when, in addition, the individual's lack of total dominion over his species-directed functions is pointed out, most people remain unconvinced. Yet, when there is question of grave and absolute precepts of natural law, one would expect, if not that men would spontaneously recognize their obligations, at least that the well-disposed should acknowledge them when clearly presented. On the other hand, while well aware of this unsatisfactory situation, theologians seem certain of the validity of their arguments.

This article is presented in the conviction that the theologians are right, but that the laymen are not wrong: those elements of the argument from natural law most capable of producing strong intellectual and emotional impact would seem, for the most part, to have been left only implicit in the more common presentations. The purpose of this study is to seek out in detail such elements and to render them explicit. It seeks to explore a bit further than usual into that concrete human nature which founds the natural law and to stimulate discussion which may ultimately lead, in more competent hands, to a psychologically more effective position than is now available, a position which will confront men's consciences with both perception and feeling of the evil of contraception.

In Part 1 certain relations between man's psychology and the natural law are stressed. Part 2 analyzes human sexual activity in terms of natural law, and the relations of sex to the total person, to other men, and to God are discussed. Part 3 applies the principles developed in Part 2 to the matter of contraception. The basic argumentation is philosophical. But when theology provides an additional insight or useful analogy, we have not hesitated to use it.

THE NATURAL LAW

The Catholic Church's rejection of contraceptive intercourse is firm and clear. But what are the intrinsic reasons for this rejection? A priori, they might be of two kinds: strictly theological (i.e., based upon the deposit of faith alone and therefore belonging to divine positive law) or philosophical (based upon things knowable by natural reason, though wholly coherent with theological positions). As Protestants have not been slow to point out, there would seem to be small grounds in Scripture for a strictly theological position;[1] nor does tradition in its other forms make up for this lack. In point of fact, the papal documents which have specified the Catholic position seem to argue from revelation very little if at all; rather, the emphasis is upon the natural law and upon the role of unaided reason in the establishing of the norms of human conduct. The arguments adduced by moralists have followed along this same path.

Now, the very concept of a morality based upon the nature of

[1] This is not to say that Onan's punishment was solely for his violation of the levirate law, without reference to his practice of *coitus interruptus*. (For a recent, non-Catholic acknowledgment of the traditional interpretation, cf. Richard M. Fagley, *The Population Explosion and Christian Responsibility* [New York, 1960], pp. 115–17). But then the detestability of his action would seem to spring from a natural obligation rather than a positive divine law.

man as related to God is not only foreign to Protestant thought but is rejected with hostility as being antithetical to the Protestant theology of original sin and of justification.[2] Clearly, then, any argument based upon the natural law will have no value whatever for a dogmatic Protestant. It is of some importance nonetheless to establish a mode of approach which can, if sufficiently elaborated, show the Church's anticontraceptive position to be continuous with and in full harmony with the views of Scripture and, indeed, to be in some sense demanded by these latter even if not provable by them. The explicitations of the natural-law argument which we proffer will, it may be hoped, furnish such a basis for the relating of that law itself to the abundant data of revelation on sex and marriage.

Often, too, non-Catholics woefully misunderstand "the natural law",[3] even though making use themselves, unknowingly, of fundamental aspects of the concept. For these reasons it will not be out of place to begin the discussion with a few remarks directed to what should still be rather exciting concepts: "nature" and "natural law". Such a procedure will, moreover, enable us to locate more clearly the subsequent discussion in terms of Scholastic morality and to see that discussion as a legitimate enlargement of the standard natural-law approach.

Consider, first, the concept of "nature" itself. By refinement and penetration of the Aristotelian definition, "Nature is a source or cause of being moved and of being at rest in that to which it belongs primarily in virtue of itself and not in virtue of a concomitant attribute",[4] one arrives at the well-known Scholastic defini-

[2] Cf. Stanislas de Lestapis, S.J., *La limitation des naissances* (Paris, 1958), pp. 36–39, for extensive references to a wide range of Protestant theology on this point.

[3] Cf., by way of example only: Alvah W. Sulloway, *Birth Control and Catholic Doctrine* (Boston, 1959), pp. 57–73; Joseph Fletcher, *Morals and Medicine* (Princeton, 1954), pp. 92–96, 222–24; Glanville Williams, *The Sanctity of Life and the Criminal Law* (New York, 1957), pp. 59–62.

[4] Aristotle, *Physics,* 192[b] 21–23; translation from W. D. Ross, *Works of Aristotle* 2 (Oxford, 1930).

tion: the nature of a thing is its essence considered as a principle of operation.[5] It is this aspect of operation which, due to the Boethian and Platonic tradition, is constantly being submerged and is in continual need of reassertion.[6]

Created beings are incomplete:[7] what they are is not what they are intended to be. The higher they stand in the scale of being and the more perfect they are in themselves, the more radically and comprehensively are they in need of completion. This completion they achieve by their own activity and operation, acquiring what is lacking, developing what is already possessed. A nature, then, is not a static thing, a mere ability to operate in a given way. Rather, it is the whole complexus of drives, tendencies, intrinsic modes of development which are the internal principle of the creature's activity. A nature is what a thing is, precisely as in tension towards what it is meant to be in its fulness. A nature is the subsistential urge of what is incomplete, striving to become fully itself.

The end and purpose of this striving is simply the creature

[5] Cf., by way of example, the discussion given in Eduardus Hugon, O.P., *Cosmologia* (*Cursus philosophiae Thomisticae* 2; Paris, 1927), pp. 255 ff.

[6] According to Boethius, "Natura est unamquamque rem informans specifica differentia"; *Contra Eutychen et Nestorium* 1, 57–58, in *Boethius, The Theological Tractates,* ed. and tr. H. F. Stewart and E. K. Rand (New York, 1918), p. 80. It is worth comparing the last half of this section in Boethius, in which he includes Aristotle's definition as given above, with Section 2, 1 of the *Physics,* whence that definition is drawn. Boethius' theological interests as well as his Platonism lead him towards the most general and immutable definition possible. Aristotle, however, goes on to supplement his basic definition by the following two: "The form indeed is 'nature' rather than the matter; for a thing is more properly said to be what it is when it has attained to fulfilment than when it exists potentially" (193[b] 6–8; Ross, *Works*). "We also speak of a thing's nature as being exhibited in the process of growth by which its nature is attained" (193[b] 12–13; ibid.).

[7] The radical incompleteness of which we are speaking throughout this section lies far deeper than the merely sexual incompleteness of male or female found in some created beings and is not to be restricted to this latter or confused with it.

fulfilled.[8] Such an end is intrinsic and its achievement is not a matter of free option: the creature is bound, under pain of perpetual incompleteness, so to act in virtue of what it now is as to develop towards its own fulness.

In the world below man and, indeed, in the human world as well, to the extent that man is subject to the laws of that lower world, no creature, despite all its efforts, achieves an ultimate completion. Completion and fulfilment cannot even be conceived at this level save as transitory, as a momentary balance between growth and decay, as a playing of a useful role for one scene, as a process whose use lies only outside itself. Thus it is that nature (or Nature) has come to signify the whole in terms of which the individual natures of atoms and flowers and wolves, and in one aspect men, alone have meaning, that totality which may be conceived as being perfected, as evolving to its fulness through the rise and decline of the individual natures acting within it.

Only persons can stand outside this Nature. Only persons are capable of an ultimate fulfilment, of a completion which transcends all process. Only persons have, in this sense, integral natures. Personal perfection is the perfection of an individual nature, not merely of Nature, precisely because the person possesses an eternal destiny.[9]

---

[8] This end, then, is "nature" in its fullest sense. Whatever is directed away from or is incompatible with this nature, the perfected being, is unnatural.

[9] The crucial importance of the concept of "person", naturally knowable and yet unknown outside the Judeo-Christian lineage, is seen in the impossibility of finding any save social (Natural) significance for the individual in other frameworks of thought. Thus, e.g., the statisms of Plato and Aristotle; thus, the nonsignificance of the individual in Stoic and Hindu thought—and all this despite the awareness of some kind of human spirituality and immortality. Indeed, it is only through the fact of the resurrection of the body, i.e., the ultimate immortality of the whole person (as distinguished from the nonpersonal, disembodied soul) that human existence achieves individual meaning. Yet, it is on this same level that we know of the glorified Mystical Body of Christ, in terms of which alone the individual will have eternal meaning—though still a personal meaning, through union of person with Persons. The ultimate value and meaning of the human person is knowable only by revelation. It is this

Man, then, can know his incompleteness; he can see what he now is and discover the direction of fulfilment by scrutiny of his own nature in body and mind and spirit. God has so created man that man can help to create himself. Precisely as a free agent, man is more strongly bound than the rest of creation, under the intrinsic sanction of ultimate and eternal frustration, to achieve himself fully. This bond of obligation, which is man's free nature, is the natural law, that law which God legislates by His very act of creation. All, then, that is knowable about man through psychology, history, or any of the sciences is relevant to the natural law, is part of the natural law.

This law lies, evidently, outside man's control. It is God's act of creating that founds it. Man's total nature and all his strivings are by very definition under God's exclusive dominion. Man's perfection and goal are unchangeable, for they enter into the very definition of what man is. Man, then, acts well, or morally, when he acknowledges this dominion by free choice of what leads to his true fulfilment in accord with what he already is; he sins when he denies this dominion by freely denying to his operations and activities their ordination towards his total fulfilment.

In concrete cases, an individual nature may be defective in its substance or its functioning, through the intervention of some extrinsic agency. Freely to accept this situation is no moral fault; it is rather the virtue of truth. But to induce such defectiveness is morally evil. One may guiltlessly be born with mental or physical defects; one may not make oneself defective without the radical disorder of freely choosing to be other than one is constituted to be.

In all that follows, we shall assume that the choice of any given mode of operation is fully free and deliberate. It is to the mode of operation, which is the object of free choice, that we shall alone turn our attention.

---

fact, perhaps, which should form the primary principle of connection between the philosophy of man and theology.

HUMAN SEXUALITY

Before we can ascertain the moral quality of contraception, we must understand human nature in its sexual aspect. Three levels of such understanding are in vogue today.

The first level regards human sexuality as merely physiological, having meaning only in terms of the immediate effect upon the individual. Thus, it sees nothing of the natural in sex and nothing of the ordination of sexuality to something beyond itself. At this level of understanding, sexual activity has no meaning or value save individual pleasure, and it becomes impossible to distinguish fornication or adultery from the chaste coition of saints, or even to divide natural intercourse from masturbation or bestiality; for the merely physiological activity of the individual is much the same in each case.

A higher and less inadequate level sees human sexuality still as merely physiological but also as truly natural. Thus, the division of the species into male and female is seen to tend, through sexual desire, to copula and the generation of offspring, whose slow biological development requires long nurture and training if they are to come to viable maturity. Sex appears as something essentially directed outward, toward another. It is meaningless for the individual except in so far as it retains this ordination through another towards adult offspring, the replenishment of the species. To destroy this ordination is to cancel the very significance of sex as such. The physiological fact of two sexes has no other explanation than the greater genetic values obtained for the species by means of sexual reproduction.

This physiological insight into man's sexual nature is, as such, truly and necessarily a datum for human morality. Yet this insight is as valid for many species of brute as it is for man; one suspects, then, that no human moral problem related to sex can be adequately treated on even this second physiological basis alone. Certainly, Christian moral teaching on fornication or adultery can be built upon such a basis only if this basis be enlarged by explicit consideration of the psychological and social nature of sexual activity. Moreover, even physiologically, a merely physiological treatment is inadequate; for in man sexual maturation and the desire for heterosexual activity is critically dependent upon an underlying psychological maturation. Finally, a too exclusively physiological approach to sex treats sex, in fact, not as a natural aspect of man but as a nature in its own right.

Unfortunately, however, in the heat of controversy many Catholic arguments against contraception give an impression of stopping at precisely this level.[10] Higher levels of insight are present only implicitly. It is hardly surprising that such arguments are misunderstood and thought to be merely physiological in character.[11] We would suggest that, even within their own context, the more or less traditional presentations seem to call for further development if such misunderstanding is to be avoided.

One may rise, however, to a third level of insight, which sees sexuality in man as physiological, indeed, and natural but also as something far more. It is *human* sexuality, a sexuality penetrated, modified, and elevated by human rationality and distinctively human emotions. Such insight, however, confronts us with a wealth of fact and image greater than we can properly handle; it

[10] Cf., by way of example only: Alphonse M. Schwitalla, S.J., "Contraception", *Catholic Encyclopedia, Supplement* 2 (1951); Eduardus Genicot, S.J., *Institutiones theologiae moralis,* ed. I. Salsmans, S.J., 14th ed. (Brussels, 1939), 1, 320–21; 2, 499; Gerald Kelly, S.J., "Catholic Teaching on Contraception and Sterilization", *Linacre Quarterly* 21 (1954): 110–13; John J. Lynch, S.J., "Another Moral Aspect of Fertility Control", ibid. 20 (1953): 118–22; A. Vermeersch, S.J., *De castitate,* pp. 267–68. Cf. also the interesting discussion: E. J. Mahoney, *American Ecclesiastical Review* 79 (1928), 133; John A. Ryan, ibid. 79 (1928), 408; John M. Cooper, ibid., p. 527; H. Davis, ibid. 81 (1929), 54.

[11] Whatever the impression occasionally made, Catholics have long insisted on the nonphysiological aspects of sexuality: the child is a new potential member of the Body of Christ; human love is a true end of marriage albeit secondary; it is gravely sinful forcibly to separate love from copula: cf., e.g., Pius XII's condemnation of AIH: *AAS* 43 (1951): 850. Cf. also the approaches taken by Josephus Fuchs, S.J., *De castitate et ordine sexuali* (Rome, 1959); Gérard Gilleman, S.J., *The Primacy of Charity in Moral Theology,* tr. William F. Ryan, S.J., and André Vachon, S.J., from 2nd French ed. (Westminster, Md., 1959).

confuses us by the vast and difficult problems its very richness raises. Many of these problems have yet to be fully solved, and it lies outside our present purpose and our competence to detail either the problems or such solutions as have been found. But there is one class of problems, of great importance for the present topic, which we shall attempt roughly to sketch and to follow with some indication of the direction their solutions might take.

This class of problems arises from the fact that adequately human sexuality seems to be a contradiction in terms, a natural conjoining of utterly disparate and opposed elements. Consider, for example, the essentially individualistic character of sense pleasure. How, then, can the most intensely pleasurable and absorptive of all bodily activities be at once source and sign and consummation of a lofty spiritual love? Yet so it is in fact, explain it as we will. It is true, of course, that whole cultures have existed and still exist in which coition is identified with male gratification and the begetting of children for family or clan, but with nothing beyond. But this very fact will help us in a little while to understand the solution.

As another example, not wholly unrelated to this last, there seems no doubt that, though stringent social conditions may work to the contrary, yet it is mutual, sexually-based love that naturally draws man and woman together, and it is their desire and need for mutual, sexual complementation and companionship that is the dominant motivation for marriage, though the ordination to children is certainly present and taken for granted. Yet, on the other hand, the whole of human sexuality is biologically and otherwise meaningless save in terms of reproduction.

One has in sexual relations the seeming contradiction of two antithetical loves: the love of another as an object of desire, as something one uses for one's own gratification, and the love of another as a personal subject to be reverenced and served for that other's sake and own intrinsic value. Or still again, what are we to say of the double fact that, on the one hand, the whole of every human being is saturated on all levels, both conscious and unconscious, with the species-directed instincts of his sexuality, and, on the other hand, each human being is a person, of individual and incommunicable value, independent and transcendent of the species, not requiring sexual intercourse or procreation for his fulfilment? This last question, as the most fundamental, we shall deal with first. We shall establish in greater detail the facts and the problem and then seek a solution through an analysis of the ultimate purpose subserved by human sexuality.

Sex suffuses the whole human being. The cells of one's body are stamped genetically, all male or all female. The body's chemical constitution, height and weight, skeletal and muscular structuring, blood composition and heartbeat, biological age and metabolism, resistance to disease, recuperative powers, longevity, delicacy and perceptiveness of sensation—to say nothing of intensity of sexual drive and the more obviously sexual physical differences—are all deeply and characteristically affected by and linked to one's sex. Not only the body, however; one's whole psychology and not, as we have come to see, merely one's consciousness is permeated by one's manhood or womanhood: spontaneous interests, natural aptitudes, degree of responsiveness, objectivity and vigor of mind, regard for law, esteem for religion, even one's prayer and personal relations with God are colored and modified by one's sex.[12] Nor is the sexual nature of man restricted to time. Though marriage and sexual intercourse cease with death, yet, as we know from the status of our Lord and our Lady, one's distinctive sexuality is retained eternally.

Yet, what is male in a man is, in all its manifold temporal aspects, ordered towards the adequate fathering of a family; what is female in woman is directed towards motherhood. But, since everything in a man is male and everything in a woman is female, all levels of a person's being possess an ordination towards parenthood.

It is nonetheless equally clear that the human person as such is not subordinated to parenthood or to any other created good

---

[12] These points are excellently elaborated in Lucius F. Cervantes, S.J., *And God Made Man and Woman* (Chicago, 1959), pp. 1–140.

whatsoever, however true it may be that one must make use of such goods in achieving that fulfilment of the in-created law of his nature which will bring him into full harmony with God's will for him.[13] The person transcends the species even as he transcends civil society. In one fundamental sense, species and society exist only for the good of the person. The person is incommunicable and unique; his value, therefore, is in some sense absolute and, certainly, irreplaceable.

Moreover, just as one may argue that all in man is ordered towards parenthood, so one may, with equally firm and solid basis in fact, argue that all in man is ordered, for example, towards civil society. For man's sexual activity is ordered to the maintenance of population, and ordered in such a way that it is to be restricted rather than used when the civic good so requires. His very life is submitted to hazard at the just will of the state in time of war. His economic abilities and activity, his knowledge of the sciences and of the arts, his virtues and spiritual development are all ordered towards making the civil society better. Similar arguments can be easily constructed to show how all levels of human existence are ordered to virtue or to economic prosperity or to the contemplation of truth, etc.

The reason that such seemingly conflicting positions are all true in their own way is this: the *person* is at once sexual and social and virtuous and all the rest. But the person acts in virtue of his nature. Wherefore, the person is made perfect in so far as he freely wills all the proper, mutual interorientations of his nature. The person transcends the species only by rationally working for the good of the species, just as he transcends the state not by rugged individualism but by laboring for the true good of civil society. But the good sought under each aspect must be the *ultimate* good of species, state, etc., or the unity with the good of the person disappears. It is only in terms of the ultimate good towards which

---

[13] We do not wish to enter here into the important but difficult question as to the role of sexual fulfilment had man not fallen; nor do we wish to state whether the absence of a strict need of such fulfilment is, in the present order, naturally knowable.

human sexuality is directed that the mode in which sex is rightly to be used and the person's transcendence of sex can be grasped.

The ultimate end of human sexuality is not carnal pleasure or companionship or marriage or children or the family or civil society, though it includes and requires all of these; for none of these is perfective of the person as such. The ultimate purpose of human sexuality, as of all else, is to raise the person and, through him, other persons to the most pure and exalted possible love of God. In so far as this can be achieved without sexual activity, sexual activity is unnecessary for a person.

But in the ordinary case, sexual activity is one of the most powerful aids available to lift one to such love of God.[14] For sexual pleasure, even as pleasure, is in its fulness other-directed. The fulness of sexual activity leads not only to another but to love of that other and, through that other, to children. Thus, love is drawn first to one's spouse, then to one's children, and finally, through one's family, to the whole of human society; a family tied up within itself and its friends is as truly stunted, though not as badly, as the couple so tied within their selfish mutuality as to wish no children. Each step in the over-all process of familial growth requires a further outgoing, a truer love, a more open moral attitude. Thus, the love of God, which urges on and motivates these steps or, if absent, is prepared for by them, is rendered more free of the obstacle and hindrance of self-centered loves.

Consequently, a truly human sexual life can in no sense be a compromise or balancing of two antithetical loves: love of the other as a thing and love of the other as a person. The first of these loves is, in its totality, sinful by virtue of its reduction of the dignity of a human person to the status of a mere means to another person's wishes — the penultimate malice of all social sin.

---

[14] Cf. August Brunner, *A New Creation,* tr. Ruth Mary Bethell (London, 1955), pp. 66–67, 71–72, 81–84. In this and the references which follow, unless something else is indicated, the material cited will give a fuller and more highly developed treatment than that to which we are held by the purpose of the present article.

Sexual love, even in its beginnings, must somehow be already striving to desire the other's good as a person. One enjoys sexual pleasure rightly only in the service of the other. The woman yields to the man for the sake of *his* physical satisfaction, to show him love, to open companionship to him, to bear him children, and to make him, far above man and husband, a father, to ground him in society, and so on. The man *serves* the woman by placing his gratification in subordination to hers, yielding to her his seed to make her fruitful, by reciprocating her love, cherishing and protecting her in her childbearing and nurturing, making her a more perfect person through motherhood, etc.

It is clear, then, that the fact that mutual love is felt to be the most proper and natural reason and motive for marriage is a fact wholly in accord with the ends and purposes of sexual relations. It is clear, too, that though an ordination to children is always present in so far as children will contribute to the ultimate end of sex and marriage, yet they are not required even when they can be had—as in the case of the marriage of those who by common consent vow themselves to virginity.[15]

This approach to three of our problems seems only to render the first-mentioned one the more intractable: How can all this lofty talk of flights of spiritual love for God and one's partner and all mankind be reconciled with the brute fact that all sense pleasure is by its very nature selfish—sexual pleasure most of all?

The root of the solution is, of course, the fact that, unlike other sense pleasures, human sexual pleasure in its mature perfection requires a partner for its achievement, a partner who is a person, not a thing.[16] For coition, then, to be human at all, it must take place as an interpersonal act, each person recognizing and reverencing the person who is, at the very least, the source of his own pleasure. Coitus is, consequently, a communication between persons, nonmediated and direct. But it is more. It

---

[15] Cf. Genicot, op. cit. 2, 492; Brunner, op. cit., pp. 85, 87–88.
[16] Cf. Cervantes, op. cit., p. 252.

is a most intimate sensible language and natural sign and symbol of love.[17]

A natural sign is something knowledge of which leads spontaneously and by its very fact to the knowledge of something else. A sensible sign of something immaterial is a symbol if it leads to the knowledge of its object by means of its own sensible likeness or analogy to that object. Both sign and symbol can become part of a language by being used by an intellectual being to communicate his thoughts and interior dispositions.

Some of the naturally symbolic aspects of coition appear at once when one considers how a description of the act of intercourse is at the same time a description of deep and mysterious personal relationships. In coition the woman gives and surrenders herself to the man by complete openness, receptiveness, submission, and a full unfolding of herself to this sole partner. The man, on his part, gives himself to the woman through his entrancement with her, his finding of his satisfaction in her alone, his yearning to protect this soft helplessness, his penetration and permeation of her with his very substance, his focusing of all his attention and activity, dominance and responsibility exclusively upon this one woman. Coitus is, then, an external union of man and woman in symbolism of their internal union and pleasure in one another.

Moreover, coitus is the physiological act of procreation. It is the condition for fusion of the male principle with the female. It prepares for the becoming of two in one flesh—the flesh of their common child into which the substance of each has merged and about which all their future activity centers. The yielding of one's body to another is, thus, the natural symbol of willingness to become father or mother, of yearning to make one's partner mother or father, of the love which desires that exalted physical, mental, and spiritual maturity for one's partner which comes only from parenthood. Only through their children does the woman gain the peculiar richness and warmth and

---

[17] It seems almost absurd to offer a single reference for that to which the whole history of art and literature bears witness, but Fr. Cervantes' last chapter provides a good outline around which to group one's data.

fulness of motherhood; the man, the deep responsibility, sobriety, long patience, and quiet nobility of fatherhood. Coition is not merely the condition for but the symbol of the creative act of God; it reflects, by intention, not only His creativity but the love of His eternal providence over each being He has created.

But the gift of self, the becoming two in one flesh, can never be total, for no created person is wholly accessible to any other; and true love for another person is essentially conditioned upon reverence for that in the other which remains solely his and God's. Neither party can give all that he is to any created being; and, conversely, any attempt to grasp the totality of another person is to seek to possess him as an object — one ceases to give to that other and seeks rather one's own profit.[18] But this radical incommunicability of persons is also stated in the very physical limitations of coitus — the two bodies can never wholly interpenetrate and be dissolved one into the other; and any attempt to pass this limit turns incompleteness into agony.[19]

Further still, in even the most intimate of created relationships there still remains the existential loneliness and the nonabsoluteness of the human person who is the recipient of one's love. The deeper the love, the more clearly does it call out for an absolute transcendence of itself and its beloved, a transcendence achieved in part in children, in part, with and through them, in civil society, yet never fully achieved save in the transcendence of God, who is Love.[20] And this call for transcendence of all created love is also symbolized in coition by its being a mere condition for conception, in its inability to effect offspring save by His intervention. For coition is *pro*creation; God alone creates.

This symbolism of sexual intercourse is, as mentioned, immediate and natural. It speaks all that it has to say — the dedication of one's self to the perfecting, as person, of another — whatever its

[18] Cf. Brunner, op. cit., pp. 93–95.

[19] Consider in this regard John Milton, *Paradise Lost* 8, 622–29; cf. also Brunner, op. cit., pp. 99–100.

[20] Cf. Gabriel Madinier, "Spiritualité et biologie dans le mariage", in *Limitation de naissances et conscience chrétienne* (Paris, 1950), pp. 199–201.

speakers may wish or intend. As natural to them, it is not within their power to change. To the extent, it is true, that the concept of the person is lacking in a culture, the higher tones in the sexual relationship will be muted and inaudible; but the act itself continues to speak its message, even though unheard. When the day arrives for a culture to come to the understanding of revelation and the human person, the true nature of the act of coition is gradually recognized as something long heard but not attended to.

But sexual activity is not merely symbolic; it is a language. Not only is there the objective order of symbol; there is the intentional one of those who activate the symbolism. Rational beings are called upon so to will, in accord with their nature, as to become more fully themselves. In the case of sexuality, their obligation is to will the meaning of their actions in so far as they can grasp it. They must rise ever higher spiritually so that they can speak ever more sincerely and perfectly the full word of mutual love.

Long before one can in fact utter this word in its total richness, however, one can freely choose and will so to utter it and consent in advance totally to its full meaning. Such a free and deliberate consent to this integral, but as yet unrealized, meaning of coitus is marriage.

The bond and covenant of marriage is indissoluble; for if the whole person has been given, what ground is left for taking back? Marriage is, in its perfection, monogamous; for though one man can give himself to many women, his gift being through multiplicable substance and activity, yet his gift cannot be perfect towards many. He is unable to order his loves for each wife through and in one another as he does his loves for God, his wife, his children, his fellow men. Thus, matrimony establishes by solemn vow a permanent state of union between two persons which issues gradually and through effort in the full life of the family.

In short, this covenant of marriage is a mutual pledge and promise to offer continually to the other all those actions of body and attitudes of heart and mind by which the various significations and fruits of coition are achieved.[21] It confers on each partner, in consequence, the right to these same actions and attitudes from the other. Since the total signification and fruit of coition can be summarized as familial love, the marital bond is the mutual right and duty to do with love all that pertains to the founding, raising, and progress of the family.

The "goods of marriage" are achieved, then, in their completeness, only to the extent that the partners fully intend and mean in every act, especially of coition, all the love and particular gift of self which that act objectively means and says. Since in man's fallen condition the tendencies to self-love—to the reduction of other persons to the rank of means to one's own ends, to make persons things—are deep and strong, and since these tendencies show themselves with peculiar violence where sexual pleasure is in question, then the permanent commitment to the total eradication of self-love, which is the marriage contract, is a commitment to a lifelong asceticism and disciplining of oneself, not only in mind and affection but also in body.[22]

Marriage provides, indeed, the proper and holy context for the easing of sexual concupiscence, but it would be a most grave error to regard marriage as making licit unrestrained sexual activity.[23] On the contrary, of its very nature, marriage requires an ever-greater human control of coition and all that accompanies it, an ever-greater awareness of *who* one's partner is and what one is seeking to say ever more perfectly to him or her by the word of love which is coitus. Indeed, this ever-deepening spiritualization of sexual relations—and all others—between husband and wife may progress to the point where even at the moment of mutual orgasm both are elevated in prayer, rejoicing in God for the gift of union He gives them, with each other and Himself. Thus, from the very beginning of married life, the twofold effort towards self-control and towards the awareness of God's creative presence

[21] Cf. John C. Ford, S.J., "Marriage: Its Meaning and Purposes", *Theological Studies* 3 (1942): 333–74, esp. 349–64.

[22] Cf. de Lestapis, op. cit., pp. 191–93, 199–218.

[23] Cf. Pius XII, *AAS* 43 (1951), 851–53.

during intercourse must regulate the actions of the young couple. It is this which is so beautifully expressed in the account of young Tobias' wedding night: "Sara, arise and let us pray to God today and tomorrow and the next day, because for these three nights we are joined to God; and when the third night is over, we will be in our own wedlock. For we are the children of saints, and we must not be joined together like heathens that know not God."[24] Thus, in truth, coition is the "marital act," the symbol of the marital state in its fulness.

All that we have said thus far has rested at the level of man's nature. But God has re-created man into a new order, giving him a share by similitude in His own inner, tripersonal life. Thus, man is given a superior nature with its own new and exalted tendencies, exigencies, and strivings towards a new and higher goal of fulfilment, in the Spirit, through the Son, to the Father, in the ultimate glory of the direct vision of the Godhead. The Scriptures show us that all levels of sexual love and activity have been reordained towards a still loftier spiritual end than that natural to them: the upbuilding of the Body of Christ. The conjugal love symbolized by coition is now itself the symbol of the love between Christ and His Church, of the nuptials of the Lamb.[25] And transcending all created orders of love, the mysterious and eternally fruitful mutual love of the three Persons is now known as the ultimate reality reflected by conjugal union.[26]

One final point, however, remains to be considered: Has not this discussion implicitly rejected the traditional thought of the Church, who continues the Old Testament tradition which insists that the primary end of marriage is not mutual love and personal self-giving but rather the procreation and raising to adulthood of offspring? Has there not been a sleight of hand replacing this primary end by the secondary ends? The answer is no. The discussion of this point can serve as a summary of this section.

[24] Tob 6:22; 8:4–10.
[25] Cf. Eph 5:23–32; Ap 19:7, 9; 21:2, 9–10; Mt 9:15; 22:2–12; Jn 3:29.
[26] Cf. de Lestapis, op. cit., pp. 163–68.

Although the terms "primary end" and "secondary end" of marriage are in standard use today, their sense is perhaps best revealed by going back to the lucid terminology used by St. Thomas. Thomas distinguishes sharply between the more, or less, *essential* ends of marriage (i.e., those pertaining to what is constitutive of marriage) and its more, or less, *excellent* ends.[27] The drive from the twofold sexuality of human nature, through copula, to the child leads to the most essential end, the new human adult. Were there no such sexual process, there would be no question of the special type of human love institutionalized in marriage.

Nonetheless, this physiological end is the least excellent of all the ends of marriage and therefore least ultimate. The far loftier ends of sex and marriage presuppose the lower sexual ordination but elevate it and transmute it by reason of their superiority. It is of some interest to note that in the Church's *Rituale,* in all the beautiful marriage ceremony, there is only one brief reference, in the final prayer after the marriage itself is over, to the procreation of children.[28] The nuptial Mass contains several references to children, but they receive little emphasis; here also it is the mutual love and total companionship which gain all the stress.[29] In fine, then, the most essential but least excellent end of marriage is called "the primary end" because it is the natural goal of the process constituting conjugal relations; it is that which first must be, but only so that it may be transmuted.[30]

---

[27] Cf. *Sum. theol., Suppl.,* q. 49, a. 3; q. 65, a. 1.

[28] Cf. *Rituale Romanum,* ed. 1925: Ritus celebrandi matrimonii sacramentum; *Priest's Ritual,* ed. Benziger (New York, 1949), pp. 247, 261.

[29] Cf. *Missale Romanum:* Missa votiva pro sponso et sponsa.

[30] Cf. Bernard J. F. Lonergan, S.J., "Finality, Love, Marriage", *Theological Studies* 4 (1943): 477–510.

THE EVIL OF CONTRACEPTION

At the beginning of our discussion we called attention to the fact that the laws of human psychology form an essential part of the natural law. This fact we then used to look more closely into the natural law in so far as it governs man's sexual behavior. Special attention has been focused on the general moral principles which flow from the symbolic nature of coition. We now apply these principles to show the moral evil, i.e., sinfulness, of contraception. We have already discussed the objective aspect of sin, its being a willed violation of a nature, a transgression of the existential law of God. Subjectively, however, sin is essentially pride. And pride is the assent to falsehood—not precisely to the telling of a lie, but to the content of the lie—a deliberate unconforming of the person with reality. This is the protosin, the prevarication of Adam: to assent to the lie that man is his own master, that man bears dominion over himself, that man may subject his person and his nature to ends (or idols) of his own fashioning rather than to those ordained by God's creative act.

But Satan is the unclean spirit as well as the essential liar and falsifier from the beginning. The uncleanness springs from the falsehood. The whole of sexual morality can be summed up in the phrase: one may not lie against or falsify the truth of the natural word of love. Thus, concretely, a man pledges by coition the gift of himself to the beloved; but if he is already another's, he lies and is an adulterer. If circumstances are such that he cannot give the fulness of commitment to his partner, he lies and is a fornicator. Perversions are yet worse. Not only do they represent a lie, the heart being kept from agreement with the symbol, but they falsify the symbol itself. They are a mock symbol of the pure beauty of interpersonal love; but they are a true symbol of something monstrous.

What better symbol could there be of isolation of one's person from reality, of self-willed and self-pitying loneliness, of the bleak sterility of self, loved in itself, than masturbation? Sodomy is a genuine symbol of sentimental shallowness of character, of perpetual juvenility and adolescent ambivalence, as well as of radical contempt for one's own sex and for all sex. And so on into the depths. Yet these puerile monstrosities are called love and passed off as such, adding to the basic lie of impurity the consent to the known unreal, the fraudulence of shoddy forgery.

It is to this company of perversions that contraceptive intercourse belongs. The woman who uses a diaphragm has closed herself to her husband. She has accepted his affection but not his substance.[31] She permits him entrance but does not suffer him to be master. So, also, by any form of sterilization a woman deprives her husband's seed of its power over her body. She accepts his headship only in so far as she can subject it to her own will. The sign and symbol of wifely submission, of patriarchal authority, is made over covertly to serve the purposes of a weakly uxorious male and a domineeringly feminist wife.

Sometimes the man will use a condom for the same reasons; sometimes for more characteristically masculine reasons of selfishness. In either event he no longer dominates his wife as person, he does not permit his activity to penetrate her; he takes no responsibility for her. Her helplessness is deceptive—if she is not armored, he is without efficacy. He worships her with his body—but not enough to share with her his substance.

Thus, such mates perform what appears to be the act of love but is only a sham; they lie to one another in their bodies as in their hearts. They take that which says perfect union and corrupt it till it can express only mutual pleasure. They abuse the symbol of the gift of one's self to another till it betokens precisely the withholding of this gift.

Such people will say: "You are wrong. It is just the fact of our mutual love that leads us to contraception. We are not seeking irresponsible pleasure. We use contraceptives only in those circumstances in which even the Catholic Church permits or even advises her members to refrain from further procreation. Indeed, your

[31] Cf. de Lestapis, op. cit., p. 183.

strictures on contraceptives might with better effect be applied to the unnatural practice of rhythm."

That those who use contraceptives to control the size of their families often do so under the impulse of mutual love is no more to be doubted than that homosexuals act under such an impulsion— and these two loves are similarly, though not equally, shallow. Lying at the root of each is the assumption that the unique mode of expression of true love is sexual. All love is reduced to sexual love, in consequence, or subordinated to it in value.

Love that is profound, however, does not deliberately frustrate its most nearly adequate mode of expression. Thus, a man who truly loves his wife would die rather than be once unfaithful, rather than retract his gift to her for even a short hour to give it to another. His gift was to be integral; even one such retraction would spoil that integrity and deprive him of an unspotted gift to give his wife. The man who thinks little of this shows only how little he knows of the depth of love.

So with contraception. Even one act is a consenting to the building of a barrier to their most intimate communication. In one single act the integrity of their mutual word of affection is sacrificed to their pleasure; for if they were willing to sacrifice their pleasure, the word could be left intact and pure for the day when it might again be uttered. That first contraceptive act declares that, much as one loves the other, one does not love enough to forgo the pleasure of intercourse so that he or she might reserve for the other the most fitting expression of that love. For these lovers, much less than the best is quite good enough for their beloved. That they do not regret such a loss is scarcely proof of the greatness of their conjugal love.[32]

Before we consider the morality of the use of "the unnatural practice of rhythm", it will be well to finish the indictment of

[32] Characteristic as such insensitivity to the true demands of love is of those using contraceptives, even so, one can only marvel that a man should be willing to have a doctor probing into the secret chambers of his wife to fit her with a diaphragm or cap, when by the man's own self-sacrifice such profanation could be avoided. Cf. also ibid., p. 190, n. 1.

contraceptive methods, so that we may compare the two approaches under all aspects.

What has been said thus far has been chiefly concerned with the effect of contraception on the personal donation of husband and wife. But, we recall, coitus proclaims not a closed love-of-two but an open love, transcending the two to find its fulfilment, by the reception of God's creative act, in children. The word of coition speaks not children but the openness of both husband and wife to the creative activity of God. It is a religious act, a submitting of human choices and desires to God.

But contraceptives destroy this ordination towards procreation. The couple using contraceptives offer each other an ersatz symbol of procreative love. Their act does not bespeak the desire for the other's fulness of parenthood; it symbolizes a flat rejection of God's intervention. They are two alone at this moment and refuse to transcend themselves; their pleasure in each other is corrupted at its core.

Sigmund Freud was no friend of Christian morality and in his earlier days, at least, he strongly favored contraception;[33] yet twenty years later he regarded the psychological essence of perversion as just this severance of the act from its intrinsic relation to procreation:

> It is a characteristic common to all the perversions that in them reproduction as an aim is put aside. This is actually the criterion by which we judge whether a sexual activity is perverse—if it departs from reproduction in its aims and pursues the attainment of gratification independently. You will understand therefore that the gulf and turning-point in the development of the sexual life lies at the point of its subordination to the purposes of reproduction. Everything that occurs before this conversion takes place, and everything which refuses to conform to it and serves the pursuit of gratification

[33] Cf. Sigmund Freud, *Collected Papers,* ed. James Strachey (London, 1924), I, 237–39.

alone, is called by the unhonoured title of 'perversion' and as such is despised.[34]

In the light which Freud himself and those who have followed him have thrown on the permeation of the whole person by sexuality, it is hardly surprising that such a rending of sexuality by contraception tears apart the deep roots of the human personality.

More profoundly, those who use contraceptives have consented to the old lie that they are masters of themselves. Man's reason is meant to show him what God has made him to be, so that he may become what God has meant him to be. Reason is not a new God, a private household deity which creates man a new creature of what sort it pleases. It has, it is true, the physical power to do so, but it does so only at the price of the destruction of man.

A wholly different viewpoint can be gained of the intrinsic malice of contraception if we consider it not as a violation of the natural symbol of conjugal love but as a violation of the sacramentally elevated and supernatural symbol of the union between Christ and His bride, the Church. Christ's generative activity upon the Church is not, with respect to every member, absolutely continuous. He gives grace freely; and He conditions it upon human co-operation, whether in the reception of the sacraments or in good works. But when He gives His grace, it is not inoperative or sterile; deliberately to reject His grace and to deprive it of all possibility of its fertilizing one's soul is not a trivial matter.

Thus, there are those who at Christmas or Easter are moved by longing for the joy and peace and warmth of soul they recall from happier years; and under the impulse of this sentimentality and pseudo love for "the good and gentle Jesus" they deliberately receive Him in Communion into souls dead in mortal sin. There are also those who render His grace sterile by going to confession and positively blocking the efficacy of absolution in their souls by wilfully holding back one of their mortal sins. Spiritual contracep-

---

[34] Sigmund Freud, *A General Introduction to Psychoanalysis,* tr. Joan Riviere (Garden City, N.Y., 1935), p. 277.

tion is a sacrilege; its symbol, physical contraception, though not itself sacrilegious, partakes of the same malice.

Contraceptive intercourse is also a repudiation of the graces of sacramental marriage or is, at least, a disbelief in their efficacy. God, through His Church, both denounces contraception and proffers the graces to regulate the size of one's family by continence. Disbelief in the one truth implies disbelief in the other.

What can be said of the morality of periodic continence or rhythm? How can one maintain what we have said about the symbolic nature of coition and yet state that the coitus of a couple who know with certainty that conception is impossible, who want it to be impossible, and who would not have intercourse if it were not impossible, is symbolically valid?[35]

The morality of coition, in the case of those making use of rhythm, may not properly be disjoined from the fact of continence. Continence is, especially for the husband, a real hardship, a painful discipline. Thus, continence itself is a symbol of sorrow that children are not to issue from subsequent marital union; it is a sign of regret for the necessities imposing its practice. It proclaims, consequently, the effects of original sin—in this sense paralleling the religious vows—and stands for the submission of man to God in penitence and reparation.

In this fallen order, continence itself, rightly entered into, can be a more tender and full expression of marital love than coitus; for the husband undertakes it for the love of his wife or of his children or of the child yet to be. It is an act of sacrifice of self for others' good. Thus, it can render succeeding coitus more deeply expressive by giving it more to say of sacrificial and other-directed love.

Moreover, periodic continence is by its nature apt to lead more rapidly to the fulness of marital chastity, that progressive purification of sexuality of all selfish elements and its unending spiritualization.[36]

[35] We are stating the problem in strong theoretical form, not implying anything as to practical chances of success in the use of rhythm.

[36] Lest there be any misunderstanding, by such "spiritualization" we do not mean less frequent intercourse, but the performance of intercourse in a more spiritual manner, whether coitus be rare or very frequent.

Thus, again, coition becomes richer in meaning, not poorer. It is quite true that such continence, to be effective, must be vastly more than the mere repression or holding in leash of violent appetites, only to turn them loose without restraint when the sterile period arrives. It requires a deep and abiding asceticism, as much in the sterile period as in the fertile, albeit differently in each. The mind and imagination must be controlled, the eyes held in check, penance practiced, interest in prayer and spiritual things cultivated, energies diverted, the sacraments frequented. Yet some such efforts must enter into every Christian marriage if the couple is to arrive at a purely selfless sexual life.

Returning to the question raised about a possible denaturing of the symbolism of coition by the intent of the husband and wife, we may note first that the act retains objectively its full value. If there is some moral evil inherent in rhythm, it is not a perversion of the symbol but a lie against it, analogous to fornication. Now, do the couple who properly practice rhythm have a mind and heart opposed to what their act says? If, indeed, they positively exclude the ordination to children from their moral activity by selfishness, even without alteration of the physical act, turning what is meant to be always open to the child and to God into a closed love-for-two, then they sin. But if they use rhythm selflessly — as its very nature leads them to try to do — their psychological state remains open to God's creative activity, the more evidently because they could close themselves securely by contraceptives. They know the child cannot result from their sterile union; but they also know, in virtue of the persevering openness of their moral attitude, that conception might very well follow if they neglect continence.

More basically, however, coition does not say the creation of the child but its procreation. Coition places one of the necessary conditions for conception, i.e., impregnation, but does not effect conception or guarantee it. It does say a desire on the part of both for children, a rational and human desire, based on the good of the child-to-be and of one's partner. But it is this very desire that leads, by supposition, to the practice of rhythm. Unperverted coition says conjugal love, a love which finds fulfilment only in a familial relationship. But this natural familial relation is general and somewhat indeterminate, not specified naturally to any given number or spacing of children. The couple's mind and heart can be fully conformed to what their act of coition says at the same time that they specify this indeterminacy by their intention to avoid conception here and now.

In summary, then, each single act of coition is a natural sign of the full, mutual, procreative love of the two partners. Coition is the symbol of natural marriage and of supernatural, which latter is, in turn, the symbol of Christ's union with His Church. Contraception is evil because it falsifies this sign. Contraception is wrong because it is a fictitious symbol of love, a substitution of what, in truth, symbolizes monstrous selfishness for what symbolizes utter self-giving.

FURTHER READING

Father Quay lays out his views on the meaning of sexuality somewhat more fully in his text *The Christian Meaning of Human Sexuality* (San Francisco; Ignatius Press, 1985). See also his "Conscientious Catholics and Birth Control: A Response to Father Overberg", *Fidelity* 5, no. 2 (Jan. 1986): 29–34.

Father Quay is also one of the most able critics of the revisionist position that there are no intrinsically evil acts. He has engaged in debate with Father Richard McCormick, S.J. See Quay's "Morality by Calculation of Values" in *Theology Digest* 23 (1975); it has been reprinted in *Readings in Moral Theology,* no. 1: *Moral Norms and Catholic Tradition,* ed. by Charles E. Curran and Richard McCormick, S.J. (New York: Paulist Press, 1979), pp. 267–93; McCormick's response to this piece appears in the same volume, pp. 309–15. See also Quay's "The Disvalue of Ontic Evil", *Theological Studies* 46 (1985): 262–86; Father McCormick's response appears in his "Notes on Moral Theology", *Theological Studies* 47 (1986): 85–86. Of interest as well are Father Quay's "The Unity and Structure of the Human Act", *Listening* 18, no. 3 (Fall 1983): 245–59; and "The Theological Position and the Role of Ethics", pp. 260–74 in the same volume.

Of interest, too, might be chapter two, "Christian Marriage", of my book *Humanae Vitae: A Generation Later.*

2

THE ENCYCLICAL *HUMANAE VITAE:*
A SIGN OF CONTRADICTION

by
Dietrich Von Hildebrand

Dietrich Von Hildebrand is one of the leaders in the modern philosophic school, the school of objectivistic phenomenology, a school of thought that can boast John Paul II in its numbers. Von Hildebrand can claim to be one of the architects of the developments in the Church's teaching on marriage. Many have observed that Church documents in the later part of this century have given increased attention to the concept of conjugal love and to love as the *meaning* of marriage, as opposed to procreation, which is its *end.* Von Hildebrand's writings have greatly deepened our understanding of the meaning of love within marriage. Certainly the centrality of conjugal love to marriage is not a new concept in the Church (cf. Tertullian), but it has only begun to receive the elaboration it deserves. The encyclical *Casti Connubii* certainly did not neglect the concept, but Von Hildebrand wrote one of his first important books on the subject of marriage and love before *Casti Connubii.* This book, *In Defense of Purity,* remains a classic.

Von Hildebrand provided one of the first lengthy defenses of *Humanae Vitae* with the pamphlet *The Encyclical* Humanae Vitae: *A Sign of Contradiction.* His treatment does not ignore the procreative meaning of the sexual act, but, rather than placing the crux of the argument there, he argues that the very meaning of

47

marriage and the sexual act as an act of total self-donation grounds the Church's opposition to contraception. This idea, of course, has become the centerpiece of the John Paul II's teaching on *Humanae Vitae.* As do most of the other authors in this collection, Von Hildebrand takes great pains to explain how human sexual love is not merely a biological or an animal function. He explains how sexual love is the natural and right expression of spousal love, whereby the human person actualizes one of his or her greatest desires, the desire for union with one who will help complete and perfect him or her. Von Hildebrand treats quite fully another important theme of *Humanae Vitae:* that spouses are cocreators with God in the act of bringing forth new life. This fact makes contraception, in Von Hildebrand's terms, "a fundamental sin of irreverence" against God. Von Hildebrand also counters well a charge made frequently at the time of *Humanae Vitae,* the charge that the Church's teaching was based on a static view of nature.

What is printed here is a portion of the pamphlet *The Encyclical* Humanae Vitae: *A Sign of Contradiction* (Chicago: Franciscan Herald Press, 1969).

2

THE ENCYCLICAL *HUMANAE VITAE:* A SIGN OF CONTRADICTION

by *Dietrich Von Hildebrand*

I

I. MARRIAGE AS A COMMUNITY OF LOVE

The very meaning and value which marriage possesses of its own cannot be understood if we fail to start from the central reality of the love between man and woman. And here, let us be frank, we touch on what used to be a kind of scandal in Catholic writings on marriage. One heard much of the *will* of the flesh, the remedy for concupiscence, and mutual help and assistance, but one heard very little of love. We mean the love between man and woman, the deepest source of natural happiness in human life, the great, glorious love of which the Canticle of Canticles says: "If a man shall give all the substance of his house for love, he shall despise it as nothing."

In contradistinction to the general silence concerning this love, Pope Pius XII was eloquent:

> The charm exercised by human love has been for centuries the inspiring theme of admirable works of genius, in literature,

in music, in the visual arts; a theme always old and always new, upon which the ages have embroidered, without ever exhausting it, the most elevated and poetic variations.[1]

It is shocking that in the past the real, valid motive for marriage has been for the most part overlooked, that the intrinsic relation of this type of love to a full mutual self-donation in bodily union has been ignored. Compared with this great, noble, and basic incentive, which the Canticle of Canticles says "is strong as death," the isolated desire of the flesh is superficial and secondary. Who can deny that it is this love which shakes the soul of man to its very depths, which marks the deepest experience in the natural realm of human life? Certainly, there is a broad scale in the potential of men for love, in the depth and completeness of love. Leonardo da Vinci said: "The greater the man, the deeper his love." Great loves, such as that between Leonore and Florestan in Beethoven's *Fidelio,* or St. Elisabeth of Hungary and her husband, or St. Louis of France and his wife, may be rare and presuppose great and deep personalities, but in every human being who has ever experienced a real love, limited and imperfect as it may be, it is the great, dynamic human experience in his life.

If we wish to understand the nature of spousal love, this glorious heritage of paradise, and the God-willed valid aspect of the sexual sphere, we should read the Canticle of Canticles open-mindedly. We should not think of the analogical meaning, but take it in its original literal sense; then we can breathe the atmosphere of this love, and see the sublimity of bodily union when experienced as the ultimate God-given mutual self-donation. And, when we have grasped the beauty of the literal sense, we should consider the implication of the fact that the Liturgy uses it as an analogy for the relation of the soul to God, and uses it in the Office of the Blessed Virgin. Should it not be clear that only something which is noble on the human level can be used as an analogy for the supernatural relation of the soul to Christ? Why

[1] *The Pope Speaks,* ed. Michael Chinigo (New York: Pantheon, 1957).

does the sacred author use this relation and not that of friendship, such as the one uniting David and Jonathan?

2. ERRORS CONCERNING MARRIAGE

Puritanical Distrust of Spousal Love

Some Catholic authors in undertaking to praise spousal love deprive it of its ecstatic ardor, of its splendor and unique *intentio unionis* (desire for union), thus detaching it consistently from the sexual sphere, from the bodily union; others, again, look down on spousal love and interpret its ecstatic character, its unique splendor, as a mirage, an illusion. Some ten years ago a famous Catholic philosopher even went so far as to claim that this type of love is nothing but a disguised sex instinct and that only in so far as *agape* exists between the spouses does their relationship deserve to be called authentic love. Most Catholic authors in the past, however, ignored the existence of this love entirely, simply omitting it when speaking of marriage.

It cannot be stated with sufficient emphasis that the time has come for us to do away with the gnostic and puritanical suspicion of spousal love, love in the most specific sense, of which the Canticle of Canticles speaks in such a unique way.

Let us be existential; let us see that the love between man and woman is a specific category and type of love, even if we prescind from the sphere of sex, that it is a beautiful and glorious reality which is destined by God's will to play a fundamental role in man's life, and that this love is the classical motive for marriage, that marriage is precisely the fulfillment of this love.

And it is this love which we call "spousal love."

Misunderstanding of the Sexual as Mere Instinct

Still another basic error bars the way to the understanding of the true meaning and value of marriage. Every approach to the sphere of sex in man which considers it a mere subdivision of the realm of instincts and biological urges having no intrinsic relation to the spiritual sphere, like thirst and the need of sleep, the meaning of which is to be found in an extrinsic end which they serve, is bound to prevent an understanding of the true nature and meaning of sex. As soon as we assume that the nature and the meaning of sex in man can be treated as a mere biological reality, we have blinded ourselves to the mystery of the sphere of sex—to the meaning and value which it can have, on the one hand, and the terrible moral evil of impurity, on the other.

If sex were really nothing more than a biological instinct, such as thirst or hunger, it would be incomprehensible why the satisfaction of an instinct implanted in man's nature by God should be something immoral outside of marriage, especially if it led to procreation. To consider the sexual sphere as a subdivision of instincts is to reduce the immorality of impurity to the mere violation of a positive commandment.

We cannot grasp the mystery embodied in this sphere until we grasp that its deepest meaning consists in being a unique fulfillment of spousal love and its desire for union. We must realize that this sphere is essentially ordained toward the constitution of a lasting, irrevocable union, the union to which spousal love aspires, and which is sanctioned by God; only then can we grasp the real sinfulness of every isolation of the satisfaction of sexual desire from the constitution of this God-sanctioned union. Only when we understand that the sexual act implies a mutual, irrevocable self-donation and is by its very nature called and destined to constitute an indissoluble union, can we see the desecration involved in sexual satisfaction outside of marriage.[2]

---

[2] In the original a section follows entitled "Spousal love as 'forma' on the sexual

The conjugal act, in its natural structure, is a personal action, a simultaneous and immediate cooperation of husband and wife, which, owing to the very nature of the agents and the propriety of the act, is the expression of the reciprocal gift, which, according to the word of Scripture, effects the union "in one flesh."[3]

We could also apply to the conjugal act the admirable words of St. Ambrose in speaking of the kiss: "Those who kiss one another are not content with the donation of their lips, but want to breathe their very souls into each other."

3. THE VALUE OF SEX AS THE EXPRESSION AND FULFILLMENT OF SPOUSAL LOVE AND THE SIN OF ISOLATING IT

We must, finally, free ourselves from seeing in the bodily union something evil, for the toleration of which in marriage one must desperately try to find a reason. We must learn to see that the bodily union, destined to be the fulfillment of spousal love and an ultimate mutual *self-donation,* is as such something noble and a great mystery, a sacred land which we should approach with deep reverence and never without a specific sanction of God; and that precisely because of this nobility and sacred mystery, because of the great value which it is destined to realize, every abuse is a terrible sin, and even contains something sacrilegious.

In stressing that it is a grave error to see the sexual sphere and the sexual act as something evil as such, we are far from denying that the isolation of the sexual sphere is not only a theoretical error but a widespread tendency of our fallen nature. The sexual

---

sphere and the Freudian error of reversing this truth". The following two paragraphs of the present section are from that section; the rest is omitted.

[3] Ibid.

sphere has also, when isolated and separated from spousal love and the mutual self-donation in marriage, an enormous attractive power. The danger of being caught and seduced by this aspect of the sexual sphere is indeed a great one and it lurks in the greater part of mankind. In my book *In Defense of Purity* I have dealt at length with this powerful fascination.[4] Whenever anyone gives in to it and undertakes to satisfy an isolated sexual desire, we are confronted with the grave sin of impurity, an outgrowth of evil concupiscence and a desecration. This sin includes a mysterious betrayal of our spiritual nature. But this in no way entitles us to look at the act of bodily union as something evil. It becomes evil through its isolation. Precisely because it is something noble, deep, and mysterious in its God-ordained relation to two becoming one flesh in the sublime love union of marriage, its abuse is a terrible desecration. To conclude that something is evil as such because its abuse constitutes a terrible sin and because in our fallen nature the tendency for such abuse is great is obviously completely illogical. Should we look on intellectual work and scholarship as something evil in itself, because it certainly produces in many persons a proud attitude, because it fosters pride? Or should we see in reason something evil because of the danger of rationalism?

No! Great and terrible as is the danger of impurity, true as it is that in our nature there lurks the tendency to respond to the appeal of the isolation of sex, this in no way alters the fact that the valid, real meaning of this sphere is to be a field of fulfillment for spousal love and that the original, valid aspect of the marital act is its function of being a mutual self-donation in the sacred bond of marriage, the constitution of an irrevocable union, and that it is thus as such not something evil, but on the contrary something great, noble, and pure.

Thus, instead of saying that the sinful satisfaction of sexual desire becomes legitimate through marriage, we should say that the sexual act, because it is destined to be the consummation of

---

[4] Baltimore: Helicon Press, 1962. [This book is now available under the title *Purity* from the Franciscan University Press, Steubenville, Ohio.]

this sublime union and the fulfillment of spousal love, becomes sinful when desecrated by isolation.[5]

4. FALSE REACTION TO THE PURITANICAL SUSPICION OF MARRIAGE: IDOLIZATION OF SEXUAL PLEASURE

Many Catholics consider the widespread positive attitude to the sexual sphere a great advance over the puritanical prudery and hypocrisy of the Victorian age. But incomparably worse than the puritanical attitude, in which the sexual act as such was considered base and evil, is the currently fashionable opinion that experience of sexual pleasure belongs to "self-fulfillment," that this pleasure is a divine gift which we should enjoy without restraint. This opinion falsifies the meaning and nature of the sexual sphere so radically that it becomes impossible to understand the meaning of the marriage act as the expression and fulfillment of wedded love, of mutual self-donation, of a union of love. The marriage act becomes even more degraded than in the puritanical view: the latter was at least recognizing its mysterious character when it considered sex a source of the mystery of iniquity, whereas in the contemporary view sex is considered a mere means of pleasure. In my book *In Defense of Purity* I have described two negative aspects which are found in the sexual sphere in addition to the aspects willed by God. The puritanical position saw in the sexual sphere only the two negative aspects, overlooking the positive character which discloses itself only in the light of spousal love. But the opinion current today separates pleasure from its function of serving the love union and makes it an end in itself; stripped thereby of all its depth, sex is even more misunderstood than in the Puritanical view.

Moreover, the term "love" is completely misused by many

[5] [The next section, omitted here, is entitled "Marriage as a *'Remedium Concupiscentiae'*".]

Catholics. They are blind to the nature of spousal love and attempt to reduce it to "sex-appeal." Even when some admit that sexual intercourse without love is something negative, love is in fact taken to mean something completely peripheral, basically a sensual desire, which lacks all the characteristics of love in general as well as those of spousal love in particular. It is of the greatest importance to stress that the question of birth control must be considered in the light of the mystery of true love and its fulfillment in bodily donation and never in terms of sexual attraction—today so often called "love." For isolated sexual pleasure is often—as in the widely circulated discussion of the encyclical *Humanae Vitae* by the German Professor Fritz Leist—thought to be the motive for marriage. (This consistently leads to the defense of promiscuity—under the title of "pre-marital relations" or "trial marriage"—and of homosexuality as a source of self-fulfilling pleasure.) This will become clearer when we briefly reflect on the distinctive marks of spousal love—that is, of love between man and woman.

5. ESSENTIAL DIFFERENCES BETWEEN TRUE SPOUSAL LOVE AND ISOLATED SEXUAL DESIRE

Many say: The sexual drive is obviously the specific mark of spousal love since this type of love presupposes the difference between the sexes. To that I reply: Certainly, but the difference between man and woman is not purely biological. After all, in the spiritual sphere there is also a complementary difference. In an essay, "Friendship between the Sexes," which appeared in my book *Man and Woman,* I treat of this spiritual, complementary difference, this specifically spiritual fecundation of each other, this completion of man and woman, which creates a special situation.[6]

[6] *Man and Woman* (Chicago: Franciscan Herald Press, 1965; paperback—Chicago: Henry Regnery Company, 1968). [This book is being republished by Sophia Institute Press, Manchester, New Hampshire.]

Indeed, it is no accident that great men saints have often found in women their most faithful and understanding followers, and conversely.

Spousal love is also characterized by another mark, namely, that the *intentio unionis* [intention of union] contained in every love, the longing to participate in the life of the beloved, the longing for a special type of communion, reaches its high point here. In every love we hasten spiritually to the other; in every love we turn to him to encounter him fully as a person and we yearn for a requital of love—for a real communion between personal beings is possible only when we look into one another in this reciprocal gaze characteristic of love. Only in love do we present our countenance fully to the other and truly disclose ourselves to him. And this attains a totally new character in spousal love. This love aims at marriage, and I am not as yet thinking of bodily union but of the union of two individual lives. Surely it is an awesome thing that two human beings want to lead *one* life, that they wish to live together, to carry one name, that they unite their lives and share everything with each other! Spousal love is also characterized by the fact that it is the purest I-thou communion. In *Metaphysik der Gemeinschaft*[7] [Metaphysics of community] I distinguish these two fundamental dimensions of communion: the I-thou communion, where two persons stand face to face, and the we-communion, where persons stand side by side and turn together toward a third object. These two dimensions of communion are normally present to a certain degree in every relationship, but the relationship is characterized according to the dimension that is dominant and proper to it. I would say that, in general, friendship is a we-communion where persons stand side by side and together turn toward common goods and values and share mutual interests. In spousal love, on the contrary, love itself is specifically the theme. Here, an explicit I-thou situation predominates, always with the longing for the attainment of the ultimate union in the mutual interpenetration of souls in love. Naturally, this implies

---

[7] Regensburg, Germany: Habbel, 1954.

that the beloved person as well as the mutual love becomes thematic in a unique way.

Still another mark of spousal love must be discussed — namely, what we call "being-in-love." This expression is so often misused that some believe that this is really nothing else but being sexually attracted to another. But this is an unfortunate error. The point here is that there are two radically divergent phenomena. Certainly, being in love includes the fact that the charm of the other sex discloses itself in a unique manner in the beloved. The shining forth of the beauty and mystery of the feminine as such to the man and of the masculine as such to the woman belongs to the state of being in love. Indeed, these are embodied in the beloved, in him alone. The decisive point is that in the true state of being in love the charm of the other sex is exclusively embodied in the beloved, as Petrarch says so beautifully of Laura, *che sola a me par donna* (who alone seems woman to me). This mark of being in love is the clearest antithesis to "sex-appeal," to more sexual attraction. Regarding the other only as sexually fascinating and experiencing an isolated sensual desire represents a phenomenon radically different from the true state of being in love. In this state the beloved stands before us as something immeasurably precious; his beauty awakens reverence in us. We are not yet referring to an especially deep being-in-love, but only to the phenomenon of being-in-love as such. Anyone who is truly in love gazes upon the other with the awareness that "I am not worthy of her," although with his whole heart he hopes that his love may be requited.

As long as I find someone only sexually attractive, as long as this person awakens only sexual desire in me, I in no way look up to him because of this. In the case of truly being in love, I am drawn into a dimension of depth, I become more sensitive and more reverent. In the case of isolated sensual desire, where I find someone merely enticing, I am drawn into the periphery. I even become less sensitive, less reverent. In the true state of being in love the beloved stands before me as a person in a unique way. I take him fully seriously as a person. In a mere sensual attraction the partner is an object for my satisfaction. In the case of truly being in love the whole charm of the other sex is embodied in the one beloved person, whereas in sensual desire the other is just *one* good representative of the other sex among many. The other is only one example that I happen to find. The real state of being-in-love—as long as it really lasts—possesses absolute exclusiveness. It is impossible, from the purely psychological point of view, to be in love with two people at the same time. This psychological exclusiveness (we are not yet touching the moral question) is grounded in the essence of "being in love." In the mere sexual attraction to the charm of a person we do not find the least trace of this exclusiveness. On the contrary, it is accompanied by the thought: this one today, tomorrow another, *delectat variatio* [variety delights]. This attitude is typically represented by Don Juan in Mozart's marvelous opera; he says to Leporello: "I would be unfaithful to the female sex were I to attach myself to one." This is the most emphatic antithesis to being in love. Here the female species is the specific theme and then only under the aspect of unalloyed sexual allurement. Every individual woman is merely an example of the species woman. For the person in love, on the contrary, the charm of the other sex can fully unfold itself only in the individual personality of the beloved; only thanks to his whole personality does the charm begin to glow and speak in its mysterious radiance, only against the background of all the other personal values of the one he loves. Needless to say, the quality of the sensual is entirely different in these two cases. (When I speak of sensual appeal, I have in mind the whole sphere of the sexual and whatever is psychologically and spiritually connected with it.) In the case of the person truly in love, the mystery of sex shows its true face in all its depth, in its mysteriousness which calls for reverence, in its moving quality, because it is formed by love; in the other case, we have only a caricature of the mystery of sex, because sex is isolated and separated from the spiritual person. With this caricature there inevitably goes a de-personalization. Whoever is seized by sheer sexual desire is himself de-personalized; he does not act as a person in that moment. Also, the one to whom he turns is not considered as a person, but is treated as a thing.

How much more noble and reverent, more aware, and consequently more lovable is a man made by love! How much richer the cosmos becomes for him and how he is led even to a greater religious depth! For one truly in love the sun shines more brightly, nature becomes more beautiful, his entire life is elevated to a higher plane. The person is then loosed from the shackles of habit which so dominate us, becomes emancipated from the dangers of conventionality, awakens much more to the hierarchy of values. The Canticle of Canticles expresses this when it says that the man who would give up all the possessions of his house for his love would regard the sacrifice as *nothing*.

Thus, we see how false it is to confuse the true state of being in love with isolated sexual attraction. And it is important to recognize that the terms "love" and "being in love" today often denote two *completely antithetical* attitudes. Nowadays, we commonly hear such objections as: Certainly, I admit that there happen to be extraordinary men with a great capacity for loving: this is very beautiful indeed, but it is something I am not endowed with and therefore for me being in love is simply being sexually attracted by someone. To this we can answer that an extraordinary love, the love-potential of a Romeo, is not under discussion. Even a completely simple, undifferentiated man who in no way rises above the ordinary, if he falls in love once in his life, exhibits the essential characteristics of being in love which separate it from mere sexual craving. Even in this man the loving attitude will be an experience completely different from an isolated sexual desire. In the latter instance, he will not at all think of uniting his life with that of the other; he will not think of marriage.

Still another element to be stressed in spousal love is the unparalleled happiness which is the fruit of this love. The mere ability to love bestows a singular happiness, not to mention the great happiness of love requited and of the union it results in. But this should not mislead one into believing that he can seek the happiness of love as an end for which the partner is a mere means. The authentic happiness of love is in reality a gift superabundantly granted. In the very instant in which he sees the other person as a mere means to happiness, he no longer loves and thus *cannot attain* the happiness proper to love.

There are many things which are ruined from the outset when they are considered in a means-to-an-end relationship. They must be taken seriously in themselves. If I listen to a Beethoven Symphony only because I wish to experience a wonderful feeling; I will then experience nothing. I must be focused on the symphony and immerse myself in its beauty; I must forget myself; and so it is in love. One should not forget that happiness is a result of love and not the motive for love. The motive for love is the preciousness, the beauty, the goodness which the other possesses, the value of this unique personality in its entire beauty. Love is a value response. But in all isolated sexual desire the opposite is true: the sham-happiness of mere sexual pleasure can be directly pursued and the other person can be considered exclusively as a means.

Spousal love alone constitutes the organic link to the sensual sphere, a sphere essentially foreign to every other love, such as friendship, the love of a mother, the love of a child. This does not exclude that in fact sexual instincts oftentimes creep into other types of love. But in such cases it is always more or less a perversion or at least a foreign body that has been added and not something which is in its very quality and nature ordered to be an organic fulfillment and expression of that love. Everyone who has an understanding of the nature and qualitative character of love and of sex, and who has not fallen prey to unrealistic abstract theories having a mythological character, such as Freud's pan-sexualism, can clearly see that it is only spousal love which has this organic relation to the sexual sphere. Spousal love is organically connected with it and finds in this sphere in a special way its expression and fulfillment. The mystery enclosed in this sphere possesses an incomparable depth.[8] In a certain sense the sexual in every man is his "personal secret." There is therefore a profound significance in the fact that the Biblical word "to know" also

[8] See *In Defense of Purity.*

signifies the marital act. Thus, the marital act is an ultimate self-donation, a giving of self. And because this sphere possesses a unique mysteriousness, it can become the vehicle and expression and fulfillment not only of the union desired by love, but also of the full and irrevocable mutual consent to become one—that is, of the clearly expressed *will* to an indissoluble union and bond, a will which organically grows out of love and which can in no way be separated from it if this spousal love is really present. This will can appear without it in marriages misleadingly labeled "marriages of convenience" (made for financial and other considerations). The mutual consent of the will (the *consensus*) to unite can therefore be given without love, but true spousal love can never be separated from the desire for this *consensus,* for the explicit and permanent bond.

We must therefore reject the application of the words "love" and "being in love" to an "abandonment" motivated by mere isolated sexual attraction, where in reality the individual flings himself away. This is a desecration of the mystery of sex, turning it into the *mysterium iniquitatis* [mystery of evil] of impurity. Such an isolated sexual desire is the exact antithesis to true love.

It should thus be clear that the grave error of seeing the primary, valid aspect of the sexual sphere as a mere realm of instincts is not corrected when, as at times today, people urge that it be considered something positive, while still overlooking the fact that its essential meaning is the fulfillment of spousal love. Whether one sees sexual desire in a positive or in a negative light is not the decisive point. One must see that this instinct is precisely not destined to remain an instinct like other instincts, but to become an expression of spousal love and an ultimate self-donation serving the union of both spouses. And even if one sees it merely as something parallel to the spiritual union, a kind of analogy in the bodily sphere, one still remains blind to the mystery, to the high value of the *mysterium unionis* [mystery of union] and to the *mysterium iniquitatis* [mystery of evil] in its abuse.

6. PRUDISHNESS, NEUTRAL ATTITUDE
OR REVERENCE AND MODESTY?

This character of mystery is especially overlooked today, and many proclaim it to be a great step forward that instead of a puritanical reticence, one now speaks in an open and neutral manner of this sphere. In reality, this is no progress at all. Little as the prudish attitude does justice to this sphere, the neutral attitude does still less.

The right antithesis to the puritan attitude is the reverent approach to this sphere in its character of mystery which excludes by its very essence every neutralization. It is erroneous to believe that a sense of shame can only indicate a response to something negative, for there are different types of shame; for instance, a virtuous man will want to hide his face when he is publicly praised. There is one kind, a noble modesty, which is a response to the intimate and mysterious character of a thing; and to misinterpret this bashfulness and modesty, which is called for in the sphere of sex, as mere prudery, is to exhibit the same deplorable blindness and superficiality which confuses humility with servility, and purity with frigidity. Indeed, this neutralization reveals the most disastrous failure to understand this sphere in its ecstatic and mysterious character and its essential intimacy.

7. SPOUSAL LOVE AND
THE IRREVOCABLE UNION OF MARRIAGE

We must thus start with an understanding of the meaning and value of marriage as the closest love union between man and woman, as constituting the most intimate human I-thou communion, the irrevocable bond which Christ elevated to a sacrament.

This union is constituted by the consensus of the spouses—that is, the lifelong mutual self-donation is constituted by the expressed will of the partners, solemnly pronounced before God and thereby, as it were, entrusted to God. The *intentio unionis* of spousal love finds its valid expression in this consensus and its fulfillment in the irrevocable union constituted by this consensus. It reaches, however, a still new fulfillment in the conjugal act, in the consummation of the marriage, with the full, accomplished self-donation, whereby they become "two in one flesh." Who can fail to grasp the grandeur and beauty of marriage and the bodily union which it essentially implies if he contemplates without prejudice the words of the Lord referring to the indissolubility of marriage?

> Because of the hardness of your heart he wrote you that precept. But from the beginning of the creation God made them male and female. For this cause a man shall leave his father and mother, and cleave to his wife, and the two shall become one flesh. Therefore now they are no longer two, but one flesh. What therefore God has joined together, let no man put asunder (Mark 10, 5–9).

Not the slightest connotation is to be found in these words which would justify a suspicious attitude toward love or the bodily union. That the bodily union is seen as the fulfillment of love clearly appears from the emphasis on the becoming one and the mutual self-donation. No mention is made of procreation. The words of Genesis clearly refer to this love: "Wherefore a man shall leave father and mother" (Gen. 2; 24). And the sublime words in which the indissolubility of marriage is expressed. "What therefore God has joined together, let no man put asunder," clearly disclose the depth and grandeur of the union constituted by the marital act: this love union was sealed by God and therefore it is not dissoluble by man. No unprejudiced mind can read and understand these words, receive them in all their solemnity in his soul, without being aware of the abyss which separates this conception of marriage from the gnostic, puritan approach so often found among Catholics.

8. THE SUPERNATURAL TRANSFORMATION OF MARRIAGE

And does not the fact that Christ granted to marriage the dignity of a sacrament, which means not only something sacred but also a source of special graces, disclose the high meaning and value of marriage?

It is not possible within the framework of this brief work to broach the most sublime aspect of marriage as a sacrament. But we wish to stress that spousal love also is called to be transformed by Christ; indeed, only in Christ and through Christ can the spouses live up to the full glory and depth to which this love by its very nature aspires. As Pius XII stated:

> But what new and unutterable beauty is added to this love of two human hearts, when its song is harmonized with the hymn of two souls vibrating with supernatural life! Here, too, there is a mutual exchange of gifts; and then, through bodily tenderness and its healthy joys, through natural affection and its impulses, through a spiritual union and its delights, the two beings who love each other identify themselves in all that is most intimate in them, from the unshaken depths of their beliefs to the highest summit of their hopes.[9]

The transformation of spousal love by Christ does not, however, make it lose its specific feature of spousal love. To quote the late Pontiff again:

> God with His love neither destroys nor changes nature, but perfects it; and St. Francis de Sales, who well knew the human heart, concluded his beautiful page on the sacred character of conjugal love with this twofold advice: "Keep, O husbands, a tender, constant, and cordial love for your wives.... And you, wives, love tenderly, cordially ... the husbands whom God has given you."
> Cordiality and tenderness, then, from one side and from the other. "Love and faithfulness," he used to say, "always create

[9] Allocution to newlyweds, Oct. 23, 1940.

intimacy and confidence; thus the saints were wont to give many demonstrations of affection in their marriages, demonstrations truly amorous, but chaste, tender, and sincere."[10]

II

I. THE MEANING OF MARRIAGE AND
THE PRINCIPLE OF SUPERABUNDANT FINALITY

.To this sublime love union God has confided the coming into being of a new man, a cooperation with His divine creativity. Could we think of any thing more beautiful than this connection between the deepest love communion, the ultimate self-donation out of love, and the creation of a new human being? A deep mystery is here offered to us, which calls for reverence and awe. But we can grasp the grandeur and depth of this connection only if we first understand the meaning and value of marriage as a love communion and the meaning and value of the marital act as the consummation of this ultimate union to which spousal love aspires. We can appreciate the mysterious character of the link between the marital act and the birth of a new person only if we have understood its finality as an instance of the principle of superabundance and not as an instrumental finality in which the conjugal act is looked at as a mere means for procreation. And it must be most emphatically stated that understanding the meaning and value of marriage as a love union *does not minimize but rather enhances the link between marriage and procreation.*

This will become clear as we examine briefly the nature of the principle of superabundance and its difference from merely instrumental finality.

[10] Ibid.

We cannot deny that one end of knowledge is to enable man to act; our entire practical life, from the most primitive activities to the most complicated ones, presupposes knowledge. Moreover, a still more sublime end of knowledge is to enable us to attain the moral perfection and sanctification which is the presupposition for our eternal welfare. And yet, if these can rightly be called the ends to which knowledge is destined, knowledge has undoubtedly also a meaning and value of its own; and the relation to the ends it serves has the character of superabundance. This is a typical case of a finality in which the end is not the exclusive *raison d'être* of something.

This kind of finality differs patently from the instrumental finality which is in question when we call a surgical instrument a means for operating, or money a means for procuring ourselves a good, or teeth a means for the mastication of food. The main difference between instrumental finality and the finality that we have called the principle of superabundance consists in the fact that in instrumental finality the being which is considered as a means is in its meaning and value completely dependent upon the end, whereas in superabundant finality, it has a meaning and value independently of the end to which it leads.

In the instrumental finality the *causa finalis* [final cause] determines the *causa formalis* [formal cause]; in the superabundant the *causa formalis* differs from the *causa finalis*.

In the case of a knife, the end (cutting) determines its entire nature; its meaning is identical with serving this end, and its value depends upon its function as a means. Its only *raison d'être* is to be a means for cutting. This is a typical instrumental finality.

In instrumental finality, the end is the exclusive *raison d'être* of the means; in superabundant finality, the good serving the end has also a *raison d'être* in itself.

We saw above that the intrinsic meaning and value of marriage consists in its being the deepest and closest love union. We saw that in its mutual self-donation and in its constitution of a matchless union, the conjugal act has the meaning of a unique fulfillment of spousal love. But to that high good, which has a meaning and value in itself, has been entrusted procreation. The same act, which in its meaning is the constitution of the union, has been superabundantly made the source of procreation; thus, we must speak of procreation as the end—but not in the sense of mere instrumental finality. Though we may consider the sexual instinct in animals as a mere means for the continuation of the species, as an end in the sense of an instrumental finality, this is patently impossible with respect to the love between man and woman or to their union in marriage.

Occasionally, it has been conceded that in their subjective approach the spouses need not look at marriage and the conjugal union as a mere means in the instrumental sense; but the claim continues to be made that objectively the relation between a union of love and procreation has the character of an instrumental finality. It is claimed that God has implanted in their hearts the love between man and woman and the desire for a conjugal union as a mere means for procreation. But in arguing thus, one has not understood the real character of the link between marriage and procreation.

We touch here on a general and dangerous tendency to overlook the very nature of the person and to assume that the kind of instrumentality that is to be found in the biological realm can be extended to the spiritual realm of man. As long as instincts or urges are in question, their inner logic and *ratio* goes, so to speak, over the head of the person. It is true that neither man's intelligence nor his free will establishes the meaningful direction of an instinct such as thirst or the desire to sleep. God has given to these instincts and urges their meaningfulness without involving man's intelligence; this finality is similar to the one found in merely unconscious physiological processes. In so far as the experienced urge or instinct of thirst, for instance, is at stake, we thus rightly say that its *raison d'être* is to procure for the body the necessary liquid, and that God has installed it as a means to that end.

But when it comes to the spiritual acts of the person, such as willing or loving or experiencing contrition, we can no longer assume that in the eyes of God they have no meaning in themselves but are only means linked to an end by a finality similar to that of the instincts or urges. We must not forget that God takes man as person so seriously that He has addressed Himself to man, and that it depends on man's free response whether or not he will attain his eternal destiny. St. Augustine expressed this when he wrote: "He who made you without you, will not justify you without you." The spiritual attitudes of man have a meaning and a *ratio* [ordering] in themselves, and they can never be treated as having their real significance independently of the person; they involve a person's intelligence and his freedom, his capacity to respond meaningfully, and not an impersonal, automatic finality going over the person's head. Consequently, it is impossible to see them as having their real significance beyond and independently of the person's conscious experience. Man is not a puppet for God, but a personal being to whom God addresses Himself and from whom He expects a meaningful response.

This devalorization and degradation of the spiritual human attitudes is incompatible with the character of man as a person, his character of *imago Dei* [image of God]; it ignores the very fact that God has revealed Himself to man and also the way in which man's redemption took place.

It may be objected: Does not God often use an evil attitude as a means for something good in the life of the individual and especially in the history of mankind? May not an attitude which is evil in itself become a means leading to something good? Yes, indeed, but the *felix culpa* [happy fault][11] does not remove from the fault its morally negative character and does not entitle us to look at a moral decision as something which acquires its real meaning only in its possible function as *felix culpa,* instead of seeing its primary meaning in its moral value or disvalue.

The kind of finality which we have in mind when we say that God's providence makes out of evil something leading to a good differs obviously also in a radical way from the instrumental

[11] [This refers to the sin of Adam, often referred to as a "happy fault" because it necessitated the coming of Christ.]

finality with which we are confronted in the biological sphere. It is not a finality which is rooted in the nature of something, but a free intervention of God's providence, using something in a direction which is even opposed to its nature and meaning. It would obviously make no sense to say that the end of moral evil is to lead to something good; that would be to claim that the very nature of a moral fault makes it a means for bringing about a good. The *culpa* [fault] is as such *infelix* [unhappy], and that it may become *felix* [happy] is owing to an intervention of God, which never entitles us to say that this is the objective, valid meaning of moral guilt in God's eyes. God does not judge man according to whether or not his sins later on prove to be a *felix culpa* but according to their intrinsic sinfulness. Thus, we see that the merciful intervention of God, making a good grow out of evil, in no way reduces the role of man to that of a puppet.

2. THE MEANING OF MARRIAGE AND ITS PRIMARY END

Coming back to our topic, we must state that it is incompatible with the very nature of the person to consider the deepest human spiritual experiences as mere subjective aspects of something that, in God's eyes, is a means for an extrinsic end. It would be seeing man in a merely biological light if we assumed that love between man and woman, the highest earthly good, is a mere means for the conservation of the species, that its objective *raison d'être* is exclusively to instigate a union which serves procreation. The God-given, essential link between love of man and woman and its fulfillment in the marital union, on the one hand, and the creation of a new person, on the other hand, has precisely the character of superabundance, which is a much deeper connection than would be one of merely instrumental finality.

But let it be stated again emphatically: to stress the meaning and value of marriage as the most intimate, indissoluble union of love does not contradict the doctrine that procreation is the primary end of marriage. The distinction we have made between meaning and end, as well as the insight that marriage has a value of its own besides its sublime value as source of procreation, in no way diminishes the importance of the link between marriage and procreation; it rather enhances the link and places it in the right perspective.

3. WHY ARTIFICIAL BIRTH CONTROL IS SINFUL

We can now see more clearly the difference between natural and artificial birth control. The sinfulness of artificial birth control is rooted in the arrogation of the right to separate the actualized love union in marriage from a possible conception, to sever the wonderful, deeply mysterious connection instituted by God. This mystery is approached in an irreverent attitude. We are here confronted with the fundamental sin of irreverence toward God, the denial of our creaturehood, the acting as if we were our own lords. This is a basic denial of the *religio,* of our being bound to God; it is a disrespect for the mysteries of God's creation, and its sinfulness increases with the rank of the mystery in question. It is the same sinfulness that lies in suicide or in euthanasia, in both of which we act as if we were masters of life.

Every *active* intervention of the spouses that eliminates the possibility of conception through the conjugal act is incompatible with the holy mystery of the superabundant relation in this incredible gift of God. And this irreverence also affects the purity of the conjugal act, because the union can be the real fulfillment of love only when it is approached with reverence and when it is embedded in the *religio,* the consciousness of our basic bond to God.

To the sublime link between marriage and procreation Christ's words on the marriage bond also apply: "What God has joined together, let no man put asunder." This becomes still clearer when we consider that the mystery of the birth of a man not only should[12] be essentially linked to wedded love (through the conjugal act, which is destined to be the expression and fulfillment of this love), but is always linked to a creative intervention of God. Neither wedded love nor, still less, the physiological process of conception is *itself capable* of creating a human being with an immortal soul. On this point Pope Paul VI quotes the encyclical *Mater et Magistra:* " 'Human life is holy,' Pope John XXIII reminds us, 'and from conception on it demands the immediate intervention of God!' " (*Humanae Vitae,* 13). Man always comes forth directly from the hand of God, and therefore there is a unique and intimate relation between God and the spouses in the act of procreation. In a fruitful conjugal act we can say that the spouses participate in God's act of creation; the conjugal act of the spouses is incorporated into the creative act of God and acquires a serving function in relation to His act.

We thus see that artificial birth control is sinful not only because it severs the mysterious link between the most intimate love union and the coming into existence of a new human being, but also because in a certain way it artificially cuts off the creative intervention of God, or better still, it artificially separates an act which is ordained toward co-operation with the creative act of God from this its destiny. For, as Paul VI says, this is to consider oneself not a servant of God, but the "Lord over the origin of human life" (*Humanae Vitae,* 13).

This irreverence, however, is exclusively limited to *active* intervention severing the conjugal act from its possible link with procreation.

The conjugal act does not in any way lose its full meaning and value when one knows that a conception is out of the question, as when age, or an operation for the sake of health, or pregnancy excludes it. The knowledge that a conception is not possible does not in the least taint the conjugal act with irreverence. In such cases, if the act is an expression of a deep love, anchored in Christ,

[12] See under 5 below, "The Order of What Is and the Order of What Ought to Be in Marriage."

it will rank even higher in its quality and purity than one that leads to a conception in a marriage in which the love is less deep and not formed by Christ. And even when for good and valid reasons conception should be avoided, the marital act in no way loses its *raison d'être,* because its meaning and value is the actualization of the mutual self-donation of the spouses.[13] The intention of avoiding conception does not imply irreverence as long as one does not actively interfere in order to cut the link between the conjugal act and a possible conception.

Nor is the practice of rhythm to avoid conception in any way irreverent, because the existence of rhythm—that is to say, the fact that conception is limited to a short period—is itself a God-given institution. In Section 6 we shall show in greater detail why the use of rhythm implies not the slightest irreverence or rebellion against God's institution of the wonderful link between the love union and procreation; it is in no way a subterfuge, as some Catholics tend to believe. On the contrary, it is a grateful acceptance of the possibility God has granted of avoiding conception—if this is legitimately desirable—without preventing the expression and fulfillment of spousal love in the bodily union.

4. TWO CONCEPTS OF NATURE IN "HUMANAE VITAE"

In order to understand the decisive difference between natural and artificial birth control we must be aware that the concept "nature" can have various meanings.

On the one hand, "nature" can signify the purely factual order of creation, especially material and biological creation. On the other, however, the same word can signify the essence of profoundly significant relations endowed with a high value.

---

[13] Even when conjugal love has grown cold, the marital act remains morally allowed, as long as worthily fulfilled and not desecrated by an impure attitude, since the right of the partner to one's body was granted in the marital consensus.

That the time between the conception and birth of a man is nine months and not eight or ten months is merely a factual datum. It could just as well be otherwise, and this fact bears no significant value. That the openings of the esophagus and the windpipe are so close together in man that one can choke easily is certainly a fact, but it is not a deeply meaningful relation which has a value. On the contrary, injuries could be averted were this not the case. But quite different, for instance, is the fact that love brings happiness. This is not something merely factual; it is deeply meaningful and bears a high value. This is also true of the fact that a deep union of two persons is constituted in mutual love. Indeed, it is of meaning and value that this reciprocal love is the only path leading to a spiritual union that is much deeper and more authentic than any amalgamation, any fusion, in the impersonal world. This fact, which is rooted in the nature of love and the personal I-thou communion, is the bearer of a high value. No one can reasonably say that this fact could be otherwise. It could not be otherwise, because it is a significant, intelligible, and necessary intrinsic relation. Similarly, it would betray extraordinary value-blindness not to see the depth and sublimity of this relation, but to regard it as something indifferent.

However, the *essential* difference between the two concepts of nature is not that in the one case we are confronted with an intelligible necessary fact and in the other with a mere empirical fact, but rather that in the one relations are deeply meaningful and possess a high *value,* and in the other they are only factual.

It is certainly true that for the faithful Christian both kinds of "nature" proceed from God and are therefore reverently accepted. Nevertheless, nature in the purely factual sense does not constitute something in which man ought not to intervene when there are reasonable grounds for seeking a change (in some circumstances he is even *obliged* to intervene). But intervention in nature in the second sense, where meaning and value are grounded in the essence of a thing, has a completely different character. For this nature contains in its very meaning and value a unique message from God and calls upon us to respect it.

This applies most of all to relations which constitute a deep mystery. Any violence done to these is particularly presumptuous on the part of man the creature. It is the usurpation of a right which man does not possess; it reflects a desire to play the role of God and Providence.

The confusion of these two concepts of nature has kept many from a proper understanding of the encyclical *Humanae Vitae*. They do not understand that it is not a merely factual or exclusively biological connection but rather a great and sublime mystery that God has entrusted the generation of a human being to the intimate union of man and wife who love each other in wedded love and who in becoming "two in one flesh" participate in the creative act of God. This is gloriously expressed by a prayer of an ancient Fulda ritual: "O Lord our God, who created man pure and spotless and thereafter ordained that in the propagation of the human race one generation should be produced from another by the *mystery of sweet love.*" The relation expressed here is thus not a merely factual one, but a staggering mystery, an ineffably deep and glorious fact. It is therefore a false argument to say: Why shouldn't man be allowed to regulate birth by artificial means, when God, after all, gave man control and dominion over nature and in the Old Testament made him the master of creation? Why is it allowed in medicine to take out the uterus, to transplant hearts, and perform many kinds of operations, but forbidden to intervene and modify nature in the case of the regulation of births? All those who argue in this way do not understand the radical difference between these two cases, because they confuse the two concepts of nature. As long as we remain within the realm of the purely "factual," we are not morally forbidden to intervene. But when we deal with meaningful relations which possess a high value in themselves, and when, as in this case, we deal with a mystery which we can contemplate only with the deepest reverence, then every artificial intervention is a flagrant moral wrong.

A Static or a Dynamic Concept of Nature?

It is more than regrettable that the terms "dynamic" and "static" have been used in the polemic against the encyclical and its concept of nature. These typical shibboleths have taken on a particularly demagogic character in contemporary philosophical discussions. They appeal to irrational emotions and muddle the objective state of affairs. I have treated extensively the various confusions that lie behind these concepts in my book *Trojan Horse in the City of God.* [14]

5. THE RELATION BETWEEN
BIOLOGICAL NATURE AND THE PERSON

One might object: Co-operation in the creation of a new human being is, after all, confined to the *physical act;* this co-operation can even take place when no union of love is present; therefore, it is a purely biological datum; it is bound neither to reciprocal love nor to the consensus of marriage, and can even be the result of the crime of rape.

But this objection overlooks the deep connection between biological nature and the person, and in two ways. First, the fact that in human nature many things are *de facto* the result of physical processes does not in the least cancel the truth that these physical processes *should* be the expression of *spiritual* attitudes. Secondly, not everything that is *connected* with biological conditions is itself biological.

[14] Chicago: Franciscan Herald Press, 1968.

The Order of What Is and the Order of What Ought to Be in Marriage

The *meaning* of the conjugal act is, as we have said, the ultimate fulfillment of the union desired by spousal love. It represents a unique gift of self, a gift that presupposes not only love, but also consensus—the volitional act necessarily aspired to by the type of love we termed spousal love and initiating the irrevocable bond of marriage. We have seen the grave sin in every profanation of the conjugal act, every isolation of it from mutual love and the consensus. This is the source of all *impurity.* On the other hand, the *active,* artificial isolation of this act from the possible genera-tion of a human being constitutes a sin of *irreverence* towards God. This is usurping a right not given to the creature.

That conception is possible even when the sanctioned love union is absent does not deny that God has entrusted procreation to the wedded act, which ought to be a love union sanctioned by consensus.

Here we touch upon a profoundly mysterious area of creation, where what is can either coincide with what ought to be or deviate from it. This is most clearly seen in human freedom: man *can* do what he *ought not* do. He can freely initiate a causal sequence independently of whether he should or should not do so. He can use his freedom in a way opposed to that for which his freedom was granted to him. On the one hand, a causal sequence is not deprived of its efficacy because men abuse it. On the other hand, the fact that this causal sequence *should* serve an end endowed with value is in no way suspended by this abuse. This relation of oughtness remains unchanged and keeps its full validity and reality. Precisely for this reason, every deviation from it is a sin.

When, therefore, someone enters into marriage for, let us say, financial reasons and thereby separates the consensus from its proper context, the marriage is certainly valid; but this does not deny that marriage should be the most intimate union of love, that this union is its meaning, and that God has given it as such to man.

Similarly, the superabundant finality of this union of love

remains a relation ordained by God, one which *ought* to exist between the union of love and the generation of a new human being, even though sexual intercourse performed without any love or outside of marriage can lead to conception.

We must endeavor to understand more deeply this mysterious structure of the cosmos: *an infraction of a moral obligation does not in itself cancel the factual order* — that is, the causal efficacy inherent in physical and physiological processes will not be destroyed when we do not act as we ought to; *but neither is the fact that something is morally binding affected by its not being done.*

We must acknowledge this great gift, which God grants to men: He entrusts to man's free will the task of harmonizing things as they are with things as they ought to be. This is man's great dignity and awesome responsibility. In order to divine the meaning of the cosmos in the light of God and understand His message in it, we must take into account how things ought to be and not restrict ourselves to the mere factual order. Therefore, the fact that a man can be generated through sexual intercourse without any love in no way nullifies the mysterious truth that God has entrusted the coming into being of a man to an indissoluble love communion.

Physiological Processes and the Creation of Human Life: Is Artificial Birth Control ever a Merely "Biological" Intervention?

Moreover, the conception of a human being, even when it takes place without the prescribed connection with marital love, is not a mere biological fact. Our entire spiritual and personal life is bound to physiological conditions in various ways, but it is not for this reason a biological reality. Indeed, even baptismal grace or the Real Presence of Christ is attached to an outward sign. In the entire cosmos, then, we repeatedly find this dispensation of divine Providence: realities of a very high order are connected with inferior conditions. But this does not permit us to see only the latter.

The creation of an immortal human person by God through the cooperation of the married couple is therefore in itself never a biological occurrence, though it requires biological conditions. Therefore, the fact that biological laws connect the conjugal act with the creation of a human person does not justify our considering the rupture of the connection only a biological intervention. An extreme case makes this immediately clear: a fatal shot through a man's head is not simply a "biological intervention" but a murder, because a man's life was connected with the physiological processes that were frustrated.

Artificial birth control is thus no mere biological intervention but the severing of a bond which is under the jurisdiction of God alone.

Biological vs. Personal Values

In order to justify artificial birth control some people invoke the superiority of personal values over biological values. It is undoubtedly true that personal values rank higher than biological values. But the generation of a new human being, a spiritual person who is an image of God, clearly bears not only a biological value but also an eminently personal value. Whoever is blind to this cannot speak meaningfully of personal values. Again, the fact that the coming into being of a new person is bound by God to the most tender love union is a great mystery which obviously also cannot be regarded as the bearer of a merely biological value. The superabundant finality that binds the becoming of a new human being to the love union in a special way even draws the one who understands it *in conspectu Dei* — before the face of God.

6. WHY ARTIFICIAL BIRTH CONTROL IS SINFUL
BUT THE RHYTHM METHOD IS NOT

The distinctions we have made above between the two concepts of nature shed new light upon the whole problem of artificial birth control. Above all, we are now in a position to see more clearly the decisive difference between rhythm and artificial birth control. We can now meet more decisively the objection: "Is it not also irreverent to have the explicit intention of avoiding the conception of a new human being without totally abstaining from the conjugal act?"

In the first place the value and meaning of the conjugal act is not affected by the married couple's certainty that it cannot lead to conception. Having seen that this act in its very meaning is a unique expression of spousal love and a mutual donation of self, grounded in consensus, we now understand more clearly that this act is not only allowed, but is possessed of a high value even when conception is not possible. This meaning and value is explicitly recognized in the addresses of Pius XII, in the Council decree *Gaudium et Spes,* as well as in the encyclical *Humanae Vitae.*

In the second place it is definitely allowed *expressly* to avoid conception when the conjugal act takes place *only* in the *God-given* infertile time — that is, only by means of the rhythm method and for legitimate reasons. One would have to be blind to the meaning and value of the conjugal act to say that complete abstinence is morally required when conception is to be avoided for legitimate reasons.

It is clear, therefore, that in the intention itself of avoiding another child for serious reasons there is not the least trace of irreverence toward the mysterious fact that God has entrusted the birth of a person to the spousal love union. We see that only during relatively brief intervals has God Himself linked the conjugal act to the creation of a man. Hence the bond, the active tearing apart of which is a sin, is realized only for a short time in the order of things ordained by God Himself. This also has a meaning. The fact that conception is restricted to a short time implies a word of God. It not only confirms that the bodily union of the spouses has a meaning and value in itself, apart from procreation, but it also leaves open the possibility of avoiding conception if this is desirable for serious reasons. The sin consists in this alone: the sundering by man of what God has joined together—the *artificial, active* severing of the mystery of bodily union from the creative act to which it is bound at the time. Only in this artificial intervention, where one *acts against* the mystery of superabundant finality, is there the sin of irreverence—that is to say, the sin of presumptuously exceeding the creatural rights of man.

Analogously, I may very well wish (and pray) that an incurably sick and extremely suffering man would die. I may abstain from artificially prolonging his life for a matter of hours or days. But I am not allowed to kill him! There is an abyss between desiring someone's death and euthanasia. In both cases the *intention* is the same: out of sympathy I desire that he be delivered from suffering. But in the one case I do nothing that might prolong his suffering, whereas in the other I actively intervene and arrogate to myself a right over life and death that belongs to God alone.

Only when we see the *divinely ordained limits to our active intervention,* the limits that define what is allowed and that play a great role in the whole moral sphere, can we perceive the abyss separating the rhythm method from the use of all kinds of contraceptive devices.[15]

It is therefore desirable that science discover improved methods for ascertaining the infertile days. Pope Pius XII said that he prayed for this, and so should all Christians. Paul VI expresses this wish in *Humanae Vitae,* 24.

As soon as we see the abyss separating the use of rhythm from

---

[15] This distinction between *active intervention* on our part and *letting things take their course* is also drawn in another situation: though no Catholic spouse is allowed to use contraceptive means, he is still not allowed to refuse the marital act even when his partner employs contraceptive means. Here also the distinction between the active and passive attitude is morally decisive.

artificial birth control, we have answered the question: why should artificial birth control be a sin if the use of rhythm is allowed? And as soon as we see clearly the sinfulness of artificial birth control, we can and must repudiate the suggestion that it is the proper means of averting dangers that menace marital happiness or averting overpopulation. No evil in the world, however great, may be avoided through a sinful means. To commit a sin in order to avoid an evil would be to adhere to the ignominious principle: the end justifies the means.

FURTHER READING

Dietrich Von Hildebrand was a prolific author. It may confuse the reader to list all his works here. Many are available as reprints from Sophia Institute Press. Those that may be of particular interest and relevance are *Purity* (Steubenville, Ohio: Franciscan University Press, 1989); *Man and Woman* (Chicago: Franciscan Herald Press, 1965; to be reprinted by Sophia Institute Press); *Marriage* (Manchester, N.H.: Sophia Institute Press, 1984). His *Trojan Horse in the City of God* (Chicago: Franciscan Herald Press, 1968) was a prophetic description of the chaos in the Church; and his *Transformation in Christ* (Manchester, N.H.: Sophia Institute Press, 1990) has become a spiritual classic. See also the chapter on "Reverence" in *Liturgy and Personality* (Manchester, N.H.: Sophia Institute Press, 1986).

3

POPE PAUL VI TO THE TEAMS OF OUR LADY,
Rome, May 4, 1970

On May 4, 1970, Pope Paul VI gave a talk on the meaning of marriage to the Teams of Our Lady, a lay association of married couples. As Father Marc Calegari's editorial note to this talk stated, he attributed great importance to this talk; he believed it to be Pope Paul VI's fulfillment of his own call for a fuller treatment of marriage that would help spouses understand the teaching of *Humanae Vitae*. Cardinal Roger Etchegaray, in a talk to the Teams of Our Lady in October 1979, commemorated Pope Paul VI's talk and referred to it as a "prolonged commentary" (*un prolongement, une reprise*) on *Humanae Vitae*.[1] He cites Paul VI's Teams of Our Lady talk as evidence that, contrary to the opinion of some, Paul VI did not allow a cloak of silence to envelop *Humanae Vitae* but that he energetically promoted its teaching. In one of his early talks condemning contraception, Pope John Paul II pointed to the magisterial force of the Church's teaching by noting that it had been advanced by the Council and by his predecessors, most notably by Paul VI in *Humanae Vitae* and in his talk to the Teams of Our Lady, among other discourses.[2]

---

[1] "Allocution de Mgr. Etchegaray aux foyers des 'Equipes Notre Dame'", *La Documentation Catholique* 1760 (Mar. 18, 1979): 271–73.

[2] John Paul II, to the Research Teams' Liaison Center (C.L.E.R.) and to the Federation of Organizations for Research and Promotion of Natural Methods of Family Planning (F.I.D.A.F.), Nov. 3, 1979. (*L'Osservatore Romano*, no. 49 (Dec. 3, 1979), p. 15.

Father Henri Caffarel has written a commentary on the talk.[3]

In this talk, Pope Paul VI indicates his sensitive understanding that couples may initially find the Church's teaching difficult to live by, both because of the affliction of original sin and also because we are living in an age of rampant eroticism. He assures spouses that marriage is a means to sanctification and that God will provide the graces necessary for couples to be faithful to the moral demands of their vocation. He elaborates on the important theme of *Humanae Vitae* that, in having children, spouses are collaborators with God.

This is an unpublished translation by Father Marc Calegari. A translation by John Drury has been published as "Christian Witness in Married Life" in *The Pope Speaks* 15, no. 2 (Summer 1970): 119–28.

[3] Father Henri Caffarel, *Sexualité, Mariage, Amour* (Paris; Editions de Feu Nouveau, 1970). This commentary has been translated into English: *Marriage, Sexuality, Love* (Melbourne; A.C.T.S. Publications no. 1581, Aug. 10, 1970). I owe the references in this and the two previous footnotes to the assistance of Father Marc Calegari.

3

POPE PAUL VI TO THE TEAMS OF OUR LADY

Rome, May 4, 1970*

Dear sons, dear daughters,

1. May we, first of all, thank you from the bottom of our heart for your faith-inspired words, for the night prayer offered for our intentions, and also for your commitment to the fostering of vocations. And we want to tell you how great is our joy as we welcome you this morning, and as we speak, through you, to the 20,000 couples of the Teams of Our Lady. You were telling us a moment ago how your movement has spread throughout the world and how concerned you are to live with Christ and to make his will an integral part of your daily living of married love. You constitute small teams of Christian couples whose object it is to help one another spiritually, supported in your efforts by the

* Note: On July 31, 1968, two days after the publication of *Humanae Vitae*, Pope Paul VI, during his regular Wednesday audience, remarked that the encyclical had "clarified a fundamental chapter ... in the field of marriage, family and morality". He added, however, that "the Magisterium of the Church could and perhaps should return to [this] immense field with a fuller, more organic, and more synthetic treatment". Cf. *AAS* 60 (1968): 527.

Was this talk to the Teams of Our Lady meant to be that "fuller, more organic, and more synthetic treatment" mentioned by Paul VI twenty-one months earlier?

All that can be answered is that in no subsequent address or document did Paul VI comment more extensively on marriage, family, and *Humanae Vitae*. This alone would make the talk eminently worthy of attention and study.

presence of a priest. How could we not rejoice in this? Dear sons and daughters, the Pope heartily encourages you and invokes the blessing of God upon your work.

All too often the Church has seemed to hold human love suspect, but this impression is erroneous. And so today we want to tell you plainly: no, God is not the enemy of the great realities of human life, and the Church does not in the least underestimate the values lived every day by millions of couples. Quite the contrary, the Good News brought by Christ the Savior is good news also for human love, which, like everything else, was excellent in its origins—"And God saw that it was very good"[1]—it too was corrupted by sin, and it too was redeemed, so that it has become, through grace, a means of holiness.

Marriage in the Lord, a Call to Holiness

2. Like all who are baptized, you are, in fact, called to holiness, according to the teaching of the Church solemnly reaffirmed by the Council.[2] But you are to pursue that goal in your own way, in and through your life as couples.[3] It is the Church that teaches us: "By grace, husband and wife are made capable of leading a holy life"[4] and of making their home "a domestic extension of the Church's sanctuary".[5]

You are certainly familiar with these thoughts. How tragic for our times that they have been forgotten. We wish to meditate on them with you for a few moments in order to strengthen once

---

[1] Gen 1:31.

[2] Cf. Second Vatican Council, Dogmatic Constitution *Lumen Gentium*, Nov. 21, 1964, no. 11: *AAS* 57 (1965): 15–16.

[3] Ibid., no. 41: *AAS* 57 (1965): 47.

[4] Second Vatican Council, Pastoral Constitution *Gaudium et Spes*, Dec. 7, 1966, no. 49.2: *AAS* 58 (1966): 1070.

[5] Second Vatican Council, Decree *Apostolicam Actuositatem*, Nov. 18, 1965, no. 11: *AAS* 58 (1966): 848.

again, if need be, your will to live generously your Christian and human vocation in marriage[6] and to cooperate together in the great design of God's love for the world, which is to form a people "for the praise of his glory".[7]

I

MARRIAGE

Man and Woman, He Created Them

3. As Holy Scripture teaches us, marriage, before being a sacrament, is a great natural reality: "God created man in the image of himself, in the image of God he created him, man and woman he created them."[8] We must always refer back to this first page of the Bible if we wish to understand what a human couple, husband and wife, is and ought to be.

Psychological analyses, psychoanalytic studies, sociological surveys, philosophical reflections can certainly shed light on sexuality and human love, but they would delude us if they neglected this fundamental teaching given to us from the beginning: the duality of the sexes was willed by God, so that man and woman together might be the image of God and, like him, a source of life: "Be fruitful, multiply, fill the earth and subdue it."[9]

Moreover, a careful reading of the Prophets, the Wisdom Books, and the New Testament shows us the significance of this funda-

---

[6] Cf. Second Vatican Council, Pastoral Constitution *Gaudium et Spes,* nos. 1, 47–52: *AAS* 58 (1966): 1025–26, 1067–74.

[7] Eph 1:14.

[8] Gen 1:27.

[9] Gen 1:28.

mental reality. We are taught not to reduce it to physical desire and genital activity but to discover in it how the qualities of man and woman are complementary, to discover the grandeur and frailty of married love as well as its fruitfulness, and to discover how married love can serve as an introduction to the mystery of God's design of love.

Education in an Erotic Atmosphere

4. This teaching retains its full value today and strengthens us against the temptation of a ravaging eroticism. This phenomenon represents an aberration, and it should at least alert us to the distressful state of a materialistic civilization that has an obscure realization that in this mysterious domain is to be found, as it were, the last refuge of a sacred value. Will we be able to rescue it from an engulfing sensuality?

Faced with a pervading eroticism, cynically fostered by a greedy industry, we must at least know how to prevent its damaging effects on the young. We must encourage an education that helps the child and the adolescent, without obstructing or inhibiting them, to become gradually aware of the power of the drives awakening within them, to make these drives an integral part of their developing personality, to control the increasing strength of these drives so as to achieve full affective as well as sexual maturity, and in this way to prepare themselves for the gift of self through a love that will give to that gift its true dimension, in an exclusive and definitive manner.

Marriage, One and Indissoluble

5. The union of man and woman differs radically, in fact, from every other form of human association. It constitutes a unique reality, namely, the couple, founded on the mutual gift of self to

the other: "And they become but one flesh."[10] The irrevocable indissolubility of this unity is the seal affixed to the free and mutual commitment of two free individuals who "henceforth are no longer two, but one flesh".[11] They are but one flesh, one couple—we could almost say one being. Their unity will take on social and juridical form through marriage and will be manifested by a community of life that finds fruitful expression in their sexual self-giving.

This means that by their marriage, husband and wife express a desire to belong to each other for life and, to this end, to contract an objective bond, whose laws and requirements, far from being a kind of slavery, are a guarantee and a protection, a real support, as you yourselves realize from your day-to-day experience.

Married Love

6. This gift of self is not, in effect, a fusion. Each personality remains distinct and in no way loses its identity in the mutual gift of self. Rather, each personality is strengthened. It affirms itself. It matures and develops throughout the course of married life, in accordance with that great law of love: give yourselves one to the other, so as to be able, together, to give yourselves to others.

Love, in fact, is the binding force that gives this community of life its strength. Love is the force that makes this community ever richer and more perfect. The whole person participates in this exchange of love, the whole person, at the deepest levels of its own mysterious inner being, with all its affective, sensory, sexual as well as spiritual dimensions, thus forming ever more perfectly that image of God that it is the couple's mission to make present and visible day by day as they live out the joys and trials of life—so true is it that there is more to love than just love.

There is no married love that in its deepest joy is not an

[10] Gen 2:24.
[11] Mt 19:6.

impetus towards the infinite and does not by reason of its very dynamism aim to be total, faithful, exclusive, and fruitful.[12]

It is in this perspective that sexual desire finds its full significance. The marriage act is as much a means of expression as it is a means for husband and wife to know each other and to share with each other. It supports and strengthens their love, and in the fruitfulness of this act the couple finds its total fulfillment: in the image of God the couple becomes a source of life.

The Christian knows that human love is good by reason of its origin. And if, like everything else in man, it is wounded and deformed by sin, it finds in Christ its salvation and redemption. But is this not the lesson of twenty centuries of Christian history? So many couples have found the path to holiness in their married lives, in this community of life, which is the only one founded on a sacrament!

II

IN THE LORD

A New Creation

7. As the work of the Holy Spirit,[13] the rebirth of baptism makes of us new creatures,[14] "called as we also are to live a new life".[15] In this splendid undertaking of the renewal of all things in Christ, marriage, which has also been purified and renewed, becomes a new reality, a sacrament of the New Covenant.

See how in the first chapters of the New Testament, as at the

---

[12] Cf. Paul VI, Encyclical *Humanae Vitae,* July 25, 1968, no. 9: *AAS* 60 (1968): 486–87.

[13] Cf. Titus 3:5.

[14] Cf. Gal 6:15.

[15] Rom 6:4.

beginning of the Old Testament, a couple makes its appearance. But whereas Adam and Eve were the source of the evil that spread over the world, Joseph and Mary are the summit from which holiness reaches down to every corner of the globe. The Savior began his work of salvation by this virginal and holy union, in which he reveals his omnipotent will to purify and sanctify the family, this sanctuary of love and cradle of life.

Union "in the Lord"

8. Since then, everything is transformed. Two Christians wish to marry; St. Paul forewarns them: "You are no longer your own."[16] They are members of Christ, both of them, "in the Lord". Their union, too, is made "in the Lord", like that of the Church. And this is why their union is a "great mystery",[17] a sign that not only represents the mystery of Christ's union with the Church but, what is more, contains this mystery within itself and radiates it through the grace of the Holy Spirit, who is its life-giving soul.

For it is indeed the very love that is proper to God that he imparts to us so that we may love him and also love one another with that divine love: "Love one another as I have loved you."[18] For Christian spouses the very manifestations of their tenderness are permeated with this love that they draw from the heart of God. And if the human source of this love were in danger of drying up, its divine source is as inexhaustible as the fathomless depths of God's tenderness.

This tells us the depth and richness of the intimate communion toward which married charity tends. It is an interior spiritual reality that transforms the couple's community of life into what could be called, according to the authorized teaching of the

[16] 1 Cor 6:19.
[17] Eph 5:32.
[18] Jn 13:34.

Council, "the domestic Church",[19] a true "cell of the Church", as our beloved predecessor John XXIII expressed it on the occasion of your pilgrimage of May 3, 1959.[20] It is a basic, germinal cell—the smallest, to be sure, but also the most fundamental in the body of the Church.

The Fullness of Christian Love

9. That mystery in which married love is rooted and that throws light on all its forms of expression is the mystery of the Incarnation, which elevates our human potentialities by penetrating them from within. Far from despising these potentialities, Christian love raises them to their fullness with patience, generosity, strength, and tenderness, as St. Francis de Sales liked to emphasize in praising the married life of St. Louis.[21]

For if the fascination of the flesh is dangerous, the temptation of angelism is no less dangerous: a human reality that is looked at with contempt is quick to reassert itself. Therefore, aware that they carry their treasures in earthen vessels,[22] Christian spouses strive with humble fervor to apply in their married life the advice of St. Paul: "Your bodies are members of Christ . . . , temples of the Holy Spirit . . . ; therefore, glorify God in your body."[23] "Wedded in the Lord", husband and wife henceforth can unite only in the name of Christ, to whom they belong and for whom they must work as active members of his body. They cannot, therefore, make use of their body, notably insofar as it is the

[19] Second Vatican Council, Dogmatic Constitution *Lumen Gentium*, no. 11: *AAS* 57 (1965): 16.

[20] John XXIII, Address to the Teams of Our Lady, May 3, 1959: *Discorsi, messaggi, colloqui del Santo Padre Giovanni XXIII,* I, p. 298.

[21] *Introduction to the Devout Life,* pt. III, chap. 38, "Instructions for Married Persons".

[22] Cf. 2 Cor 4:7.

[23] 1 Cor 6:13-20.

principle of generation, except in the spirit of Christ and for his work, since they are members of Christ.

The Fruitfulness of the Couple

10. As "free and responsible collaborators of the Creator",[24] Christian spouses thereby see their physical fertility take on a new dignity. Their impulse to unite sexually is life-bearing and permits God to give himself children. When they become father and mother, the spouses discover to their amazement at the baptismal font that henceforth their child is a child of God, "born again of water and the Spirit",[25] and that this child is entrusted to them that they may watch over his physical and moral growth, yes, but also over the beginnings and development and maturing in him of the "new man".[26] This child is no longer merely the infant they see with their eyes, but no less what they believe to be "an infinity of mystery and love that would dazzle us if we were to see it face to face".[27] Thus, education becomes truly a service of Christ, as he himself said: "What you do to one of these little ones, it is to me that you do it."[28]

And if it should happen that the adolescent closes himself to the efforts of his parents to educate him, then these parents painfully partake in their very flesh in the Passion of Christ faced with the refusals of man.

---

[24] Paul VI, Encyclical *Humanae Vitae,* no. 1: *AAS* 60 (1968): 481.

[25] Jn 3:5.

[26] Eph 4:24.

[27] Emmanuel Mounier to his wife, Paulette, Mar. 20, 1940, in *Oeuvres* 4 (Paris: Seuil, 1963), p. 662.

[28] Mt 25:40.

The Mystery of Parenthood

11. Dear parents, God has not entrusted such an important task to you[29] without at the same time giving you a marvelous gift, his love as a Father. Through parents who love their child in whom Christ is living, it is the love of the Father that is poured out in his beloved Son.[30] Through the authority of the parents, it is his authority that is exercised. Through their devotedness, his providence is exercised, that of a "Father from whom all fatherhood takes its name in heaven and on earth".[31] In this way, through the love of his parents, the baptized infant discovers God's fatherly love and, as the Council tells us, has his "first experience of the Church".[32] Of course, the child will become aware of this only as he grows older; but through the tender care of his father and mother, God's love is already nurturing and developing in him his life as a child of God.

This indicates how splendid is your vocation, which St. Thomas Aquinas rightly compares to the ministry of the priesthood: "Some persons propagate and conserve the spiritual life by a ministry that is only spiritual, and this belongs to the sacrament of orders. Others do it by a ministry that is both physical and spiritual; this takes place in the sacrament of marriage, which unites man and woman so that they may have children and rear them for the worship of God."[33]

Couples who bear the heavy burden of being childless are, nevertheless, also called to cooperate in the growth of the People of God in many ways.

---

[29] Cf. Second Vatican Council, Declaration *Gravissimum Educationis,* Oct. 28, 1965: *AAS* 58 (1966): 728–39.

[30] Cf. 1 Jn 4:7-11.

[31] Cf. Eph 3:15.

[32] Second Vatican Council, Declaration *Gravissimum Educationis,* no. 3: *AAS* 58 (1966): 731.

[33] *Contra Gentiles,* IV, 58.

The Duty of Hospitality

12. This morning we only want to draw your attention to hospitality, which is an outstanding form of the married couple's mission and apostolate. Consider St. Paul's injunction to the Romans: "Be zealous in your practice of hospitality."[34] Is this not addressed first of all to couples? And in formulating it, was he not thinking of Aquila and Priscilla and of their hospitality, which he had been the first to enjoy in the home that later would welcome the Christian community?[35] In our days, when life is so hard for many people, what a blessing it is to be welcomed "into this miniature Church", as St. John Chrysostom expressed it,[36] to enter into its tenderness, to discover its maternal care, to experience its mercy, so true is it that a Christian home is "the gentle smiling face of the Church".[37] This is an irreplaceable apostolate, which is yours to carry out generously. It is an apostolate proper to the couple, with areas of activity particularly well suited to it: preparing engaged couples for marriage, helping newly married couples, and aiding couples in trouble.

If you support one another, what tasks can you not carry out both in the Church and in the City of Man? We call upon you with great confidence and much hope to undertake them: "The Christian family loudly proclaims both the present power of the Kingdom of God and the hope of the blessed life to come. Thus by its example and its testimony it convinces the world of its sinfulness and enlightens those who seek the truth."[38]

[34] 12:13.

[35] Cf. Acts 18:2–3; Rom 16:3–4; 1 Cor 16:19.

[36] *Homily 20 on Ephesians*, no. 6: *PG* 62:143.

[37] Phrase coined by a member-couple of the Teams of Our Lady, cited by H. Caffarel, in *Anneau d'Or*, no. 111–12; *Le mariage, ce grand sacrement* (Paris: Feu Nouveau, 1963), p. 282.

[38] Second Vatican Council, Dogmatic Constitution *Lumen Gentium*, no. 35: *AAS* 57 (1965): 40–41.

III

A CALL TO HOLINESS

On the Journey of Love

13. Dear sons and daughters, as you well know, it is by living the graces of the sacrament of marriage that you journey with "untiring, generous love"[39] toward that holiness to which we are all called by grace.[40] It is not an obligation arbitrarily imposed that calls us to holiness but rather the love of a Father who desires that his children attain their full potential and maturing and find their total happiness. Moreover, to arrive at this goal, you have not been left to your own resources, since Christ and the Holy Spirit, "those two hands of God", according to the expression of St. Irenaeus, are unceasingly at work on your behalf.[41]

Do not therefore let yourselves be led astray by the temptations, difficulties, and trials that arise along the way. Do not be afraid, when necessary, to go against the tide of thought and opinion of a world ruled by paganized standards of behavior. St. Paul warns us: "Do not conform yourselves to this world, but be transformed by the renewal of your spirit."[42]

And do not be discouraged in moments of weakness. Our God is a Father full of tenderness and goodness, filled with concern and overflowing with love for his children, who have to struggle on their journey. And the Church is a mother who desires to help you live to the fullest this ideal of Christian marriage. She reminds you, along with the beauty of this ideal, of all its demands.

---

[39] Ibid., no. 41: *AAS* 57 (1965): 47.
[40] Cf. Mt 5:48; 1 The 4:3; Eph 1:4.
[41] Cf. *Adversus Haereses,* V, 28, 4: *PG* 7:1200.
[42] Rom 12:2.

Thinking, Willing, Acting Right

14. Dear sons, chaplains of the Teams of Our Lady, you know by a long and varied experience that your consecrated celibacy makes you particularly available to couples, to be for them, on their journey toward holiness, active witnesses of the love of the Lord in the Church.

Day after day you help them "walk in the light".[43] You help them to think right, that is, to evaluate their behavior and see to what extent it conforms to the truth. You help them to will right, that is, to direct their wills, as responsible persons, toward the good. You help them to act right, that is, gradually to bring their lives, in spite of the risks inherent in human existence, into harmony with that ideal of Christian marriage that they are generously pursuing.

Who does not know that it is only little by little that man succeeds in bringing order to his manifold tendencies and in making them an integral part of his personality, until at length he harmonizes them in that virtue of married chastity wherein the couple find their total human and Christian potential and fulfillment?

This work of liberation, for that is what it is, is the fruit of the true freedom of the children of God. Their consciences must be respected and also educated and formed, in an atmosphere of confidence and not of anxiety. In such an atmosphere, moral laws are seen not as coldly inhuman, abstractly objective, and remote prescriptions; instead they serve to guide the couples on their journey. When husband and wife, in fact, make the effort, patiently and humbly, without allowing themselves to be discouraged by setbacks, honestly to live up to the profound demands of a sanctified love, then moral laws, which exist to recall these demands, are no longer rejected as a hindrance but recognized to be a powerful help.

---

[43] Cf. 1 Jn 1:7.

The Good News for Couples

15. The journey undertaken by husbands and wives, like every human life, has many stages; and, as you know from your experience over the years, it also includes difficult and painful periods. But this must be said loudly: anguish and fear should never be the lot of persons of good will, since, after all, is not the Gospel good news also for husbands and wives? And for all the demands it makes, is it not a profoundly liberating message?

It is naturally distressful to realize that one has not yet achieved interior freedom, that one is still subject to the impulses of instinct. It is distressful to discover oneself almost incapable at a particular moment of respecting the moral law in such a fundamental area. Yet this is a decisive moment when the Christian in his confusion, instead of giving way to sterile and destructive feelings of rebellion, makes his way humbly to the staggering discovery of what it means to be a man before God, a sinner before the love of Christ the Savior.

Easter Mystery

16. All progress in the moral life starts with this radical awareness of what it means to be a man and a sinner before God. The couple having thus been "evangelized" in the depths of their being, husband and wife discover "with fear and trembling",[44] but also with wonder and joy, that in their marriage, as in the union of Christ and the Church, the Easter mystery of death and resurrection is being accomplished.

In the midst of the large Church, this small Church then knows itself for what it is in reality, a community—weak, sometimes

---

[44] Phil 2:12.

sinful and penitent, but forgiven—on the road toward holiness, "in the peace of God which surpasses all understanding".[45]

This does not at all mean that spouses are shielded against all failures: "Let him who prides himself on standing take care lest he fall."[46] They are not dispensed from the need of persevering effort, sometimes in cruel circumstances that can only be endured by realizing that they are participating in Christ's Passion.[47] But at least they know that the moral demands of married life, which the Church recalls to them, are not intolerable and impracticable laws but a gift of God to help them discover, by means of their own weaknesses and looking beyond them, the riches of a fully human and Christian love. And for this reason, the spouses do not at all have the anguished feeling that they have in some way reached a dead end, and that in some instances they are perhaps sinking into sensuality as they abandon all reception of the sacraments or even as they rebel against a Church they consider as inhuman. Nor do they have the anguished feeling that they are becoming hardened by reason of an impossible effort that threatens their harmony and emotional balance or even the marriage itself. Instead, husband and wife will open themselves to hope, a hope founded on the certainty that all of the Church's resources of grace are available to help them on their journey toward the perfection of their love.

CONCLUSION

The Apostolate of Bearing Witness

17. It is in the light of these perspectives that Christian couples, in the midst of the world, live the good news of salvation in Christ

---

[45] Phil 4:7.
[46] Cf. 1 Cor 10:12.
[47] Cf. Col 1:24.

and progress toward holiness in and through their marriage, with the light, the strength, the joy of the Savior.

These are also the major orientations of the apostolate of the Teams of Our Lady, beginning with the witness of their own lives, which has so great a force of persuasion. Restless and feverish, our world wavers between fear and hope, and many young people are unsure as they set out on the road that opens before them. Let this be for you a stimulus and a call. With the power of Christ you can, and therefore you should, accomplish great things. Meditate on his words. Receive his grace in prayer and in the sacraments of penance and the Eucharist. Strengthen one another, bearing witness to your joy in a simple, discreet manner. A man and woman who love one another, the smile of a child, peace in a home are a sermon without words but an astonishingly persuasive one. In it everyone can already glimpse quite clearly the reflection of another love, a love infinitely attractive.

Towards a New Springtime in the Church

18. Dear sons and daughters, you are the living, active cells of the Church. Thanks to the family life lived in your homes the Church presents almost tangible proof of the power of redeeming love and brings forth her fruits of holiness. As faithful and happy couples who have been proven and tested by experience, you are preparing a new springtime for the Church and for the world. Already the first signs of this new age fill us with intense joy. Seeing you here and united in spirit with the millions of Christian couples spread throughout the world, we are filled with an irrepressible hope; and in the name of the Lord, we say to you with confidence: "In this way let your light shine in the sight of men, so that they may see your good works and give praise to your Father who is in heaven."[48] In his name we call down an abundance of divine graces on you and your beloved children, on all the couples

[48] Mt 5:16.

of the Teams of Our Lady and their chaplains, particularly on our esteemed Father Caffarel. We wholeheartedly wish our Apostolic Blessing to be a pledge of these graces.

Before giving this Blessing, we would like to say a prayer with you, an Our Father, which we will recite together for all the intentions of your movement:

> For all the couples who are members of the Teams of Our Lady, and also for the widows who are likewise members of the movement;
>
> For their children, that God protect them and inspire vocations among them;
>
> For couples who are suffering or are undergoing times of trial;
>
> Finally, that an ever growing number of husbands and wives discover the riches of Christian marriage.
>
> Our Father . . .

FURTHER READING

Father Calegari's translation of *Humanae Vitae* is available from Ignatius Press (1983). For further post–*Humanae Vitae* reflections by Pope Paul VI on marriage, see Jean Guitton, *The Pope Speaks: Dialogues of Paul VI with Jean Guitton,* trans. Anne and Christopher Fremantle (New York: Meredith Press, 1968), and three talks of Pope Paul VI, "The Genesis of 'Humanae Vitae' " (July 31, 1968), "What the Encyclical Is and Is Not" (August 4, 1968), and "Prayers Sought for the Encyclical" (August 11, 1968), in Andrew Bauer, ed., *The Debate on Birth Control* (New York: Hawthorne Books, 1969), 30–41.

4

THE MEANING OF CONTRACEPTION

by
Mary Rosera Joyce

Mary Rosera Joyce, in her own right and in collaboration with her husband, Robert Joyce, has been working for a long time to effect a true sexual revolution, to foster real sexual liberation. A great promoter of friendship as the proper and best relationship between the sexes, she attempts to show that sexuality is much more than mere genitality; rather it is a way of relating to the whole person, to the spirit and soul as well as to the body. While appreciating the value of both suppression and sublimation of sexual feelings, she argues that the most positive response to sexual feelings is to integrate them into one's whole way of responding to the world, especially in the mental and emotional intercourse one has with others. She argues that communion and communication are at the heart of relationships. Thus, the failure to reflect upon one's own thoughts and feelings and to incorporate one's sexuality into the practice of expressing one's intimate thoughts and feelings with another retards one's ability to engage in interpersonal relationships.

As has been noted, one of John Paul II's major contributions to our understanding of sexuality is his comparison of the meaning of sexual intercourse to language. This concept appeared in the works of a few theologians long before it became a part of the language of the Church. Mary Rosera Joyce's book *The Meaning of Contraception* was written before *Humanae Vitae* was issued. The passages excerpted here exhibit her employment of the image of language and lying as analogues for sexual intercourse and contraception. The second piece excerpted puts these images to work in explaining the differences between contraception and methods of natural family planning.

The essays printed here are portions of the book *The Meaning of Contraception* (New York: Alba House, 1970). "An Authentic Comparison" is chapter six, pp. 25–28; "The Art of Regulating Conception" is chapter eight, pp. 41–47.

4

THE MEANING OF CONTRACEPTION

by
Mary Rosera Joyce

AN AUTHENTIC COMPARISON

The similarity between the communication of coital intercourse and the communication of verbal dialogue seems to be a strong basis for an elucidation of the meaning of contraception.

Both forms of human intercourse are voluntary or personally chosen actions. Both result in conception. Coital intercourse is fruitful in the conception of a child. Verbal intercourse is fruitful in the conception of ideas and the development of these ideas in the womb of the mind. The words expressed in verbal dialogue are physical sounds produced by physical organs, and are voluntarily spoken. Once the words are physically uttered, the physical aspect of the movement of sound takes its own course, just as the generative substance takes its own course once it is voluntarily expressed in coital union.

Each form of communication is both communal and conceptional in nature. The experience of being-together, and conceptional fruitfulness, are correlative values in both verbal and coital intercourse. In verbal dialogue, this communal aspect of communication is expressed by the feeling tone of the voice, attitudes of the person, gesticulation with the hands, certain bodily movements and facial expression. And in coital intercourse, the communal relationship is expressed in a still more extensive bodily articulation of presence and feeling. Despite the striking differences that exist between mental and coital intercourse, the similarity of these acts is substantial enough to be revealing.

In both forms of communication, not all acts of intercourse result in conception. One person may try to express an idea to another repeatedly before the other understands. The generative power of the mind is not always ready for activation. Similarly, not every act of coital expression is actually generative.

On the basis of these similarities between the mental and more properly sexual forms of human intercourse, contraception is like communicating words of love to one's spouse while preventing the sound waves of these words from reaching the other person. We can imagine that ear stopples or chemicals might be used to prevent the conception of ideas in the womb of the mind. In each of these ways, the act of communicating is internally separated from its mentally generative power.

Though the above examples seem farfetched and unrealistic, they do help to expose the meaning of separating an interpersonal action from a power internally structured in this action. More realistic examples of interference with mental communication, and ones more proportionate to the nature of mental life and expression, are lying, rationalization, refusal to receive the words of another in listening, or closing one's mind in the face of someone who is cherished as a loved person. All of these actions can be done without the use of devices, chemicals or surgery. But they are separations of a human action from one of its powers and are comparable with contraceptive separation.

Lying is an internal separation of a communicative act from its power to express and generate judgments truthfully. In his reflection upon his own judgments, the person judges them to be true, false or doubtful. If he tries to communicate as true a statement that he himself judges to be false, he separates his act of communication from his reflective judgment. This separation is not effected when he speaks in such a way to his dog, or to a wall, but only when the act of communication is fulfilled by being received through the listening and judging powers of another person. It is possible to communicate judgments by gestures, nods and other signs, as well as by speaking. But the meaning of the term "communicative act" in the definition of lying, when the act is one of speaking, is much more complex than simply uttering articulated sounds into the air. It is an interpersonal act that is not communicative unless accompanied by listening. As a communicative act, speaking is a sharing with another person who has a right to know what the speaker judges to be true, false or doubtful. When separation is offered under the guise of union, or falsity under the guise of truth, the lie comes into existence. Where there is no communal relationship, as in a case where the other person has no right to such a relationship, and where force is being used, the articulation of statements and other signs to express as true what is judged to be false does not fulfill the definition of a lie. Such speech is as different from interpersonal or communal speech as copulation under the force of a rapist who has no right to union is different from the coital act.

At times, there are truths that other persons should not know. Some truths should not be expressed. But these situations can be sustained without lying. When speech is internally separated from judgment, truth is not simply being withheld. It is made to become a guise for a statement that the speaker internally judges to be false.

In verbal communication, then, lying is an act which prevents the conception of truth right within the very act of presenting something as true. In coital communication, contraception is an act which prevents the conception of life right within the very act of presenting that which conceives life. These definitions and descriptions of lying and contraception reveal their basic similarity.

Rationalization is an internal form of lying in which the person prevents the conception of truth in his own mind. The chemical manipulation of germ-producing processes via the anovulant pill, and the mental manipulation of sources of judgment done by rationalizing, have much in common. Also, the closing of one's

mind while pretending to listen is comparable to the use of a
diaphragm while pretending to receive the conceptive substance
of the husband.

Though contraception seems to be more physical in nature,
and lying more mental in nature, both are separations of personally chosen communicative action from a power internally structured in this action.

THE ART OF REGULATING CONCEPTION

The regulation of conception may be not only a good, but also a
necessity, for any given family. Just as the principal cause of
conception, the coital act, is meant to be treated as a human art,
conception regulation should be treated as a fully human *art,* and
not just a matter of scientific technology. Conception regulation
is primarily the regulation of the whole person in his coital
activity, an *art* that incorporates scientific technology without a
utilitarian abandonment to it. Since the power to generate new
life is a power of the whole person, the regulation of this power
should be a matter of self-regulation and not merely a control of
biology.

Just as there are times when truth should not be spoken, there
are times when children should not be conceived. But the act of
refraining from speaking differs essentially from the act of internally separating speech from its power truthfully to express and
generate judgments in the mind of another. Similarly, the act of
refraining from coital activity differs essentially from the act of
internally separating coital union from its generative power.

By their very nature, some coital acts do not engage their
generative power. These acts simply do not have the natural result
of generation, though they are still internally united with their
generative power. Internal union of act and power does not imply

a necessary activation of the generative power by the coital act. Because he has the freedom to choose whether or not he will engage in coital activity at all, the human person is free to choose between generative and non-generative coital acts. And his freedom to choose whether or not he will engage in coital activity is much greater than his freedom to choose whether or not he will eat food; the latter choice is more deeply conditioned by organismic necessity than the former.

As the generation of new persons is a marital action shared by two persons contemporaneously, the regulation of conceptions should be a marital act shared by two persons at once. Conception regulation by periodic continence is impossible without both persons sharing the choice and responsibility at once. For this reason, it is proportionate to the marriage relationship itself. With contraception, on the other hand, one person at a time can easily use means for preventing conception.

Besides engaging both persons together, the art of periodic continence involves the total person of each. It includes psychic, mental and spiritual action as well as physiological consideration. While contraception is an investment of birth control in devices and chemicals, periodic continence is an investment in the whole person. Devices such as the calendar and thermometer are used as helps for integrating the process of ovulation into personal knowledge and understanding. Conception regulation, if it is to be proportionate to the person and to the marriage relationship between two persons, should be as psychological and as spiritual as it is physical. And it should be as psychic, spiritual, physical and interpersonal *in its method* as marital love itself.

When conception control is wholly invested in devices and chemicals, and no effort made to assimilate the generative power into personal knowledge and understanding, these items become substitutes for a fully human art. The effort to follow, through scientific means, the rhythms of fertility can hardly be compared to the simple, direct and efficient suppression of this rhythm by the anovulant pill, or to the internal separation of this rhythm from the coital act by other contraceptives. Conception regulation by periodic continence respects the real distinction between the coital act and its generative power, but contraception reduces the distinction to a separation.

When people think that human generation is solely a biological event rather than a totally human event, it is then logical to think that a control of the generative power ought to be a control of biology alone. However, contraception does not control, but suppresses, biology. There is a great difference between control and suppression. For instance, controlling the activities of a two-year-old child is essentially different from suppressing his activities by staking his feet to the ground. Similarly, controlling the human generative power by knowledge of ovulation and by periodic continence is essentially different than forcefully putting the generative power out of action and out of attention with contraceptives.

When the generative power is put out of action, and out of attention, in the very act that would render this power active, it is radically separated from its human context. The person tries to reduce this power to the level of mere biology. By separating the generative power from its totally human context, contraception is an attempt to biologize, and thus to depersonalize, this power. Consequently, the separation is a dehumanization and a devaluation of the personal nature of the human generative power. With contraception, the person intends to render a potentially generative interpersonal action non-generative; with periodic continence, what would be a potentially generative interpersonal action is not engaged.

But it has been argued that periodic continence, while it respects the physiological rhythm of persons, interferes with their psychic rhythm. It is claimed that the coital expression of love must be turned on and off artificially, and that the spontaneity of emotion is violated. Many say that though the coital act and its generative power are not separated by periodic continence, the very persons who are two in one flesh are separated. Periodic continence is declared to be just as artificial as contraception.

But if this is the case, would it not likewise be that a mother who is faced with the tremendous challenge of controlling the behavior of her two-year-old runabout may readily say that this demand for control interferes with her psychic desires and tendencies? If she abandons the challenge and ties the child to a tree or stakes his feet to the ground, she will be more free to follow spontaneously her own psychic life. It is clear that in this latter case she is imposing an exceedingly artificial existence on the child, but it is not so clear that in the first case she is really imposing an artificial existence on herself. Human effort and control are not necessarily artificial. It is only the lack of a creative attitude toward this effort and control that renders it, in some sense, artificial. The control of an active child is a great art, and one that requires love, respect, affirmation and knowledge on the mother's part. But suppressing rather than regulating the child's activity is no art at all.

Conception regulation by periodic continence is rarely viewed as a human art. It has been criticized as being similar to shaking hands with a friend only if he comes at a certain time of the month. But sustaining this example, contraception is like going to put on gloves or using some kind of chemical or mechanical protection before shaking hands with a friend so that contamination by his germs may be prevented. Is shaking hands really that important? The free person knows that there are other ways of warmly greeting a friend.

Insofar as he loves himself and another, the human person is free *to* express himself or *not to* express himself in any given way. If he were not free not to express a certain idea that comes to his mind, his expression would be necessitated. Unless the person is free *not to* express a thought or feeling, he is not free *to* express that thought or feeling.

Just as he is able to express thought in many ways, the human person is capable of expressing love in many ways. If coital intercourse is the only spontaneous way of communicating marital love, then the love, freedom, spontaneity and sexuality of the persons are grossly undifferentiated. But such a differentiation of the person is necessary for maturation. If periodic continence can help to differentiate persons so that love may be spontaneously expressed in more than one way, and so that the coital act may be spontaneously expressed only on the basis of respect for its generative power, then periodic continence is highly desirable for the sexual maturation of married people. As this maturation progresses, continence becomes less and less difficult, and more integrated into the art of marital life.

Such a development is required of any art. At first, the art of piano playing requires practice, exercise and work without much spontaneity. Only after the art is somewhat developed does spontaneity appear. But this developed spontaneity is much more refined and differentiated than that of the child who spontaneously pounds the piano before the discipline of lessons and practice begins. Similarly, coital activity may have an undeveloped spontaneity at first. But as it becomes modified through the art of conception regulation, this spontaneity may diminish for a time only to emerge again in a more highly developed form.

While the persons progress through the first stages in developing the art of self-regulation, the periods without coital activity may seem to be periods of continence or abstinence, or a kind of discipline similar to the discipline required in learning any art. But once the spontaneity of the art begins to emerge, periods without coital activity are no longer experienced as being negative, but rather as another kind of positive fulfillment. The use of the terms continence and abstinence actually belongs more properly to periods without food and drink, than to periods without coital activity. The need for food and drink is based upon organismic necessity. But the coital expression of love is not meant to be based on organismic necessity. For this reason, the use of the terms continence and abstinence in sexuality is almost inevitably misleading.

Since conception regulation is also coital regulation, it implies a control not only of the generative power, but also of coital activity in which the generative power internally exists. As the pianist, in performing a great work of musical art, follows the rhythm of the written score, and does not abandon it for the sake of a more emotional rhythm of his own, married persons, in performing the art of coital love-expression, may follow the rhythm of their generative power written into their lives, and not abandon it for the sake of another more emotional rhythm.

Implicit in the choice of periodic continence over contraception is a respect for the total being of the persons involved. This respect can become an essential motivator in developing the art of regulating conception. Respect for the unity of the person, as well as for the interpersonal unity of the generative power, can become the mental, emotional and spiritual leaven that married people need in order to sustain the effort and practice required by their art.

Just as any art that is good in itself can be used for negative or selfish reasons, periodic continence, an art that is good in itself, can be used for selfish reasons. Contraception, neither an art nor a good in itself, can be used for a good *purpose,* that is, to limit the size of a family where this limitation is necessary. Contraception can be used also for selfish reasons. But the positive or negative purpose for which any one of these methods is used does not make the method itself positive or negative. It is not the purpose that makes the methods different; and no purpose can ever make them the same. They are essentially different as means to an end. No selfish purpose can make periodic continence a negation in itself, and no good purpose can make contraception a good in itself.

But when a negation is used for a creative purpose, as when a child's activity is suppressed to prevent him from receiving injury in an accident, the quality of the creative purpose is affected by the negation. And the quality of a good action done for a negative purpose is affected by that purpose. A woman who creatively regulates the activities of her child for a purpose other than the good of the child himself, changes the quality of her good action. Thus any art that is good in itself, but performed for selfish reasons, becomes affected, or modified, by its purpose.

If freedom, love and sexuality are differentiated so that married people have various ways of expressing themselves to each other, conception regulation can become an art as physically, psychically and spiritually total as coital love itself. But this process of differentiation always depends for its impetus and strength upon the way in which the persons think about their human nature and sexuality. Do they have an authentic philosophy and theology of their human being and their sexuality to act as an emotional-mental leaven in their life together? Without creative *meaning,* it is difficult to live a creative life. The widespread use of contraception is symptomatic of a lack of meaning in marriage. Marital communion does not live by needs and impulses alone, but also, and most importantly, by the meanings and values of *being.* There is a great need, today, for a revolutionary metaphysics of human being and sexuality. (Cf., *New Dynamics in Sexual Love;* A Revolutionary Approach To Marriage and Celibacy, by Robert and Mary R. Joyce, St. John's University Press, Collegeville, Minnesota, 1970.)

FURTHER READING

Mary Rosera Joyce has published a commentary on *Humanae Vitae, Love Responds to Life: The Challenge of Humanae Vitae* (Libertyville, Ill.: Prow Books, Franciscan Marytown Press, 1971). She has coauthored two books with her husband, Robert Joyce: *New Dynamics in Sexual Love: A Revolutionary Approach to Marriage and Celibacy* (Collegeville, Minn.: St. John's University Press, 1970) and *Let Us Be Born: The Inhumanity of Abortion,* (Chicago: Franciscan Herald Press, 1970).

She has published articles on a variety of topics in a variety of journals. For instance, "Reflections on Women Priests", *Sisters Today* 48, no. 2 (Oct. 1976): 88–96; "What Is Sexual Freedom?" *International Review of Natural Family Planning* 1, no. 3 (Fall 1977): 271–75; "Caring for Wisdom", *Communio* 6, no. 4 (Winter 1979): 399–404; "Understanding Our Sexuality", coauthored with Robert Joyce and Sheila Fabricant, *Journal of Christian Healing* 6, no. 1 (1984): 6–13; "Polarity and Paradox in Sexuality: A Response", coauthored with Robert Joyce, *Journal of Christian Healing* 7, no. 1 (Apr. 1985): 54–55. She has published a book on sexuality for teenagers: *Friends for Teens* (St. Cloud, Minn.: LifeCom, 1990). See also her pamphlets *How Can a Man and Woman Be Friends?* (Collegeville, Minn.: Liturgical Press, 1977) and *Women and Choice* (St. Cloud, Minn.: LifeCom, 1986).

5

CONTRACEPTION AND CHASTITY

by
G. E. M. Anscombe

G. E. M. Anscombe is one of the foremost scholars of philosophy in this half century. Her work on Wittgenstein, intention, and "intentionality" are classics in the field. That such an eminent, thoroughly modern philosopher should find the Church's teaching against contraception eminently defensible may be surprising to those who wish to dismiss the Church's teaching as the outmoded teaching of a Church committed to outmoded philosophies.

Anscombe's essay was one of the earliest philosophical defenses of *Humanae Vitae* and remains one of the best. But the philosophical defense comes late in her essay. Speaking first as a Catholic Christian, she observes that the enthusiasm for contraception is incompatible with the demands of Christian discipleship. She notes how Christians have always held themselves to a higher standard in morality, especially sexual morality, than secular society. There follows a helpful explanation of many of the peculiarities of the historical condemnation of contraception, for instance, its being categorized with the sin of homicide. Very welcome is her fair treatment of the much-maligned Augustine and his argument that sex engaged in "*purely* for pleasure" is sinful, if only in a small way. In her treatment of Augustine and in the closing pages of her essay, Anscombe patiently explains the difference between sexual intercourse undertaken for purposes of assuaging lust or for the purposes of sensuality, purposes that are degrading to both partners, and true marital sexual intercourse motivated by the desire to enjoy a great pleasure with one's spouse, a purpose fully in accord with God's intent that we properly enjoy the true goods of this world.

Anscombe's work abounds in careful distinctions. Once some false positions are exposed, some historical strands clarified and connected, Anscombe begins her peerless explanation of the evil of contraception with a skillful explanation of the meaning of the word *intention*. She notes how, although both couples using "rhythm" and those using contraception may have the same "further" intention of avoiding conception, their immediate intentions differ radically. The contracepting couple intends to engage in an act and simultaneously to rob that act of its deepest meaning, whereas the abstaining couple simply refrain from engaging in an act that may lead to conception. Her argument requires and repays a careful and exact reading. Her reasoning demonstrates that if sexual intercourse is severed from its procreative meaning, philosophical consistency would necessitate the legitimizing of any and all sexual activity. She ends as she begins, noting the meaning of the call to Christian discipleship, and implores us not to succumb to the blandishments of the age.

This is a reprint of her essay printed in pamphlet form, *Contraception and Chastity* (London: Catholic Truth Society, 1975).

5

CONTRACEPTION AND CHASTITY

by
G. E. M. Anscombe

I

I will first ask you to contemplate a familiar point: the fantastic change that has come about in people's situation in respect of having children because of the invention of efficient contraceptives. You see, what can't be otherwise we accept; and so we accept death and its unhappiness. But possibility destroys mere acceptance. And so it is with the possibility of having intercourse and preventing conception. This power is now placed in a woman's hands; she needn't have children when she doesn't want to and she can still have her man! This can make the former state of things look intolerable, so that one wonders why they were so pleased about weddings in former times and why the wedding day was supposed to be such a fine day for the bride.

There always used to be a colossal strain in ancient times between heathen morality and Christian morality, and one of the things pagan converts had to be told about the way they were entering on was that they must abstain from fornication. This peculiarity of the Christian life was taught in a precept issued by the Council of Jerusalem, the very first council of the Christian Church. The prohibition was issued in the same breath as the merely temporary retention of Judaic laws prohibiting the eating of blood—no black pudding!—and the prohibition on eating the flesh of animals that had been sacrificed to idols. And in one way these may have been psychologically the same sort of prohibition to a pagan convert. The Christian life simply imposed these peculiar restrictions on you. All the same the prohibition on fornication must have stood out; it must have meant a very serious change of life to many, as it would today. Christian life meant a separation from the standards of that world: you couldn't be a Baal-worshipper, you couldn't sacrifice to idols, be a sodomite, practice infanticide, compatibly with the Christian allegiance. That is not to say that Christians were good; we humans are a bad lot and our lives as Christians even if not blackly and grossly wicked are usually very mediocre. But the Catholic Christian badge now again means separation, even for such poor mediocrities, from what the unchristian world in the West approves and professes.

Christianity was at odds with the heathen world, not only about fornication, infanticide and idolatry; but also about marriage. Christians were taught that husband and wife had equal rights in one another's bodies; a wife is *wronged* by her husband's adultery as well as a husband by his wife's. And Christianity involved nonacceptance of the contemptible rôle of the female partner in fornication, calling the prostitute to repentance and repudiating respectable concubinage. And finally for Christians divorce was excluded. These differences *were* the measure, great enough, of the separation between Christianity and the pagan world in these matters. By now, Christian teaching is, of course, *known* all over the world; and it goes without saying for those in the West that what they call "accepting traditional morals" means counting fornication as wrong—it's just not a respectable thing. But we ought to be conscious that, like the objection to infanticide, this is a Jewish-Christian inheritance. And we should realize that heathen humanity tends to have a different attitude towards both. In Christian teaching a value is set on every human life and on men's chastity as well as on women's and this as part of the ordinary calling of a Christian, not just in connexion with the austerity of monks. Faithfulness, by which a man turned only to his spouse, forswearing all other women, was counted as one of *the* great goods of marriage.

But the quarrel is far greater between Christianity and the present-day heathen, post-Christian, morality that has sprung up as a result of contraception. In one word: Christianity taught that men ought to be as chaste as pagans thought honest women ought to be; the contraceptive morality teaches that women need to be as little chaste as pagans thought men need be.

And if there is nothing intrinsically wrong with contraceptive intercourse, and if it could become general practice everywhere when there is intercourse but ought to be no begetting, then it's very difficult to see the objection to this morality; for the ground of objection to fornication and adultery was that sexual intercourse is only right in the *sort* of set-up that typically provides children with a father and mother to care for them. If you can turn intercourse into something other than the reproductive type of act (I don't mean of course that every act is reproductive any more than every acorn leads to an oak-tree but it's the reproductive *type* of act) then why, if you can change it, should it be restricted to the married? Restricted, that is, to partners bound in a formal, legal, union whose fundamental purpose is the bringing up of children? For if that is not its fundamental purpose there is no reason why for example "marriage" should have to be between people of opposite sexes. But then, of course, it becomes unclear why you should have a ceremony, why you should have a formality at all. And so we must grant that children are in this general way the main point of the existence of such an arrangement. But if sexual union can be deliberately and totally divorced from fertility, then we may wonder why sexual union has got to be married union. If the expression of love between the partners is the point, then it shouldn't be so narrowly confined.

The only objection, then, to the new heathen, contraceptive morality will be that the second condition I mentioned—near-universality of contraception where there ought not to be begetting—simply won't be fulfilled. Against the background of a society with that morality, more and more people will have intercourse with little feeling of responsibility, little restraint, and *yet* they just won't be so careful about always using contraceptives. And so the widespread use of contraceptives naturally leads to more and more rather than less and less abortion[1]. Indeed, abortion is now being recommended as a population control measure—a second line of defence.

Now if this—that you won't get this universal "taking care"—is the only objection then it's a pretty miserable outlook. Because, like the fear of venereal disease, it's an objection that's little capable of moving people or inspiring them as a positive ideal of chastity may.

The Christian Church has taught such an ideal of chastity: in a narrower sense, and in a broader sense in which chastity is simply the virtue whose topic is sex, just as courage is the virtue whose topic is danger and difficulty. In the narrower sense chastity means continence, abstention. I have to say something about this—though I'm reduced to stammering because I am a mediocre worldly person leading an ordinary sort of worldly life; nevertheless I'll try to say it even with stammering.

What people are for is, we believe, like guided missiles, to home in on God, God who is the one truth it is infinitely worth knowing, the possession of which you could never get tired of, like the water which if you have you can never thirst again, because your thirst is slaked forever and always. It's this potentiality, this incredible possibility, of the knowledge of God of such a kind as even to be sharing in his nature, which Christianity holds out to people; and because of this potentiality every life, right up to the last, must be treated as precious. Its potentialities in all things the world cares about may be slight; but there is always the possibility of what it's for. We can't ever know that the time of possibility of gaining eternal life is over, however old, wretched, "useless" someone has become.

---

[1] The exception to this in the short term is where abortion has been encouraged and contraceptives not available; making contraceptives available then produces an immediate but only temporary reduction in abortions.

Now there are some people who want this so much that they want to be totally concerned with it and to die to their own worldly, earthly and fleshly desires. It is people who are so filled with this enormous desire and are able to follow it, who pursue the course of chastity in the narrow sense—this is the point, the glory, of Christian celibacy and virginity and of vows of chastity. I think one has to know about it in order to appreciate the teachings of Christianity about chastity in a wide sense. But as I say I speak stammeringly because I'm not very well qualified.

II

Turning to chastity not in the narrower sense but in the sense in which it is simply the virtue connected with sex, the Christian Church has always set its face against contraception from the earliest time as a grave breach of chastity. It inherited from Israel the objection to "base ways of copulating for the avoidance of conception", to quote St Augustine. In a document of the third century a Christian author wrote of the use of contraceptives by freeborn Christian women of Rome. These women sometimes married slaves so as to have Christian husbands but they were under a severe temptation because if the father was a slave the child was a slave by Roman law and this was a deterrent to having children; and they practised some form of contraception. This was the occasion of the earliest recorded explicit Christian observation on the subject. The author writes like a person mentioning a practice which Christians at large must obviously regard as shameful.

From then on the received teaching of Christianity has been constant. We need only mention two landmarks which have stood as signposts in Christian teaching—the teaching of Augustine and that of Thomas Aquinas. St Augustine wrote against the Manichaeans. The Manichaeans were people who thought all sex evil. They thought procreation was worse than sex; so if one must have sex let it be without procreation which imprisoned a soul in flesh.

So they first aimed to restrict intercourse altogether to what they thought were infertile times and also to use contraceptive drugs so as if possible never to have children. If they did conceive they used drugs to procure abortions; finally, if that failed, in their cruel lust or lustful cruelty, as St Augustine says, they might put the child out to die. (The appetite for killing children is a rather common characteristic in the human race.)

All these actions Augustine condemned and he argued strongly against their teaching. Sex couldn't possibly be evil; it is the source of human society and life is God's good creation. On the other hand it is a familiar point that there is some grimness in Augustine's view of sex. He regards it as more corrupted by the fall than our other faculties. Intercourse for the sake of getting children is good but the need for sexual intercourse otherwise, he thought, is an infirmity. However, "husband and wife" (I quote) "owe one another not only the faithful association of sexual union for the sake of getting children—which makes the first society of the human race in this our mortality—but more than that a kind of mutual service of bearing the burden of one another's weakness, so as to prevent unlawful intercourse."

Augustine holds up as an ideal something which he must have known didn't happen all that much: the life of married people who no longer seeking children are able to live in continence. He considers it a weakness that few ever do this. There's a sort of servitude to fleshly desire in not being able so to abstain. But marriage is so great a good, he said, that it altogether takes vice out of this; and what's bad about our weakness is thereby excused. If one partner demands sexual intercourse out of the pressure of sexual desire, he says, the other does right in according it. But there is at least venial sin in demanding it from this motive, and if one's very intemperate, mortal sin.

All this part of his teaching is very uncongenial to our time. But we must notice that it has been a bit misrepresented. It has been said that for Augustine sexual intercourse not for the sake of getting children involves actual sin, though not mortal sin—a little bit of sin—on the part of at least one partner, the partner

who demands it. What he seems to say however is not that, but
something different; that if one seeks it out of mere fleshly desire
for the sake of pleasure, there is such sin; and this latter teaching
has in fact been constant among all the saints and doctors of the
Church who have written on the matter at all. (I will be coming
back to this.)

St Augustine indeed didn't write explicitly of any other motive
than mere sensuality in seeking intercourse where procreation
isn't aimed at. What he says doesn't exclude the possibility of a
different motive. There's the germ of an account of the motive
called by theologians "rendering the marriage debt" in his observation that married people owe to one another a kind of mutual
service. Aquinas made two contributions, the first of which concerns this point: he makes the remark that a man ought to pay the
marriage debt if he can see his wife wants it without her having to
ask him. And he ought to notice if she does want it. This is an apt
gloss on Augustine's "mutual service", and it destroys the basis for
the picture which some have had of intercourse not for the sake of
children as necessarily a little bit sinful on one side, since one must
be "demanding", and not for any worthy motive but purely "out
of desire for pleasure". One could hardly say that being diagnos-
able as wanting intercourse was a sin! St Thomas, of course, speaks
of the matter rather from the man's side, but the same thing could
be said from the woman's, too; the only difference being that her
rôle would be more that of encouragement and invitation. (It's
somewhat modern to make this comment. We are much more
conscious nowadays of people's complexities and hang-ups than
earlier writers seem to have been.)

St Thomas follows St Augustine and all other traditional teachers
in holding that intercourse sought out of lust, only for the sake of
pleasure, is sin, though it is venial if the intemperance isn't great,
and in type this is the least of the sins against chastity.

His second contribution was his definition of the "sin against
nature". This phrase relates to deviant acts, such as sodomy and
bestiality. He defined this type of sin as a sexual act of such a kind
as to be intrinsically unfit for generation. This definition has been

colossally important. It was, indeed, perfectly in line with St
Augustine's reference to copulating in a "base" way so as not to
procreate, thus to identify some ways of contraception practised
in former times as forms of unnatural vice. For they would, most
of them, be deviant sexual acts.

Contraception by medical methods, however, as well as abortion,
had previously been characterized as homicide throughout the
dark ages. And this seems a monstrously unreasonable stretching
of the idea of homicide. Not unreasonable in the case of abortion;
though some may doubt (it's a rather academic question, I think,
an intensely academic question) the good sense of calling a fertilized ovum a human being. But soon there is something of a
human shape, and anyway this is the definite beginning of a
human being (or beings in the case of a split—where you get
twins—the split occurs soon, at least within two weeks), and if
you perform an abortion at that early stage all the same you are
destroying that human beginning.

But of course the notion of homicide is just not extendable to
most forms of contraception. The reason why it seemed to be so
in the dark ages (by the "dark ages" I mean roughly from the
4th–5th centuries on to the 12th, say—I won't make an apology
for using the expression—scientifically it was pretty dark) was
that it was taken for granted that medical methods were all
abortifacient in type. We have to remember that no one knew
about the ovum. Then, and in more primitive times, as language
itself reveals with its talk of "seed", the woman's body was thought
of as being like the ground in which seed was planted. And thus
the perishing of the seed once planted would be judged by people
of those times to be the same sort of event as we would judge the
perishing of a fertilized ovum to be and hence the deliberate
bringing about of the one would be just like the deliberate bringing about of the other. So that is the explanation of the curiosity
that historically medical contraception was equated with homicide—
it was equated with homicide because they thought it was that
sort of thing, the sort of thing that destroying a fertilized ovum is.

When Aristotle's philosophy became dominant in the thirteenth century a new (but still erroneous) picture replaced that ancient one: namely that the woman provided the *matter*, and the man the formative principle of a new conception. This already made that extended notion of "homicide" look untenable—contraception that would prevent the formation would obviously not be destroying something that was already the beginning of new human life. With modern physiological knowledge contraception by medical methods could be clearly distinguished from early abortion, though some contraceptive methods might be abortifacient.

On the other hand intercourse using contraception by mechanical methods was fairly easy to assimilate to the "sin against nature" as defined by St Thomas. Looking at it like this is aided by the following consideration: suppose that somebody's contraceptive method were to adopt some clearly perverse mode of copulation, one wouldn't want to say he committed two distinct sins, one of perversion and the other of contraception: there'd be just the one evil deed, precisely because the perversity of the mode consists in the physical act being changed so as to be not the sort of act that gets a child at all.

And so the theologians tried to extend the notion of the evil as one of perversity—speaking, for example, of the "perverse use of a faculty"—so as to cover all types of contraception including medical ones which after all don't change the mere physical act into one of the type: "sin against nature".

For with contraception becoming common in this country and the Protestants approving it in the end, the Popes reiterated the condemnation of it. It was clear that the condemnation was of deliberately contraceptive intercourse as a breach of chastity, as "a shameful thing". But the rationale offered by the theologians was not satisfactory. The situation was intellectually extremely distressing. On the one hand, it would have been absurd, wouldn't it? to approve douches, say, while forbidding condoms. On the other hand, the extension of the notion of a perverse act, a deviant act, seemed strained.

Furthermore, while one doesn't *have* to be learned (nobody has to be learned) or able to give a convincing account of the reasons for a teaching—for remember that the Church teaches with the authority of a divine commission, and the Pope has a prophetical office, not a chair of science or moral philosophy or theology—all the same the moral teaching of the Church, by her own claims, is supposed to be reasonable. Christian moral teachings aren't revealed mysteries like the Trinity. The lack of clear accounts of the reason in the teaching was disturbing to many people. Especially, I believe, to many of the clergy whose job it was to give the teaching to the people.

Again, with effective contraceptive techniques and real physiological knowledge available, a new question came to the fore. I mean that of the rational limitation of families. Because of ignorance, people in former times who did not choose continence could effect such limitation only by obviously vile and disreputable methods. So no one envisaged a policy of seeking to have just a reasonable number of children (by any method other than continence over sufficient periods) as a policy compatible with chastity. Indeed the very notion "a reasonable number of children" could hardly be formulated compatibly with thinking at once decently and realistically. It had to be left to God what children one had.

With society becoming more and more contraceptive, the pressure felt by Catholic married people became great. The restriction of intercourse to infertile periods "for grave reasons" was offered to them as a recourse—at first in a rather gingerly way (as is intelligible in view of the mental background I have sketched) and then with increasing recommendation of it. For in this method the act of copulation was not itself adapted in any way so as to render it infertile, and so the condemnation of acts of contraceptive intercourse as somehow perverse and so as grave breaches of chastity, did not apply to this. All other methods, Catholics were very emphatically taught, were "against the natural law".

Now I'd better pause a bit about this expression "against the natural law". We should notice it as a curiosity that in popular discussion there's usually more mention of "natural law" in connexion with the Catholic prohibition on contraception than in connexion with any other matters. One even hears people talk of "the argument from natural law". It's probable that there's a very strong association of words here: on the one hand through the contrast, "artificial"/"natural" and on the other through the terms "unnatural vice" or "sin against nature" which are labels for a particular range of sins against chastity; that is those acts which are wrong of their kind, which aren't wrong just from the circumstances that the persons aren't married: they're not doing what would be all right if they were married and had good motives— they're doing something really different. That's the range of sins against chastity which got this label "sin against nature".

In fact there's no greater connexion of "natural law" with the prohibition on contraception than with any other part of morality. Any type of wrong action is "against the natural law": stealing is, framing someone is, oppressing people is. "Natural law" is simply a way of speaking about the whole of morality, used by Catholic thinkers because they believe the general precepts of morality are *laws* promulgated by God our Creator in the enlightened human understanding when it is thinking in general terms about what are good and what are bad actions. That is to say, the discoveries of reflection and reasoning when we think straight about these things *are* God's legislation to us (whether we realize this or not).

In thinking about conduct we have to advert to laws of nature in another sense. That is, to very general and very well-known facts of nature, and also to ascertained scientific laws. For example, the resources of the earth have to be worked on to supply our needs and enhance our lives: this is a general and well-known fact of nature. Hence there needs to be control over resources by definite owners, be they tribes or states or cities or corporations or clubs or individual people: and this is the institution of property. Laws of nature in a scientific sense will affect the rules about control that it is reasonable to have. The type of installations we need if electricity is to be made available, for example, and the way they work, will be taken into account in framing the laws of the country or city about control of this resource. The institution of property has as its corollary the "law of nature" in the ethical sense, the sense of a law of morality, which forbids stealing. It's useful, very useful, to get clear about all this; it should help us to think and act justly and not to be too mad about property, too.

It was in these various ways that the Pope spoke of natural laws in *Humanae Vitae* — the expression occurs in all these senses — and the topic of natural law in the ethical sense has not any greater relevance to contraception than to anything else. In particular, it is not because there is a *natural* law that something *artificial* is condemned.

The substantive, hard teaching of the Church which all Catholics were given up to 1964 was clear enough: all artificial methods of birth control were taught to be gravely wrong if, before, after, or during intercourse you do something intended to turn that intercourse into an infertile act if it would otherwise have been fertile.

At that time there had already been set up by Pope John in his lifetime a commission to enquire into these things. The commission consisted of economists, doctors and other lay people as well as theologians. Pope John, by the way, spoke of contraception just as damningly as his predecessor: it's a mere lie to suggest he favoured it. Pope Paul removed the matter from the competency of the Council and reserved to the Pope that new judgment on it which the modern situation and the new discoveries — above all, of oral contraceptives — made necessary.

From '64 onwards there was an immense amount of propaganda for the reversal of previous teaching. You will remember it. Then, with the whole world baying at him to change, the Pope acted as Peter. "Simon, Simon," Our Lord said to Peter, "Satan has wanted to have you all to sift like wheat, but I have prayed for thee that thy faith should not fail: thou, being converted, strengthen thy brethren." Thus Paul confirmed the only doctrine which had ever appeared as the teaching of the Church on these things; and in so doing incurred the execration of the world.

But Athenagoras, the Ecumenical Patriarch, who has the primacy of the Orthodox Church, immediately spoke up and confirmed that this was Christian teaching, the only possible Christian teaching.

III

Among those who hoped for a change, there was an instant reaction that the Pope's teaching was false, and was not authoritative because it lacked the formal character of an infallible document. Now as to that, the Pope was pretty solemnly confirming the only and constant teaching of the Church. The fact that an encyclical is not an infallible kind of document only shews that one argument for the truth of its teaching is lacking. It does not shew that the substantive hard message of this encyclical may perhaps be wrong — any more than the fact that memory of telephone numbers isn't the *sort* of thing that you *can't* be wrong about shews that you don't actually know your own telephone number.

At this point one may hear the enquiry: "But isn't there room for development? Hasn't the situation changed?" And the answer to that is "Yes — there had to be development and there was." That, no doubt, was why Pope John thought a commission necessary and why it took the Pope four years to formulate the teaching. We have to remember that, as Newman says, developments "which do but contradict and reverse the course of doctrine which has been developed before them, and out of which they spring, are certainly corrupt." No other development would have been a true one. But certainly the final condemnation of oral contraceptives *is* development — and so are some other points in the encyclical.

Development was necessary, partly because of the new physiological knowledge and the oral contraceptives and partly because of social changes, especially concerning women. The new knowledge, indeed, does give the best argument I know of that can be devised for allowing that contraceptives are after all permissible according to traditional Christian morals. The argument would run like this: There is not *much* ancient tradition condemning contraception as a distinct sin. The condemnations which you can find from earliest times were *almost* all of early abortion (called homicide) or of unnatural vice. But contraception, if it is an evil thing to do, is distinct from these, and so the question is really open. The authority of the teaching against it, so it is argued, is really only the authority of some recent papal encyclicals and of the pastoral practice in modern times.

Well, this argument has force only to prove the need for development, a need which was really there. It doesn't prove that it was open to the Pope to teach the permissibility of contraceptive intercourse. For how could he depart from the tradition forbidding unnatural vice on the one hand, and deliberate abortion, however early, on the other? On the other hand to say: "It's an evil practice if you do these things; but you may, without evil, practise such forms of contraception as are neither of them" —wouldn't that have been ridiculous? For example, "You shouldn't use withdrawal or a condom, or again an interuterine device. For the former involve you in acts of unnatural vice, and the latter is abortifacient in its manner of working. But you may after all use a douche or a cap or a sterilizing pill." This would have been absurd teaching; nor have the innovators ever proposed it.

We have seen that the theological defence of the Church's teaching in modern times did not assimilate contraception to abortion but characterized it as a sort of perversion of the order of nature. The arguments about this were rather uneasy, because it is not in general wrong to interfere with natural processes. So long, however, as contraception took the form of monkeying around with the organs of intercourse or the act itself, there was some plausibility about the position because it really amounted to assimilating contraceptive intercourse to acts of unnatural vice (as some of them were), and so it was thought of.

But this plausibility diminished with the invention of more and more sophisticated female contraceptives; it vanished away entirely with the invention of the contraceptive pill. For it was obvious that if a woman just happened to be in the physical state which such a contraceptive brings her into by art no theologian would have thought the fact, or the knowledge of it, or the use of the knowledge of it, straightaway made intercourse bad. Or, again, if a woman took an anovulant pill for a while to check dysmenorrhea no one would have thought this prohibited intercourse. So, clearly, it was the contraceptive *intention* that was bad, if contraceptive intercourse was: it is not that the sexual act in these circumstances is physically distorted. This had to be thought out, and it was thought out in the encyclical *Humanae Vitae.*

Here, however, people still feel intensely confused, because the intention where oral contraceptives are taken seems to be just the same as when intercourse is deliberately restricted to infertile periods. In one way this is true, and its truth is actually pointed out by *Humanae Vitae,* in a passage I will quote in a moment. But in another way it's not true.

The reason why people are confused about intention, and why they sometimes think there is no difference between contraceptive intercourse and the use of infertile times to avoid conception, is this: They don't notice the difference between "intention" when it means the intentionalness of the thing you're doing—that you're doing *this* on purpose—and when it means a *further* or *accompanying* intention *with* which you do the thing. For example, I make a table: that's an intentional action because I am doing just *that* on purpose. I have the *further* intention of, say, earning my living, doing my job *by* making the table. Contraceptive intercourse and intercourse using infertile times may be alike in respect of further intention, and these further intentions may be good, justified, excellent. This the Pope has noted. He sketched such a situation and said: "It cannot be denied that in both cases the married couple, for acceptable reasons," (for that's how he imagined the case) "are perfectly clear in their intention to avoid children and mean to secure that none will be born." This is a comment on the two things: contraceptive intercourse on the one hand and intercourse using infertile times on the other, for the sake of the limitation of the family.

But contraceptive intercourse is faulted, not on account of this further intention, but because of the kind of intentional action you are doing. The action is not left by you as the kind of act by which life is transmitted, but is purposely rendered infertile, and so changed to another sort of act altogether.

In considering an action, we need always to judge several

things about ourselves. First: is the *sort* of act we contemplate doing something that it's all right to do? Second: are our further or surrounding intentions all right? Third: is the spirit in which we do it all right? Contraceptive intercourse fails on the first count; and to intend such an act is not to intend a marriage act at all, whether or not we're married. An act of ordinary intercourse in marriage at an infertile time, though, is a perfectly ordinary act of married intercourse, and it will be bad, if it is bad, only on the second or third counts.

It may help you to see that the intentional act itself counts, as well as the further or accompanying intentions, if you think of an obvious example like forging a cheque to steal from somebody in order to get funds for a good purpose. The intentional action, presenting a cheque we've forged, is on the face of it a dishonest action, not to be vindicated by the good further intention.

If contraceptive intercourse is permissible, then what objection could there be after all to mutual masturbation, or copulation *in vase indebito,* sodomy, buggery[2], when normal copulation is impossible or inadvisable (or in any case, according to taste)? It can't be the mere pattern of bodily behaviour in which the stimulation is procured that makes all the difference! But if such things are all right, it becomes perfectly impossible to see anything wrong with homosexual intercourse, for example. I am not saying: if you think contraception all right you will do these other things; not at all. The habit of respectability persists and old prejudices die hard. But I am saying: you will have no solid reason against these things. You will have no answer to someone who proclaims as many do that they are good too. You cannot point to the known fact that Christianity drew people out of the pagan world, always saying no to these things. Because, if you are defending contraception, you will have rejected Christian tradition.

People quite alienated from this tradition are likely to see that my argument holds: that if contraceptive intercourse is all right

---

[2] I should perhaps remark that I am using a *legal* term here—not indulging in bad language.

then so are all forms of sexual activity. To them that is no argument against contraception; to their minds anything is permitted, so long as that's what people want to do. Well, Catholics, I think, are likely to know, or feel, that these other things are bad. Only, in the confusion of our time, they may fail to see that contraceptive intercourse, though much less of a deviation, and though it may not at all involve *physical* deviant acts, yet does fall under the same condemnation. For in contraceptive intercourse you intend to perform a sexual act which, if it has a chance of being fertile, you render infertile. *Qua* your intentional action, then, what you do *is* something intrinsically unapt for generation and, that is why it does fall under that condemnation. There's all the world of difference between this and the use of the "rhythm" method. For you use the rhythm method not just by having intercourse now, but by not having it next week, say; and not having it next week isn't something that does something to today's intercourse to turn it into an infertile act; today's intercourse *is* an ordinary act of intercourse, an ordinary marriage act. It's only if, in getting married, you proposed (like the Manichaeans) to confine intercourse to infertile periods, that you'd be falsifying marriage and entering a mere concubinage. Or if for mere love of ease and hatred of burdens you determined by this means never to have another child, you would then be dishonouring your marriage.

We may be helped to see the distinction by thinking about the difference between sabotage and working-to-rule. Suppose a case where either course will have some typical aim of "industrial action" in view. Whether the aim is justified: that is the first question. But, given that it is justified, it's not all one how it is pursued.

If a man is working to rule, that does no doubt make *a* difference to the customary actions he performs in carrying out the work he does. It makes them also into actions in pursuit of such-and-such a policy. This is a matter of "further intention with which" he does what he does; admittedly it reflects back on his action in the way I have stated. That is to say: we judge that any end or policy gives a new characterization of the means or of the detailed things done in executing it. All the same he is still, say, driving this vehicle to this place, which is part of his job.

If, however, he tries to sabotage his actions—he louses up a machine he is purporting to work, for example—that means that *qua* intentional action here and now his performance in "operating" the machine is *not* a doing of this part of his job. This holds quite without our having to point to the further intention (of industrial warfare) as reflecting back on his action. (And, *N.B.* it holds whether or not such sabotage is justified.)

Thus the distinction we make to shew that the "rhythm method" may be justified though contraceptive intercourse is not, is a distinction needed in other contexts too.

The anger of the propagandists for contraception is indeed a proof that the limitation of conception by the "rhythm" method is hateful to their spirit. It's derided for not working. But it does work for many. And there were exclamations against the Pope for pressing medical experts to find out more, so that there could be certainty here. The anger I think speaks to an obscure recognition of the difference between ordinary intercourse with abstention at fertile times when you are justified in seeking not to conceive at present, and the practice of contraceptive intercourse.

Biologically speaking, sexual intercourse is *the* reproductive act just as the organs are named generative organs from their rôle. Humanly speaking, the good and the point of a sexual act is: marriage. Sexual acts that are not true marriage acts either are mere lasciviousness, or an Ersatz, an attempt to achieve that special unitedness which only a real commitment, marriage, can promise. For we don't invent marriage, as we may invent the terms of an association or club, any more than we invent human language. It is part of the creation of humanity and if we're lucky we find it available to us and can enter into it. If we are very unlucky we may live in a society that has wrecked or deformed this human thing.

This—that the good and the point of a sexual act is marriage—is why only what is capable of being a marriage act is natural sex. It's this that makes the division between straightforward fornication or adultery and the wickedness of the sins against nature and of contraceptive intercourse. Hence contraceptive intercourse within marriage is a graver offence against chastity than is straightforward fornication or adultery. For it is not even a proper act of intercourse, and *therefore* is not a true marriage act. To marry is not to enter into a pact of mutual complicity in no matter what sexual activity upon one another's bodies. (Why on earth should a ceremony like that of a wedding be needed or relevant if that's what's in question?) Marriage is a mutual commitment in which each side ceases to be autonomous, in various ways and also sexually: the sexual liberty in agreement together is great; here, so long as they are not immoderate so as to become the slaves of sensuality, nothing is shameful, if the complete acts—the ones involving ejaculation of the man's seed—that they engage in, are true and real marriage acts.

IV

That is how a Christian will understand his duty in relation to this small, but very important, part of married life. It's so important in marriage, and quite generally, simply because there just is no such thing as a casual, non-significant, sexual act. This in turn arises from the fact that sex concerns the transmission of human life. (Hence the picture that some have formed and even welcomed, of intercourse now, in this contraceptive day, losing its deep significance: becoming no more than a sort of extreme kiss, which it might be rather rude to refuse. But they forget, I think, the rewardless trouble of spirit associated with the sort of sexual activity which from its type is guaranteed sterile: the solitary or again the homosexual sort.)

There is no such thing as a casual, non-significant sexual act; everyone knows this. Contrast sex with eating—you're strolling along a lane, you see a mushroom on a bank as you pass by, you know about mushrooms, you pick it and you eat it quite casually—

sex is never like that. That's why virtue in connection with eating is basically a matter only of the *pattern* of one's eating habits. But virtue in sex—chastity—is not *only* a matter of such a pattern, that is of its rôle in a pair of lives. A single sexual action can be bad even without regard to its context, its further intentions and its motives.

Those who try to make room for sex as mere casual enjoyment pay the penalty: they become shallow. At any rate the talk that reflects and commends this attitude is always shallow. They dishonour their own bodies; holding cheap what is naturally connected with the origination of human life. There is an opposite extreme, which perhaps we shall see in our day: making sex a religious mystery. This Christians do not do. Despite some rather solemn nonsense that's talked this is obvious. We wouldn't, for example, make the sexual organs objects of a cultic veneration; or perform sexual acts as part of religious rituals; or prepare ourselves for sexual intercourse as for a sacrament.

As often holds, there is here a Christian mean between two possible extremes. It is: never to change sexual actions so they are deprived of that character which makes sex so profoundly significant, so deep-going in human life. Hence we would not think of contraceptive intercourse as an exercise of *responsibility* in regard to sex! Responsibility involves keeping our sexual acts as that kind of act, and recognizing that they are that kind of act by engaging in them with good-hearted wisdom about the getting of children. This is the standard of chastity for a married Christian. But it should not be thought that it is against wisdom for poor people willingly to have many children. That is "the wisdom of the flesh, and it is death"[3] (there's a lot of this death around at present).

Sexual acts are not sacred actions. But the perception of the dishonour done to the body in treating them as the casual satisfaction of desire is certainly a mystical perception. I don't mean, in calling it a mystical perception, that it's out of the ordinary. It's as ordinary as the feeling for the respect due to a man's dead body:

[3] Rom. 8:6.

the knowledge that a dead body isn't something to be put out for the collectors of refuse to pick up. This, too, is mystical; though it's as common as humanity.

I'm making this point because I want to draw a contrast between two different types of virtue. Some virtues, like honesty about property, and sobriety, are fundamentally utilitarian in character. The very point of them is just the obvious material well-ordering of human life that is promoted if people have these virtues. Some, though indeed profitable, are supra-utilitarian and hence mystical. You can argue truly enough, for example, that general respect for the prohibition on murder makes life more commodious. If people really respect the prohibition against murder life is pleasanter for all of us—but this argument is exceedingly comic. Because utility presupposes the *life* of those who are to be convenienced, and everybody perceives quite clearly that the wrong done in murder is done first and foremost to the victim, whose life is not inconvenienced, it just isn't there any more. He isn't there to complain; so the utilitarian argument has to be on behalf of the rest of us. Therefore, though true, it is highly comic and is not the foundation: the objection to murder is supra-utilitarian.

And so is the value of chastity. Not that this virtue isn't useful: it's highly useful. If Christian standards of chastity were widely observed the world would be enormously much happier. Our world, for example, is littered with deserted wives—partly through that fantastic con that went on for such a long time about how it was part of liberation for women to have dead easy divorce: amazing—these wives often struggling to bring up young children or abandoned to loneliness in middle age. And how many miseries and hang-ups are associated with loss of innocence in youth! What miserable messes people keep on making, to their own and others' grief, by dishonourable sexual relationships! The Devil has scored a great propaganda victory: everywhere it's suggested that the troubles connected with sex are all to do with frustration, with abstinence, with society's cruel and conventional disapproval. As if, if we could only do away with these things, it would be a happy and life-enhancing romp for everyone; and as if all who were chaste were unhappy, not only unhappy but hard-hearted and censorious and nasty. It fitted the temper of the times (this is a rather comic episode) when psychiatrists were asked to diagnose the unidentified Boston Strangler, they suggested he was a *sex-starved* individual. Ludicrous error! The idea lacks any foundation, that the people who are bent upon and who get a lot of sexual enjoyment are more gentle, merciful and kind than those who live in voluntary continence.

The trouble about the Christian standard of chastity is that it isn't and never has been generally lived by; *not* that it would be profitless if it were. Quite the contrary: it would be colossally productive of earthly happiness. All the same it is a virtue, not like temperance in eating and drinking, not like honesty about property, for these have a purely utilitarian justification. But it, like the respect for life, is a supra-utilitarian value, connected with the substance of life, and this is what comes out in the perception that the life of lust is one in which we dishonour our bodies. Implicitly, lasciviousness is over and over again treated as hateful, even by those who would dislike such an explicit judgment on it. Just listen, witness the scurrility when it's hinted at; disgust when it's portrayed as the stuff of life; shame when it's exposed, the leer of complicity when it's approved. You don't get these attitudes with everybody all of the time; but you do get them with everybody. (It's much too hard work to keep up the façade of the Playboy philosophy, according to which all this is just an unfortunate mistake, to be replaced by healthy-minded wholehearted praise of sexual fun.)

And here we're in the region of that constant Christian teaching, which we've noticed, that intercourse "merely for the sake of pleasure" is wrong.

This can mislead and perturb. For when is intercourse purely for the sake of pleasure? Some have thought this must mean: when it's not for the sake of getting a child. And so, I believe, I have been told, some Catholic women have actually feared the pleasure of orgasm and thought it wrong, or thought it wrong to look for it or allow oneself to respond to feelings of physical desire. But this is unreasonable and ungrateful to God. Copulation, like eating, is of itself a good kind of action: it preserves human existence. An individual act of eating or copulation, then, can be bad only because something about it or the circumstances of it make it bad. And all the pleasure specific to it will be just as good as *it* is.

A severe morality holds that intercourse (and may hold this of eating, too) has something wrong about it if it is ever done except explicitly as being *required* for that preservation of human life which is what makes intercourse a good kind of action. But this involves thoroughly faulty moral psychology. God gave us our physical appetite, and its arousal without our calculation is part of the working of our sort of life. Given moderation and right circumstances, acts prompted by inclination can be taken in a general way to accomplish what makes them good in kind and there's no need for them to be individually necessary or useful for the end that makes them good kinds of action. Intercourse is a normal part of married life through the whole life of the partners in a marriage and is normally engaged in without any distinct purpose other than to have it, just *as* such a part of married life.

Such acts will usually take place only when desire prompts, and desire is for intercourse as pleasurable; the pleasure, as Aristotle says, perfects the act. But that does not mean that it is done "purely for pleasure". For what that expression means is that sensuality is in command: but that one has intercourse when desire prompts and the desire is for pleasure, does not prove, does not mean, that sensuality is in command. One may rightly and reasonably be willing to respond to the promptings of desire. When that is so, the act is governed by a reasonable mind, even though no considering or reasoning is going on. The fact that one is thus having intercourse when, as one knows, there's nothing against it, makes it a good and a chaste marriage act and a rendering of the marriage debt.

There is indeed such a thing in marriage as intercourse "purely for pleasure"; this is what the Christian tradition did condemn. Marks of it could be: immoderate pursuit of, or preoccupation with sexual pleasure; succumbing to desire against wisdom; insisting against *serious* reluctance of one's partner. In all these cases but the last both parties may of course be consenting. For human beings often tend to be disorderly and extreme in their sensuality. A simple test of whether one is so is this: could one do without for a few weeks or months in case of need? For anyone *may* be faced with a situation in which he ought to do without; and he should watch that he does not get into a state in which it is impossible for him. But we ought to remember also, what isn't always remembered, that insensibility and unjustified abstention is *also* a sin against moderation, and is a defrauding of one's partner.

Well now, people raise the cry of "legalism" (one of the regular accusations of the present day) against this idea which I have taken from the old theologians of "rendering what is owing", the giving the other person this part of married life, which is owing. It embodies the one notion, I would say, that is honest, truthful and quite general. People would rather speak of the expression of mutual love. But what do they mean by "love"? Do they mean "being in love"? Do they mean a natural conjugal affection? Either of these may be lacking or onesided. If a kind of love cannot be commanded, we can't build our moral theology of marriage on the presumption that it will be present. Its absence is sad, but this sadness exists; it is very common. We should avoid, I think, using the indicative mood for what is really a commandment like the Scout Law ("A Boy Scout is kind to animals"—it means a Boy Scout ought to be kind to animals). For if we hear: "a Christian couple grow in grace and love together" doesn't the question arise "supposing they don't?" It clears the air to substitute the bite of what is *clearly* a precept for the sweetness of a rosy picture. The command to a Christian couple is: "Grow in grace and love together." But a joint command can only be jointly obeyed. Suppose it isn't? Well, there remains the separate precept to each and in an irremediably unhappy marriage, one ought still to love the other, though not perhaps feeling the affection that cannot be commanded. Thus the notion of the "marriage debt" is a very necessary one, and it alone is realistic: because it makes no assumption as to the state of the affections.

Looking at the rightness of the marriage act like this will help in another way. It will prevent us from assuming that the pleasant affection which exists between a happy and congenial pair *is* the fulfilment of the precept of love. (It may after all only be a complacent hiving off together in a narrow love.) We ought absolutely not to give out a teaching which is flattering to the lucky, and irrelevant to the unhappy. Looked at carefully, too, such teaching is altogether too rigorist in a new direction. People who are not quite happily married, not lucky in their married life, but nevertheless have a loyalty to the bond, are not, therefore, bound to abstain from intercourse.

The meaning of this teaching "not purely for pleasure" should, I think, have a great appeal for the Catholic thinking of today that is greatly concerned for the laity. We want to stress nowadays, that the one *vocation* that is spoken of in the New Testament is the calling of a Christian. All are called with the same calling. The life of monks and nuns and of celibate priesthood is a higher kind of life than that of the married, not because there are two grades of Christian, but because their form of life is one in which one has a greater chance of living according to truth and the laws of goodness; by their profession, those who take the vows of religion have set out to please God alone. But we lay people are not less called to the Christian life, in which the critical question is: "Where does the compass-needle of your mind and will point?" This is tested above all by our reactions when it costs or threatens to cost something to be a Christian. One should be glad if it does, rather than complain! If we will not let it cost anything; if we succumb to the threat of "losing our life", then our religion is indistinguishable from pure worldliness.

This is very far-reaching. But in the matter in hand, it means that we have got not to be the servants of our sensuality but to bring it into subjection. Thus, those who marry have, as we have the right to do, chosen a life in which, as St Paul drily says, "the husband aims to please his wife rather than the Lord, and the wife her husband, rather than the Lord"—but although we have chosen a life to please ourselves and one another, still we know we are called with that special calling, and are bound not to be conformed to the world, friendship to which is enmity to God.

And so also we ought to help one another and have co-operative pools of help: help people who are stuck in family difficulties; and have practical resources in our parishes for one another's needs when we get into difficult patches.

The teaching which I have rehearsed is indeed against the grain of the world, against the current of our time. But that, after all, is what the Church as teacher is for. The truths that are acceptable to a time—as, that we owe it as a debt of justice to provide out of our superfluity for the destitute and the starving—these will be proclaimed not only by the Church: the Church teaches *also* those truths that are hateful to the spirit of an age.

FURTHER READING

Anscombe had an interesting exchange on the place of natural law in the Church's condemnation of contraception with Herbert McCabe, O.P. See Herbert McCabe, O.P., "Contraception and Natural Law", *New Blackfriars* 46 (Nov. 1964): 89–95; G. E. M. Anscombe, "Contraception and Natural Law", *New Blackfriars* 46 (June 1965): 517–21; and McCabe, "Contraceptives and Holiness", *New Blackfriars* 46 (Feb. 1965): 294–99.

Anscombe provided further defense of the Church's teaching in her essay "You Can Have Sex Without Children: Christianity and the New Offer", in *Ethics, Religion, and Politics: The Collected Papers of G. E. M. Anscombe,* vol. 3 (Minneapolis: University of Minnesota Press, 1981), 82–96. A critical response to her work has been provided by Jenny Teichman, "Intention and Sex", *Essays in Honour of G. E. M. Anscombe,* ed. by Cora Diamond and Jenny Teichman (Ithaca, N.Y.: Cornell University Press, 1979), 147–61. Brian Shanley has responded to Teichman, "The Moral Difference Between Natural Family Planning and Contraception", *Linacre Quarterly* 54, no. 1 (1987): 48–60. Readers may also enjoy her "Why Have Children", in *The Ethics of Having Children: Proceedings of the American Catholic Philosophical Association* 63 (1990): 49–53. Her most famous philosophical text most likely is her *Intention* (Oxford: Blackwell, 1957).

PART TWO

The Views of John Paul II

6

MARRIAGE AND CONTRACEPTION

by
Cormac Burke

Prior to *Humanae Vitae* it was customary for most defending the Church's teaching against contraception to attempt to explain what moral wrong was involved in violating the procreative meaning of the sexual act. Pope John Paul II (and, before him, Von Hildebrand and Quay) has expanded our awareness of the evil of contraception by taking seriously the claim of *Humanae Vitae* 12 that the unitive and procreative meanings of the sexual act are inseparable. He has clarified how contraception violates not only the procreative but also the unitive meaning of the sexual act.

Father Cormac Burke, a priest in the prelature of Opus Dei, provides a particularly persuasive presentation of this insight. He explains why is it incorrect to think that the pleasure generally incumbent upon the sexual act does not constitute the unitive meaning of the sexual act. Understanding the conjugal act as one of total self-giving, he elaborates how contraception thwarts the spouses' attempt to unite in the conjugal act. Speaking of the act of sexual intercourse as an expression of love, he notes the difference between what a noncontracepted act of sexual intercourse expresses and what a contracepted act of sexual intercourse expresses: the noncontracepted act is full of meaning and significance, whereas the contracepted act is nearly devoid of meaning. He explains how contraceptive sexual intercourse is not conducive to the spouses coming to know each other more fully and how in a contraceptive act of sexual intercourse the spouses are not able to enjoy and express fully their masculine and feminine sexual identities. Burke's work is clearly profoundly informed by the insights of John Paul II; he has made them his own and has provided us with a deeply probing analysis of the unitive meaning of the sexual act and its violation by contraception.

This article appeared in the *Linacre Quarterly* 55 (Feb. 1988): 44–55; it has been reprinted in the *Homiletic and Pastoral Review* 89, no. 4 (Jan. 1989): 9–18, and in *Creative Love: The Ethics of Human Reproduction,* ed. by John Boyle (Front Royal, Va.: Christendom Press, 1989), 151–67.

6

MARRIAGE AND CONTRACEPTION

by
Cormac Burke

I. BACKGROUND

A few preliminary remarks may help to set this theme in context. Some people maintain that the understanding of marriage which prevailed in the Church, up to Vatican II, was social or institutional. In their view, the traditional "bona" or "goods" of marriage — children, unity, perpetuity — were stressed to the detriment of the good of the spouses, which today is often described as the personalist end of marriage.

Vatican II, so they suggest, gave rise to a new understanding according to which the personalist end — the "intima communitas vitae et amoris coniugalis" (GS 48): the intimate partnership of life and love — is seen to be equally important along with the other ends; and is, in fact, seen as "independently" important, in the sense that it can stand on its own and basically has little or no relationship to the other ends.[1]

Now, to turn to our immediate concern, there are two related issues before us — two questions asking for clear and, if possible,

[1] This view, I could add in passing, has had a strong influence in the development of a canonical jurisprudence that distinguishes between the "right to procreative intercourse" and the "right to communion of life". Ultimately it is the same view as that which stresses the difference between the "biological" and the "personalist" aspects of marriage.

simple answers: a) why must the conjugal act be open to procreativity; b) why must procreation be the consequence of a true conjugal act?

Of these two issues, the first is bigger; it is of importance everywhere round the world, and of moral significance to practically all married couples. It has been the subject of intense debate for some 25 years, and at this stage, I feel, well-matured answers are available.

The second issue is of much more recent appearance. It also is intensely debated, although basically in academic circles with echoes in the press. It is of practical interest to relatively few couples. Probably it will take some years before its finer points (as in certain forms of homologous artificial fertilization) can be fully seen in satisfactory light. I feel that a clear answer to this second question will largely come in consequence of having clearly answered the first, to which, in fact, most of my remarks will be addressed. My main endeavor, therefore, will be to show why one cannot annul the procreative aspect or the procreative reference of the marital act without necessarily destroying its unitive function and significance.

II. CONTRACEPTION AND MARITAL UNION

There is a modern argument for contraception which claims to speak in personalist terms, and which could be summarized as follows. The marital act expresses love; it unites. It has, indeed, a possible procreational "side-effect" which can result in children. But since this side-effect depends on biological factors, which science today permits us to control, the procreative aspect of marital intercourse can be nullified, while leaving its unitive function intact.

Until quite recently, the traditional argument against birth control has largely been that the sexual act is naturally designed for procreation, and it is wrong to frustrate this design because it is wrong to interfere with man's natural functions. But the reply can be made, and is made that we do interfere with other natural functions, for instance when we use earplugs or hold our nose, etc., and no one has ever argued that to do so is morally wrong. Why then should it be wrong to interfere for good reasons with the procreational aspect of marital intercourse?

The defenders of contraception dismiss this traditional argument as mere "biologism"; as an understanding of the marital act that fails to go beyond its biological function or possible biological consequences, and ignores its spiritual function, i.e., its function in signifying and effecting the union of the spouses.

They feel they are on strong and positive ground here. The marital act, they maintain, is not only potentially a procreative act; it is actually and in itself a love-act, a unitive act. And, while contraception frustrates the biological or procreative aspect of the act, it fully respects the spiritual and unitive aspect and, in fact, facilitates it by removing tensions or fears capable of impairing the expression of love in married intercourse.

This is the contraceptive argument, couched in apparently personalist terms. If we are to offer an effective answer to it and show its radical defectiveness, I would suggest that we, too, need to develop a personalist argument, based on a true personalist understanding of sex and marriage.

This contraceptive argument is evidently built on an essential thesis: that the procreative and the unitive aspects of the marital act are *separable,* i.e., that the procreative aspect can be nullified without this in any way vitiating the conjugal act or making it less a unique expression of true marital love and union.

This thesis is of course explicitly rejected by the Church. The main reason why contraception is unacceptable to a Christian conscience is, as Paul VI puts it in "Humanae Vitae", the *"inseparable* connection, established by God . . . between the unitive significance and the procreative significance which are both inherent to the marriage act" (HV 12).

Paul VI affirmed this inseparable connection. He did not, however, go on to explain *why* these two aspects of the marital act are, in fact, so inseparably connected, or why this connection is such that it is the very ground of the moral evaluation of the act. Yet, I think that serene reflection easily enough discovers the reasons why this is so: why the connection between the two aspects of the act is, in fact, such that the destruction of its procreative reference necessarily destroys its unitive and personalist significance. In other words, if one deliberately destroys the power of the conjugal act to give life, one necessarily destroys its power to signify love: the love and union proper to marriage.

III. THE MARITAL ACT AS AN ACT OF UNION

Why is the act of intercourse regarded as *the* act of self-giving, the most distinctive expression of marital love? Why is this act, which is but a passing and fleeting thing, particularly regarded as an act of *union?* After all, people in love express their love and desire to be united in many ways: sending letters, exchanging looks or presents, holding hands. . . . What makes the sexual act unique? Why does this act unite the spouses in a way that no other act does? What is it that makes it not just a physical experience but a *love* experience?

Is it the special pleasure attaching to it? Is the unitive meaning of the conjugal act contained just in the sensation, however intense, that it can produce? If intercourse unites two people simply because it gives special pleasure, then it would seem that one or other of the spouses could, at times, find a more meaningful union outside marriage than within it. It would follow, too, that sex without pleasure becomes meaningless, and that sex with pleasure — even homosexual sex — becomes meaningful.

No. The conjugal act may or may not be accompanied by pleasure, but the meaning of the act does not consist in its pleasure. The pleasure provided by marital intercourse may be intense, but it is transient. The *significance* of marital intercourse is also intense, and it is not transient; it lasts.

Why should the marital act be more significant than any other expression of affection between the spouses? Why should it be a more intense expression of love and union? Surely because of *what happens* in that marital encounter, which is not just a touch, not a mere sensation, however intense, but a *communication,* an offer and acceptance, an exchange of something that uniquely represents the gift of oneself and the union of two selves.

Here, of course, it should not be forgotten that while two persons in love want to give themselves to one another, to be united to one another, this desire of theirs remains, humanly speaking, on a purely volitional level.[2] They can *bind* themselves to one another, but they cannot actually *give* themselves. The greatest expression of a person's desire to give *himself* is to give the *seed* of himself. Giving one's seed is much more significant, and in particular is much more real, than giving one's heart. "I am yours, I give you my heart; here, take it", remains mere poetry, to which no physical gesture can give true body. But, "I am yours; I give you my seed; here, take it", is not poetry; it is love. It is conjugal love embodied in a unique and privileged physical action whereby intimacy is expressed—"I give you what I give no one"—and union is achieved. "Take what I have to give. This will be a new me. United to you, to what you have to give—to your seed—this will be a new *"you-and-me",* fruit of our mutual knowledge and love." In human terms, this is the closest one can get to giving one's self conjugally and to accepting the conjugal self-gift of another, and so achieving spousal union.

Therefore, what makes marital intercourse express a *unique* relationship and union is not the sharing of a sensation, but the sharing of a *power*—an extraordinary life-related, creative, physical, sexual power. In a true conjugal relationship, each spouse says to the other: "I accept you as somebody like no one else in my life. You will be unique to me and I to you. You and you alone will be my husband; you alone will be my wife. And the proof of your

[2] We are obviously not speaking here of the gift of self which a person may make to God.

uniqueness to me is the fact that with you, and with you alone, am I prepared to share this God-given life-oriented power."

In this consists the singular quality of intercourse. Other physical expressions of affection do not go beyond the level of a mere gesture; they remain a symbol of the union desired. But the conjugal act is not a mere symbol. In true marital intercourse, something *real* has been exchanged, with a full gift and acceptance of conjugal masculinity and femininity. And there remains, as witness to their conjugal relationship and the intimacy of their conjugal union, the husband's seed in the wife's body.[3]

Now if one deliberately nullifies the life-orientation of the conjugal act, *one destroys its essential power to signify union.* Contraception in fact turns the marital act *into self-deception or into a lie:* "I love you so much that with you, and with you alone, I am ready to share this most unique power. . . . " But *what* unique power? In contraceptive sex, no unique power is being shared, except a power to produce pleasure. But then the uniqueness of the marital act is reduced to pleasure. Its significance is gone.

Contraceptive intercourse is an exercise in meaninglessness. It could perhaps be compared to going through the actions of singing without letting any sound of music pass one's lips.

Some of us can remember the love duets of Jeanette McDonald and Nelson Eddy, two popular singing stars of the early "talkies". How absurd if they had sung *silent* duets, going through the motions of singing, but not allowing their vocal chords to produce an intelligible sound—just meaningless reverberations; a hurry or a flurry of movement signifying nothing. Contraceptive intercourse is very much like that. Contraceptive spouses involve each other in bodily movements, but their "body language" is not truly human.[4] They refuse to let their bodies communicate sexually

---

[3] In this way, in fact, the uniqueness of the decision to marry a particular person is reaffirmed in each marital act. By every single act of true intercourse, each spouse is *confirmed* in the unique status of being husband or wife to the other.

[4] The "language of the body" is, of course, a key expression in Pope John Paul II's writings on sexuality and marriage.

and intelligibly with one another. They go through the motions of a song but there is no *song*.

Contraception is, in fact, not just an action without meaning; it is an action which contradicts the essential meaning which true conjugal intercourse should have as signifying total and unconditional self-donation.[5] Instead of accepting each other totally, contraceptive spouses reject part of each other, because fertility is part of each one of them. They reject part of their mutual love — its power to be fruitful.

A couple may say, "We do not want our love to be fruitful." But if that is so, there is an inherent contradiction in their trying to express their love by means of an act which, of its nature, implies fruitful love; and there is even more of a contradiction if, when they engage in the act, they deliberately destroy the fertility-orientation from which precisely it derives its capacity to express the uniqueness of their love.

In true marital union, husband and wife are meant to experience the vibration of human vitality in its very source.[6] In the case of contraceptive "union", the spouses experience sensation, but it is drained of real vitality.

The anti-life effect of contraception does not stop at the "No" which it addresses to the possible fruit of love. It tends to take the very life out of itself. Within the hard logic of contraception, anti-life becomes anti-love. Its devitalizing effect devastates love, threatening it with early aging and premature death.

At this point, let us anticipate the possible criticism that our

---

[5] "Contraception contradicts the *truth* of conjugal love". Pope John Paul II, Address, Sept. 17, 1983.

[6] This still remains true even in cases where, for some reason or another, the spouses cannot have children. Their union in such cases, just as their union during the wife's pregnancy, draws its deepest meaning from the fact that both their conjugal act and the intention behind it are "open to life", even though no life can actually result from the act. It is their basic openness to life which gives the act its meaning and dignity, just as the absence of this openness is what undermines the dignity and meaning of the act when the spouses, without serious reason, deliberately limit their marital intercourse to the infertile periods.

argument so far is based upon an incomplete disjunction, inasmuch as it seems to affirm that the conjugal act is either procreative or else merely hedonistic. Can contraceptive spouses not counter this with the sincere affirmation that, in their intercourse, they are not merely seeking pleasure, but they are also experiencing and expressing love for one another?

Let us clarify our position on this particular point. We are not affirming that contraceptive spouses may not love each other in their intercourse, nor, insofar as they are not prepared to have such intercourse with a third person, that it does not express a *certain* uniqueness in their relationship. Our thesis is that it does not express *conjugal* uniqueness. Love may somehow be present in their contraceptive relationship; conjugal love is not expressed by it. Conjugal love may, in fact, soon find itself threatened by it. Contraceptive spouses are constantly haunted by the suspicion that the act in which they share could indeed be, for each one of them, a privileged *giving* of pleasure, but could also be a mere selfish *taking* of pleasure. It is logical that their love-making be troubled by a sense of falseness or hollowness, for they are attempting to found the uniqueness of the spousal relationship on an act of pleasure which tends ultimately to close each one of them sterilely in on himself or herself, and they are refusing to found that relationship on the truly unique conjugal dimension of loving co-creativity, capable, in its vitality, of opening each of them out, not merely to one another, but to the whole of life and creation.

IV. SEXUAL LOVE AND SEXUAL KNOWLEDGE

The mutual and exclusive self-donation of the marriage act consists in its being the gift and acceptance of something unique. Now this something unique is not *just* the seed (this indeed could be "biologism"), but the *fullness of the sexuality* of the other person.

It was in the context of its not being good for man to be alone that God made him sexual. He created man in a duality—male and female—with the potential to become a trinity. The differences between the sexes speak therefore of a divine plan of complementarity, of self-completion and self-fulfillment, also through self-perpetuation.

It is not good for man to be alone because man, on his own, cannot fulfill himself. He needs others. He especially needs one other—a companion, a spouse. Union with a spouse, giving oneself to a spouse, sexual and marital union in self-donation, are normally a condition of human growth and fulfillment.

Marriage, then, is a means of fulfillment through union. Husband and wife are united in mutual knowledge and love, a love which is not just spiritual, but also bodily and a knowledge underpinning their love which is likewise not mere speculative or intellectual knowledge. It is bodily knowledge as well. Their marital love is also meant to be based on *carnal* knowledge. This is fully human and fully logical. How significant it is that the Bible, in the original Hebrew, refers to marital intercourse in the terms of man and woman "knowing" each other. Adam, Genesis says, *knew* Eve, his wife. What comment can we make on this equivalence which the Bible draws between conjugal intercourse and mutual knowledge?

What is the distinctive knowledge that husband and wife communicate to one another? It is the knowledge of each other's integral human condition as spouse. Each "discloses" a most intimate secret to the other—the secret of his or her personal sexuality. Each is revealed to the other truly as spouse and comes to know the other in the uniqueness of that spousal self-revelation and self-gift. Each one lets himself or herself be known by the other, and surrenders to the other, precisely as husband or wife.

Nothing can undermine a marriage so much as the refusal to fully know and accept one's spouse or to let oneself be fully known by him or her. Marriage is constantly endangered by the possibility of one spouse holding something back from the other; keeping some knowledge to oneself that he or she does not want the other to possess.[7] This can occur on all levels of interpersonal communication, physical as well as spiritual.

In many modern marriages, there *is* something in the spouses, and between the spouses, which each does not want to know, does not want to face up to, wants to avoid, and this something is their sexuality. As a result, since they will not allow each other full mutual carnal knowledge, they *do not truly know each other* sexually or humanly or spousally. This places their married love under a tremendous existential tension which can tear it apart.

In true marital intercourse, each spouse renounces protective self-possession, so as to *fully possess* and be *fully possessed by* the other. This fullness of true sexual gift and possession is only achieved in marital intercourse open to life. Only in procreative intercourse do the spouses exchange true "knowledge" of one another, do they truly speak humanly and intelligibly to one another, do they truly *reveal* themselves to one another in their full human actuality and potential. Each offers, and each accepts, full spousal knowledge of the other.

In the body language of intercourse, each spouse utters a word of love that is both a "self-expression"—an image of each one's self—as well as an expression of his or her longing for the other. These two words of love meet, and are fused in one. And, as this new unified word of love takes on flesh, God shapes it into a person—the child, the incarnation of the husband's and wife's sexual knowledge of one another and sexual love for one another.

In contraception, the spouses will not let the word—which their sexuality longs to utter—take flesh. They will not even truly speak the word to each other. They remain humanly impotent in the face of love; sexually dumb and carnally speechless before one another.

Sexual love is a love of the whole male or female person, body and spirit. Love is falsified if body and spirit do not say the same

[7] Obviously we are not referring here to those occasions in which, out of justice to a third party, one of the spouses is under an *obligation* to observe some secret, e.g., of a professional nature. Fulfillment of such an obligation is in no way a violation of the rights of married intimacy.

thing. This happens in contraception. The bodily act speaks of a presence of love or of a degree of love that is denied by the spirit. The body says, "I love you totally", whereas the spirit says, "I love you reservedly", The body says, "I seek you"; the spirit says, "I will not accept you, not all of you".

Contraceptive intercourse falls below mere pantomime. It is disfigured body-language; it expresses a rejection of the other. By it, each says: "I do not want to know you as my husband or my wife; I am not prepared to recognize you as my spouse. I want something from you, but *not* your sexuality, and if I have something to give to you, something I will let you take, it is *not* my sexuality."[8]

This enables us to develop a point we touched on a few pages back. The negation that a contraceptive couple are involved in is not directed just toward children, or just toward life, or just toward the world. They address a negation directly toward one another. "I prefer a sterile you", is the equivalent to saying, "I don't want all you offer me. I have calculated the measure of my love, and it is not big enough for that; it is not able to take all of you. I want a 'you' cut down to the size of my love . . . " The fact that both spouses may concur in accepting a cut-rate version of each other does not save their love or their lives or their possibilities of happiness from the effects of such radical human and sexual devaluation.

Normal conjugal intercourse fully asserts masculinity and femininity. The man asserts himself as man and husband, and the woman equally asserts herself as woman and wife. In contraceptive intercourse, only a maimed sexuality is asserted. In the truest sense, sexuality is not asserted at all. Contraception represents

---

[8] If it is not sexuality which each spouse in contraceptive intercourse gives to or takes from the other, what does each one, in fact, actually take or give? In what might be termed the better cases, it is a form of love, divorced from sexuality. In other cases, it is merely pleasure, also, be it noted, divorced from sexuality. In one case or the other, contraceptive spouses always deny themselves sexuality. Their marriage, deprived of a true sexual relationship, suffers in consequence.

such a refusal to let oneself be known that it simply is not real carnal knowledge. A deep human truth underlies the theological and juridical principle that contraceptive sex does not consummate marriage.

Contraceptive intercourse, then, is not real sexual intercourse at all. That is why the disjunctives offered by this whole matter are insufficiently expressed by saying that if intercourse is contraceptive, then it is merely hedonistic. This may or may not be true. What is true, at a much deeper level, is that if intercourse is contraceptive, then *it is not sexual*. In contraception there is an "intercourse" of sensation, but no real sexual knowledge or sexual love, no true sexual revelation of self or sexual communication of self or sexual gift of self. The choice of contraception is, in fact, the rejection of sexuality. The warping of the sexual instinct from which modern society suffers represents not so much an excess of sex, as a lack of true human sexuality.

True conjugal intercourse unites. Contraception separates, and the separation works right along the line. It not only separates sex from procreation, it also separates sex from love. It separates pleasure from meaning, and body from mind. Ultimately and surely, it separates wife from husband and husband from wife.

Contraceptive couples who stop to reflect realize that their marriage is troubled by some deep malaise. The alienations they are experiencing are a sign as well as a consequence of the grave violation of the moral order involved in contraception. Only a resolute effort to break with contraceptive practices can heal the sickness affecting their married life. This is why the teaching of "Humanae Vitae" as well as subsequent papal magisterium on the matter, far from being a blind adherence to an outdated posture, represent a totally clear-sighted defense of the innate dignity and true meaning of human and spousal sexuality.

V. WHY DOES ONLY PROCREATIVE SEX FULFILL?

Our argument so far is that contraceptive marital sex does not achieve any true personalist end. It does not bring about self-fulfillment in marriage, but rather prevents and frustrates it. But, one may still ask, does it follow that procreative marital sex alone leads to the self-fulfillment of the spouses? I think it does, and that the reason lies in the very nature of love.[9] Love is creative. God's love (if we may put it this way) "drove" Him to create. Man's love, made in the image of God's, is also meant to create. If it deliberately does not do so, it frustrates itself. Love between two persons makes them want to do things together. While this is true of friendship in general, it has a singular application to the love between spouses. A couple truly in love want to do things together; if possible, they want to do something "original" together. Nothing is more original to a couple in love than their child, the image and fruit of their love and their union. That is why "*the* marital thing" is to have children, and other things, as substitutes, do not satisfy conjugal love.

Procreative intercourse fulfills also because only in such intercourse are the spouses open to all the possibilities of their mutual love, ready to be enriched and fulfilled not only by what it offers to them, but also by what it *demands* of them.

Further, procreative intercourse fulfills because it expresses it and does not contradict it, as contraception does. It is only on life-wishes, not on death-wishes, that love can thrive. When a normal married couple have a child, they pass their child joyfully to each other. If their child dies, there is no joy; there are tears, as they pass the dead body to one another. Spouses should weep over a contraceptive act—a barren, desolate act which rejects the life which is meant to keep love alive, and would kill the life to which their love naturally seeks to give origin. There may be physical

[9] Cf. the author's essay, "Marriage in Crisis", in *Osservatore Romano* (English edition), Sept. 24, 1976.

satisfaction, but there should be no joy in passing dead seed, or in passing living seed only to kill it.

The vitality of sensation in sexual intercourse should correspond to a vitality of meaning (remembering, as we have said, that sensation is not meaning). The very explosiveness of sexual pleasure suggests the greatness of the creativity of sex. In each conjugal act, there should be something of the magnificence—of the scope and power—of Michelangelo's "Creation" in the Sistine Chapel in Rome. But it is the dynamism just not of a sensation, but of an event—of something that happens, of a communication of life.

A lack of true sexual awareness characterizes the act if the intensity of the pleasure does not serve to stir a fully conscious understanding of greatness of the conjugal experience: I am committing myself—my creative life-giving power—not just to another person, but to the whole of creation: to history, to mankind, to the purposes and design of God.

A last point should be made. The whole question we are considering is, of course, tremendously complicated precisely by the strength of the sexual instinct. Nevertheless, the very strength of this instinct should itself be a pointer toward an adequate understanding of sexuality. Elementary common sense says that the power of the sexual urge must correspond to deep human aspirations or needs. It has, of course, been traditional to explain the sexual urge in cosmic or demographic terms; just as we have a food appetite to maintain the life of the individual, so we have a sex appetite to maintain the life of the species. This explanation makes sense, as far as it goes. However, it clearly does not go far enough. The sex appetite—the strength of the sex appetite—surely corresponds not only to cosmic or collectivist needs, but also to personalist needs. If man and woman feel a deep longing for sexual union, it is also because each one personally has a deep longing for all that is in involved in true sexuality: self-giving, self-complementarity, self-realization, self-perpetuation, in spousal union with another.

The experience of such complete spousal sexuality is filled with a many-faceted pleasure, in which the simple physical satisfaction of a mere sense instinct is accompanied and enriched by the personalist satisfaction of the much deeper and stronger longings involved in sex, and not marred and soured by their frustration. If continuous and growing sexual frustration is a main consequence of contraception, this is also because the contraceptive mentality deprives the very power of the sexual urge of its real meaning and purpose, and then tries to find full sexual experience and satisfaction in what is basically little more than a physical release.

VI. WHY DOES PROCREATION HAVE TO BE THE FRUIT OF A CONJUGAL ACT?

Human life has its origins in sex. It cannot be passed on other than by sexual reproduction. The generation of each child, which marks the renewal and perpetuation of creation, is always and necessarily the result of the union of sexual differences. Modern science has made procreation possible by fusing these sexual differences without any actual union of the bodies of husband and wife. It is the teaching of the Catholic Church that this gravely violates the God-given rule and mode of procreation, as well as the use and purpose of sex within marriage. This teaching has been most recently set forth in the Instruction "Donum Vitae".[10] The few remarks that I set down here simply constitute some incidental thoughts on the topic of artificial fertilization, in line with the reasoning of the preceding pages on human sexuality.

The child is meant to be not just the fruit of sexuality in a purely biological sense, i.e., the fruit of the union, however brought about, of two cells, but the fruit of *human and spousal* sexuality. The child is—has the right to be—the fruit of the living union of two *persons*, which means the union of two souls and two bodies, not just of two *wills* with no true bodily union. A

---

[10] "Donum Vitae" ("The Gift of Life"), Instruction of the Congregation for the Doctrine of the Faith, Feb. 22, 1987.

union of wills, without a union of bodies, lacks the proper composition of parental love. It does not constitute a sufficient *human* basis for the creation of a new life, nor does the simple union of seed, without the union of bodies. The union of bodies is conjugal and human. It is the *mere* union of seed which is "biological".

A child is not meant to be the fruit of a *bodiless* union. That way his origin is less than human; he is *de-humanized* in his origins. If the child is not the fruit of true marital intercourse between the parents, fruit of that act by which they have human-sexual knowledge of one another, he is not actually *conceived.* He remains, all his life, a *product* of the "knowledge" of technology, but not an *incarnated concept* of his parents' spousal and bodily knowledge of each other.[11] Humanly, if not biologically, he will suffer the consequences. He may easily end up as a misfit in a life which he has certainly started as a misconception.

There is a certain logic in the failure of secularism to see that there is *no* right to die "with dignity" (in the sense in which they understand it), but there *is* a right to be conceived and brought into this world with dignity.

Questions of rights, of course, underlie the present debate, much of which seems to assume that the spouses have a right to children. This is not so. They do not possess such a right. The generation of a child may fulfill an *expectation* of the spouses, but it does not fulfill any *right* of theirs. They collaborate in producing the gift of life. But it is not they who really give the gift to one another. The gift is a free gift, and comes from above. In the end, it is God Who gives it or does *not* give it. God's plan for some is that they have children, and yet they circumvent His plan. Just so, there may be others to whom God does not give children and they will not accept this.

---

[11] In contraception, man and woman do not become one flesh, they do not *know* one another sexually or humanly, and there is no fruit of knowledge. In artificial fertilization, they do not know each other either; there *is* fruit, however, but it is the fruit of scientific or technological knowledge, not the fruit of spousal, sexual carnal knowledge. It is this less-than-human aspect to it which turns it into forbidden fruit.

A basic nobility of intention can no doubt be attributed, *prima facie,* to those married couples who want a child by means of homologous artificial fertilization. Nevertheless, it would be good to remember, and to remind them, that the moral issue they have to face is not just one of sexuality. It is also one of possible pride—of wanting to appropriate to themselves the tree of life and to seek its fruit on their own terms.[12]

A satisfactory answer to this whole problem will be found only by those persons who believe that God loves them more than they can ever love each other or love their real or possible children and that He, Who indeed has His mysterious ways, knows best.

[12] Even in relation to the very child whom they seek, their attitude shows a possessiveness which goes beyond the proper rights or expectations of parenthood.

FURTHER READING

Father Burke has provided an excellent introduction to marriage in his *Covenanted Happiness: Love and Commitment in Marriage* (San Francisco: Ignatius Press, 1990). See also his "Children and Values", *International Review of Natural Family Planning* 12, no. 3 (Fall 1988): 181–92; "Matrimonial Indissolubility and the Rights of Persons", *Homiletic and Pastoral Review* 88, no. 7 (Apr. 1988): 27–32, 51–52; and his *Authority and Freedom in the Church* (San Francisco: Ignatius Press, 1988).

7

PERSONAL INTEGRITY, SEXUAL MORALITY AND RESPONSIBLE PARENTHOOD

by
John M. Finnis

John Finnis is arguably one of the most distinguished moral philosophers of our time. He is especially well known for his work on natural rights and natural law. Many who know him for this work may be unfamiliar with his energetic philosophic defense of the Church's teaching on contraception.

The article printed here may not be entirely accessible to the general reader but should be of particular interest to those with philosophic training. Finnis engages in a thought experiment, not uncommon among modern philosophers, that raises the question of the difference between appearance and reality: If one can have a simulated experience that provides the same pleasure as a real experience (and one would not know that it is a simulated experience), why should or would one prefer the real experience? What the thought experiment seeks to show is that we are not simply seeking experiences with our choices; we are attempting to realize real goods.

Finnis makes good use of the thought experiment to show how masturbation is an act that seeks to provide an experience that only simulates the real sexual experience, since it has no link with the procreative good or with the good of sexual union with another. Finnis then proceeds to show that as kinds of actions, masturbation and contraceptive sex are deficient in similar ways; both are mere simulations of sexual acts ordained to real human goods. He speaks of the conjugal relationship as a friendship designed to achieve certain goods and shows that contraception acts against those very goods. In the final portion, he explains how the same principles that render contraception morally impermissible also render *in vitro* fertilization impermissible.

Many of those in the sixties who attempted to defend the Church's condemnation of contraception observed that if contraception were justifiable, so too would be many sexual acts until then considered to be perverse, and so too would many manipulations of the reproductive powers. Modern theologians have, indeed, since defended as licit many types of sexual acts always deemed by the Church to be immoral and have defended such reproductive technologies as *in vitro* fertilization. Finnis enables us to see the philosophical reasons that such acts have profound moral similarities.

This article appeared in *Anthropos* 1 (1985): 43–55. (This journal is now called *Anthropotes* or, in full, *Rivista di Studi nella Persona e la Famiglia, Anthropotes,* Istituto Giovanni Paolo II, Lateran University, Rome.)

7

PERSONAL INTEGRITY, SEXUAL MORALITY AND RESPONSIBLE PARENTHOOD

by
John M. Finnis

I

We come to understand the nature of the human person by coming to understand human capacities, which we come to understand by coming to understand human acts, which we come to understand by coming to understand the objects of those acts. The neglect of this methodological principle, a principle announced and applied by St. Thomas from beginning to end of his works,[1] can seriously distort ethical discourse.

There was a time, for example, when Christian teaching on sex was often expounded by appealing directly to the order or pattern inherent in nature, in this case, human nature. The structure of a faculty would be analysed to disclose both the end of the faculty and the proper, i.e. natural, order of means to that end. This would then be declared to be the moral order for free human acts involving the actuation of that faculty — on the ground that the natural order disclosed the will of the Creator for that faculty

Fellow of University College, Oxford.

[1] See, e.g., *I Sent.,* dist. 17, q. 1, a. 4 sol. et ad 4; *III Sent.,* dist. 33, q. 1, a. 1, sol. 1; *S. Th. I,* q. 26, a. 2 ad 2 (*"objectum praeintelligitur actui potentiae"*); q. 87, a. 3c (*"objecta praecognoscuntur actibus, et actus potentiis"*); in *II De an.,* lect. 6, nn. 304–8; in *III De an.,* lect. 9, n. 803; quaest. disp., *De an.,* a. 16 ad 8.

—on the ground that the natural order disclosed the will of the Creator for that faculty and all its uses.

Such an analysis inverts the proper order of explanation. Thus, in setting aside this mode of discourse in morals, Paul VI and John Paul II are not abandoning the Church's genuine *philosophia perennis* (perennial philosophy). Rather, they are the more faithful to its authentic fundamentals of method.

For Aquinas, as I have said, we come to understand human nature by first coming to understand what are human opportunities, i.e. human goods. For the objects of human acts of will are the intelligible goods, and the most immediately intelligible (and thus most basic) goods are those we identify when we grasp the basic principles of practical understanding.[2] St. Thomas's list of those principles is not closed, but includes life and its preservation; procreative union, education of children, "et similia" (and similar things); knowledge, especially but not exclusively knowledge of God; sociable living and communicating, and so forth; and reasonableness in choosing. . . . [3] Aquinas's name for those ultimate practical principles in which the goods are

---

[2] This becomes clear when the famous passage in *S. Th.* I–II, q. 94, a. 2c is read with *S. Th.* I, q. 80, a. 1 ad 1; q. 82, a. 4c and I–II, q. 10, a. 1c: ". . . Principia intellectualis cognitionis sunt naturaliter nota. Similiter etiam principium motuum voluntariorum oportet esse aliquid naturaliter volitum. Hoc autem est bonum in communi, in quod voluntas naturaliter tendit *sicut etiam quaelibet potentia in suum objectum* . . . et universaliter omnia illa quae conveniunt volenti secundum suam naturam. Non enim *per voluntatem appetimus* solum ea quae pertinent ad potentiam voluntatis; sed etiam *ea quae pertinent ad singulas potentias, et ad totum hominem.* Unde naturaliter homo vult *non solum objectum voluntatis, sed etiam alia quae conveniunt aliis potentiis:* ut cognitionem veri, quae convenit intellectui; et esse et vivere et alia hujusmodi, quae respiciunt consistentiam naturalem; quae omnia *comprehenduntur sub objecto voluntatis sicut quaedam particularia bona*": *S. Th.* I–II, q. 10, a. 1c; "Objectum . . . voluntatis est bonum et finis in communi. Quaelibet autem potentia comparatur ad aliquid bonum proprium sibi conveniens, sicut . . . intellectus ad cognitionem veri. Et ideo *voluntas per modum agentis movet omnes animae potentias ad suos actus,* praeter vires naturales vegetativae partis quae nostro arbitrio non subduntur": *S. Th.* I, q. 82, a. 4c.

[3] *S. Th.* I–II, q. 94, aa. 2c, 3c.

identified as goods, i.e. as desirable and to be pursued, is "the first principles of natural law."[4]

An exposition of the natural law concerning human sexuality demands precision in relation to two methodological issues often misunderstood. First, it demands precision in the understanding of the relevant first principle or first principles; in particular, as to the character of the "goods" identified in the basic principles of natural law. Secondly, the first principles by themselves are no more than "the seeds, so to speak, of the virtues";[5] their rational implications are to be unfolded in the *further* principles and moral norms which are unfolded in the *prudentia* (prudence) of the *sapientes* (the wise).[6] I call the most generic and architectonic of these further principles "intermediate principles of natural law". An exposition of sexual morality must appeal to one or more of these intermediate principles; the precise character of such an appeal is thus the second key methodological issue.

I shall not here offer a treatise on those methodological issues,[7] but rather shall indicate their bearing on our understanding of human sexuality. The first issue is the underlying theme of sections II–V below, and the second of section VI. In section VII, I apply the analysis in some reflections on the new methods of non-procreative human generation.

II

My first question, then, concerns the real human good or goods at stake in sexual action. I approach that question by seeking first

---

[4] "Lex naturae prima principia": *S. Th.* I–II, q. 94, a. 4.

[5] *S. Th.* I–II, q. 63, a. 1c; q. 51, a. 1c.

[6] *S. Th.* I–II, q. 100, aa. 1c, 3c, 11c; II–II, q. 47, a. 6c et ad 3; a. 13 ad 2.

[7] See Finnis, *Natural Law and Natural Acts* (Oxford U.P.), 1980 (= *NLNR*), p. 30 and chs. III, IV, V; Finnis, *Fundamentals of Ethics* (Oxford: Oxford U.P., Washington, D.C.: Georgetown U.P., 1983 [= *FoE*]), pp. 10–17, 20–22, 25, 47–53, 68–79.

an understanding of what it is for a human good to be *real* and *intelligible*. To do this, I propose a thought-experiment used by other Anglo-American philosophers today: "The experience machine".[8]

We imagine a machine which, by stimulating your brain while you lie floating in a tank, affords you all the experiences you choose, with all the variety (if any) you want; but you must plug in for a lifetime or not at all. What is on offer is thus a lifetime of experiences of all the sorts of things in which a human being can take pleasure and satisfaction, in the broadest and most refined as well as the most fleshly senses of "pleasure" and "satisfaction". But it is not a life of activities, achievements, fulfilments; it is a lifetime of doing nothing at all, but of just floating in a tank plugged in to a machine which creates for you the experience of satisfactions.

This thought-experiment has been used in contemporary explorations of the grand themes of Platonic and Aristotelean and Christian ethics. Two of these I just mention here: that activity is its own point (the basis, incidentally, of the principle of Catholic social teaching called the principle of subsidiarity); and that the maintenance of one's own identity is a good. It is a third point that I want to pursue here: appearances are not to be substituted for reality.

In the experience machine, even if one opts for the experience of human contact and communication, there is no actual contact or communication with anyone or anything. There is only the simulation of the experience of such contact or communication. And notice: the distinction between being in contact with the real world of communication with other people, etc., and having the complete but mere experience of being in contact with reality, is a distinction which cannot be apprehended *in feelings* or *in experience*. For, ex hypothesi, everything that feelings and experience as such can deliver is on one side of the distinction. Yet the distinction remains; by our critical intelligence we understand both the dis-

---

[8] Robert Nozick, *Anarchy, State, and Utopia,* Blackwell (Oxford, 1974), pp. 42–45; Grisez and Shaw, *Beyond the New Morality: The Responsibilities of Freedom* (Notre Dame and London: U. Notre Dame P., 1974), p. 26; Finnis, *NLNR,* pp. 95–97; Id., *FoE,* pp. 37–42. See also Aristotle, *Eud. Eth.* I, 5, 1216a.

tinction and its importance. We *understand* that the distinction between real life really lived and the self-immolating passivity of the "indeterminate blob" floating in the tank of experiences is profound and real and important. And notice again: when we reject or even question, in thought, the option of plugging in, we are grasping (understanding) that certain possibilities—e.g. the possibility of knowing and communicating with reality and real persons (not mere semblances)—are more than bare "factual" possibilities. We understand them instead as the sort of evaluated possibility that we call opportunities, i.e. as desirable and thus as good, perhaps basic human goods.

Someone on the experience machine would have no experience of inauthenticity or of lack of personal integrity. On the contrary, being free from all the anxieties and disappointments and misunderstandings that accompany the attaining of real goods in real lives and real communities, the man in the tank doubtless would have a veridical (= *seemingly* true) experience of personal integration (and, with this machine's resources, such an experience can doubtless be supplied to order!). Yet we can say that his life is, as human life, radically and virtually totally inauthentic and lacking in integrity.

For personal integrity involves, fundamentally, that one be reaching out with one's will, i.e. freely choosing, real goods, and that one's efforts to realise those goods involves, where appropriate, one's bodily activity, so that that activity is as much the constitutive subject of what one does as one's act of choice is. That one really be realising goods in the world; that one be doing so by one's free and aware choice; that that choice be carried into effect by one's own bodily action, including, where appropriate, bodily acts of communication and co-operation with other real people— these are the fundamental aspects of personal integrity. That one's feelings or "experiences" be in harmony with all these other harmonies (of person with goods, of will with deeds, and of person with person) is certainly a further aspect of that integrity, but, in an integrated life, derivatively so. A sharing of experiences can certainly help to build up a relationship between persons, but only when it takes its place within, and is in line with, some mutually chosen commitment of those persons.

III

One can choose to engage in a form of sexual activity which lacks all the constitutive elements of personal integrity. This form of activity, when chosen, goes under the name "masturbation". This act, while it lasts, isolates the individual within his or her own self-consciousness, in order to achieve an effect within that self-consciousness or "experience": the effect of self-gratification (which may or may not be rationalised as tension-allaying). The effect is achieved, characteristically, by two distinct but related causes, chosen for their effect: a stimulation of the body and, typically, a fantasising of a relationship with another person. To the extent that stimulation of the body is the operating cause of the desired effect and, in any case, inasmuch as the bodily happening of orgasm is the self-gratifying (or "tension-releasing") event desired, the body is being used as an object, in particular as an instrument of self-consciousness. For one's bodily activity, in masturbation, bears no more relationship to the real-ising of any chosen good outside self-consciousness than the choice to plug into a lifetime of experiencing the writing of great novels bears to the writing of great novels. In masturbation, one's bodily activity is not serving the transmission of human life; nor is it expressing a choice to communicate with another person; those choices and their carrying out are only simulated.

Thus there is in masturbation a threefold lack of personal integrity. First, the bodily activity is not the carrying out by me of some chosen project that involves me in my bodily life (a life that can include even contemplation, as in speculative knowing or in praying), but is rather being used as one "part" of me in the service of another "part" (self-consciousness, with no objective counterpart). Secondly, both the bodily stimulation and the fantasising activity of self-consciousness are unintegrated with real goods (such as human life in its transmission, or friendship). And thirdly, those activities are not integrated with any other real person (such as the friend with whom one might share the good of co-operating in friendship in the service of transmission of life or the community which is committed to that service). In all these respects, the lack of integrity is vividly manifested by the fact that the act simulates, by stimulus, by fantasy and by orgasmic finality, the *conjugal* act—while remaining in reality devoid of the conjugal act's real relationship, as a willed act, to the genuine goods of a procreative friendship between real persons.

I have been speaking of solitary masturbation. But its essential features are to be found in casual promiscuous sexual relations, such as heterosexual fornication or adultery often is and homosexual activity usually is. In such sexual activity, another person is present. But since there is no mutual commitment to any project beyond the achieving of effects in self-consciousness, there is simply a use of two bodies as instruments rather than one. And instead of sheer fantasising of the presence of an absent or imagined person, there is the fantasising of a genuinely personal relationship of love i.e. of devotion, or at any rate the simulating of the act that most aptly (for reasons that we shall see) can express that love.

Such is the intrinsic character of casual, promiscuous acts of fornication, adultery or homosexual sex. Of course, people often enough try to make their extra-marital sexual intercourse (i.e. sexual actions with a partner) more than masturbatory. The obvious way to seek to do this is to ensure that the bodily acts do express some sort of relatively stable common life, common commitment. But one must say, to be brief, that these attempts to transcend the masturbatory in extra-marital sex are doomed to fail. The acts of bodily intercourse still have no real bearing on any genuine human good to which the partners are committed in common; for these partners, ex hypothesi, are not committed to a procreative community, or to a procreative community that truly expresses and lives out the reality of parenthood, which is a reality of exclusiveness and permanence of this unique couple vis-a-vis the child that can in reality only ever be a child of their union. There is in the usual extra-marital relationship no common responsibility for shared goods which are relevant to what the couple subjectively experience in their sexual acts.

Finally, it should not be overlooked that there can be masturbatory sex between the spouses in a marriage. That is to say, there can be sexual activity which is chosen by either or both the spouses, not as an appropriate expression of their lasting mutual commitment and shared conjugal responsibilities, but rather as a means of simple self-gratification and/or release. This possibility, of relatively senseless sex within marriage, is a feature (I venture to say) of the experience of countless married couples, just as the senselessness of solitary masturbation is a feature of the experience of those who engage in it.

But I must repeat that palpable experience is not the criterion of senselessness or lack of integrity here, any more than it was in the case of the man on the experience machine. What is decisive is, rather, a critical judgment of the extent to which bodily activity is, or is not, the integrated expression and performance of acts of free choice really engaged with real goods, and, where relevant, with real persons related not as instruments but as cooperators in real not simulated community.

I said that the attempts of those engaged in extramarital sexual activity to transcend the masturbatory are doomed to failure (whatever they sometimes experience), because of the objective lack of integration between that sexual activity and any real community of commitment to shared *relevant* goods. So too I think we should say that the attempt of the married couple to avoid the masturbatory in their sexual activity is doomed to failure (whatever they may experience) when they choose to uncouple that activity from any real relationship to the willingness to serve life procreatively, the willingness which is the rationale of marital community. Whatever may be the appearance to the couple or to the observer, contracepted sexual intercourse is simulated, not real, conjugal intercourse.

IV

The uncoupling of sexual activity from a real relation to procreation can be found even when the couple place no physical barriers and take no "artificial" measures. What accomplishes the uncoupling is the resolution and choice to *render* what might have been procreative infertile. "Natural family planning" can be, and sometimes is, selected simply as a preferred method of contraception, i.e. of choosing against the good of human life in its transmission. Selected on that basis, it has the same moral *species* as any (other) method of contraception. There is, indeed, a certain moral hazard in talking about the rhythm "method", the Billings "method", etc.; for these expressions equivocate between a method of determining when intercourse would in fact be unlikely to result in procreation, and a method of carrying out a choice to exclude procreation from one's sexual intercourse.

The Christian teaching about periodic abstinence is frequently misrepresented and misunderstood (even by those who wish to hold to it) as a teaching that you may choose against new life (i.e. that you may make a contraceptive choice) provided that the means you employ to give effect to your choice are such-and-such (e.g. "natural", non-artificial, etc.). But that is not the teaching of the Church. Nor is it the proper resolution of the issue that confronted Pius XI and Pius XII and Paul VI, when it became possible to determine with accuracy when a woman was or would be fertile.

In the response of the Popes to that issue, the Christian teaching on life, sex and marriage, remained intact: one's genital capacities are to be activated only in full integration with a complex good, the marital good (a community of mutual, exclusive and permanent commitment in the service of new life). That full integration is disrupted by, for example, any sort of choice to exclude new life from an act from which it would or might very well otherwise follow. Hence the Christian teaching has always been that, married or unmarried, if you wish not to incur the responsibilities that accompany the transmission and creation and fostering of new life, you must abstain from sexual intercourse, lest you find yourself choosing against life (by contraception or abortion) or violating some other aspect of the marital good. In the new teaching about periodic abstinence for regulation of births, the obligation not to choose against procreation remains absolutely unchanged. But, as the recent Popes confirmed, if a married couple knows that at certain times their intercourse would willy nilly be unfruitful, then at such times their obligation to abstain ceases, inasmuch as intercourse at such times will no longer involve them in the choice between the wrong of deliberately impeding procreation and the wrong of incurring inappropriate responsibilities or burdens. They may at such times engage in intercourse if that is appropriate to make concrete and experienced the real marital good whose integrity they have done nothing to diminish.

V

The previous three sections were not directly concerned with moral judgments. Rather they sought to advance our understanding of human goods by a specific account of masturbatory sex as a realm of appearances, of apparent goods, of simulations of reality by the inducing of experiences chosen for their appeal to self-consciousness rather than for the real goods whose realisation such experiences characteristically accompany and signify. It is now time to focus on the "reality" of which these "appearances" are the simulation. I shall do so by considering, first, the reality as actualised with all the fullness that could reasonably be desired, and then the same reality as an object of the will, i.e. as a good which is choosable and available for respect, violation or rejection.

As actualised, this reality will be the conjugal life of a married couple who, over a lifetime of freely chosen and aware commitment, transmit their bodily life to new human beings whom they (in co-operation with God) create, nurture, and educate to the point where they, the children, can make a similar commitment, or some alternative integrating commitment. The exclusiveness and stability of such a relationship has as its rationale these children and the nurturing in them of a secure identity on the basis of which, in due course, to make the choices and commitments which will constitute their independence, an independence harmonised with due gratitude to their unique parents whose free and aware choices made them what they unrepeatably are.

But the good thus realised is one of those basic goods, like other forms of friendship or community, or like knowledge or practical reasonableness, which are never completed, finished off, consummated. Such goods thus differ, as ends, from projects such as making an omelette or building a bridge or putting a man on the moon, which are definite and limited goals that can be fully and definitively, once-and-for-all attained (or missed). The goal of cooperatively bringing into being new lives, and of relating to them as persons, is never exhaustively attained. It always remains as a good to-be-pursued.

So the reality of conjugal life can be considered now not as actualised but as an object of choice, as a good identified by intelligence and acknowledged and pursued or respected by acts of choice. Such acts of choice may have the transitive effect of actualising the good of a real family. But they also have the intransitive effect of constituting the character of the one who chooses.[9] For free choices are creative and constitutive, even when what they sought is denied to the chooser by the chances and resistances of the world. So the free choices of the spouses to do what they can to achieve the conjugal good constitute them as spouses and give their shared and their individual activity the real status of conjugal acts, conjugal dispositions, conjugal life.

As an object of practical understanding ("this is good, worthy

[9] See Karol Wojtyla, *The Acting Person* (Boston and London: Reidel, Dordrecht, 1979), pp. 13, 99, 108–9, 151, 160; Finnis, *FoE,* pp. 136–42; Germain Grisez, *The Way of the Lord Jesus,* vol. I, *Christian Moral Principles* (Chicago: Franciscan Herald Press, 1983), chap. 2.

of pursuit") and of will ("I freely choose to commit myself to living out this good"), the conjugal good is an integrating good.

The most integrating of all integrating goods is practical reasonableness (*prudentia*). Practical reasonableness is itself a specific aspect of human fulfillment;[10] but it is the one aspect which takes for its subject-matter the whole of one's life in all those aspects, however intimate, that can be affected by one's choices. Its claim is: to direct the way in which we seek to participate in each and any of the basic goods. It does not claim to be the supreme good, but only to be the supremely directive natural good. The point of being practically reasonable is not: being practically reasonable. Rather, it is: participating in the basic human goods, *well*.[11]

The conjugal good is not so radically architectonic. For one thing, it does not become the integrating principle of a life unless and until it is chosen, and whether or not it is to be chosen by you or me is a question whose determination is affected by the criteria of practical reasonableness. There are other forms of life integrated around other goods. Still, the conjugal good, as chosen or as choosable, *is* an integrating principle. If it is to be actualised, its requirements extend to the thoughts, the feelings, the entertained desires, the projects, the activities, the properties and investments, the testamentary dispositions, etc., of each of the spouses.

The conjugal good is complex. It is a friendship in which, as in other forms of friendship, A desires and wills the good of B for the sake of B, and B desires and wills the good of A for the sake of A, so that B's good becomes an aspect of A's good, and A's good of B's good, and the reciprocity never comes to rest, for either friend, in either friend's good alone.[12] But the conjugal good is

---

[10] S. Th. I–II, q. 94, a. 3; see also q. 63, a. 1c; II–II, q. 47, a. 7c.
[11] See Finnis, FoE, pp. 70–74.
[12] See Finnis, NLNR, pp. 141–44.

also procreative; it is a partnership with a view to[13] the transmission of the bodily human life of the spouses. These aspects of the conjugal good are, as I have said, interdependent. The intended procreativeness determines the exclusiveness and stability of the commitment to friendship. And the friendship makes the procreativeness more than a technique of reproduction of oneself, and makes possible a non-exploitive friendship between children and parents, which can be the model for all other non-exploitive friendships the child may later enter.

The conjugal good makes good sense of the spouses' free and aware choices to engage in sexual activity. *Gaudium et spes* and *Humanae vitae* rightly speak of sexual acts being capable of having meaning (*sensus, significatio, ratio*), and John Paul II pushes the analysis further to speak of the *conjugal meaning* of our bodily nature. These meanings are not to be discerned by studying simply the physical structures of the body or the biology of the reproductive process or even the psychology of masculine and feminine. I recall again the fundamental principle of Aristotelian anthropological method, which St. Thomas saw fitted so well with Christian anthropology: our nature is to be understood by understanding our capacities, our capacities by our acts, and our acts by their objects, viz. the goods that make sense of human acts. So we understand the conjugal meaning of our bodies by understanding the conjugal good as a possible and worthy object of choice. This understanding—not, of course, attained in sheer ignorance of physical, biological and psychological possibilities and patterns—enables us to understand how the relevant aspects of our psychology, our biology and our physique are capable of integrated activity in the living out of a commitment to that integrating good.

---

[13] *Humanae vitae,* 8: "Per mutuam sui donationem, quae ipsorum propria est et exclusoria, conjuges illam persequuntur personarum communionem qua se invicem perficiant *ut* ad novorum viventium procreationem et educationem cum Deo operam socient."

VI

In making moral judgments we are concerned, not with such distinctions as between the natural and the artificial, nor with respecting patterns inherent in nature (just as patterns inherent in nature). Rather we are concerned with the relations between acts of choice and the real human goods which can be favoured, respected, contemned or rejected in human choices.

Between the first principles of practical reasoning and natural law (as identified in, say, *Summa Theologiae* I–II, q. 94, aa. 2c, 3c) and *moral* norms such as we find in, say, the Decalogue, there is a logical space to be filled by a process of derivation or inference. In some cases the derivation is immediate (*statim*) and obvious; in others it requires wisdom, i.e. a reasonableness not found in everyone or even in most people.[14]

St. Thomas did not, I suggest, provide any explicit and sufficient account of this process of derivation. The history of moral philosophy, especially in the centuries since it began to seek to distinguish its method from that of theology, is in large measure the history of a search for the missing *intermediate principles*.

I have argued elsewhere[15] that there are nine or ten basic requirements of practical reasonableness—requirements which embody the sought-after intermediate principles (moral principles of the most generic type) because they afford the first premise(s) of arguments which have as their middle term a relation of the will to one or other of the basic human goods, and which conclude to relatively specific "moral principles" of the type found in the Decalogue.

Of those nine or ten, the generic moral principles which explain the moral principles and norms pertaining to chosen sexual activity are, I think, these: (I) that one's acts ought to harmonise (be integrated with) one's commitments; (II) that one ought not to use

---

[14] *S. Th.* I–II, q. 100, aa. 1c, 3c, 11c.

[15] Finnis, *NLNR,* chap. V; Id., *FoE,* pp. 72–76. Cf. Germain Grisez, *The Way of the Lord Jesus,* vol. I, chap. 7.

oneself or another as a mere means; (III) that one ought not to prefer appearances to reality, more especially when settling for appearances blocks attainment of reality by reducing the incentive to pursue it; (IV) that one ought not to choose directly against any basic human good (and human life in its transmission is such a good).

In earlier writings on contraception and sexual morality,[16] I have concentrated on this last principle. Countless theologians and laypeople have become muddled about the issue here.[17] They have misconceived the issue that confronted Paul VI as a choice between "methods" of giving effect to *one and the same overall intention,* viz. that we shall engage in sexual activity but shall not procreate. They have then declared, not unreasonably, that there is no morally significant difference between "natural" and "artificial" methods of securing that intention. But in truth that is not the situation. The choice to use a contraceptive is a choice that has but one meaning, one intentionality, viz. to suppress a basic human good, procreation, human life in its transmission. And so these theologians and their followers have stumbled on to discover that they are willing to make other choices directly against basic goods whenever their overall "intention", i.e. motivation, is to maximise overall net good (the "proportionate good"). And thus they have come to defend abortion and terror bombing and outright lying, and so forth.[18]

[16] *Natural Law in* Humanae vitae, "Law Quarterly Rev.", (1968) 84, pp. 467–71; *Natural Law and Unnatural Acts,* "Heythrop J." (1970) 11, pp. 365–87, esp. p. 387; *The Rational Strength of Christian Morality* (London: Netherhall House, 1974); *Conscience, Infallibility and Contraception* (1978), *The Month,* pp. 410–17, at p. 416; "Int. Rev. Nat. Fam. Plan" (1980) 4, pp. 128–40. For the original formulation of the argument, see Germain Grisez, *Contraception and the Natural Law,* Milwaukee: Bruce, 1964; Id., *A New Formulation of a Natural-Law Argument against Contraception, The Thomist* (1966) 30, pp. 343–61.

[17] See also Finnis, Humanae vitae: *Its Background and Aftermath,* "Int. Rev. Nat. Fam. Plan" (1980) 4, pp. 141–53.

[18] For an exposition and critique of proportionalism, consequentialism, and "teleological ethics" (including "mixed" or "moderate teleology") see Finnis, *FoE,* pp. 80–120, 133–34. Since all those methods in ethics are essen-

But in this paper I have been pursuing another explanatory source of the Christian moral principles and norms of right sexual conduct. I have been seeking to explain not only how the procreative good, properly understood, calls for integration in a wider and more integrating good (the conjugal good), but also how contracepted sex, like other forms of essentially non-conjugal sexual activity, settles for the appearance rather than the reality (and at the expense of the more arduously attainable reality). For contracepted sexual intercourse is in vital respects a simulation of *conjugal* intercourse, i.e. of intercourse that not merely contributes in some way to the stability and peace of the marriage (as a husband's resort to a good-time girl may be intended to), but that really, as an act of will bodily expressed, is adequately expressive of the conjugal good. For if one's chosen acts are to be adequately expressive of the conjugal good, one must refuse to entertain any sexual activity which involves turning against *either* the exclusive friendship of the spouses (e.g. by fantasising intercourse with another) *or* the procreativeness that is the rationale of that friendship and of its commitment to exclusiveness. If one's sexual acts merely simulate the adequate expression of the conjugal good, they violate the same generic moral principle that excludes other forms of inauthenticity, e.g. the inauthenticity of offering religious exercises that give the experience of forgiveness without actual repentance.

Regulation of births by "natural family planning" has as its rationale the resolution not to make sexual activity inauthentic by a choice to uncouple sexual activity from procreativeness. There is, you might say, a certain uncoupling, but it is accomplished not in the sexual activity of the couple but precisely in their abstention from such activity. Thus no chosen feature of their sexual activity is rendered a mere simulation of the procreative good or

---

tially arbitrary, individual proportionalists can and do "draw the line" at different points, and thus may, despite their method, adhere to this or that principle or norm of Christian teaching while abandoning and attacking others, *ad lib.* See further Grisez, *The Way of the Lord Jesus,* vol. I, chaps. 6 and 36.

of the conjugal good of which the procreative good is an essential aspect.

But contracepted intercourse has, objectively, the masturbatory feature that it simulates an aspect of the conjugal good that has in fact and in intention been excluded from it by an act which affects the reality of the sexual activity (*qua* chosen) itself. The children of that generation of parents, and the followers of that generation of theologians, have drawn the moral: if personal integrity is sufficiently preserved and respected in mutilated sexual activity of that (contracepted) sort, why not also in sexual activity of any other sort, provided that the *motivation* be realisation of *some* good, however much that good may be inharmonious or disconnected with the conjugal good as such, or however much the sexual activity, precisely as chosen, is unrelated to expressing, itself, by its chosen and/or permitted features, the integral conjugal good?

VII

The foregoing reflections help to indicate why human generation by artificial insemination or by *in vitro* fertilisation, even when restricted to married partners and accompanied by no destruction or disposition to destroy or waste any embryonic human being, is morally unacceptable.[19]

These methods involve a physical separation between sexual intercourse (if any) and reproduction. But neither that physical separation, nor its physical/biological abnormality and artificiality, precisely as such, is *per se* of direct moral significance. For the

[19] For a further discussion along these lines, but dealing also with the death-dealing aspects of IVF, see *In Vitro Fertilisation: Morality and Public Policy,* Evidence submitted to the Government Committee of Inquiry into Human Fertilisation and Embryology by the Catholic Bishops' Joint Committee on Bio-Ethical Issues on behalf of the Catholic Bishops of Great Britain (England: Catholic Information Services, May 1983).

morally significant we should look rather to the relationship between the relevant acts of choice and the conjugal good.

Generation by IVF (or, *mutatis mutandis,* by artificial insemination) involves a series of irreducibly separate acts of choice of different people: the choices of those involved in producing and collecting sperm, of the mother and those involved in collecting an ovum, of those who mix sperm and ovum, and who transfer to the womb the product of that mixing or uniting, and the choice of the mother to permit that transfer. None of these acts of choice has the character of an act of person-to-person involvement. Each takes its place in a series which unmistakably has the character of a *production process,* a mastering of materials (even if those materials, in *present-day* technology, are the "complete" gametes provided by "nature" and bearing in that form a genetic character derived from that of the respective parent).

Now the relation between product and maker is willy nilly a relationship of radical inequality, of subordination to mastery. Thus the child produced by these methods is envisaged, in the foregoing acts of choice, in a status of radical inequality with its parents. And correspondingly the parents and their agents, whatever their motivations, choose to put themselves in a position of domination which is foreign, indeed opposed, to the conjugal good.

For the conjugal good is such that to pursue it, authentically, involves the couple in a radical *submission* to the contingencies, however unforeseen, of unreserved and lifelong commitment. Among those unforeseeable contingencies is the gift and responsibility of children, whom the parents undertake, in advance and "blind", to nurture whether those children be "better or worse", richer or poorer, in health and talents.

Procreation by act of sexual intercourse profoundly embodies, expresses and enacts this submission to membership in a partnership which is a partnership of friendship and service not only between one spouse and the other but also between parents and child. For it is proper to an act of sexual intercourse that it be an act which, being an act of mutual involvement, bodily, emotionally, intelligently and freely, express and extend the whole common life of the spouses. It is a giving of self and receiving of the other, and a giving-and-receiving which is open to being complemented by the gift-and-reception of a child who will, by its very existence, express and extend the common life of the spouses. And this giving-and-receiving is also a giving and submitting of each of the spouses to the other, and a submission both to God as the creator of any forthcoming child and to service of that child in the unforeseeable contingencies of their new and never-to-be-ended role as parents. Thus, in their choices to engage in sexual intercourse, the parents of a child of sexual union envisage (at least implicitly) that child as entering their community not as an object of production, as a product of mastery over materials, but rather, though weak and dependent, as a kind of partner in the family enterprise and thus on a plane of fundamental equality with them.

The structure of their choice is thus concordant with the conjugal good, properly understood in its richness as the procreative form of *community* or *friendship*. The (*re*)*productive* character of IVF and artificial insemination renders the choices to engage in them structurally opposed to that conjugal good.

FURTHER READING

In footnote 16 to this article, Finnis lists some of his earlier writings on contraception and sexual morality. He has since coauthored a substantial article that develops a quite different (but complementary) case against contraception: Germain Grisez, Joseph Boyle, John Finnis, and William E. May, "Every Marital Act Ought to Be Open to New Life: Toward a Clearer Understanding", *The Thomist* 53 (1988): 365–426, reprinted in *The Teaching of Humanae Vitae: A Defense* (San Francisco: Ignatius Press, 1988). See also his "Conscience, Infallibility, and Contraception" and *"Humanae Vitae:* Its Background and Aftermath", *International Review of Natural Family Planning* 4, no. 2 (Summer 1980): 128–40, 141–53. Other works of interest are his *Natural Law and Natural Rights* (Oxford: Clarendon Press, 1980); "The Natural Law, Objective Morality and Vatican II", in *Principles of Catholic Moral Life,* edited by William E. May (Chicago: Franciscan Herald Press, 1980), 113–49; *Fundamentals of Ethics* (Washington, D.C.: Georgetown University Press, 1983); and *Moral Absolutes: Tradition, Revision, and Truth* (Washington, D.C.: The Catholic University of America Press, 1991).

Certain elements of Finnis' moral analysis, shared by Germain Grisez, have met with considerable criticism. See Ralph McInerny, "The Principles of Natural Law", *American Journal of Jurisprudence* 25 (1980): 1–15; John Finnis and Germain Grisez, "The Basic Principles of Natural Law: A Reply to Ralph McInerny", *American Journal of Jurisprudence* 26 (1981): 21–22; Russell Hittinger, *A Critique of the New Natural Law Theory* (Notre Dame, Ind.: University of Notre Dame Press, 1987); Janet E. Smith, "Natural Law: Does It Evaluate Choices or Acts?" *American Journal of Jurisprudence* 36 (1991): 171–201; and Appendix Four in my *Humanae Vitae: A Generation Later;* Robert P. George, "Recent Criticism of Natural Law Theory", *University of Chicago Law Review* 55 (1988): 1371–1419. Many of these articles and others are collected and commented on in Finnis, ed., *Natural Law,* vols. 1 and 2 (Aldershot, England; Dartmouth Publishing Company, 1991).

8

THE PERSONALISM OF JOHN PAUL II
AS THE BASIS OF HIS APPROACH
TO THE TEACHING OF *HUMANAE VITAE*

by
John F. Crosby

The dispute about contraception is not simply a dispute about some minor ethical matter involving how to limit family size, nor is it about the authority of the Church or some such question; rather, it is, as Pope John Paul II insists, a dispute about the very truth about the human person and the meaning of human existence. John Crosby's essay explains this claim. In commenting on the thought of John Paul II, Crosby has the distinct advantage of being, as is John Paul II, a phenomenological philosopher who takes personalism as the foundation of his philosophy. Crosby is emerging as one of the foremost interpreters of the thought of John Paul II.

Personalism for its moral judgments does not look first to the will of God, divine law, or natural law as the foundation for moral truths. Rather it takes the truth about man as its foundation—a truth that differs not at all with the will of God or divine law or natural law—but a truth that is in ways more accessible to man than other avenues to truth. It is, after all, the phenomenon of which he has the most direct experience, to which he has most direct access.

Crosby carefully outlines the "subjective" foundations of John

Paul II's thought and shows how this emphasis is fully compatible with the claim that there is an objective moral order, an order that is more deeply understood when one understands the subjectivity or interiority of man. John Paul II maintains that being "self-giving" is central to the human person and bases much of his explanation of the evil of contraception on the claim that contraception destroys the self-giving power of sexual intercourse.

This article is taken from *Anthropotes* 5, no. 1 (May 1989): 47–69. It was originally presented at a 1988 conference of the Pope John Center and published in *Trust the Truth: A Symposium* on the Twentieth Anniversary of the Encyclical *Humanae Vitae* (Braintree, Mass.: Pope John Center, 1991), pp. 37–63. This present article is an expanded version of that paper. Permission to reprint this article was granted to the Publisher by the Pope John XXIII Medical-Moral Research and Education Center, 186 Forbes Road, Braintree, MA 02184 (Telephone: 617-848-6965).

8

THE PERSONALISM OF JOHN PAUL II
AS THE BASIS OF HIS APPROACH
TO THE TEACHING OF *HUMANAE VITAE*

by
John F. Crosby

In his address of September 17, 1983, the Holy Father said that "it is not sufficient that it [the encyclical, *Humanae vitae*] be faithfully and fully proposed. . . . " This seems at first glance surprising, for it is, as everyone knows, relatively rare for a Catholic pastor or teacher, or for that matter even the Bishops' Conference of a country, to present the teachings of the encyclical "faithfully and fully". Those who do present it fully usually give evidence thereby of their faithfulness to the entire magisterium of the Church. And yet the Holy father said that this is not enough; it is indispensable, of course, but not enough. His sentence continues: "but it also is necessary to devote oneself to demonstrating its deepest reasons".[1] No-one in the church has done more than John Paul himself to advance this work of finding "the deepest reasons" for the moral teachings of the Church concerning man and woman; indeed, one of the most precious legacies of his pontificate will surely be his

This article is a somewhat expanded version of the paper which the author presented at the conference on *Humanae vitae* at Princeton University, August, 1988. The conference, which stood under the motto, "Trust the truth", was organized by the Roman Academic Center of New York.

[1] Cf. *Familiaris consortio,* para. 31.

own profound and original reflection on the foundations of these teachings.[2] But long before he was elected Pope and while he was still only Karol Wojtyla, he was already doing original philosophical and theological work which is very rich in what it says and implies about "the deepest reasons" for the teachings of the Church on marriage, parenthood, chastity.[3] In the present paper I want to draw on all these sources, and to offer a brief introduction to those philosophical themes in the thought of the Pope which form the basis of his preferred way of presenting the teachings of the encyclical, *Humanae vitae*. But I do not aim at developing completely his arguments for these teachings; my primary concern is with the philosophical foundations on which John Paul attempts to build his arguments.

Where does the Holy Father look for the reasons which underlie the moral teachings of the Church? Does he look right away to the will of God? Does he say that God has forbidden the use of artificial contraception, and that we ought to obey God whenever He exercises his authority? Not at all; though his reflection is theological, and refers repeatedly to God, he does not appeal to any divine prohibition. Or if one insists on saying that God prohibits artificial contraception, the Holy Father will ask in turn, But why does God prohibit it? And his answer is that it is opposed to "the truth about man", as he likes to say, and that this is in a

[2] I refer of course in the first place to the series of 133 addresses at the Wednesday audiences which began in 1979 and extended to 1984 and which was devoted to developing a "theology of the body". The definitive Italian text is Giovanni Paolo II, *Uomo e donna lo creò*, Rome 1987. I will in the following quote from the English translations which appeared in *L'Osservatore Romano* and which have been published in four paperback volumes by the Daughters of St. Paul, Boston, under the following titles: I: *Original Unity of Man and Woman* (1981); II: *Blessed Are the Pure of Heart* (1983); III: *The Theology of Marriage and Celibacy* (1986); IV: *Reflections on Humanae Vitae* (1984). My references will be to these volumes.

[3] Here we have to do primarily with *The Acting Person*, Dordrecht 1979 and *Love and Responsibility*, New York 1981. Karol Wojtyla also wrote certain papers which are important for the subject of this study: these will be introduced below.

sense a deeper answer to the question. There is a truth about who we are, about our bodies, our masculinity and femininity, and above all, about our personhood, and about our creaturehood; it is this truth, and ultimately the God who is Truth, but not any legislative will of God, which is the ultimate basis for the norms for responsible procreation as enunciated in *Humanae vitae*. If someone does not accept these norms, his problem is usually not in the first place with the norms, but with his whole philosophy and theology of human nature; he has to begin with rethinking his philosophy and theology if he is ever going to see the reasonableness of the norms. This is why Karol Wojtyla said in 1978: "It seems that we can consider as the deepest level of this event [the struggle surrounding the encyclical] the controversy and the struggle over man, over the value and meaning of human existence . . . ."[4]

The Holy Father develops this idea by saying (in *Familiaris consortio*, no. 32, among many other places) that the person who takes contraception for granted, and sees in it a morally harmless way of avoiding conception, does not just have a slightly different understanding of human nature from the Christian one, but a fundamentally different one. He holds that to the acceptance of artificial contraception there corresponds one vision of the human person, and to the rejection of it there corresponds an entirely different vision of the person. The norms taught in the encyclical, then, do not just concern the marital practice of spouses in their child-bearing years; they raise the whole question of the truth about man and woman and about the human person. If the Holy Father goes to a lot of trouble to explain these norms, it is not because he is onesidedly obsessed with them, but because he is aware of this vaster truth about man on which they depend, and because he feels keenly his calling to proclaim this truth in its integrity.

[4] *Die anthropologische Vision der Enzyklika Humanae vitae*, in *Von der Koenigswuerde des Menschen*, Stuttgart 1980, 182. This paper first appeared in "Lateranum", XLIV (1978), no. 1, with the title "La visione antropologica dell' Humanae Vitae."

We are about to discuss this truth as the Holy Father sees it. But first we need to get acquainted with one other idea of his about its importance; he thinks that it is *pastorally* of the utmost importance to trace the norms of *Humanae vitae* back to the truth about man and woman. He thinks that we need this truth, not just in order to *understand* the norms of the encyclical, but also in order to *live* in accordance with them. In other words, it is not just theologians but also spouses who need to know the "truth about man" which underlies the prohibition of contraception.[5] And the reason is this: without any insight into this underlying truth, the norm seems to be outside of us, and is felt to be an imposition, or at least a burden. But in seeing how the norm grows out of the truth about man, and how we *live in the truth* of our being by acting according to the norm, it is internalized, made our own, and thus ceases to be a burden even when it requires considerable sacrifice of us. In his major philosophical treatise John Paul reflects on this process of internalization, and says: "The tension arising between the objective order of norms and the inner freedom of the person is relieved by truth, by the conviction of the truthfulness of good. But it is, on the contrary, intensified and not relieved by external pressures, by the power of injunction and compulsion".[6] Hence the supreme pastoral importance of bringing out in a convincing way the truthfulness of the moral norms taught by the Church. The human person is so made for the truth, that he can live it only if he understands it. This of course does not mean that a Catholic is excused from a norm which he does not yet fully understand; it just means that the faithful owe it to themselves as persons to do everything they can to develop their understanding of the norms of the Church, and that the Church owes it to the faithful to do everything she can to build up their understanding of what she teaches. And I might add that she owes this to them, in the view

---

[5] Cf. *Familiaris consortio,* no. 34. As will often be the case throughout this study, our reference here is not to the most important passage in John Paul's writings which illustrates what we are ascribing to him in the text, even less is it to the only such passage; it is simply to one exemplary passage.

[6] Karol Wojtyla, *The Acting Person,* 166.

of John Paul, not just because their understanding of the norms facilitates their compliance with the norms, but in the first place because she takes them seriously as persons by leading them beyond a blind obedience and by educating them to a rational obedience, an *obsequium rationabile,* as St. Paul calls it.

One can see how congenial to the mind of John Paul the motto of our conference on *Humanae vitae* is: Trust the Truth. In other words: trust the truth about man and woman; it can win, as nothing else can win, the allegiance of spouses. Do not teach the norms of conjugal morality apart from the anthropological truth which grounds them; be confident in the power of truth to do what the norms, taken in isolation, are impotent to do, and impotent even if they are supported by compulsion, namely to enter into the heart and appeal to our freedom.

But enough of introduction. We want now to get acquainted with this so compelling "truth about man" and to understand why John Paul deserves to be called a kind of prophet of this truth. Though we will study the "truth about man" with a view to understanding better the teaching of *Humanae vitae,* we do not, I repeat, claim to develop a complete argument for this teaching; we are primarily concerned with presenting the anthropological vision of the Holy Father on the basis of which one could then (in another article) develop his preferred arguments for the central teaching of the encyclical. We limit ourselves in this way because we are well aware that even after the Christian vision of the human person has been secured there remain various difficulties which one has to deal with in trying to draw the right ethical conclusions about the regulation of births. But this in no way calls into question the supreme importance of the anthropological foundation of the ethical analysis; without this foundation the ethical analysis is doomed to failure.

It is natural to begin by asking what *the* most important single element is in the "adequate anthropology" of the Holy Father, as he also calls his attempt to formulate the "truth about man". This most important single element, and most fundamental element, is not difficult to find; it is this, that each human being is a person.

This is why I have chosen in my title to speak of his "personalism" rather than of his anthropology. We do not have to hear John Paul talk for long before we realize that he is fascinated with, and in awe of, the personhood of man.

We begin by speaking of his distinctive way of approaching the study of the person. Though this will indirectly introduce us to his vision of the human person, it is only in the second and third section that we will speak directly of it.

I. THE BEING OF THE PERSON AS REVEALED IN THE "SUBJECTIVITY" OF THE PERSON

In analyzing the structure of the person John Paul goes beyond the philosophical tradition which he inherits in a remarkable way: he makes much of the conscious experience which the person has of himself. This tradition had defined the person, to quote the classical formula of Boethius, as an "individual substance of rational nature", but it did not, it precisely did not express itself in terms of self-presence, subjectivity, inter-subjectivity, interiority, solitude, communion. Now John Paul, while of course entirely affirming the substantiality and the rationality of the person, does speak, indeed makes a point of speaking, and takes a particular delight in speaking, in just these "subjective" terms. Thus he commonly discusses the nature of the person in terms of *interiority* and of *inwardness* (just as *Gaudium et spes* does in para. 14). This is nothing other than the belonging of the person to himself (of which we shall speak directly below) *as it is experienced from within by the person.* Here is another example. In his extraordinarily profound meditation on the first three chapters of Genesis he observes that the account of the creation of man in chap. 2 is more subjective than the "priestly" account found in chap. 1, by which he means that only in chap. 2 do we read of such things as the *solitude* of man before the creation of woman, and of the *experience of shame,* both of its absence and then, after the fall, of its presence. This subjective approach fascinates John Paul, who marvels at the fact that it is found in so archaic a text as Genesis 2. He centers his meditation mainly around this second and more subjective account of creation.

One has to understand correctly this interest of the Holy Father in personal subjectivity. He does not think that he is departing from the *being* of the person, and studying instead only *psychological experiences* in the person; even less does he think that there is nothing more to the being of the person than such experiences. He knows well that the person has a being and a structure as person whether he is consciously present to himself or not. *But he thinks that in the conscious self-presence of the person we have a uniquely intimate access to the being of the person.* When, for example, John Paul studies the human person through the experience of sexual shame, he gives not just a psychological but a deeply personalist reading of this experience, which he explicitly calls a metaphysical reading of it.[7]

We could say that there are for John Paul two extremes to be avoided in our understanding of consciousness and being in the human person. We must not reduce the being of the person to consciousness, as if the person were real as person only in conscious self-presence. But we must also not separate being from consciousness in the person, as if the deeper, more metaphysical being of the person in no way communicated with the conscious self-presence of the person and lay entirely outside of consciousness. The Pope thinks that this deeper being of the person is actualized in conscious self-presence, and is thus reflected in conscious self-presence, and this far more than had been generally recognized in pre-modern thought, and he thinks that this self-presence should be used more as a source for the deepening of our image of the human person.[8]

---

[7] Karol Wojtyla, *Love and Responsibility,* chap. 3, section 2, "The Metaphysics of Shame". And in his commentary on Genesis he gives a *theological* reading of the experience of sexual shame.

[8] On this whole subject see above *The Acting Person,* chaps. 1 and 2.

And why should it be used more? What is to be gained by supplementing the older, more objective approach with this more subjective approach? In a very important but neglected little essay entitled, "Subjectivity and the Irreducible in Man",[9] which is surely one of his boldest philosophical statements, he claims that the objective approach, left to itself, runs the danger of losing what is distinctive of man as person. He goes so far as to claim that the whole Aristotelian metaphysics runs the risk of "reducing man to the world", of failing to do justice to the proprium of man, to what makes him a person. He says that there is a *cosmological* focus of the Aristotelian tradition which needs to be completed by a more *personalist* focus, which is characterized by studying man not only in terms of substance, potentiality, and the like, but also of self-presence and self-donation, and thereby studying him in all his concreteness and specificity. And he thinks that as a matter of historical fact the recourse to subjectivity in the last few centuries has enabled many thinkers to achieve a more adequate vision of man as person, and to achieve it without any least concession to subjectivism.[10]

Here we can say a word about the "phenomenology" of the Pope. I find that very many people would like to understand just what it is in his thought which gets called phenomenological; they are not sure what this term means, but are intrigued at its being applied to the thought of a Pope. Well, one answer, not an exhaustive answer, but part of the answer, is that phenomenological philosophy has cultivated the study of personal subjectivity, and that the method and even many of the results of this philosophy can serve to enrich the Christian personalism towards which John Paul is working.

---

[9] In *Analecta Husserliana,* VII, Dordrecht 1978, 107–14. This article was just recently published in Polish in "Ethos" 2/3 (1988), 21–28.

[10] If one considers, as Josef Seifert has tried to show in his metaphysical treatise, *Essere e persone,* Milano 1989, that being in the most proper sense is personal being, then it follows that the "subjectivity" through which Karol Wojtyla proposes to study man as person is a subjectivity through which the most properly objective reality is revealed.

Now his interest in the subjectivity of the person shows itself in his way of explaining the teaching of *Humanae vitae*. He starts from the self-donation which is enacted in the sexual union of spouses. In what follows we will have much to say about this self-donation, but already now we can see that spousal self-donation is by its very nature something consciously lived through; spouses could not possibly perform this self-donation without being aware of it; they are necessarily present to themselves as donating them-selves to each other. John Paul proceeds to argue as follows: "The act of contraception introduces a substantial limitation within this reciprocal giving and expresses an objective refusal to give to the other all the good of femininity and masculinity."[11] He often expands this thought by saying that as a result of resorting to contraception the self-donation of each spouse inevitably gets eroded by the attitude of selfishly using the other for one's own gratification. This almost implies that the disorder involved in contraception cannot remain entirely unknown to contracepting spouses, but that they can find it in their own self-experience if only they look deeply enough. For if self-donation is by its very nature something consciously lived through, then, one would think, self-donation compromised by selfishness cannot remain completely outside of the consciousness of the spouses.

Notice that other ways of explaining the teaching of *Humanae vitae* are not as "subjective" as the one which is so congenial to John Paul and to his personalism. If for instance one starts from the anti-life character of contraception, or if one starts from the impiety of contraception (as John Paul himself often does), then one starts from facts which may or may not be experienced by contracepting spouses; they are not essentially embedded in our self-experience in the same way as compromised self-donation is.

In his important paper of 1978, "La visione antropologica dell'*Humanae vitae*",[12] Karol Wojtyla carried out an extremely

---

[11] Allocution of September 17, 1983; cf. *Familiaris consortio,* para. 32.

[12] I refer here to the German translation, *Die anthropologische Vision der Enzyklika "Humanae vitae",* especially the section entitled "Subjektivitaet", 186–92. See my note 5 above.

careful textual comparison of *Humanae vitae* with the chapter on Christian marriage in *Gaudium et spes,* and came to the conclusion that the latter text deals with the wrong of contraception in primarily objective terms, whereas the encyclical deals with it in more subjective terms. His main point is that in speaking of the inseparability of the unitive and procreative "meanings" of the marital act, the encyclical speaks of the act as consciously performed and experienced by the spouses. Karol Wojtyla saw in this more subjective approach a significant "progress" of the encyclical over the conciliar text.

But of course this subjective approach of John Paul is not to be confused with subjectivism (any more than the subjective emphasis of the encyclical could be confused with a concession to subjectivism). John Paul does not mean that contraceptive intercourse simply weakens the experience of self-donation; he means that it compromises the *reality* of self-donation, and that it is this deformed reality which can be experienced. Nor does he mean that there is a merely empirical connection between contraception and compromised self-donation; he means that there is an intrinsically necessary connection between them, that there is an inexorable personalist logic whereby the one leads to the other. Nor finally does he mean that if spouses using contraception should not be able to find in their self-experience anything in the way of sexual selfishness, then they are free of this selfishness and are not guilty of any moral disorder; he means that in their intercourse there is an "*objective refusal* to give to the other all the good of masculinity and femininity" (my italics) and hence an objective moral disorder. In order to grasp the breadth and balance of John Paul's thought one has to dwell on the fact that in the very passage where he probes the *subjectivity* of the contracepting spouses, he speaks of the *objectivity* of their refusal.[13]

John Paul thinks that the more subjective approach to the

---

[13] We will understand better the objectivity of this refusal after we have gotten acquainted with the place of the body in the makeup of human nature according to John Paul.

teachings of the encyclical, besides being deeply congenial to his own mind, is also pastorally indispensable, that it is exactly the approach required by our age.

> [The author of the encyclical] was undoubtedly aware of that particular sensibility of modern man which refers to the subjectivity of his acting and his experience. The development in modern philosophy of the anthropological subject corresponds to this sensibility. It follows from our analysis that this sensibility does not lead man to the position of pure subjectivism. *On the contrary, by grasping the objective moral order in being conscious of himself as subject, he is enabled to understand in a more mature way the authenticity, the reasonableness, the beauty of this order* [my italics]. Perhaps it is precisely then that we achieve what St. Thomas wanted to express when he spoke of the "participatione legis aeternae in rationali creatura".[14]

We get a glimpse here of the boldness with which John Paul attempts to unite *vetera* and *nova,* to unite the traditional and the modern.

So far we have simply spoken of the subjective approach for which John Paul has such a great affinity, and though this has introduced us to his personalism and to his understanding of the relation between being and consciousness in the human person, we must now make the attempt, if we are going to throw new light on the teaching of *Humanae vitae,* to speak more directly about his vision of the human person.

2. THE PARADOXICAL STRUCTURE OF THE HUMAN PERSON

When talking of man as person, John Paul often quotes a line from *Gaudium et spes;* indeed, there is I think no other conciliar text which he quotes as much as this one. In para. 24 the Council fathers say "that man, though he is the only creature on earth

---

[14] Ibid., 192 (my translation from the German).

which God willed for its own sake, cannot fully find himself except through a sincere gift of himself". The Holy Father is taken with the paradoxical structure which is here ascribed to the human person: each human person is so much a being of his own that he can only be willed for his own sake, and yet he is not so much a being of his own as to be able to live for himself and be happy in the solitude of his own being, he has instead to make a gift of himself to another in order to gain that being of his own which belongs to him as person. The Pope thinks that much of the "truth about man" is epitomized in this conciliar expression of this paradoxical structure. Let us see what he has to say about each of the two terms of the paradox; let us hear him first on the selfhood of the human person, and then on the need which the human person has for communion with others.

Persona est sui iuris et alteri incommunicabilis. Freely rendered, a person is a being who belongs to himself and who is not a part or property of anything else. Each person is so much a being of his own, is so strongly gathered into himself and anchored in himself, that he resists being incorporated into any totality in which he would be a mere part, serving only to build up the totality; he is rather a totality of his own, a world for himself. The thought can be expressed in the famous terms of Kant: each person is an end in himself and is never to be treated, whether by himself or by another, as an instrumental means for realizing some result.[15]

As one sees in this Kantian formulation, this basic truth about the person gives rise to a basic moral norm; the selfhood of the person gives rise to the norm directing us to respect persons in this far-reaching "being of their own" which they have as person, and to abstain from all using, owning, absorbing of persons. This norm, which for John Paul is *the* first principle of morality—he calls it the "personalist principle"—is so strong as to hold even for

[15] See, above all, *The Acting Person,* chap. 3. But for a briefer statement of his thought on the selfhood of the person see *Love and Responsibility,* 21–24, or his lectures *Die personalistische Konzeption des Menschen,* in *Elternschaft und Meschenwuerde,* Vallender-Schoenstatt 1984, Wenisch (ed.), 27–43, especially 30–36.

God. In his early work, *Love and Responsibility,* he says, "This principle has a universal validity. Nobody can use a person as a means towards an end, no human being, not even God the Creator. . . . if God intends to direct man towards certain goals, he allows him to . . . know those goals, so that he may make them his own and strive towards them independently".[16] This is why the passage in the Pastoral Constitution, 24, which John Paul so loves to quote, speaks of man being willed by God *for his [man's] own sake.* The Holy Father means that God is simply recognizing the personhood of man by willing him, and also ruling him, for his own sake. He often says that we, when we respect persons and abstain from all using and violence towards them, are simply participating in that vision of them and love for them which God has.[17] But what above all concerns us at the present moment is not so much the personalist norm, and its validity even for God, but the underlying truth about the selfhood of the person which is reflected in it, the truth that the person is *sui iuris* and *alteri incommunicabilis,* that is, in an incomparable sense he is himself and he is not any other.

This is what John Paul says about the *being* of the person. He also has something to say about the *acting* of the person. He makes his well-known distinction between "what happens in man" and what man "does himself", calling the former an "activation" and reserving the term, "acting", for the latter.[18] "What happens in man" would comprise instincts, drives, and whatever else springs up in us outside of our selfhood and with a spontaneity of its own. One sees how acting expresses the being of one who belongs to himself as person, it is just because the human person belongs to himself, that he does not just endure what happens in him, but can act through himself. If the human person were not gathered into

[16] Karol Wojtyla, *Love and Responsibility,* 27.

[17] See for example John Paul II, *Original Unity of Man and Woman,* Boston 1981, 116, 132. (This is the first of the four volumes which contain all the allocutions of the Holy Father's five-year catechesis on human love; see my note no. 3 above.)

[18] *The Acting Person,* chap. 2.

himself in the sense of being *sui iuris et alteri incommunicabilis* he would entirely lack the inner ontological resources, so to speak, for acting through himself.

We cannot fully understand the thought of John Paul on the acting of the person without considering the person *in his relation to truth*. He often explains himself on this point in exactly that subjective way discussed above. Thus in one place he explains it by reflecting on the experience of solitude. Feeling himself into the account of Adam naming the animals, he interprets this act of naming as the act of understanding the truth about the non-personal beings around him.[19] And in understanding this truth Adam acted through himself and so came to himself, began to experience himself; in going out to the truth of things around him he returned to himself, and began to experience his personal selfhood and to develop an interiority. But in this self-experience he realized how different he was from all the beings around him, and in this realization he experienced a deep solitude. This is a solitude which we too experience in our relation to nonpersons, and experience in proportion as we understand the truth about them. It is clear that this solitude is not *a merely psychological* experience, detached from the being of the person; it is nothing but an experience of this being, it is an experience of that ontological structure of belonging to oneself of which John Paul speaks. Perhaps we could even say that it is an experience of what Boethius had called, using the language of Aristotelian metaphysics, the proper substantiality of the person. The main point for us is that we act through ourselves and experience our selfhood through our relation to the truth of beings, and that we cannot act through ourselves and experience our selfhood if we lose our orientation towards truth.

He also discusses the more properly moral acting of the person,

[19] *The Original Unity of Man and Woman,* 43–49, cf. also John Paul's address at the Catholic University of Lublin, June 9, 1987. See my commentary on this address, *Dialektyka podmiotowosci i transcendencii w osobie ludzkiej* (*The Dialectic of Subjectivity and Transcendence in the Human Person*), in "Ethos" 2/3 (1988), 57–65.

and explains why it is possible only in relation to the "truth about good". When we feel the appeal of good things, even objectively good things, we are at first in danger of being dominated by them, of being subject to a "moral determinism" which tends to prevent us from acting through ourselves. Only in breaking through to the "truth about good" do we gain that spiritual distance to goods which lets us act through ourselves towards them.[20] Through that spiritual distance we experience something like the solitude of Adam naming the animals; we grow in that interiority and subjectivity in which the ontological structure of the human person is lived through and experienced.

Thanks to his subjective approach to the human person John Paul is able to bring to light a very significant though easily overlooked feature of our acting in relation to the truth about good. He says that this acting should not be exclusively understood in terms of the good to which it is directed; there is also a reflexive element in all acting, that is, the agent also has to do with himself. This is perhaps nowhere so clear as in conscience; when we feel some moral imperative in conscience, however strongly we are drawn outside of ourselves by the good which imposes the obligation, we are at the same time drawn within ourselves, and are aware of disposing over our very selves in the performing of the action, in other words we are aware that our acting involves self-determination. Just as in all cognition we are not only aware of some object, but also present to ourselves as cognizing, so in all acting in relation to good we not only affirm some object outside of ourselves but also determine ourselves; self-determination is to moral acting what self-presence is to cognition.

In thus probing the subjectivity of acting we can develop further our understanding of the selfhood of the person. For John Paul often says[21] that self-presence and self-determination express the fact that the person is an end in himself and even in a sense

---

[20] *Love and Responsibility,* 115; cf. also *The Acting Person,* chap. 3, sections 7 and 9, and chap. 4, section 3.

[21] For instance in *Die personalistische Konzeption des Menschen,* 34.

exists for his own sake; if the *whole* meaning of his acting were the cognizing of some object outside of himself or the promoting of some good outside of himself then, he would be drawn off of himself towards that object or that good in a manner inconsistent with his belonging to himself.

Let us now see what follows (from John Paul's account of selfhood and self-determination) for the understanding of the teachings of *Humanae vitae.*

1. The personalist principle, as we saw, says that the person, being *sui iuris et alteri incommunicabilis,* must never be merely used but always also affirmed for his own sake.[22] This implies for John Paul the wrongness of one way of trying to explain the condemnation of contraception, and thus at least points indirectly in the direction of the right way of defending it. He means the "rigorism" according to which the whole meaning of the sexual union of spouses is to be an instrumental means for raising up offspring.[23] If that were so, it would of course follow that contraceptive intercourse is inherently disordered and irrational. But the premise contradicts the personalist principle; spouses would violate each other as persons if in their intimate relations they merely used each other for the sake of procreation, and God would violate them as persons if He gave them the sexual drive merely to use them for this purpose. Notice that the nobility of the purpose does not help at all in removing the moral disorder which comes from using persons.

2. But from this it does not follow for John Paul that one can give a personalist defense of contraception, *for contraception also violates the personalist principle,* and this violation goes far towards explaining the wrongness of contraception. In other words, it is not only non-contraceptive marital relations performed according the spirit of this "rigorism", but also contraceptive marital relations, which violate the truth about the person. While it is obvious that

[22] Cf. *Love and Responsibility,* 40–44.
[23] Ibid., 57–61.

the former violate the personalist principle, it is not equally obvious that the latter violate it, and so we shall have to examine more closely the depersonalizing character of contraception. But we have made an important start by identifying the personalist principle as the principle which according to John Paul controls the ethical analysis of contraception.

3. This personalist principle helps us understand why John Paul teaches, as the Church has always taught, that the act of contraception is intrinsically wrong and can never be made right by any amount of good results which it might lead to. It is not so difficult to see that the violation of a person, as when one makes a slave of him, is intrinsically wrong, and that the good consequences of enslaving him are irrelevant to the rightness or wrongness of enslaving him. If then John Paul can show that contraception does indeed violate the personalist principle, it will hardly be surprising if he teaches that the wrongness of contraception is an intrinsic wrongness. I touch here of course on a vast subject, which I cannot do justice to in this paper; but the subject should not pass unmentioned.

4. John Paul's understanding of selfhood and self-determination underlies his teaching on the possibility of abstinence. If abstinence were easy, the teaching of *Humanae vitae* would have caused no controversy; everyone would then agree that the only medically sensible way of spacing out births would be abstinence, which would be much preferable to powerful new drugs or to unreliable devices. But very many people think that the abstinence which is typically required of a couple which refuses contraception is not only difficult but is in fact more than human nature can bear. John Paul responds that such people often fail to understand the personhood of man and woman; they think that human beings have to live at the beck and call of their drives and wants; they overlook their power of acting through themselves and of determining themselves. He often calls attention to the paradox that the same people who exalt man into a promethean position when it comes to the technological manipulation and domination of the

world and of themselves, fail to treat him even as a person when it comes to the task of him mastering and forming his drives and urges: they make him first a god and then a beast, without ever getting closer to the truth that he is in fact an incarnate person.[24]

But the human person, for all his selfhood, does not exist through himself, and does not suffice for his own happiness. "He can find himself only by making a sincere gift of himself", as that Council text says. If the human person through his selfhood reflects God, then through his being made for communion with other persons he reflects the inner-trinitarian life of God. In his commentary on Genesis John Paul ventures the opinion, cautiously, that this being made for communion with others is perhaps an even more significant fact about man than his selfhood.[25] As we would expect, John Paul often explains interpersonal communion in a subjective way, as when, in the same commentary, resuming his discussion of solitude, he says, "Man's solitude . . . is presented to us not only as the first discovery of the characteristic transcendence peculiar to the person, but also as the discovery as an adequate relationship 'to' the person, and therefore as an opening and expectation of a communion of persons".[26]

It is important to add that John Paul not only stresses the necessity of each person living by self-donation, *but also of being received by the one to whom he gives himself;* this too belongs to the full finding of oneself in communion with other persons.[27]

Now what is the most perfect form in which one human person makes a sincere gift of himself to another human person? In a marvellous passage in his early work, *Love and Responsibility,* Karol Wojtyla explains the answer which he has always given to this question: the most radical self-giving of one human person to another human person occurs between man and woman in spou-

---

[24] Cf. his allocution at the Catholic University of Lublin, June 8, 1987.
[25] *The Original Unity of Man and Woman,* 72.
[26] Ibid.
[27] See for instance Ibid., 128–34.

sal love.[28] Here we have a love which is more than just benevo-
lence towards the other, and even more than the readiness to make
sacrifices, even very great sacrifices, for the other; here we have a
giving of oneself, and not only that, but a *surrender* of oneself to
the other, and the will of each to come to belong to the other.
Indeed, the abandonment of each spouse to the other goes so far,
he observes, that one might well wonder how this abandonment
is compatible with the selfhood of each spouse. How can a person,
who as person belongs to himself, ever make himself belong to
another, how can he even want to belong to another? "The very
nature of the person is incompatible with such a surrender".[29]
Karol Wojtyla answers that in fact spousal self-surrender is *rendered
possible* by the belonging of the person to himself. *Precisely because*
the person belongs to himself, and is handed over to himself, he
can dispose over himself by giving himself away spousally.[30]
And he gives a further answer. One can see that a further answer
is necessary as soon as one notices that the belonging of the person
to himself also renders possible the act for example of selling
himself as a slave or of throwing himself away in some other
manner; if he did not belong to himself as person he could not
dispose over himself like this. The further answer is that in giving
oneself away spousally one precisely does not throw oneself away
but rather gives oneself in such a way as to gain oneself and to live
and thrive as a personal self who is *sui iuris* and *alteri incommunicabilis.*
He says that spousal love bears witness in a particular manner the
words of Our Lord: "He who would save his soul shall lose it, and
he who would lose his soul for my sake shall find it again" (Matt.
10:39).

Notice that many modern thinkers who start from the selfhood
and self-determination of the person go on to develop some
notion of autonomy, or of man as a subject of rights, which
excludes the possibility of self-donation. But John Paul knows

---

[28] *Love and Responsibility,* 95–100.
[29] Ibid., 96.
[30] Cf. also *Die personalistische Konzeption des Menschen,* 34–36.

how to find a new personalist approach to self-donation *precisely on the basis of selfhood and self-determination.*

But we have not yet given a complete account of John Paul's personalist analysis of self-donation; we have to consider not only the person who gives himself spousally but also his partner, the one to whom he gives himself. If I experience my partner as merely sexually attractive I will not be able to perform any act of spousal self-donation. I have first of all to apprehend my partner as person and to experience his or her sexual attractiveness only in relation to his or her personhood. And why? Why does my self-donation to the other require this cognition of the other as person? Because I can act through myself and determine myself in a properly personal way only by acting in relation to the "truth about good"; as we saw, only this truth lets me gain a spiritual distance to good and loveable beings and thus gain that spiritual space which I need in order to determine myself with respect to them. But it is almost the most important part of the truth about the goodness and loveableness of the other that he or she is a person. The fact, then, that I am a person and thus belong to myself is only a necessary but not a sufficient condition for me performing the act of spousal self-donation. I have also to apprehend the *other* as person and thus stand in the truth about the goodness of the other.

So much, then, on the paradoxical structure of the person according to John Paul. To summarize: on the one hand, the person exists in selfhood, with a being of his own, as a world for himself, but on the other hand, he is made for self-donation, and can live as personal self only by basing his existence on self-donation.

We indicated above some of the consequences which follow from the selfhood of the person for the ethical question of contraception; let us now indicate one of the main consequences which follow from the self-donation which, according to John Paul, the human person is made for.

All of his thought on spousal self-donation stands in the closest relation to his thought on marriage. In marriage a man and a woman achieve that complete belonging of each to the other for which they long as a result of their spousal love. A man and a woman with no interest in marriage could not possibly, John Paul would say, love each other with a spousal love. But more to the point of the present study is the fact that self-donation is not only the soul of marriage but is also the soul of the marital act; the whole *raison d'être* of the sexual union of the spouses, according to John Paul, is to express and to enact their spousal surrender to each other and their spousal belonging to each other. He loses no opportunity to protest against a purely biological consideration of sexual intercourse; the only way to understand it for what it really is, is to consider it from the point of view of the person, that is, from the point of view of spousal self-donation.[31]

Let us suppose that the marital act had nothing to do with self-donation, and in fact that it had no deep personalist significance, and were not distorted by being considered in a purely biological way; let us suppose that it were nothing more than the gratification of sexual concupiscence. Then it would be very hard to make an ethical case against contraception; it would be impossible to make any argument based on the inseparability of the unitive and procreative meanings of sexual relations, for one would have abolished the unitive meaning, which of course does not consist in physical union but in the union of persons. Most people can readily see that there is something morally relevant about the bond between the bodily expression of spousal self-donation, and the coming into being of a new human being, even if they are often unclear as to exactly which ethical consequence they should draw; they see that such a bond is deeply meaningful, and that there is hardly any other human act or experience which would be more appropriately endowed with procreative power. But nobody could possibly find any moral relevance in the bond between the selfish gratification of sexual concupiscence and the coming into being of a new human person. On the contrary, one would have to judge this bond to be an unfortunate fact of nature, one would even have to say that such a way of coming into

---

[31] Cf. for instance *Love and Responsibility,* chap. 5.

existence is unworthy of a new human person. When then contemporary men and women, strongly influenced by consumerist materialism, can see nothing more in sexual relations than entertainment, devoid of any deeper personalist content, then it is only natural that they will find the Church's teaching on contraception unintelligible; indeed, it would be strange and unnatural if, having driven self-donation out of human sexuality, they had any moral objections to the use of contraception. But if they can learn from John Paul how spousal self-donation is the soul and the form of sexual intimacy, and why sexual intimacy becomes untruthful and depersonalized in the absence of any spousal self-donation, then they might recover some sense of the deep human meaning and mystery which lies in the procreative power of sexual union, and then the idea of sterilizing the sexual union would become for them, at the very least, ethically quite problematical.

Here we see the makings of a powerful personalist argument for the teaching of *Humanae vitae*. It is certainly not the only argument which can be made; I stress it because of the way it grows out of John Paul's analysis of self-donation. But the argument cannot be developed further without first enlarging the underlying personalism. The reader should bear in mind that the task we have set ourselves in this study is not the completion of any of the arguments for the teaching of the encyclical, but an exposition of the personalism of John Paul which makes certain of the arguments possible.

3. THE NUPTIAL MEANING OF THE HUMAN BODY

There is an all-important category in the personalism of John Paul of which we have as yet said very little: the human body. If one takes a certain view of the body, if one separates it from the person, maintaining a kind of dualism of the person and his body, than one gets a personalism which really is subversive of many Catholic moral teachings. Though the term dualism is not regularly used by John Paul, it lends itself naturally to expressing the position opposed to his own. Since this term can express very various meanings and confusions of meanings, it is important that the reader take in exactly that meaning of dualism which emerges from the following, and that he take John Paul's critique of this dualism as a critique precisely of it and not of other dualisms.[32]

An American feminist calling herself a Catholic recently defended any and all kinds of sexual relations between man and woman (and between man and man, and woman and woman), saying that *God does not care what we do with our bodies, but only how we treat each other as persons.* She apparently did not consider the possibility that a person's body forms such a unity with the person himself that the way men and women treat each other's bodies determines whether they respect each other as persons. One would misunderstand the dualism which this feminist expressed if one thought that she, or rather the mentality which she represents, rejected entirely the possibility of self-donation, or that it regarded all sexual activity as inherently selfish. No, the representatives of this mentality might speak in praise of self-donation; what characterizes their mentality is a certain "spiritualism", that is, *the idea that self-donation is not tied to this bodily expression rather than that one, and is not necessarily incompatible with any particular bodily expression. This means that self-donation springs out of the interiority of the person and has complete freedom in seeking its bodily expression, which can in principle be any exercise of sexuality.*[33] If persons get estranged

[32] One often calls by the name of dualism the position that there is a substantial distinction between body and soul in man, that is, a distinction such as is presupposed for the continued existence of the separated soul after death and before the resurrection of the body. Obviously John Paul and any other Christian thinker as well maintains this dualism. This is dualism in a sense very different from the dualism of which we speak in the text; it is a dualism which is in no way antagonistic to the nuptial meaning of the body, and in fact further reflection would show that it is even presupposed by the nuptial meaning of the body.

[33] When I speak here of "spiritualism" I do not mean a Platonic metaphysics of the soul and a failure to do justice to the unity of soul and body. I speak of spiritualism and of dualism, not in a Platonic or in a Cartesian sense, but in

from their bodies like this, then it becomes very hard indeed for them to make any sense at all of *Humanae vitae* and of other Catholic teachings on sexuality and procreation.

In the writings and addresses of John Paul we can find at least two causes of this dualism, or two reasons why it is so difficult for modern men to understand the real unity of the person with his body.

1. In his allocution of April 8, 1981, which belongs to the catechesis on human love, he said:

> The whole development of modern science, regarding the body as an organism, has rather the character of biological knowledge, because it is based on the separation, in man, of that which is corporeal in him from that which is spiritual. Using such a one-sided knowledge of the functions of the body as an organism, it is not difficult to arrive at a way of treating the body ... as an object of manipulations. In this case *man ceases, so to speak, to identify himself subjectively with his own body, because it is deprived of the meaning and the dignity* deriving from the fact that this body is proper to the person [my italics].[34]

2. The other factor tending to estrange the person from this body is not a specifically modern factor, nor does it have any special connection with modern technology; it is the sexual concu-

---

the sense in which Fabro in effect ascribes them to Kierkegaard when he says that Kierkegaard's thought is characterized by "a diffida contro ogni prevalere dell'esteriorita" (Introduzione al *Diaro*, I, Brescia 1980, 68). Perhaps one could say, in deliberate oversimplification, that we speak in the text of a spiritualism and dualism which in the modern world derives more from Luther than from Descartes. It is the spiritualism/dualism which underlies much Protestant situation-ethics. The Cartesian spiritualism/dualism is in any case anti-materialistic, whereas we refer in the text to a dualism/spiritualism which is commonly found among largely materialistic thinkers who want to have nothing to do with the metaphysics of a spiritual soul. This whole subject needs further investigation, which would stand very much in the service of the development of John Paul's personalism.

[34] John Paul II, *Blessed are the Pure of Heart*, 263.

piscence which has taken over in human nature since the fall. John Paul discusses sexual concupiscence far more extensively than the first factor, and in fact what he has to say about it forms a particularly rich part of his catechesis on human love.[35] He says that as a result of the fall there occurred

> a certain constitutive break within the human person, almost a rupture of man's original spiritual and somatic unity. He realizes for the first time that his body has ceased drawing upon the power of the spirit. . . . The body, which is not subordinated to the spirit as in the state of original innocence, bears within it a constant center of resistance to the spirit, and threatens, in a way, the unity of the man-person. . . . The structure of self-mastery, essential for the person, is, in a way, shaken to the very foundations in him. . . . [36]

As a result, the masculinity and the femininity of the human body are no longer transparent to the personhood of men and woman, but begin to exercise an attractive power which is detached from the preciousness and loveableness which they have as persons. Man and woman then desire each other for sexual gratification, and not to perfect their belonging to each other. This disappearance of the person from sexuality leads to, or rather is, that dualism which John Paul deprecates.

But one might at first wonder whether, for all his deprecation of dualism, there are not elements of it in his own thought. As we saw, John Paul's reflection on the self-determination of the person leads him to an important distinction between what happens in man and what man does through himself. This means that there are two poles in the makeup of human nature: there is the more passive pole which is the principle of undergoing, enduring, and there is the pole of selfhood and self-activity. In *The Acting Person* Karol Wojtyla is in fact willing to adopt a widely-used terminology, and to distinguish between "person" and "nature" in man, and in one place in this work he even goes so far as to say

---

[35] See, above all, ibid., 19–152.
[36] Ibid., 50–51.

that person and nature "divide the human being, as it were, into two worlds".[37]

The problem is that the person-nature distinction is very commonly understood in a dualistic sense, and that it is very commonly used by those who argue for the liceity of contraception; they say that the biological processes which are manipulated by contraception belong to what is merely "nature" in man, and that human beings are simply exercising the self-possession which belongs to them as "persons" when they practice this manipulation.

And yet John Paul does not hold the dualism. For he maintains in this same work, and in fact argues here at length, that person and nature in man, distinct as they are in idea, are nevertheless not distinct beings, they rather belong to one and the same being.[38] The same human being who is characterized by personal selfhood, is characterized by nature; the very one who acts through himself in freedom also undergoes and endures. I cannot discuss now all of his arguments for the unity of man; I will limit myself to just one of them, a typically subjective one. "When man acts, the ego has the experience of its own agency in action. When, on the other hand, there is something happening in man, then the ego does not experience its own agency and is not the agent, *but it does have the experience of the inner identity of itself with what is happening* [my emphasis] . . . ".[39] In other words, when I act through myself in freedom, and then undergo that which happens in me, I experience not two different experiencing subjects, but one; I experience that it is the same subject who now acts and now undergoes. Person and nature, then, though sharply distinct in idea, belong to the same human being.

But if we want to find John Paul's deepest insights into the error of the dualism, we should look not just at what he says about *the ontological unity of person and nature in man,* but also and above all at what he says about *the task of integrating nature into the*

[37] *The Acting Person,* 79.
[38] Ibid., 71–90.
[39] Ibid., 80.

life of the person. I would try to render his train of thought in the following way.

Self-donation belongs to man as person, as we saw; it belongs to him no less than selfhood and self-possession. The supreme self-donation between human persons is spousal self-donation. We explained these things above without any reference to the body. But now John Paul adds: this spousal self-donation can be fully expressed and enacted only when a man and a woman in marriage become one flesh (Genesis 2, 24). Though sexual attraction, in its origin, is a matter of nature, springing up in us on its own, and existing at first outside of our interiority, it is destined to be drawn into our interiority. Then it can lend an entire dimension to the self-donation of persons which would otherwise be missing. This means that the sexual drive is not merely related to the person as something to be dominated by the person, it is related much more intimately to the person than that, *it is related as something to be incorporated into the life of the person,* for in marriage it provides the person with a medium for a deeper and more perfect performance of an act which springs from the depths of his selfhood and interiority. This potential of the masculinity and the femininity of the human body to serve the supreme self-donation of persons is[40] what the Holy Father calls the "nuptial meaning of the human body". This aptitude of the body to serve the communion of persons, and to make possible a plenitude of communion which would otherwise be missing, gives us a profound disclosure of the dignity, the nobility of the human body, and shows forcefully the error of a Manichean hatred of the body. But more to our present point: this aptitude to be incorporated into the deepest life of the person shows that the body belongs to the being of the person and is not an object for the person, and that the person is not entirely free in seeking the bodily expression of his inner acts.

One might ask whether this entirely refutes the dualism. What if someone were to interpret the thought of John Paul as follows: the spouses can confer the meaning of self-donation on their

[40] Subject to the qualification introduced in the next paragraph.

bodily union, and then their bodily union comes to express self-donation, but only as a result of this conferral; if they do not confer this meaning then their bodily union is merely bodily union and has nothing to do with self-donation. Is this not still the dualism? This question forces us to bring out into the open the aspect of John Paul's teaching which decisively refutes the dualism. It is this: their bodies have nuptial meaning, and their bodily union has the meaning of self-donation, *independently of any subjective act of conferring which they might perform.* This is why the bodily union of man and woman in the absence of spousal self-donation and of spousal belonging to one another (that is, the bodily union of fornication or adultery) has something untruthful, it "says" as it were too much, more than is really meant. This means that a certain self-surrender of man and woman to each other is objectively effected by their sexual union, whether they want this or not; they do not have the power to render their sexual union harmless, to keep their personhood out of it, and to deprive it of its meaning of self-donation. The untruthfulness comes from the discrepancy between this objective self-surrender and the subjective absence of spousal love.[41] We spoke above of the person disappearing from sexuality; now we have to qualify this and say that there is a certain sense in which the person cannot disappear from sexuality. John Paul expresses all this, if I read him correctly, when he says that spouses, in truthful sexual relations, employ a

---

[41] Dietrich von Hildebrand expresses a related thought in his great work, *In Defense of Purity* (the original German title is *Reinheit und Jungfraeulichkeit*), 21–26. He says that in all sexual intimacy there is enacted an incomparable self-disclosure of each partner to the other, a unique revelation of the most intimate secret of each partner, and he says that this self-revelation is enacted whether the man and woman want it or not. This is why sexual union, as soon as it is isolated from marriage and from any spousal self-donation, effects a terrible *desecration* of each, a terrible *self-squandering* of each. This idea of self-surrender through self-revelation, and of self-squandering as the result of irresponsible sex, adds something to the analyses of Karol Wojtyla/John Paul. There is an important study waiting to be written on the understanding of man and woman, of sexuality, chastity, purity in the writing of von Hildebrand and of John Paul.

"language" which is not of their own making.[42] We find, then, that the nuptial meaning of the body does not exist merely as conferred by the spouses, it is rather pre-formed in the nature of man and woman, and is so strong a reality that it constitutes a norm for their subjective intentions; and it cannot be ignored without persons misusing each other.

Let us now recall the ethical issue which serves to focus the personalist analysis of this study, that is, the issue of contraception. It is true that the reflection of the last paragraph only referred to the wrongness of fornication and adultery. But we do not have far to look in order to find some bearing on contraception.[43]

We just saw that the subjective intentions of men and women do not suffice to render their sexual relations worthy of themselves as persons; these subjective intentions can remain good only by conforming to the objective laws governing the bodily expression of them. But then the question arises: are there perhaps other such objective laws governing the intimate bodily union of man and woman? Could it be that the nuptial meaning of the body requires other elements besides self-donation if sexual union is to be worthy of the person united? Does it also require an openness to the procreative power of sexual union? Could it be that spouses inevitably fall out of the attitude of respect for truth and respect for each other as persons when they sterilize their sexual union? *In any case, the whole discussion is put on a new level as soon as one abandons the spiritualistic attempt to explain the ethics of contraception in terms of internal intentions and begins looking for the objective laws, grounded in the nuptial meaning of the body, which govern truthful sexual intimacy.*

[42] Cf. John Paul II, *The Theology of Marriage and Celibacy,* 313.

[43] Of course the nuptial meaning of the body has a bearing on all kinds of other issues of sexual and marital morality. To give just one example: John Paul rethinks the idea that one of the purposes of marriage is the *remedium concupiscentiae,* and says that this does not mean that marriage legalizes the unbridled exercise of concupiscence, but rather that it relieves concupiscence in the sense of making sexual desire serve the union of persons and making it more dependent on the nuptial meaning of the body.

It would, by the way, be a mistake to think that John Paul gives up his preferred subjective approach when he comes to the task of establishing these objective laws. He thinks that these laws make themselves felt in the deeper subjective experience of men and women, and can be experienced from within precisely as objective laws. He himself often explores the nuptial meaning of the body through the subjectivity of spouses.

4. TOWARDS DEVELOPING THE PERSONALISM OF JOHN PAUL: THE CONTINGENCY OF THE HUMAN PERSON

We conclude with a few observations on one direction in which the personalism of John Paul might be developed so as to throw still more light on the teaching of *Humanae vitae*.

The fact that the human person is a composition of personal selfhood and of nature gives us evidence of the contingency of the human person. An absolute being would have to be pure selfhood, pure interiority, it would have to be nothing but personal selfhood and to lack anything in the way of nature, any principle of undergoing and enduring. The nuptial meaning of the body gives further evidence of the contingency of the human person; for an absolute being could not be subject to norms which did not originate in its interiority. Now it seems to us that *this category of the contingency of the human person* needs to be brought forward and thematized, and indeed developed with the same thoroughness with which John Paul has developed the self-donation of the person, or the nuptial meaning of the body. In thus exploring the contingency of the human person one would not merely subsume the human person under a general metaphysical category and in this way depart from the personalism of John Paul: one would rather develop and modify what has been said about the selfhood of the person. One would come to see that the human person not only stands in himself, he also stands in another, that is, he exists through God. As person he belongs to himself; as creature he belongs to God. To try to understand more deeply this paradox of personal existence is a great task of Christian personalism. And in fact it is entirely possible, as far as I can see, to explore the contingency of the human person in the same subjective way in which John Paul explores other aspects of the human person.[44]

What especially concerns us is that the contingency of the human person is rich in moral relevance, surely no less so than the selfhood of the human person. And it is rich in moral relevance for our subject of contraception, as the Holy Father himself well knows. In his allocution of September 17, 1983, says that spouses using contraception "assume the qualification not of being cooperators in God's creative power, but the ultimate depositaries of the source of human life"; this can only be understood on the basis of the contingency and creaturehood of the human person. And the contingency of the person not only has its own moral relevance; it also underlies the moral relevance of other elements of John Paul's personalism, such as the nuptial meaning of the body. It is not enough to see the objectivity of the nuptial meaning of the body; we have also to approach it in piety, in the reverence of a creature, in order to grasp fully the moral relevance of it.

And yet it happens all the time that a philosopher or theologian, while seeming to profess the contingency of the human person, evacuates it of its moral relevance.[45] This gives us the challenge, not just to insist on this moral relevance and on the various norms grounded in it, but to go back to the contingency of the human person and to try to understand it more deeply. In this way one

---

[44] I have attempted in my forthcoming book, *The Paradoxical Structure of Personal Existence,* Boston 1990, after trying to work out the rightly understood autonomy of the human person, to examine the contingency of the person both in a "metaphysical" and in a "subjective" way.

[45] This seems to me to be the tendency of for example J. Fuchs, *Das Gottesbild und die Moral innerweltlichen Handelns,* in *Stimmen der Zeit,* Bd. 202, Jg. 109, H 6 (June 1984), 363–82. See the critique of Fuchs by J. Seifert, *Gott und die Sittlichkeit innerweltlichen Handelns,* in *Forum Katholischer Theologie,* Jg. 1, H 1 (1985), 27–47.

might develop a little further the personalism of John Paul, rendering explicit what is already present in it, and so perhaps even enhance its power of throwing new light on the moral teachings of the Church, including the teaching of the encyclical *Humanae vitae.*

FURTHER READING

See also, John Crosby, "Reflections on the Foundation of Karol Wojtyla's Philosophy of the Person", in *Karol Wojtyla: Filoso Teologo, Poeta,* Proceedings of the First International Colloquium on Christian Thought (Rome 1984) 25–37; "The Creaturehood of the Human Person and the Critique of Proportionalism", in *Persona, Verita è Morale: Atti del Congresso Internazionale di Teologia Morale* (Rome, April 7–12, 1968) 195–200, also published in *Anthropotes* 2 (1987) 195–99; "The Personalist Foundations of Bioethics", *The Linacre Quarterly* 55: 3 (1988) 43–55, also published under the title "Man as Person: A Personalist Approach to the Spiritual Nature of Man", in *Creative Love* ed. by John F. Boyle (Front Royal, Va.: Christendom Press, 1989).

9

POPE JOHN PAUL II AND *HUMANAE VITAE*

by
Janet E. Smith

Pope John Paul II has provided us with a full "theology of the body" to reinforce the teaching of *Humanae Vitae*. That this theology is so compatible with *Humanae Vitae* may be less surprising when it is recognized that views of John Paul II may have had a significant influence on the contents of *Humanae Vitae*. He was on the special commission that advised Paul VI on the subject of birth regulation; he did not attend any meetings, but he did provide a response to the majority report.[1] He also was influential in the writing of *Gaudium et Spes,* the Vatican II document on the Church in the modern world; the views of marriage set forth there are echoed in *Humanae Vitae*. Finally, Pope Paul VI was reportedly reading *Love and Responsibility* when he wrote *Humanae Vitae*. He has made major contributions to our understanding of contraception as a violation of the goods of marriage.

This article appeared in *International Review of Natural Family Planning* 10, no. 2 (Summer 1986): 95–112 (now *International Review*).

---

[1] "Les fondements de la doctrine de l'église concernant les principes de la vie conjugale", *Analecta Cracoviensia* 1 (1969): 194–230.

9

POPE JOHN PAUL II AND *HUMANAE VITAE*

by
Janet E. Smith

Pope John Paul II has made teaching about human sexuality a major part of his pontificate; on nearly every visit to countries around the world, he has taken care to reiterate the Church's opposition to artificial means of birth control. Many who have read the writings of John Paul II say that they are difficult to read, that he has a rather impenetrable style. That may be true for some of his works, but I am among those who find his works not only challenging, but at the same time lucid and illuminating. Those I know who, in particular, are familiar with his writings on family life and sexuality all say the same thing: These views are exciting.

Some may ask, when one is referring to papal teachings, what can one possibly mean by the word "exciting"? Now, since I am from the University of Notre Dame, you will not be surprised to find me using football examples to clarify my points. We have a definite understanding of excitement at Notre Dame—it generally means a last minute winning field goal in the Notre Dame stadium— but this is not the way that I am using the word here. It is more like the excitement one finds in the works of St. Thomas, for instance. Fewer people find excitement there than in football— but seekers after truth will know what I mean. St. Thomas and the pope have had profound insights into the nature of man and the world in which man lives; it is a privilege to be able to learn from them the truths which they have grasped. Thomas' method was appropriate in his time, and John Paul II has found interesting and captivating ways of conveying to our age the truths he sees.

And it is not just people of arcane or unusual tastes—people like myself, who think possession of an encyclical more exciting than season tickets to the Notre Dame football games—who find the pope's views exciting. It will please you to know that many young people, indeed, even students at Notre Dame, upon being introduced to the pope's views and arguments, find them extremely provocative and illuminating. He is a thinker whose views, because of their philosophic rigor and because of the challenge which they present to the modern age, simply must be taken seriously.

In fact, I am going to say something which I hesitate to say, because it will undoubtedly seem extravagant and sound like I am a cheerleader for the quarterback at the Vatican: I believe the pope's book *Love and Responsibility* deserves placement on any list of the Great Books of the Western World. At this point I would like to mention that I teach in a Great Books Program at Notre Dame. We spend a fair amount of time in that program determining what qualifies as a Great Book; there is little quarrel that books such as Homer's *Odyssey* and *Iliad,* Augustine's *Confessions,* and Dante's *Divine Comedy* belong on such a list; these books qualify if only because they have held the interest of every generation since they were written. We conjecture that they have had such an enduring appeal since they address the great questions which plague all men, questions which help us determine what sense we can make of the world around us and our place in it. I maintain that the pope's book belongs in this group, since I think generations to come will read his book—they certainly should do so, for if they do they will find that it boldly confronts questions we all have about life and offers a way of viewing human relationships which, if accepted, would radically alter the way in which we conduct our lives.

Love and Responsibility is the first of the pope's major works on human sexuality. Paul Johnson, in his fine biography of Pope John Paul II, tells us that Pope Paul VI was reading this work as he wrote *Humanae Vitae* and that he was greatly influenced by it.[1] Since he has assumed the pontificate, John Paul II has energetically tried to put before the public the truth about human sexuality; he has given three series of talks on human sexuality. The first series focused on a few key passages from Genesis, published by the Daughters of St. Paul under the title *Original Unity of Man and Woman;* the second series was a reflection on key passages from Matthew, published under the title *Blessed Are the Pure of Heart;* and he recently finished the third series, published under the title *Reflections on Humanae Vitae.* This essay, in three sections, shall draw upon all these writings.

Since many find the pope's method intimidating, I shall try first to make his approach more accessible by trying to explain the ways in which the pope's talks are innovative; I shall try to diminish the intimidating power of such words as "phenomenological" and "personalistic"—terms frequently used to describe the pope's philosophy. I shall try to show how this method and approach are very appropriate for our times.

In the second part of the talk, I shall lay out the main lines of the pope's teaching on sexuality. Again, some of his terms are unusual and in need of explication. The most interesting phrase used by John Paul II is "language of the body". The pope speaks of the body as the "expression of the person"; he teaches that the "language of the body" must express the true meaning of sex. This way of speaking about the body and sex offers a view of sexuality which clarifies the purpose of sexuality and provides us with invaluable guidance on the place of sexuality in our lives.

The third portion of the talk will point out how John Paul II explains why natural means of family planning are morally permissible, whereas artificial contraception is not. Of special interest here will be his claim that "self-mastery" leads not to repression but to freedom, the freedom to express not lust, but love.

---

[1] Paul Johnson, *Pope John Paul II and the Catholic Restoration* (Ann Arbor, Michigan: Servant Publications, 1981), 32–33.

THE POPE'S APPROACH

John Paul II is so modern that even many devout Catholics, appreciative of his relentless defense of Catholic doctrine, do not seem to know what to make of him. He is regularly described as a "phenomenologist" and what term is more intimidating than "phenomenology"? And what is this "personalism"? Are not all defenders of the truth "scholastics" or "neo-Thomists"? Are not all reliable moral philosophers, natural law ethicists?

Now, although it may be heresy in some circles—and circles that I frequently spin in—it must be said that "scholastic" is not a strict synonym for all true philosophy. The word scholastic, of course, refers to works that are written under the influence of the philosophy of St. Thomas; they are generally recognizable because they follow a certain method and use a certain vocabulary; more importantly, of course, they are committed to a certain metaphysics, a certain world view. Often it is the students of St. Thomas who find the pope's works hard going because he does not explicitly use Thomas' method or his vocabulary. Phenomenology is one of the modern schools of philosophy which is largely distinguished for its method; it does not use the tight definitions of Thomism or any other tradition, but attempts to use common language to analyze human experience and by means of this analysis to unfold basic truths of existence.

I am an expert neither in Thomism nor phenomenology, but I believe I know enough about both approaches to say that the pope has blended the two in a way which enables him to arrive at insights about reality which are fully consonant with the Thomistic and Catholic view of the world, but which also grow out of the experience of a twentieth-century man. Unlike Thomists, the pope does not start with distinctions and definitions, though they often soon follow. He starts with human experiences that we all have had and by asserting values we immediately find attractive. His use of the phenomenological method does not mean a rejection of Thomism—indeed Pope John Paul II has reiterated the teaching of Leo XIII that the philosophy of Thomas is to have primacy of place among Catholics; and the pope himself is thoroughly familiar with the writings of St. Thomas. Yet there is something in his manner of proceeding which is somewhat foreign to Thomists.

Let me make my point in this way. Thomas' discussion of law plays a large part in his moral philosophy: he links eternal law, divine law, natural law, and human law. The writings of the Church often follow such a pattern; for instance, *Humanae Vitae* begins with a few statements about God as the Creator and man's role as Co-creator with God. The document goes on to explain how human behavior must be in accord with the laws of nature, which are the laws of God. Let me be quick to say that I find nothing wrong—and even everything right—with this method of proceeding. But there is more than one way to get to Rome, more than one way to discover and teach the truth.

Phenomenologists are concerned to provide accurate descriptions of the way things are, of the nature of reality—descriptions not predetermined by definitions, but rooted in common experience. The pope shows himself to be a penetrating student of the human person in all that he writes. What makes his writings on human sexuality exciting and appealing is that he is able to take experiences which we all have had and make sense of them. He not only describes them well, he also explains what these experiences mean for us and helps us to reflect how we should respond and act on the basis of these experiences.

The pope concentrates on several fundamental human experiences in his works on sexuality: He speaks of *solitude* as an "original" human experience; he observes that we all long for another to complete us; he describes well the intensity and welcomeness of the *attraction between the sexes;* and he helps us see that we experience love between the sexes as a *gift.* It is through the "language of our bodies" that we express our desire to make this gift of ourselves to another. It is out of such universal human experiences that the pope composes his teaching on human sexuality. The second part of this essay shall provide some elaboration on his descriptions of these experiences.

The pope's "personalism" means that he places the human person at the center of his ethical analysis. When the pope moves beyond describing human experience to showing what makes for moral or immoral human behavior, he does not begin explicitly with the principles of natural law. The pope's point of entry is different; he starts with a statement of value which he expects all to accept; he starts with the principle that man has an intrinsic value and that it is never right to treat him as a means to an end. His foremost concern is how each and every act we perform conforms with what is in accord with what human dignity demands. Thus, his is called a *personalistic* philosophy; it takes as its main point of departure and has as its main concern the human person.

Our century has been unparalleled in its disregard of the value of the human person; Nazi and Communist atrocities and the holocaust of abortion show that many in our times do not share this value. But perhaps we can say that thinking men have come to realize that one must never compromise the inherent rights of the human person—we should always respect the inherent dignity of man, for we know all too well the consequences of any violation of this value. So, in a sense, the value the pope uses as his starting point is one which the experience of this century has taught us to hold dearly. The rootedness of the pope's teaching in common experience—and particularly twentieth-century experience—begins here and pervades his work.

The pope's personalism can be explained in this way: It is the claim that the inherent dignity of man entitles him to a certain kind of treatment and obligates him to a certain kind of behavior. That is, the pope teaches that man should never be used as a means nor treat others as a means and that this is as true in the realm of human sexuality as it is in any other realm. Moreover, he argues that human acts must respect the nature, not only of the human person, but of reality; he argues that sex has a meaning which must be respected. Shortly we shall see how his phrase "language of the body" reflects the intertwining of this need to respect the inherent meaning of sex and the need to respect the dignity of the human person.

LANGUAGE OF THE BODY

Since his reflections on *Humanae Vitae* presuppose an understanding of his prior teachings on sexuality, let me quickly sketch out these teachings. This is just a sketch. I will not be able to do full justice to the depth and complexity of his argument—indeed, I will be leaving out major as well as minor points—but I would like us to have a few fundamental concepts before us.

Let me again note that the pope constantly stresses the fundamental dignity of man: we are never simply objects to be used; we are persons with an inherent dignity that requires that our personhood always be respected. Ultimately, the only way to respect another fully is to *love* him or her and to work for what is best for the person; it is never to use another for one's own selfish desires. That is the background against which the pope places all his other teachings.

Another foundational observation is that all of us sense ourselves as being fundamentally alone and in need of another to complete us; the pope's skillful and sensitive reading of *Genesis* as a story which captures this poignant human need is in itself a remarkable achievement. The pope tells of Adam's delight at seeing another who is "bone of his bone and flesh of his flesh". He describes well how we respond to the attraction to one of the opposite sex, and especially to the shared attraction as a gift, a precious gift which helps us complete our own personhood. Thus, our desire for complete and full union with the other is extremely powerful.

The pope teaches us clearly the difference between this desire as found in man before original sin and this desire after original sin. He observes that, before the Fall, this desire was completely in the control of our progenitors. But now we easily recognize that our desires are disordered, that we are inclined not to use our sexuality to express our love for another person, but that often this desire is simply lust for the body of the other person. This lust tends to see the other person as an object, not as a spiritual being which should never be used as an object, not as a person which deserves to be loved.

So we have here at least four concepts which we should keep in mind: (1) The dignity inherent in the human person means that he or she is never to be treated as an object, therefore, if we respect the dignity of the other, we shall love him or her, not use him or her; (2) there is a fundamental human need for union with another; (3) this union is experienced as the mutual exchange of the gift of selves; and (4) the desires which draw us to this union are, as the result of original sin, disordered. A fifth important concept is this, that, through the grace made available by Christ's redemptive act, we are able to regain the control of our desires.

In his *Reflections on Humanae Vitae,* John Paul II draws upon these and a few other basic concepts as he attempts to justify the teachings of that document. He does not seek to comment upon the whole document but continues his interest in how using contraception affects the human person; again he does not reject or ignore the arguments from natural law, but incorporates the natural law perspective into his concern for the needs of the human person.

Throughout his writing on love and sexuality, John Paul II distinguishes the subjective emotions allied with love and the need to ground these emotions in an objective appraisal of the beloved and in an objective recognition of universal values. That is, he teaches forcefully that we so much love to be in love that we often deceive ourselves about the true qualities of the beloved; he counsels that lovers must be very careful not to love only the exterior attractiveness of the beloved, but also to love the interior qualities of the beloved. It is only if we truly know who the beloved is that we can truly love. And those who truly love each other, desire to make a complete gift of themselves to the other. This is one of the key arguments for the pope's defense of *Humanae Vitae;* he makes the rather startling claim that the use of contraception, in fact, makes quite impossible that full and complete union which we seek to have with our beloved. This claim derives in great part from the central Catholic doctrine which he reiterates: that man and woman are not just souls within bodies, but that the human person is the union of the soul and the body.

The pope uses an unusual phrase to describe the relation of the soul to the body: He says that the body is the "expression of the human person," that is, we express who we are through our bodies. The argument in his *Reflections on Humanae Vitae* is that we must use the expressions of the body honestly and that there must be a correspondence between what our bodies do and what we, as true lovers, intend. It is in this context that John Paul II uses the phrase "language of the body"; he wants to teach us what the truth is we should be expressing with our bodies in our sexual relationships.

The following passage gives some of the "flavor" of the pope's approach to this matter:

> As ministers of a sacrament which is constituted by consent and perfected by conjugal union, man and woman are called *to express* that mysterious *"language" of their bodies in all the truth which is proper to it.* By means of gestures and reactions, by means of the whole dynamism, reciprocally conditioned, of tension and enjoyment—whose direct source is the body in its masculinity and its femininity, the body in its action and interaction—by means of all this *man,* the person, "speaks" [my emphases].[2]

The pope is claiming that certain of our bodily actions have an inherent meaning which we must respect; for example, that there is an objective truth to the meaning of sex to which we must conform our behavior. This is where the pope has recourse to natural law; he reiterates the claim of *Humanae Vitae* that there is an inseparable connection, established by God, between "the unitive significance and the procreative significance which are both

[2] John Paul II, *Reflections on Humanae Vitae* (Boston: Daughters of St. Paul, 1984), 32.

inherent to the marriage act". John Paul II argues that these two significances of the marriage act are truly inseparable; they are the truth about sex. The pope maintains that the "language" of the body must express the truth of the marriage act.

The pope denies that this respect for natural law is a recourse to legalism. Again, he roots all his explanation in an argument about what is good for the human person. Thus, he attempts to show us that it is not against man's desires, that is, against the dynamics of a love which desires complete union with another, to conform to the meaning which sex has of both procreation and union. To deny our procreative powers, to withhold deliberately this power from sexual union is to make the union less than what it ought to be; it is to offer only a part of ourselves, not the whole of ourselves to the beloved. And this reduced offering is particularly serious in that it robs the sex act of what makes it ultimately most unitive; it robs it of the ability for two to become one flesh through the new life they could create. That is, he is saying that the sex act which is not open to procreation is not truly unitive, and since union is what we seek through the sex act, we are working against our own desires when we use contraception.

The pope explains the evil of contraception in this way:

> It can be said that in the case of an artificial separation of these two aspects, there is carried out in the conjugal act a real bodily union, but it does not correspond to the interior truth and to the dignity of personal communion: *communion of persons*. This communion demands in fact that the "language of the body" be expressed reciprocally in the integral truth of its meaning. If this truth be lacking, one cannot speak either of the truth of self-mastery, or of the truth of the reciprocal gift and of the reciprocal acceptance of self on the part of the person. Such a violation of the interior order of conjugal union, which is rooted in the very order of the person, *constitutes the essential evil of the contraceptive act* [my emphases].[3]

[3] Ibid., 33.

The evil of contraception, then, is that it belies the truth which the "language of our bodies" should be expressing: the truth that we are seeking complete union with the beloved.

Let me show the richness of this phrase, "language of the body", a bit further. We have heard the phrase "body language" and that phrase, I think, is not so very different from what the pope means by "language of the body". Our bodies do convey very clear messages in the way that we position them and move them. As I have stated, John Paul II is claiming that certain acts of the body have inherent meaning which should not be violated. What does it mean to say that some acts of the body have inherent meaning?

An example from verbal language should help to clarify this claim. Certain words have fairly unambiguous meanings and carry with them certain obligations. Most everyone has felt betrayed by someone who has said "I love you." Most of us take this to mean "I will care for you", "I will treat you kindly", "I will not hurt you." Many have learned that some use these words to seduce us into serving them in different ways, perhaps into giving them gifts and even perhaps into having sex with them. When we later learn that these words did not carry the meaning we believed them to have, we feel betrayed; we feel used; we feel lied to.

Is it right to say that certain actions, like certain words, carry inherent meaning? The best example of this, I think, can be found in scripture, when Judas kisses Christ. Is not a kiss a sign of affection, of friendly feeling? But Judas uses a kiss to do an unfriendly thing—to betray Christ. With his kiss he has lied to Christ—he is not expressing affection with this kiss.

John Paul II is saying that the sex act carries with it an inherent meaning: it says among other things "I find you attractive"; "I marvel and rejoice in your existence"; "I am grateful for the gift of yourself and wish to make a gift of myself to you." He also maintains that the act says "I wish to become wholly one with you and to accept the possibility of enjoying the good of procreation with you." In other words, one must accept and mean what sex itself means, that is, one must accept both the unitive and procreative aspects of sex. The pope says that this is what the body expresses when it engages in sex, and that if the person engaging in sex does not intend this meaning, then he is not telling the truth with his body. Thus, contraceptive sex involves the body in a lie. The persons engaging in this type of sex are not communicating openly and honestly with their bodies. They wish to deny one of the inherent meanings of sex: the possibility of procreation. Having sex includes the meaning that we wish to become one with another; denying the power of procreation means that one does not wish for complete union.

I explain this teaching to my students in this way: While we may desire to have sex with many people, it is when we are willing to have children with another that we know we are in the realm of love, not lust. Having a child with another is the most profound sort of union which one can have with another (to whom one is not already bonded by means of blood-ties). One's very genetic structure becomes mingled with another's genetic structure to create a new human being, for which the parents share a lifetime of responsibility. Raising that child together creates more and more bonds between the two. Thus, the most profound union is possible only for those who wish to unite by having children. (Of course, if a couple for some physiological reason is not able to have children, this does not detract from the fact that their love is the kind that seeks to achieve that depth of union.) To use sex to express only physical desire and not the desire for total union with the other is to belie the nature of sex. To have sex without being open to procreation diminishes the union one is having with one's beloved; the individual treats his partner like one with whom he does not wish to have union—like one with whom he does not wish to have children. An individual demeans his love, he demeans his beloved, by not expressing desire for union of this depth.

In short, the pope is saying that the sex act itself says: "I love you so much, I wish to experience the ultimate union with you, the possibility of having a child." He is saying that if one does not mean this when one has sex, one is telling a lie with one's body.

The pope expands the seriousness of the falsehood told through contraceptive sex when he refers to the teaching of *Humanae Vitae* that God is a silent partner in sex. God is the one who created male and female and made sexuality the most profound way in which their bodies communicate. He wrote into the sex act its meaning of union and procreation. Those practicing contraceptive sex, then, are not only lying with their bodies to one another, they are, in a sense, betraying and misusing a good which God has given to them. And, again, one of the goods they are denying is the good of parenthood, and the good of the union which comes through parenthood. Children are a gift from God, not a punishment, as today's world so often thinks. Children are a gift which brings to true fruition the loving union of a couple. Indeed, a child is a shared creation by God and the lovers; God has chosen to bring new life into this world through the union of lovers and to deny Him the opportunity to work in this fashion is to abuse the meaning which He has written into sex.

Sex without contraception, then, carries with it the opportunity for the most profound expression of one's gift of oneself to another: one is not holding back one's own fertility—which is an integral part of oneself—nor is one refusing to accept the fertility of one's beloved partner. The couple does not tell God that they are dissatisfied with the way He arranged matters, but work in cooperation with the arrangement God has established.

Clearly, although this doctrine may "sound good", it is not easy to live by. Married couples often find it to be a responsible and loving decision to limit their family size. They do not wish to have the language of their bodies tell a lie, but they, perhaps for reasons of health or finances, may decide that it would not be good to have more children at a certain time. The Church does not teach that couples must have as many children as biologically possible. The Church sees as one of the chief purposes of marriage the formation of children to be citizens of the Kingdom of God. Any parent will tell you that supplying such formation requires an enormous amount of learning, time, and energy and there are limits to how many children one can do this for, given the other obligations one has in life. The Church recognizes that responsible parents often will wish to limit their family size; it teaches that there is a way to do this which maintains respect for human dignity and for the nature of sex.

Recently I have read arguments in the press that the pope shows lack of concern for women, who, if they do not use artificial contraception may be burdened by too many children. Yet, throughout his writings, the pope makes clear that it is women more often than not who are the greater victims in a disorderedness in the sexual realm. In several places in his writings, he reaffirms Pope Paul VI's prediction that contraception is not a liberator of women, but is more likely to be used as a means to exploit women. Many of my conversations with women have borne out the pope's teaching. Many women I know have been exploited or have allowed themselves to be exploited by contraception. But even further, many of them feel degraded by the use of contraceptives; they do sense that it is a blow to their human dignity and integrity to be taking chemicals or using artificial devices which work against their fertility. Women using natural family planning (NFP) nearly always feel revered and treasured by their husbands, for they sense that their husbands respect them as persons. An analysis of the difference between NFP and contraception should help explain why many women discern such a difference between the two.

There are many ways to explain the difference between artificial contraception and NFP. The most-straightforward explanation goes like this: (a) there is nothing wrong with wanting, for good reasons, to limit one's family size and (b) there is nothing wrong with married couples either having sex or not having sex; thus, since it is not wrong to want to limit your family size and there is nothing wrong with not having sex, it follows quite smoothly that there is nothing wrong with not having sex because you want to limit your family size.

I think that line of reasoning is unassailable but it does not usually serve to answer all the objections of those who, at least at first, have trouble understanding the difference between NFP and artificial contraception. They think that both couples using contraception and those using NFP do not want children, so what is the big difference about how they achieve this end? They wonder how a couple who is using NFP can truly be open to procreation, to having children.

The difficulty here arises from too narrow an understanding of the word "open". "Open" does not mean wanting a child *now;* it means having done nothing to *close out* the possibility of having children. There is an odd phrase used currently to describe sex without contraception: such sex is called "unprotected" sex. This phrase may help us here. Those using NFP are having "unprotected" sex; though the couple may be quite certain that they cannot conceive at this point, they have done nothing to close out the possibility of a child. A woman does not make herself periodically infertile, nature does; thus, in having sex during the infertile periods, she has not done anything to close out the possibility of having children; nature closes that possibility. And, since she has no obligation to have sex, in not having sex during her fertile period, she also does no wrong in abstaining. To use the phrase of the pope, the couple using NFP are not telling a lie with their bodies; they are still allowing sex its full, natural meaning. In short, the naturalness of NFP is obvious: It recognizes fertility as a good and does nothing to deny this good; it operates fully in accord with the laws of nature, which are the laws of God.

This, though, is not quite the pope's line of reasoning. In line with his personalistic philosophy, he emphasizes the positive effects of NFP for the human person. John Paul II puts great stress on the power of responsible use of periods of abstinence to aid man in regaining the mastery of himself which was his before original sin. He argues that the use of artificial or technological means allows him to avoid this mastery, and thus diminish the dignity of man. Man relies upon technology to do for him, what he cannot—or will not—do for himself. Self-restraint or continence is not a means of birth control in the same way that artificial means are, for continence does not require artificial devices; it requires strengthening the powers and virtues of the human person. John Paul II tells us that "mastery of the self" is indispensable for the human person. He insists that NFP helps us learn to control our desires; it helps us acquire virtue and strength. On the other hand, artificial means of birth control do not help us develop interior strength.

The pope continues to develop the theme of "language of the body" along with this theme of "self-mastery". Those who do not have self-mastery are not able to use their bodies to express exactly what they wish to express. They are unable to perceive or express the profounder values of love. These are the pope's words:

> Concupiscence of the flesh itself, insofar as it seeks above all carnal and sensual satisfaction, makes man in a certain sense blind and insensitive to the most profound values that spring from love and which at the same time constitute love in the interior truth that is proper to it.[4]

The pope argues that sexual union should be the product of the desire to express love for another, not the outcome of ungovernable passion. If an individual is driven by his desires to have sex rather than by love, he risks treating the beloved as an object to satisfy those desires, not as a person with whom to share love. Thus, the control of the passions gained through periodic abstinence is not a negation of passion. It is a means of affirming respect for one's partner. The control enables individuals to respect each other, for those who have control are able to use sexual union to express their love, not to use their beloved solely as a means of satisfying their physical desire.

The pope does not underestimate the effort that will need to be made to learn to respect one's beloved fully and to gain self-mastery. He counsels us to have regular recourse to the graces to

[4] Ibid., 63.

be gained through prayer and especially the sacraments of penance and the Eucharist, for these are the means that Christ instituted to heal our weaknesses and make us whole.

The value of the product of such an effort also ought not to be underestimated. Self-mastery not only "enhances man's dignity"; it also "confers benefits on human society". The pope cites a passage from *Humanae Vitae* which speaks of the goods of self-control:

> This self-discipline . . . brings to family life abundant fruits of tranquility and peace. It helps in solving difficulties of other kinds. It fosters in husband and wife thoughtfulness and loving consideration for each other. It helps them to repel the excessive self-love which is the opposite of charity. It arouses in them a consciousness of their responsibilities. And finally, it confers upon parents a deeper and more effective influence in the education of their children. For these latter, both in childhood and in youth, as years go by, develop a right sense of values as regards the true blessings of life and achieve a serene and harmonious use of their mental and physical powers.[5]

The pope tells us that use of NFP will make us better spouses and parents; our self-control in matters of sex will permeate other areas of our lives where we need self-control in order to deal with our marriages and our children. And also of great importance is the excellent example we will be for our children when we attempt to convince them of the proper place for sex in their lives.

This connection between the proper use of sexuality, the strength of marriage, and the healthiness of children and consequently of society as well is, I think, the reason why the pope has made human sexuality a constant theme of his pontificate. Mother Teresa constantly reminds us that love and peace must begin at home, and, if we establish loving and peaceful relationships there, they will spread to the rest of the world. The pope is spreading a similar message when he implores us to be true to our human

[5] Ibid., 46.

dignity in sexual matters; he maintains that integrity in sexual matters will permeate the rest of our lives.

CONCLUSION

At the beginning of this talk, I spoke of the pope's book *Love and Responsibility* as a Great Book, because it addressed fundamental questions facing man and because I thought that, if we were to live by its message, our lives would change radically. His message, a message which promises to liberate us from the sexual permissiveness of our times and from the heartbreak which follows from this permissiveness, is truly exciting. Consider how much happier many will be if they can escape the emotional trauma which results from sexual license. Think of the prospect of fewer "unwanted" pregnancies and the reduction of poverty and dislocated lives which follow "unwanted" pregnancy. Think of the happiness which will result from wives and husbands who love and respect each other. Ponder the joyful ramifications of fewer broken homes. The Church has been accused of being obsessed with sex and sexual sins, but those who understand how close is the nexus between sex, love, family, and human happiness will realize the importance of the pope's message.

With this essay, I hope I have made somewhat clearer the pope's impressively thorough teachings on sexuality. When I told a friend that I was going to talk on the pope's phenomenological method and his personalistic approach, he responded that he understood those terms very simply: The pope is a phenomenal person. Well, I agree. His is a voice which our age desperately needs to hear; let us open our ears and be glad.

FURTHER READING

I treat of the views of John Paul II extensively in my book *Humanae Vitae: A Generation Later;* see chapter four, 107–18, and chapter eight. The following bibliographical information is taken largely from there.

John Paul II's instructions on marriage and contraception have been published by the Daughters of Saint Paul in four volumes: *The Original Unity of Man and Woman: Catechesis on the Book of Genesis* (Boston: St. Paul Editions, 1981); *Blessed Are the Pure in Heart* (Boston: St. Paul Editions, 1983); *The Theology of Marriage and Celibacy* (Boston: St. Paul Editions, 1986); and *Reflections on Humanae Vitae* (Boston: St. Paul Editions, 1984). One talk was omitted from the final series, a talk entitled "Living According to the Spirit", November 14, 1984.

See also Karol Wojtyla, *Love and Responsibility,* trans. by H. T. Willetts (New York: Farrar, Straus, Giroux, 1981); *The Acting Person,* trans. by Andrzej Potocki (*Analecta Husserliana* v. 10; Boston: D. Reidel Publishing Company, 1979), and *Familiaris Consortio: The Role of the Christian Family in the Modern World* (Boston: St. Paul Editions, 1981). On the tenth anniversary of *Humanae Vitae,* John Paul highlighted some of the connections between *Humanae Vitae* and *Gaudium et Spes.* This talk has been published in a volume entitled *Fruitful and Responsible Love* (New York: Seabury Press, 1979).

Few scholars have done any extensive work on the Pope's teachings on sexuality. Perhaps the most useful brief summary of his teachings is to be found in Richard Hogan, "A Theology of the Body", *The International Review of Natural Family Planning* 6, no. 3 (Fall 1982): 227–312 (rpt. from *Fidelity,* December 1981). Useful too is Daryl J. Glick, "Recovering Morality: Personalism and Theology of the Body of John Paul II", *Faith and Reason* 12, no. 1 (1986): 7–25. While his book *Sex, Marriage, and Chastity* (Chicago: Franciscan Herald Press, 1981) is not explicitly about John Paul II's teachings, William May nonetheless worked to integrate the Pope's teaching into his book. See also A. Mattheeuws, S.J., "De la Bible à 'Humanae vitae'. Les catéchèses de Jean-Paul II", *Nouvelle revue théologique* 111, no. 2 (March–April 1989): 228–48.

PART THREE

The Sanctity of Life

10

WHO IS LIKE THE LORD, OUR GOD?

by
Carlo Caffarra

This article was given as the keynote address for a conference held in Rome to celebrate the twentieth anniversary of *Humanae Vitae*. Monsignor Caffarra, director of the John Paul II Pontifical Institute for Marriage and the Family, spoke about the connection between God's creative power, the life of man, and the life-giving powers of man. Many of the dissenters from *Humanae Vitae* charged that the Church was guilty of "physicalism" or "biologism", that is, of granting undue importance to the biological power of the sexual organs and acts to generate new life. They argued that such biological processes should be subordinated to man's spiritual nature. Caffarra, while not taking on these charges directly, provides a response. He argues that man's being is utterly contingent upon God's creative action and thus that man is utterly beholden to God. He further argues that the modern age is very wrong to make of the body a thing, rather than seeing the body as a gift from God, one that puts man in contact with the divine, and through its fertility in contact with God's creative power.

Moreover, he, again rather indirectly, addresses the charge that the Church has not taken into account historical circumstances in her unyielding condemnation of contraception. Caffarra argues that moral norms are transcendent of history and that to say that there are no such norms established by an eternal God is to evacuate the ethical experience of ultimate meaning. He unites his focus on the creative power of God and man and this need for transcendent norms when he observes that both concepts are rooted in the dignity of man. He demonstrates that the use of contraceptives violates the dignity of man since it entails a rejection of the goodness of being; it reveals that man is deciding for himself what is good rather than assenting to the good of being that God wishes to transmit through the sexual act. Caffarra also argues that the nature of the dignity of man is falsified when the conscience is understood to be creative rather than to be a faculty that listens to the divine voice.

This talk provoked a controversy when some theologians objected to Caffarra's citation of the Church's dictum that the one who contracepts should be viewed as one who commits homicide. What Caffarra's critics failed to note is that neither Caffarra nor the Church was attributing moral equivalency to murder and contraception. Rather, they were speaking of an analogy of meaning between the two: both murder and contraception are violations against the good of life; the murderer intends to destroy a life that has begun, while the contraceptor intends not to let life begin.

This appeared as "*Humanae Vitae:* Twenty Years Later", in *Humanae Vitae: 20 Anni Dopo* (Milan: Edizioni Ares, 1988), 183–95.

WHO IS LIKE THE LORD, OUR GOD?

by
Carlo Caffarra

The celebration of the twentieth anniversary of the encyclical *Humanae Vitae* (H.V.), in the context of this solemn academic act of inauguration and in this university, which is related in a special way to the Bishop of Rome, cannot be reduced to a mere ceremony. It must be the occasion for reflecting ever more deeply on the ultimate meaning of the doctrine that was taught in that papal document and which has already been sufficiently illustrated during the past twenty years. Allow me, from the outset, to present this meaning in a synthetic form.

Humanae Vitae represents one of the most intense moments of the Church's Magisterium, because it defends the point of encounter between God and man: it affirms the glory of God and the supreme dignity of man, called to find fulfillment in the gift of self. In a word: what is at stake is the cause of God *and* of man.

I. THE ENCOUNTER OF GOD WITH MAN: "THE GLORY OF THE ONE WHO MOVES ALL THINGS"

It is well known that the problem for which Paul VI meant to offer a solution was not the licitness or illicitness of contraception.

More exactly, it was the licitness or illicitness of a *particular* method of contraception: chemical contraception.

During the past twenty years, we have been able to see the deep-lying *roots* of this problem, of what is at first sight a very particular problem. The roots have come to light: they are planted within the relationship of man with God the Creator.

There are experiences in human life so filled with "mystery" as to arouse in man the admiration and wonder that are at the source of every metaphysical and religious research.

One of these is wholly singular in its evident simplicity: no one of us has come into being by his own decision; each one has discovered that he had come to be. This "factualness" of our existence can be explained—and has been explained—in three ways: each one of us is the fruit of *chance*—each one of us is the fruit of an inexplicable *necessity*—each one of us is the fruit of a free act of God's *creative love.* To affirm that we have come into being by chance makes it impossible, with any consistency, further to affirm the presence of an indestructible meaning in our existence. To affirm the necessity of our coming into being makes it impossible, with any consistency, further to affirm the existence of a reason for which it is worthwhile living, a reason more important than life itself. To affirm a divine creative act at the origin of our coming into being leads to the further affirmation of a dependence on God that is *radical* (that concerns the very act of being), a dependence into which the human subject is called to enter ever more profoundly in order not to fall back into the nothingness from which it was drawn. It is in the space opened up within this threefold explanation that *free will* is called to make a decision and to decide the supreme destiny of the person. Either we are born by chance, we die by chance, and live by chance, so that the exercise of free will is reduced to the possibility of all possibilities, or we are born by necessity, die by necessity, and live by necessity, so that the person is reduced to a meeting point of impersonal forces, governed by impersonal laws: not "I" am but "one" exists; not "I" die but "one" dies; not "I" live but "one" lives. Or we are born through the act of a freely creative love, each of us called to consent to a love that—if it is obeyed—brings man from his mortal existence into the eternity of *being,* from his vanity into the light of *truth,* from his original solitude into the communion of *goodness.* The first two explanations are the ruin of a freedom that, by rejecting the creative act as ultimate explanation of our existence, is led either to the tedium of pure experimentalism (= *pure* possibility—casuality) or toward the despair of blind fatalism (= *pure* necessity). Placed between these two existential abysses, free will emerges in the choice of an obedience to a divine law that leads to life.

Someone will ask: What has all this to do with H.V.? The past twenty years have clearly shown not only that all of this has something to do with H.V. but also that this is the *true, ultimate* "cause of contention" that has arisen around the encyclical.

Allow me to begin in an extremely simple way. We begin our Creed by saying: "I believe in God, the Father almighty, *Creator...* " We can ask ourselves: "When did God create me?" Only one answer is possible: at the very moment of my conception, for it is not possible that there should be any instant of my existence that is not the term of God's creative act.

That is why the Council spoke of the human procreative act as being a certain cooperation with God's creative love (cfr. *GS* 50).

On the basis of these simple reminders, it is possible to pursue our reflection. The exercise of conjugal sexuality, when it is fertile, constitutes the mysterious tangential point between the created universe of being *and* God's creative love; it is even the point at which this creative love comes *within* the created universe of being, with a view to the *new* term of its potency. At that moment—the moment when a fertile conjugal act is completed—a *new* created person becomes *really* and *proximately* possible. The man and the woman have the responsibility of respecting this possibility *or* of rejecting it, destroying it through contraception. The fertility inherent in the conjugal act is not a merely biological fact. It brings the spouses, objectively, into a real relationship with God the Creator, whether or not they are conscious of the fact.

When they are placed in this relationship, their free will is called to its supreme act: to acknowledge that God is the Creator of every person or to acknowledge that man is the creator of man. That is: either that man, in the very act of his being, is entrusted to a freedom that transcends him, or that man is entrusted exclusively to himself, in the casuality or the impersonal necessity of the event of his coming into being.

Paul VI had seen prophetically the progressive dimming of the splendor of the glory of God in the created universe of being: "egent gloria Dei" (Rom 3:23).

Many facts have indeed occurred in these twenty years as tragic confirmation of this prophecy. Allow me briefly to recall at least two of these.

The first is the progressive *artificialization* of the exercise of human sexuality. Everyone knows that one of the main points of H.V. is the affirming of an inseparable connection between the procreative and unitive meanings. This affirmation comes directly from a *central* thesis of Christian anthropology: the thesis of the substantial unity of the human person. To the extent and by reason of the fact that the fertile conjugal act expresses and actualizes the unity of the conjugated *persons* in their reciprocal gift of self, this act cannot of itself exclude what constitutes the human person in integral unity. The fertile conjugal act, to the extent and by reason of the fact that it sets the conditions for the biological process that can lead to the conception of a new human person, cannot help being the language of conjugal love. This view of the conjugal act, which is specific to H.V., brings together in unity *both* the biological dimension *and* the spiritual dimension, for neither is the former exclusively biological nor the latter exclusively spiritual. The body is *personal,* and the person is *corporeal.*

When this Christian vision of the human person becomes obscured in the human conscience, two things of particular gravity occur in spiritual life: the first is described in H.V.; the second has taken place, by logical necessity, during these past years.

The first is the separation of sexuality from procreation, a separation expressed in contraception. Going more deeply into this first fact, we see that this separation implies a relationship of the person to his body, considered in terms of *use,* bringing with it a consistent and progressive depersonalization of the body itself. The human body is then a merely biological reality of which we can—we must—make use to achieve certain ends. From the spiritual and cultural point of view, this reification of the body is an event of tragic import for many reasons: because the body is, in reality, constitutive of the person; because every interhuman relationship is always mediated in and through the body, so that the reification of the body leads to the reification of the person as such and to the progressive building up of a culture in which the utilitarian and hedonistic norm takes the place of the personalistic norm.

The second thing that has happened is the separation of procreation from sexuality, a separation expressed in artificial procreation. If, indeed, the biological dimension is no more than that, if it is exclusively biological, it can, as such, be replaced by a technical procedure if there are reasons for doing so. Only the person, in its irrepeatable singularity, is irreplaceable: "something" can always take the place of "something"; "someone" can never take the place of "someone".

If we reflect carefully on this twofold separation, we can see that in either case there is an identical logos, one same internal law. This can be grasped by observing the concept of reason and liberty that is operative in this vision. Reason is not capable of grasping, of seeing a *truth* of human corporality, an intrinsic "meaning" inscribed in this corporality that cannot be defined in terms of use *calculated* with a view to the achievement of preestablished ends. During these twenty years, the existence of an ulterior truth that is *something more* than this has even come to be denied. The existence, that is, has been denied, within human corporality-sexuality-fertility, of a preciousness, a goodness, a beauty that cannot be otherwise than *venerated.* In a word: *technical* reason has taken the place of *ethical* reason. To be more precise: the procreative faculty belongs to human *making* and not to human *acting.* The problems, then, that this reason has to confront are those of efficiency (contraceptives that are more and more safe;

artificial procreative procedures whose results are more and more certain); the problems also of balancing, calculating the various possible gains with the possible losses.

Within this rationality, liberty is no longer conceived nor experienced as responsibility before God the Creator and supreme Lawgiver, but as responsibility for achieving a good with the least possible number of losses: a good that liberty itself constitutes, by its own decision.

I have spoken of an *artificialization* of human sexuality. I hope I have shown the meaning and content of this process. Aristotle, and more clearly still St. Thomas, had already clearly distinguished two fundamental significations of *practical reason.* One connotes the exercise of a rationality, the implementation of a plan that is autonomously conceived through the manipulation ("artificium") of a material that receives its form only from and in this plan. The other connotes, on the contrary, the exercise of a rationality, the implementation of a plan that is not invented but discovered, not discussed but venerated, through the obedience of a liberty that submits to truth.

What H.V. has taught, by affirming the inseparable connection between the unitive meaning and the procreative meaning, is that human sexuality can be lived not in the context of the first type of rationality but only in that of the second. There is also a consequential chain of further artificializations: passing from the separation of sexuality from procreation to the separation of procreation from sexuality, to the artificialization of the familial society, through the separation of biological motherhood-fatherhood from the gestational and the legal.

This first fact—the artificialization of human sexuality—which in these twenty years has shown the *veritas per contrarium* of H.V., has been, at one and the same time, the cause and the effect of a second fact that has involved Catholic thought more directly and more intimately.

As Dante writes at the beginning of the third canto, the glory of God "per l'universo penetra e risplenda / in una parte più e meno altrove" (penetrates in splendor through the universe / in one part more and in another less). There are places in the created universe of being in which the glory of God shines forth and lets itself be seen with particular splendor. One of these is the *fertile* conjugal act. In this and through this, indeed, a space is opened up in the created universe for a creative act of God, a holy place in which God shows his creative love. When the truth taught by H.V. became obscured in the conscience of contemporary man, this could not fail to bring about, inevitably, a profound crisis in the understanding of the relationship of man to God the Creator: a relationship that is the *heart,* at one and the same time, of metaphysical reflection, of ethical reflection, and of religious experience.

The second fact that has tragically confirmed the prophecy of H.V. is, precisely, the progressive *evacuation of ethical experience.*

Man has ethical experience—as Plato had already clearly and wonderfully expressed in the *Crito*—when his freedom is challenged, provoked, by an unconditional and absolute exigency. Augustine gives an incomparable description of this "provocation" in the first chapters of the twelfth book of *De Civitate Dei* when he analyzes the fall of the angels. The creature, endowed with a spiritual subjectivity, is placed in a situation of *unstable* ontological equilibrium. As a creature, coming from nonbeing, it is changeable in its being, exposed to error in its thinking, inclined to solitude in its willing. Insofar as it is spiritual, it can find its fulfillment only in God himself, becoming alive in the life of God, true in the light of the Word, loving in the gift of the Spirit. Discarding its mutability is the *supreme* act of its liberty, establishing the person in the fullness of being, in truth and in love, *or* making it fall into the mutability of nonbeing, into the meaninglessness of error, into the desert of egoism. In ethical experience, man finds himself precisely at the "point" in which time and eternity meet, within his liberty: he is called to rise and find fulfillment through the wisdom of the Word and the love of the Spirit.

That is why, when man rises to the ethical stage, he no longer takes a minimal or ultimate interest in the *historical* possibilities, consequences, results of his acting: he is situated above any such calculation. When Crito explained to him all the consequences of his decision to undergo rather than to commit an injustice, Socrates could give as his only answer: what you ask is unjust, and injustice may never be committed. Abraham, when asked to sacrifice his only son, the son of the Promise, has no interest for the consequences this sacrifice will have for his descendants: his ultimate interest is obedience to the Lord and not the historical consequences of his action.

When is ethical experience evacuated? When it is reduced to being the commitment to bring about *the triumph* of justice in the world and is not experienced as the absolute and unconditional requirement to *act* with justice in the world; when it is the commitment to maximalize the goods of this world (the premoral goods), while minimizing as far as possible the (premoral) evils; when it is not experienced as the pure and simple exigency of "doing good and avoiding evil". But here we need a reflection of great theoretical rigor.

St. Thomas writes that "the ultimate end of man cannot be the good of the universe" (1, 2, q. 2, a. 8, ad 2um), because the whole good of the universe is a *created* and therefore a *limited* good, whereas only the uncreated Good is the supreme vocation of man. Man's supreme dignity consists *in this,* and nothing else: "ut, licet sit ipsa mutabilis, inhaerendo tamen incommutabili bono, id est Summo Deo beatitudinem consequatur" (St. Augustine, *De civitate Dei,* 12, 1; PL 41, 349). This immediate and direct relationship to God, that man is called to institute through his liberty, is the basis for the absolute and unconditionable character of the moral norm, separating it, for its *essential* diversity, from any other norm of human acting. In fact, these other norms govern human acts for the achievement of a good that is created and limited and, as such, merits not an ultimate, absolute, and unconditional interest but only an interest that is penultimate, relative, and conditional; moral norms, on the contrary, govern human acts for the attainment of the uncreated and unlimited Good: the only Good that deserves to be loved with all one's heart, all one's soul, all one's might. Disobedience to the former type of rule, bringing about a limited evil, can always be justified for the avoidance of a greater evil: by definition, in fact, every finite evil can suppose one that is greater. Disobedience to the moral norm, generating an evil that is *infinite* by reason of its term, can never be justified by the avoidance of a greater evil, for the simple reason that a "greater than the infinite" does not exist.

Ethical experience is evacuated when it no longer breathes the air of eternity; that is, when it is affirmed that there does not exist any moral norm governing man's intraworldly acts that does not admit of exceptions; when it is affirmed that man's experience is ethical when he balances goods and evils that are always limited, with a view to making a choice that, in time, maximizes the former and minimizes the latter. It is evacuated because it ceases to be the "serious case" in life.

What has been happening, precisely, during these years since H.V., in a wide sector of Catholic thought?

The doctrine of the encyclical is the defense of the sanctity of a place where the glory of God penetrates and shines forth more than elsewhere, a holy space where God manifests his glory as Creator. It is not by chance that, at the beginning of the encyclical, there is a reference to the great text of the letter to the Ephesians in which the author contemplates the Fatherhood of God as the source of all parenthood in heaven and on earth. On what condition could this teaching be contested? And what consequences would follow from this contestation?

The radical condition was that no event, no act belonging to man's intramundane action, should have in itself and of itself an import, a meaning, a decisive value for man's relationship to God the Creator and supreme Lawgiver. In scholastic language let us say: there would not exist "acts which, *per se* and in themselves, independently of circumstances, are always seriously wrong by reason of their object" (Ap. Exh. *Reconciliatio et Poenitentia,* no. 17). What would have been the consequence of denying the doctrine of H.V.? It has been very well described by one of those denying this doctrine: "Many theologians are arguing that one cannot isolate the object of an act and say that it is *always* wrong in *any* conceivable circumstances" (R. McCormick, "Notes on Moral Theology 1977", *Theological Studies* [1978]: 76–103). The two denials—of the teaching of H.V. and of the existence of acts that are intrinsically wrong, i.e., of the absolute character of moral norms—became closely linked, influencing one another. They showed how Paul VI's defense of the sanctity of the conjugal act was, basically, only the confession and praise of the glory of God, who "penetrates with splendor through the universe", as the great theologian Karl Barth recognized at once, immediately after the publication of the encyclical. It was, basically, only the fulfillment of a duty pertaining to the pastor of the Church: to prevent ethical experience from being evacuated.

Although, considered in itself, the problem solved by H.V. is a very specific one in the general context of ethical reflection, the solution given affects and guides the solution of the deepest problems of human existence and therefore also of ethics.

2. THE DIGNITY OF MAN: "GLORIA DEI VIVENS HOMO"

I said at the beginning that H.V. is the defense not only of the glory of God but also of the *dignity* of man. In this second part of my reflection I should like to demonstrate this briefly, always in the light of what has been happening during the past twenty years.

The two causes—that of God's glory and that of man's dignity—are inseparable, according to Catholic teaching. God does not make his glory shine forth over man's ashes. Rather, to quote the famous dictum of St. Irenaeus, the glory of God is the living human being.

In what sense is the doctrine taught by H.V. the defense of man's dignity? In what sense does the contestation of H.V. during these twenty years carry with it—even contrary to the intentions of its authors—the pathogenic germs of a destruction of the dignity of man? In this second part, I should like to reply to these two questions.

2.1. To reply to the first question, we have to start once again from the central affirmation of the encyclical: the inseparable connection of the unitive and the procreative meaning in the conjugal act. This inseparability, as we have seen, can be broken from a twofold standpoint: by separating sexuality from procreation or by separating procreation from sexuality.

The inseparable connection between conjugal sexuality and procreation derives from the Catholic vision of conjugal communion as a communion of love, as a communion of love ordained to the gift of life.

It is first of all the consequence of the Catholic vision of conjugal communion as a communion of love: contraception is the negation of the *truth* of conjugal love. In the text already quoted, St. Augustine defines the essential difference between the choice made by the faithful angels and that of the fallen angels in this way: "dum alii constanter in communi omnibus bono, quod ipse illis est Deus, atque in ejus aeternitate veritate charitate persistunt, alii sua potestate potius delectati, velut bonum suum sibi ipsi essent, a superiore communi omnium bono beatifico ad propria defluxerunt" (*De civitate Dei,* cit.; PL 41, 349). At this point we must briefly refer to the theodramatic character of created love, of which conjugal love is a singular form. This theodramatic character is rooted in what we called awhile ago the *ontologically* unstable equilibrium of the spiritual creature. Possessing its *own* act of being and not able to be reduced to the evanescent form of a divine *Unum,* possessing a true and proper liberty, the spiritual creature may consider as *its own* the good that has been given to it and make the choice of a self-love that is exclusive and excluding. Or, acknowledging its own being *as a gift,* it can decide to find self-fulfillment in the gift of self. The issue for every created spirit is *entirely* contained in this aut-aut: the grain of wheat, falling into the ground, *either* does not die and remains alone *or* dies and bears fruit. The contraceptive act comes within this logical sequence as one of the two possibilities inherent in every created love and therefore also in conjugal love. In fact, at the moment when the two spouses give concrete expression to their conjugal love, there is something they do not intend to bestow reciprocally on one another: the capacity of each to make the other respectively father/mother. Love says of every being and to every being: "How beautiful, how good it is that you *are!*" For, as I said, love affirms the goodness of being, not of *my* being. The contraceptive act says: "It is not beautiful, it is not good that you should be what you are!"—that is, that you should be fruitful, capable of giving life. "A superiori communi omnium beatifico bono ad propria defluxerunt", writes St. Augustine, as we have seen. We have here the headlong fall of created liberty from one degree in the order of being to a degree that is infinitely inferior. What is actually meant by "How beautiful, how good it is that you are!"? It means the recognition, the veneration, the praise of the goodness of being as such, the preciousness of being as such: a goodness and preciousness deriving from the supreme Good. And this is the act of love that brings the created person into eternity, into truth, into communion. What, on the contrary, is meant by "It is not beautiful, it is not good that you should be!"? It means denying the goodness of being, its intrinsic beauty, and therefore the decision to bring in something else. The shrewdness of futility has taken the place of the certainty of truth, and the convenience of each has taken the place of the communion of charity.

The quality of the person and the quality of his/her love: by denying, with a denial that does not admit of exceptions, the licitness of contraception, H.V. recalled human persons—called to live in conjugal love—to their supreme capacity: the capacity to love in truth, just as, in the very same year, *Sacerdotalis coelibatus* recalled to the same supreme greatness the man who is called to live in virginal love.

Conjugal communion in love is ordained to procreation. The evident and obvious destruction of this finalization through contraception reveals for us another dimension of the defense, by H.V., of the dignity of man.

As was recently underlined, in the corpus of law that was in force until 1917, the Church used a very strong expression with regard to whoever—married or not—had recourse to contraception: "tamquam homicida habeatur". The equivalence, or better, the analogy that canon law established for centuries between homicide and contraception no longer surprises us if we look not exclusively at the material nature of the behaviour in the two cases but rather at the intention or movement of the will that has recourse to contraception. Ultimately, in fact, the decision is rationalized and motivated by the judgment: "It is not good that a new human person should exist." The fall that occurs, ontologically and ethically, within the conjugal love, as we have just been saying, continues in relation to the potential person, also in the relationship between the couple and the potential new person. The antilove inherent in contraception is identically antilife, since there is always implicit in it the refusal of the goodness of being, the refusal to exclaim: "How beautiful, how good it is that you should exist!": "ad propria defluxerunt", exactly as St. Augustine wrote.

We have come in this way to discover the ultimate sense in which, by affirming the inseparability of sexuality from procreation, H.V. has defended the dignity of man. It is the affirmation of the truth of love as destiny of mankind, and the affirmation of the goodness and beauty of being. H.V. is part of the endeavor to reconstruct a culture of truth and love that characterized the pastoral ministry of Paul VI.

The inseparable connection of procreation with sexuality that, without being explicitly affirmed, is implicit in H.V. has become necessary in these last years on account of the new artificial procreative procedures. The instruction *Donum Vitae* did no more than develop systematically what was already fundamentally the teaching of H.V.; it carried further the Church's commitment to the defense of human dignity.

The dignity, in the first place, of the spouses and of their conjugal love. With respect to procreation, the spouses, indeed, can never be reduced to the ones who provide the germinal cells so that a technician, through appropriate manipulation, can set in motion the procreative process. Nor can the conjugal act be reduced to the action of producing these cells.

The dignity of the "concepiendus", who cannot be brought into the universe of being through an activity that establishes a relationship of "dominion". Persons cannot be *made;* they can only be *generated.*

To affirm the reciprocal indwelling of the unitive and the procreative meanings within the fertile conjugal act is to recognize the specific greatness of the spiritual creature, unique in the created universe of being. To recognize that its proper "modus", the *measure* of its being, its proper "species", that is, its intrinsic beauty, and its proper "ordo", that is, its inner law, cannot be reduced to the *modus-species-ordo* of any other creature. The defense of God's "cause" has coincided perfectly with the defense of the "cause" of man: this coincidence is central to the whole encyclical.

2.2. The contestation of this coincidence during these twenty years—contrary, no doubt, to the intentions of those who have led and are leading it—has now fully demonstrated the antihuman, because antitheistical, force with which it is charged. This is the delicate ecclesial situation with which I should like now to deal briefly in concluding my reflections.

I shall begin by ascertaining a fact. Among the reasons given for defending the licitness of contraception, not the least in importance were and are the (supposed) demands of conjugal love. If now we ask ourselves to what extent the widespread contraceptive mentality has promoted the well-being of the conjugal community, our assessment can only be tragically negative. We have reached the point where even the value of the conjugal community as such has been called in question, with the attempts made under some civil regulations to give equal value to any type of union whatsoever. We have reached the point of the refusal to allow any kind of legal defense for the right to life of the conceived but as yet unborn human person. We have reached the point of the pure and simple production of human persons for use in experimentation. These facts have their own inherent logic and call for serious reflection.

I have referred to an antihuman, because antitheistical, force that is present in the contestation of H.V. I should like to speak now about that.

The most sacred thing in man is his moral conscience, because in it we have God's original revelation of his glory to mankind. John Henry Newman has written incomparable reflections on this subject. It is in our conscience, indeed, that the call rings out to the Covenant with God, the divine voice that summons us, with unconditional and absolute power, to communion with the Lord. What exists, in God's sight, is not the human race but the individual human being: every single person is willed in and for himself. And this relationship between the single person and the Single One is rooted in the moral conscience ("solus cum Deo": GS 16). To be uprooted from the moral conscience is to lapse, inevitably, into useless rhetoric about historical tasks, the general sense of human history, and the like. The "scientific seriousness" in which this type of discourse is often wrapped is in reality only the fig leaf used in trying to cover the shame of futility. And so every attack against the moral conscience pollutes not only the course of man's whole spiritual life but also its very *source.*

It seems to me that, in these twenty years since H.V., the moral conscience has been attacked from three points of view by those contesting the encyclical.

The first is the denial of the existence of intrinsically illicit acts, on the grounds that, where intramundane human action is concerned, there do not exist moral norms that admit of no exception. With this twofold negation, the moral conscience ceases to be the place where the order of divine wisdom penetrates the concrete, daily experience of each person. Precisely in the person's temporal experience, which is *his* experience; precisely in the progress toward eternal life, which is the meaning of remaining in time, the person ceases to be "sola cum Deo" and becomes "sola cum seipsa". That is what Augustine had already observed: "*ad propria* defluxerunt". In no one of the choices that are woven into the tissue of our daily life does man meet with an unconditional factor that is "intimior intimo suo" because it is "superior superiori suo".

But, underlying this first attack, there is a *second:* the most serious that the spiritual history of humanity has ever known. It is the affirmation of the *creativity* of conscience. Conscience is no longer the place for listening to the divine voice; it is itself the source that makes the *ultimate decision* as to what is morally licit or illicit in the intramundane action of man. The ecclesiological aspect in affirming the creativity of conscience is well known: it is denial of the existence of a moral Magisterium in the strict sense, with competence in relation to the intramundane action of man. These last twenty years have seen precisely the development of the theory excluding the existence of such a competence.

A moment's reflection will show that this twofold attack springs basically from denial of the truth of creation. It was not by chance that the attack started precisely from the contestation of H.V., which—as we have seen—is the pure and simple affirmation of this truth. When the splendor of the creative act is obscured precisely where it shines forth most brightly, in the fertile conjugal act, man is deprived of the best possibility of receiving its illumination, and the moral conscience is lost.

But what is man when he suffers violence in his most sacred possession, his moral conscience? Deprived of what allows him to rise above all else, because it brings him into direct and immediate relationship to his Creator, he becomes no more than part of a whole: the consensus of the majority, the consensus on common values, creates the norms for action. But when you try to see *on what* there is consensus, you find it is something that grows smaller and smaller and, finally, is purely formal in character; or else, that whoever cannot consent, inevitably foregoes respect for his dignity. Has it not been agreed that the person already conceived but not yet born is not a person and does not deserve absolute and unconditional respect? And so, every year, millions of innocents are done away with. Socrates already warned his young friend Crito that, in questions of this kind, the criterion is not the opinion of the majority but the truth itself, while he clearly foresaw the tragic end for himself in a society of consensus: the elimination of the just man.

Precisely because H.V. has defended the "cause of God", it defends the "cause" of man: the sanctity and individuality of his moral conscience, of his dignity.

CONCLUSIONS

As exergue for these pages, I took the words of the psalm: "Quis sicut Dominus Deus noster, qui habitat in coelis et humilia respicit?" It seemed to me that no biblical expression could better sum up what has been happening in these twenty years. Who is like the Lord our God, who dwells in the heavens? The encyclical H.V. takes its origin from the certainty that no one and nothing is like the Lord our God: that the Glory of God can be attributed to no one else. But Revelation itself tells us that the Lord, who has no equal, lets his glance rest on creatures. And he looks in a way that is wholly singular, unique, on one of these: the spiritual creature. As the object of this glance, the spiritual creature "in tanta excellentia creata est ut, licet sit ipsa mutabilis, inhaerendo tamen incommutabili bono, idest summo Deo, beatitudinem consequatur" (*De civitate Dei,* loc. cit.). The encyclical H.V. takes its origin from the will and the commitment not to allow man to be demeaned from this great dignity and screened from God's downward glance: "ut non evacuetur Crux Christi".

Christ's redemptive act restores man to the dignity of his primal origin, fully revealing the splendor of the Father's glory and giving man a part in that splendor. For, in the end, everything passes away. Only two realities are eternal: God, of his essence, and the spiritual creature, by participation.

FURTHER READING

See also Msgr. Carlo Caffarra, "Conscience, Truth, and Magisterium in Conjugal Morality", in *Marriage and Family* (San Francisco: Ignatius Press, 1989), 21–36.

PART FOUR

Theological Argument

II

A COVENANT THEOLOGY
OF HUMAN SEXUALITY

by
John F. Kippley

John Kippley is another thinker, along with several others in this volume, who seems to have anticipated John Paul II's major contributions to our understanding of human sexuality and the Church's condemnation of contraception. Kippley was one of the first to come to the defense of *Humanae Vitae* both intellectually and practically. Kippley is not only trained in theology but is also a man who has nearly unparalleled familiarity with the practical realm. He founded and has directed for 21 years the Couple to Couple League, an organization dedicated to helping married couples teach other couples the sympto-thermal method of natural family planning. Thus, with this experience and as a married man, he should be immune to the criticism that those who defend the Church's condemnation of contraception remain blind to the realities of married life.

To say that Kippley writes primarily for the general reader and that his writing is wonderfully accessible for that reason is not to suggest that his thinking is unsophisticated or without scholarly foundation. Kippley combines careful scholarship with the ability to provide examples and arguments that are clear and simple to grasp. As a theologian, he starts with revelation but also insists that what is revealed to us can be seen to be true by thoughtful reflection on lived experience. His basic thesis on the meaning of sexuality is rather dazzling for its clarity and simplicity (and its ability to be applied to a wide range of sexual moral issues). He argues that the basic truth about sexual intercourse is that it is meant to be a renewal of the marriage covenant. Contraception violates this covenant because it belies the total self-giving that spouses pledge to each other on their wedding day; the use of sexual intercourse for any reason other than for expressing and being true to this pledge is an immoral use of sexual intercourse.

This essay is the first chapter of Kippley's book, *Sex and the Marriage Covenant: A Basis for Morality* (Cincinnati, Ohio: The Couple to Couple League International, 1991).

Chapters of that book 2 and 3 apply this theology to sex outside and within marriage respectively. Chapter 5 is about conscience; chapter 6 extensively documents the teaching of the Church about the birth control issue, and chapter 7 addresses the question of infallibility of the teaching of *Humanae Vitae*. Chapters 8 through 16 address other facets of the birth control controversy. It is available at bookstores and through the Couple to Couple League, P. O. Box 111184, Cincinnati, OH 45211.

II

A COVENANT THEOLOGY
OF HUMAN SEXUALITY

by
John F. Kippley

I. THE BASIC CONCEPT

1. *Introductory Notes about Theology*

The fundamental meaning of theology is still summed up in the brief expression of St. Anselm, "Faith seeking understanding" (fides quaerens intellectum). The most obvious implication of that statement is that theology is not identical with faith, and certainly no theology is identical with God's revelation. What God has revealed is contained in Sacred Scripture and Sacred Tradition, and its content is presented to us and clarified for us by the teaching authority established by Jesus Christ himself in his Church.

Theology uses the data of God's revelation and attempts to explain certain aspects of it. For example, God's revelation says very clearly, "Thou shalt not commit adultery", but God does not say *why*. Theology starts with the commandment and attempts to explain why.

Once you recognize that theology is not identical with the content of faith, then it is easy to understand that there may be more than one way of seeking to explain the faith, i.e., more than one theology. That doesn't mean that every theology is equally good; any given theology may be more or less adequate for explaining the faith. In fact a theology may be quite adequate at one point in history but less adequate at another. For example, one theology may explain the evil of adultery primarily in terms of the injustice done to the innocent party. At a time when mutually agreed upon adultery was unthinkable, that explanation may have been very helpful. However, at a time of moral degradation as evidenced by mutual spouse-swapping, that explanation may be no less true but it may be less helpful than a theology which focuses on the divinely intended marital meaning of sexual intercourse.

A limited comparison can be made between theology and scientific theories. Moral theology seeks to explain the natural moral law; scientific theories seek to explain the natural physical law. The comparison will read more easily if we treat any specific theology as a theory—an effort to explain non-physical reality.

A theory has value insofar as it applies to the greatest number of cases. A major purpose of a theory, whether it be in the field of physics or morality, is to show a unifying theme, principle, or "law" which is applicable to all of the observable cases. In the physical sciences, a theory is first of all derived from observation. Then if more and new data are observed which do not fit into the previous formulation of the theory, an effort will be made to modify the theory or to replace it with a new one. However, the new theory still has to explain the older data; it cannot rest content with an explanation which is suited only to the new observation. From the point of view of the "laws of the universe", a theoretical law attempts to account for the regular occurrences observed. If the statement of a "law" is changed, it is not because there was a change in nature but because new observations enabled the scientist to see more of nature and then forced him to account for the new observations as well as the old. The statement of a physical law is nothing more than a theoretical expression which has gained universal acceptance. It is an effort to explain that which *is* in the physical order, and the discovery of greater detail about *physical being* may well force the revision of previous theoretical statements which did not account for all that was there but only for that part which was initially observed.

A theory is more valuable if it is simple. The simpler it is, the more universal it will be, and the more universal, the more of *being* it will explain. The natural scientist yearns for the ultimate physical theory which will explain and unify everything. This, of course, will never eliminate the more complex and detailed explanations which are subordinate to, dependent upon, and congruent with the more general theory.

The above comparison may be helpful to explain why there can be different theologies. Furthermore, just as insight can be gained into the physical laws of the universe by witnessing ecological disasters, so also insights can be gained in moral theology by witnessing the moral disasters that have followed widespread disobedience to God's laws. Such insights help to explain why there can be progress in moral theology.

There are, however, real limitations to this comparison because of very real differences in the subject matter of the natural sciences and theology. To conclude this comparison quickly, let us simply note that the physical sciences are based on the human experience of repeated observations, but sound moral theology is ultimately based on God's revelation including that He created man and woman in His own image and likeness.

God has already revealed the answers to the great problems of man—who created the universe, the nature of God, the nature and destiny of man, and salvation. He has revealed that He is the Creator, that He is Love and that man is made in His image and likeness. However, after these matters have been accepted on faith as the great realities of life, we are still left with the duty of showing how various forms of behavior either are loving or are not loving, either do or do not enable man to live up to his calling to perfection in the likeness of Christ. The prime statement about man being made in the image and likeness of God who is Love does not spare us from the duty of trying to construct lesser statements to cover both specific actions and whole areas of related activity. That's what moral theology is all about.

Or at least that's what good moral theology should be doing. However, it is possible for moral theologians to get off track and to work their way into blind alleys; and probably the easiest way for this to happen is for theologians to concentrate their attention so exclusively upon their fellow human beings that they lose sight of God and His order of creation. I think that's what has happened all too commonly in the moral theology dealing with birth control, i.e., in the writings of the dissenters from *Humanae Vitae.*

In the entire birth control controversy, there has been such emphasis on the "problem of contraception" for married people that this problem has been isolated from the over-all "problem of sexuality." (Is there any age group over childhood and before senility for which sex does not provide some sort of a challenge or problem?) One serious aspect of this narrowing of perspective is that it impedes the development of a theology of sexuality that can be applied to the widest possible scope of sexual problems. Another serious aspect of this restricted vision is that instead of seeing contraception in the light of an over-all theology of sexuality, theories are developed to solve only the problem of contraception and are then applied to other problem areas. For example, if one theorizes that suppression of the tendency to express affective love in intercourse is evil, the theory is very quickly applied to pre-marital relations as well. Thus, while seeming to "solve" one problem, the theory creates more.

One of the weaknesses inherent in much of the theorizing that has taken place about birth control is that it has proceeded from the less known to the better known. That is, it has been centered around contraception (a less known) and then is applied to the better known (fornication, adultery, sodomy), having the effect of undermining the traditional teaching on these as well (or at least not being able to show why they are evil).

Any good moral theology must first of all be true to God's revelation; it must make some aspect of the Lord's order of creation a bit more understandable by those who are called to live and love in the image and likeness of God. Secondly, any good moral theology must be true to man. Therefore it will challenge what stems from greed, laziness, lust, etc. within us. We may not like it because it reflects the challenge of walking with the Lord, but we have to admit within ourselves that it has the ring of truth. It will come as no surprise that I hope that such will be your judgment about the covenant theology of sex.

2. A Covenant Theology of Sex

Let us start with a section from *Familiaris Consortio* in which Pope John Paul II called for theology to explain and uphold the teaching against marital contraception:

> I feel it is my duty to extend a pressing invitation to theologians, asking them to unite their efforts in order to collaborate with the hierarchical magisterium and to commit themselves to the task of illustrating ever more clearly the biblical foundations, the ethical grounds, and the personalistic reasons behind this doctrine. Thus it will be possible, *in the context of an organic exposition,* to render the teaching of the Church on this fundamental question truly accessible to all people of good will. . . . (emphasis added).
>
> A united effort by theologians in this regard, inspired by a convinced adherence to the magisterium, which is the one authentic guide for the people of God, is particularly urgent for reasons that include the close link between Catholic teaching on this matter and the view of the human person that the Church proposes: *doubt or error in the field of marriage or the family involves obscuring to a serious extent the integral truth about the human person* in a cultural situation that is already so often confused and contradictory. In fulfillment of their specific role, theologians are called upon to provide enlightenment and a deeper understanding, and their contribution is of incomparable value and represents a unique and highly meritorious service to the family and humanity (n.31; emphasis added).

In 1983–1984, the Pope gave a series of lectures in which he developed his "theology of the body" to provide an answer to his own request, but his statements above make it clear that he did not intend to rule out other efforts. As a point of historical fact, I developed the covenant theology of sexuality in the mid-Sixties, and I have been encouraged by the fact that in many ways it corresponds very closely with the theology of the body developed by Pope John Paul II.

What I intend to do now is to express a basic theological statement which is at the heart and core of the covenant theology of sex, and then explain it. Then, after I have shown how this covenant theology is rooted in Sacred Scripture and Christian personalism, I will explain how this reaffirms Christian teaching (1) about authentic love and sex, and (2) against the various forms of sexual immorality including contraception. Please note that the morality of birth control is not considered in isolation. Rather, I contend that unnatural forms of birth control are immoral for the same basic reason that adultery, fornication, and sodomy are immoral. I believe that such a unified approach is in accord with the call of Pope John Paul II for a theological effort "in the context of an organic exposition" as quoted above. In short, while the consequences of various sexual sins may be different, I believe that the ultimate reason for the objective evil of all sexual sins is the same. They all fail, in one way or another, to be a sign of the committed and caring love pledged at marriage; they all fail to be a renewal of the marriage covenant.

3. The Core Statement

The core statement of the covenant theology of sex is simplicity itself:

> "Sexual intercourse is intended by God to be at least implicitly a renewal of the marriage covenant."

It can be embellished slightly by rephrasing the last part of the statement:

"Sexual intercourse is intended by God to be at least implicitly a renewal of the faith and love pledged by the couple when they entered the covenant of marriage."

It can be rephrased further in *secular* terms:

"Sexual intercourse is meant to be a renewal of the couple's own marriage covenant, a symbol of their commitment of marital love."

Or, in its most secular form:

"Sexual intercourse is meant to symbolize the self-giving commitment of marriage."

Secular phrasing is helpful for conveying the idea to students in schools where religion is not taught and/or where it cannot be taught that sexual intercourse is truly a marriage act and is honest and finds its meaning only within marriage. As an aside, I want to respond to the easily imagined challenge that this concept could not be taught in an American public school because it might be seen as reflecting a religious belief. The response is threefold. (1) Most just laws reflect the *natural moral law* which has been codified in the Ten Commandments, so there is no difference in teaching that man is not meant to steal from others or the government and teaching that man is not meant to have sex outside of marriage. (2) The ordinary language of cultures all over the world—both in time and in place—support the notion that sexual intercourse is meant to be a marital act. Any culture which has a taboo on adultery or which sees pre-marital sex by engaged couples as less good than marital sex supports the notion that sex is meant to symbolize the commitment of marriage. (3) Such basic non-sectarian norms of human behavior simply must be taught at every level and place of education, or alleged education is simply not human education, and that, of course, is the problem with much education today.

4. *Marriage Is the Key*

The Catholic faith teaches that sex is a gift from God even though that gift is frequently misused. Any reading of the Bible or even secular literature quickly shows how frequently and in how many ways men and women have misused the gift of their sexuality, and from the biblical statements we can arrive at the core statement that sex is intended by God to be a renewal of the marriage covenant.

There is no direct biblical statement that sex is intended by the author of creation to be a renewal of the marriage covenant. However, we can arrive at the statement by deduction. As will be shown in Chapter 15, "Biblical Foundations", adultery, fornication, homosexual behavior, contraception, masturbation, and bestiality are all condemned by Sacred Scripture. Thus the only form of sexual intercourse not condemned by Sacred Scripture is non-contraceptive intercourse between a man and woman who are married to each other. I will use the term "honest sex" or "honest sexual intercourse" to designate the sex act taught by Scripture and Tradition to be good: mutually voluntary, non-contraceptive intercourse by a validly married couple.

That leads to an obvious question: what is there about marriage that makes morally good the same physical act that is morally evil outside of marriage? Or to put it the other way, if honest sexual intercourse is (or can be) a moral good within marriage, why is it evil for those who are not married to each other? Certainly God knows that the degree of emotional love felt by unmarried persons is sometimes much stronger than that felt by many married couples. To sharpen the focus a bit more: if Jim and Jane love each other, why is it the grave matter of mortal sin for them to have sexual intercourse on the day before they marry but good for them to celebrate their marriage with honest sexual intercourse after they have married?

The answer is that when they married, they freely entered into a covenant of God's making. They solemnly promised before God and their fellow man that they would exercise caring love for each other from that time until death will separate them. They gave themselves, each to the other, without reservation. This is what makes marriage so wonderful. Each person knows his or her own sins and imperfections; each knows that the other has his or her sins and imperfections. Yet they give themselves, each to the other, in caring love, without reservation, for better and for worse, for life. They become "two in one flesh".

Within marriage, sexual relations have the potential of renewing this great act of self-giving love. With their minds and with their wills, they have irrevocably committed themselves to each other in marriage. (To emphasize what they have done in getting married, I like to use the phrase, "They have *committed* marriage.") They have united their persons and their lives spiritually. Now with their whole persons, soul and body, they have the right to express the oneness of their persons in the oneness of the full sexual union.

Two things need to be noted about marital sexual intercourse. First of all, it is a *unique* sign of their marital commitment. Of all the things they do as a married couple, this (along with its preparatory actions) is the only action that is morally right *only* for married couples. There are, indeed, many other acts that in fact they do with each other which reflect their marriage covenant— common meals, financial sharing, common living quarters, and literally hundreds of little acts of kindness, but these could also be practiced if one were living with a relative or even a very close friend. Both the Bible and the Catholic Church make it clear that sexual intercourse is intended by God to be a unique expression of love—that of marital love and commitment.

The second thing that needs to be noted is that while sexual intercourse is meant to be a unique sign of marital love, it is not always an appropriate sign of love. For example, who could call it loving behavior on the part of a husband to insist upon sexual relations when his wife is sick with the flu? (More on this below.)

The fact of unpleasant realities that may occur in any given marriage in which sexual intercourse seems far removed from the caring love of their marriage day does nothing to undermine the covenant theology of sexuality. On the contrary, it reaffirms it. To improve a poor marital relationship, a couple need to reflect on the marital meaning of sex; they need to see sexual intercourse as a physical sign of the caring, the tenderness, the intimacy they pledged at marriage. They need to consider that their physical nakedness at times of marital relations should reflect the openness and self-abandonment that they offered to each other in their marriage covenant. Married spouses understand—and some learn only through hard experience—that sexual relations can be experienced as signs of intimacy only when there is first of all a spiritual intimacy between them. Indeed, marriage is the key to understanding the mystery of human sexuality.

In summary, we have seen that God has revealed that sexual intercourse is a good act only within marriage, and we have seen that God creates a oneness out of the will of man and woman to marry which makes it good for them to express that oneness in the one-fleshness of honest sexual intercourse. What can we conclude except that God intends for their sexual union to be a unique sign, a symbol of their marriage union?

The next question which arises is this: "Once they are married, is the sex act intended to reflect the caring love the couple promised to each other?" To put it another way, "Can a husband demand sex from his wife no matter how harshly he has treated her? Does the teaching of St. Paul that a wife is to be submissive to her husband (Eph 5:22) and that she should give him his conjugal rights (1 Cor 7:3) mean that he is entitled to marital relations even if he should be drunk and abusive?"

The answer is to be found in the context of each of the passages above. St. Paul also commands that husbands are to love their wives "as Christ loved the Church and gave himself up for her" (Eph 5:25). Is that not both a beautiful and yet very forceful statement that husbands are to love their wives with a self-sacrificing love? Furthermore, in the passage of First Corinthians, Paul taught that "the husband should give to his wife her conjugal rights and likewise the wife to her husband" (1 Cor 7:3).

In the strict sense of conjugal rights that are necessary for the validity of marriage, such rights are limited to honest sexual intercourse. That is, the lack of kindness and affection do not nullify a marriage, but the refusal to engage in sexual intercourse—ever—would provide grounds for nullity.

However, in a looser sense we can say that conjugal rights extend beyond sexual intercourse. Spouses also have a right to affection from the other spouse and at a bare minimum they have a right not to be abused. When one spouse acts against these rights, his or her claim to the right to sexual intercourse is correspondingly reduced.

The point I am making is that within marriage a couple are called to keep alive the faith and the love—a caring love—they promised when they married. Perhaps the clearest statement of this continuing obligation to keep renewing their original pledge of love is found in the first and last sentences of Paul's famous discourse on marriage:

> Be subject to one another out of reverence for Christ . . . Let each one of you love his wife as himself, and let the wife see that she respects her husband (Eph 5:21,33).

From this combination of biblical data and personalist reflection, I believe that it is legitimate and even necessary to conclude that God intends that sexual intercourse should be at least implicitly a renewal of the marriage covenant.

At least implicitly . . . The words "at least implicitly" are important. A husband and wife are not required to intend explicitly that their marital relations should be a renewal of their marriage covenant. Having this concept of marital sexuality firmly in mind can certainly give more meaning to their exercise of their marital rights, and is therefore desirable, but it is not necessary.

What is meant by the words "at least implicitly" is that the spouses, either individually or together, may not act *against* the self-giving love they promised at marriage. What is called marital rape would be an example of one spouse acting against the marriage covenant; the couple mutually agreeing to engage in spouse swapping would be an example of both spouses acting against the marriage covenant. As we shall see later, contraceptive behavior is also a mutual act against the marriage covenant.

5. The Christian Teaching about Love

Before applying the covenant theology of sex to specific sexual behaviors, we must ask if there is a specifically Christian teaching about love that applies to the love of husband and wife as well as to their love for their children and others.

What Jesus taught about love was a doctrine of bittersweet love. "Love your enemies and pray for those who persecute you . . . " (Mt 5:44–30). "Come to me all who labor and are heavy laden, and I will give you rest . . . My yoke is easy, and my burden light" (Mt 11:28–30). "If anyone wants to come after me, let him deny himself and take up his cross daily and follow me" (Lk 9:23). "A servant is not above his master" (Jn 13:16).

The teaching of Jesus was not limited to words. His whole life portrayed the love of God for man, and certainly the love of one spouse for the other cannot exceed the love God has for that same spouse. And what do we see in the life of Jesus that illustrates God's love for each of us? Born in humble surroundings, fasting, overcoming temptations, teaching others and being rejected, accepting his suffering, and finally his passion and death on the cross.

The point is this: there is nothing in the teaching of Jesus Christ that indicates that love is easy. In fact, everything points the other way. As we shall see, when He taught about the permanence of marriage, certainly a teaching about sexual love, His disciples understood the great difficulty implied by His teaching, and some of them wondered why a man should marry at all if he couldn't get rid of a bothersome spouse. Marriage is sweet, but the fullness of God's revelation that marriage is truly permanent adds a dimension that at times becomes bittersweet, a burden—even if a light one, a yoke—even if an easy one.

The next point is this: Is there any reason for a Christian to think that other aspects of Christ's teaching about marital love will necessarily be other than bittersweet? On what possible grounds can the Christian argue that because the teaching against marital contraception involves certain difficulties, he or she can thereby ignore it?

The conclusion is that it should not be surprising if the teaching of Jesus Christ about marital love and sex contains the same element of bittersweet that is found in His teaching about marriage itself.

II. THE USEFULNESS OF THE COVENANT THEOLOGY OF SEX

As noted above, Pope John Paul II has asked theologians to illustrate "ever more clearly the biblical foundations, the ethical grounds, and the personalist reasons" behind the teaching against marital contraception. Furthermore, he said, "Thus it will be possible, *in the context of an organic exposition,* to render the teaching of the Church on this fundamental question truly accessible to all people of good will" (emphasis added). I believe that "an organic exposition" means treating the morality of birth control in the context of other sexual behaviors such as fornication, adultery and sodomy.

The covenant theology of sex fulfills the requirements for a useful theology as noted by the Pope (biblical, ethical, personalist), and in the rest of this chapter I will address each of these criteria plus several others that I think are necessary for a theology to be useful today. In short, I propose to show, very briefly in most cases, that the covenant theology of sex is (1) simple, (2) biblical, (3) ethical, (4) personalist, (5) theological, and (6) ecumenical. Furthermore, it lends itself to "an organic exposition," and thus it (7) distinguishes between marital and non-marital sex and (8) provides a key for understanding not only the evil of contraception but also the evil of adultery, fornication, sodomy and other sexual behaviors condemned as objectively sinful by the Catholic moral tradition. I believe that the covenant theology of sex is also (9) realistic. It provides a terminology that avoids the sometimes austere quality of previous theological terms and also avoids the subjective mushiness and inaccuracy of much of contemporary talk about sex, love and marriage. Finally, (10) it provides both a norm and an ideal.[1]

1. *Simple*

Any two people who are mentally and spiritually capable of committing themselves to marriage are also capable of understanding this covenant theology of sex and marriage. In fact, if a couple either cannot or will not understand or admit the elements or beliefs involved in this concept of marriage and sex, then it is questionable whether their proposed union should be called a Christian marriage. What are these elements or beliefs?

1. God the Creator has created us, loves us and knows what is good for us.

2. God has created the human relationship of marriage and has told us that marriage lasts for a lifetime. In short, God's creative love has determined the basic rules of marriage.

3. Christian marriage is a covenant which is much more than a contract. The whole purpose of human contracts is to spell out very definite limits to what is covered, and they can be changed by mutual consent. However, a covenant entails unlimited liability. This has been traditionally stated in the marriage vows as "in sickness and in health, for richer and for poorer, and for better and for worse."

4. When you marry, you make no pledges at all about having

[1] Many of the ideas in this section appeared in a previous article: John F. Kippley, "A covenant theology of sex", *Homiletic and Pastoral Review* (August–September 1983), 22–32.

romantic feelings toward your spouse, either always or occasionally. Rather, you are promising to exercise caring love of the kind described by St. Paul in 1 Cor 13: "Love is patient and kind . . . "

5. Sexual intercourse is intended by God to be a sign of your marriage commitment, your pledge of caring love for better and for worse. It symbolizes both the covenant relationship that God has created and your own personal entry into that covenant with each other and with God.

It needs to be said in connection with the fourth point that although one cannot pledge that he or she will always "feel" well-disposed to the other spouse, each does have an obligation to invite and nourish such feelings as much as is reasonably possible. Indifference is the common opposite of love within marriage, so each spouse is obliged not to be indifferent but to try to feel good about his or her spouse and to encourage such feelings in return by, for example, thoughtful anniversary and birthday gifts and by frequent compliments.

Each of the previous five points is basic for understanding Christian marriage and could be elaborated upon at length, but in their brevity they should be comprehendible by everyone capable of entering marriage.

2. Biblical

What could be more biblical than a theology of sex based upon the covenant, probably the most basic theme of the Bible? The application of the covenant theme to marriage was first developed by the prophet Hosea. Through His words, God revealed the highly personal nature of His love for His people as the love of a faithful husband for his wife. Hosea even called Israel a whore for her unfaithfulness to Yahweh. In Hosea, God used marriage to reveal something about His covenant with his people; and in Ephesians 5, Paul used the covenant of Christ and His Church to reveal something about marriage. With this sort of biblical precedent, it is certainly legitimate to search for the meaning of sexual intercourse in terms of the covenant of marriage. In short, the covenant theology of sex is based upon and is in accord with all of the biblical concepts of sex, love, covenant, and marriage. It accepts both the eroticism of the Song of Songs and the self-oblation of 1 Corinthians 13 as constitutive of married love.

Specifically, the covenant theology is biblical because it allows for an interpretation of Genesis 38:10 that sees here the sin of contraception as a sin against a covenant. As is shown in Chapter 15, "Biblical Foundations", Onan was not the only one to violate the Law of the Levirate in this specific situation, for his father and younger brother also disobeyed it by default. However, Onan engaged in the act called for by the Levirate "covenant" but contradicted it. The sin for which the sacred authors tell us he was punished was not the violation of the Levirate which he would have violated if he had merely refused to have intercourse with Tamar; rather it was his participation in the covenanted act and his contraceptive invalidation of it that was so sinful that he was punished while the other Levirate-violators in his family were not.

The covenant theology is in accord with St. Paul's self-styled concession to married people about not refusing each other except perhaps for a while by mutual agreement lest they be tempted by lack of self-control (1 Cor 7:3–6). Whether the abstinence be for prayer or more secular values, the covenant theology merely states that when they do come together again, it must be a valid renewal of the marriage covenant.

It is, of course, in accord with the further Pauline teaching in Ephesians 5 where the self-sacrificing love of Christ for His Church is held up as the model for a husband's love for his wife. The new covenant was made in the blood of Christ shed for His Church for its holiness, and this covenant theology calls for a somewhat analogous death to self in order to promote the holiness of each marriage.

The covenant theology is biblical in the sense that it calls for those values and attitudes which are specifically and habitually rejected by the world—a radical teaching on fidelity to the marriage covenant, an attitude of denial of self and trusting surrender to Christ, and an attitude toward material goods that tends to place one among the Bible's little people, the *anawim,* rather than among society's beautiful people.

Finally, the covenant theology of sex actually takes its start from all the biblical teaching about sex, a teaching which condemns all forms of intentional orgasmic sexual behavior except honest, non-contraceptive intercourse between husband and wife.

3. *Ethical*

Pope John Paul II has called for theologians to show "the ethical grounds" for the evil of contraception. Ethics is different from moral theology; for while moral theology takes its start from revelation, ethics limits itself solely to the use of reason. Its first principle is "Do good and avoid evil", and it seeks to demonstrate by reason the goodness or evil of certain actions.

Such an effort is best undertaken by moral philosophers, and this book makes no claims to provide any sort of in-depth ethical analysis. However, what I will do in Chapter 2, "Sex Outside Marriage", is to make use of a philosophical tool called "ordinary language analysis" to illustrate that sex is supposed to be a marriage act and that non-marital sex is wrong.

In ethical terms, the great evil of marital contraception is that it is intrinsically dishonest. It pretends to be an act of love, but it destroys the act as a symbol of the self-giving promised at marriage. Contraceptive behavior is "getting" behavior, not giving behavior, whether one or both spouses are in the "getting" mode. As such, one form of contraceptive behavior is essentially no different from another, and they may all be reduced to masturbation.

4. *Personalist*

The emphasis in this theology of sex is on what two persons have willed to do in entering the covenant of marriage, creating the two-in-one-fleshness revealed by God in Genesis. This theology does not in the least contradict the more physiological theologies applied to the marriage act, but its emphasis is on the freely-willed self-donation that made their desired union a marriage. That is, instead of focusing on the natural orientation of the human sexual organs or even on the anti-procreative (and therefore anti-marital) meaning of contraception, it focuses first and foremost on what each spouse did in making the commitment of marriage. In effect, it says: "Be honest with yourself. You made an unreserved gift of yourself in marriage. Don't contradict your gift of self through acts of contraception, acts of sex with serious reservation."

5. *Theological*

Nowhere in Scripture are to be found the words, "Sexual intercourse is intended by God to be at least implicitly a renewal of the marriage covenant." Yet, that concept is contained in Scripture. Just about every imaginable form of sexual activity is mentioned in Sacred Scripture, but the only form that is recognized as legitimate is that of marital intercourse. I think it is indisputable that God has revealed that sexual intercourse is intended to be essentially covenantal. In short, theology goes beyond the mere quotation of Scripture and attempts to put things together; when Scripture provides an answer to what is right or wrong, theology attempts to explain why.

6. Ecumenical

Any theology which proposes to be ecumenical today must be biblical and have its roots in a Tradition that at one time was accepted by those whom Protestants recognize as their spiritual ancestors. The proposed covenant theology of sex is certainly biblical, and it is also firmly rooted in a Tradition that in America, at least, was vocalized even more by Protestants than by Catholics. It is an undeniable fact of American history that in the 19th century, anti-contraceptive laws were passed by Protestant legislatures for a largely Protestant America. Looking for documentation of Protestant Church positions on birth control prior to Lambeth of 1930, I was told by Professor Paul Ramsey of Princeton that I was wasting my time trying to prove the obvious. That is, so universal was this belief that it simply would not have been the subject of Church statements any more than we would expect today a statement that stealing is immoral.

However, the memory of this historical Tradition has been lost to contemporary Christians. At every opportunity afforded, I ask groups of Catholics and Protestants how many are aware that until 1930 no Christian Church had ever accepted contraception as morally permissible. Perhaps three in 100 might know that bit of Christian history; small wonder that *Humanae Vitae* has been so widely regarded simply as a papal idiosyncrasy rather than an affirmation of a Tradition universally held by all Christian churches until 1930 and reaffirmed in one way or another by every Pope since then with the exception of the short-reigned John Paul I.

There is some reason to hope that the memory of Protestant opposition to unnatural forms of birth control will be revived. A small book published in 1989 lists 99 Protestant theologians who taught against Onanism, including actual quotations from 66 of these. Martin Luther, John Calvin, and John Wesley were strongly opposed to unnatural birth control, with Luther calling it a form of sodomy, Calvin calling it the murder of future persons, and Wesley saying it could destroy your soul. In his introduction to that section of the book, the author states: "We have found not one orthodox theologian to defend Birth Control before the 1900s. NOT ONE! On the other hand, we have found that many highly regarded Protestant theologians were enthusiastically opposed to it, all the way back to the very beginning of the Reformation."[2]

7. It Can Distinguish . . .

Because the belief that sexual intercourse is meant to be a renewal of the marriage covenant is based solidly on the biblical concepts of covenant, marriage, and love, it can distinguish between marital and non-marital sex. Before marriage, there is simply no covenant to renew; therefore non-marital sex pretends to be what it is not and cannot be, so it is simply dishonest sex, a lie. That holds true whether the sexual activity is the premarital sex of an engaged couple, the experimental sex of teenagers, or adultery. Whatever the situation without the marriage covenant, sexual relations are intrinsically dishonest and immoral.

Such an understanding of sex is radically different from the soft calculus of much of contemporary talk about sex. For example, one high school text says: "Sexual union should always take place in the context of love—of genuine concern for both your own welfare and that of the other. Your relationship should bring happiness and growth to both of you. You will, therefore, consider the possible consequences of your words and actions, and you will not risk hurting yourself or another unnecessarily."[3]

Or again; "Rather, according to both the laws of society and the Gospel of Jesus, what is wrong or immoral is what hurts or risks hurting yourself or others unnecessarily, without sufficient reason."[4]

---

[2] Charles D. Provan, *The Bible and Birth Control* (Monongahela, Pa.: Zimmer Printing, 1989), 63.

[3] Michele M. McCarty, *Relating* (Dubuque: W. C. Brown, 1979), 56.

[4] McCarty, 50.

Examples could be multiplied both from the same high school text or others. My criticism about this way of talking about chastity is not that the author is probably trying to discourage pre-marital sex—obviously a good intention. Nor would I deny that such reasoning contains large grains of truth. The point is rather that such talk is essentially a soft calculus that does not say a firm biblical "no" to anything. It implies that the people involved will be able to calculate the possible harm to be done and will refrain from sex because of such possible consequences, but nowhere does it say that sex outside of marriage is simply a lie and an act of fornication even if the two people manage to rationalize their way around all the obstacles and think they have "sufficient reason" for taking those risks of hurting themselves or others. Such talk is an invitation to calculating and rationalizing. Given the tendency of passion once aroused to interfere with clear and reasonable thinking—even if calculus were all that was needed—this kind of "explanation" is ultimately seductive.

By ignoring the absolute prohibition on fornication as in the examples cited, modern authors erode consciousness of the sovereignty of God. As Father Richard Roach, S.J., puts it, "God's sovereignty is violated whenever we knowingly and freely break an absolute prohibition."[5]

However, the concepts that sex is meant to be a renewal of the marriage covenant and that non-marital sex is a violation of the God-created meaning of sex operate on a different plane entirely—the plane of discipleship rather than consequentialism. I agree that the unhappy consequences of non-marital sex need to be pointed out again and again, but I insist that any theology of sex and that any discussion of sex in a religious environment must go beyond the pragmatic to the biblical foundations and to the symbolic meaning of sex as a renewal of the marriage covenant.

---

[5] Richard R. Roach, S.J., "From What Are They Dissenting?" *International Review of Natural Family Planning* 4:4 (Winter 1982), 338.

8. *Applies to All...*

As has already been indicated, the understanding that sexual
intercourse is meant to be a renewal of the marriage covenant
provides a clear explanation for the evil of non-marital intercourse
whether it be technically adultery or fornication, whether between
lovers or with prostitutes: there is no covenant to renew. Sodomy
between homosexuals is condemned on precisely the same grounds
as fornication between heterosexuals: there is no valid marriage
covenant to renew. The evil of bestiality should be apparent
without further elaboration; and if the whole meaning of freely-
willed sexual actuation is to renew at least implicitly the mutual
love and faith pledged at marriage, then the evil of the essentially
self-centered act of masturbation is apparent.

Granted, with the covenant theology of sex, all of this becomes
very simple and deductive, but who ever said that a theology
about matters that affect every man and woman had to be complicated or understandable only to those trained in philosophy and
theology?

9. *Realistic Terminology*

Too much of the talk about sex within marriage uses terminology
that is inaccurate or misleading; sometimes it appears to be the
result of wishful thinking. For example, one priest-teacher of
college theology told his students that at the instant of marital
orgasm the floodgates of sanctifying grace were opened. When
the students asked my opinion as a married layman, I had to say
that the professor was confused between grace and sperm count.

More typical is this: "The act of sexual intercourse between
two people is, in itself, beautiful and good."[6] That's misleading
because as it stands it makes no distinction between marital and

[6] McCarty, 49.

non-marital intercourse, nor does it address the real situation within marriage when intercourse is sometimes neither good or beautiful.

Another inaccurate, misleading statement: "The Church understands the act of sexual intercourse to be the ultimate expression of love and fidelity between two people."[7] The author goes on to qualify that the Church means married people so in the context the flaw of not mentioning marriage is corrected. However, my first objection is to the phrase, "ultimate expression of love and fidelity". Precisely what does that mean? "Ultimate expression" is a fuzzy, imprecise phrase that may conjure up visions of ecstasy but can mean different things to different people. My second objection is that the description uses the verb "to be" in the sense of "sexual intercourse is the ultimate expression . . . " There is a world of difference between "meant to be" and "is".

Real life examples. Every priest, marriage counselor, and married couple with any honesty and realism can come up with real life examples that mock the notion of marital sex as good, beautiful, and the ultimate expression of love, fuzzy as it is. John has sat in front of the TV screen all Sunday afternoon completely engrossed in football. The combination of beer and provocative cheerleaders has steered his imagination towards sex. He calls into the kitchen to his wife who feels neglected and hates beer breath, "Go get yourself ready for 'making love' at half-time. Should be about another 10 minutes." Translated "Go put in your diaphragm and foam because I want relief of sexual tension instead of watching the half-time show." Love? Beauty? Ultimate expression of love and fidelity? Absurd, but too frequently that's what is being fed to young people in supposedly Christian education today.

In the fall of 1989 as I was working on this book, I received three letters in three days from women complaining about their marital situations. In each case, the husband was insisting upon complete fellatio. Sometimes it was a substitute for periodic

[7] McCarty, 49.

abstinence; at other times it was in place of normal genital-genital intercourse.

In another case, a woman called to say she and her husband had been practicing "NFP" (natural family planning) for eight years, having taken instruction from a program not associated with the Couple to Couple League (CCL). All during this time they had practiced mutual masturbation instead of sexual self-control during the fertile time. Then she happened to read in CCL's book on NFP, *The Art of Natural Family Planning,* that such activity is "contrary to the Christian tradition of sexual morality which holds that deliberate ejaculation must take place only within the vagina" (70). Her phone call was not to criticize us, but simply to find out if we had a priest on staff to whom she might "go to confession" over the phone. (We don't.)

The last case I will mention was a letter from a man who responded to a fund appeal letter in which I had mentioned the difficulty of finding couples who were interested in natural family planning. He wrote to tell me that if we taught couples "NFP" as he and his wife practiced it, couples would be breaking down the doors. He then described their practices of completed oral and anal sex during the fertile time.

The point I am trying to illustrate is that too much of what passes for "marital sex" has nothing to do with authentic marital love, and some of it is nothing more than marital sodomy, the same sort of perverse activities that constitute homosexual sex. That's why any talk about marital sexuality has to distinguish between morally good and morally bad sexual activity.

Evaluate closely the statement, "Sexual intercourse is meant to be at least implicitly a renewal of the marriage covenant." Such terminology easily recognizes the difference between what sex *should be* and what it frequently *is.* The use of "meant-to-be" clearly implies a standard set by the Creator above and beyond the intentions of the participants. It carries within it the norm that sexual intercourse is intended by God as a sign of marriage, not just affection regardless of marital status.

The phrase "at least implicitly" recognizes that it is not necessary that married couples consciously tell themselves or each other, "Let us renew our marriage covenant."

The fact that the whole statement is built upon the marriage covenant provides a concrete, objective norm, and the notion that sex is meant to be a renewal of that covenant places each act of sex within the standard of the valid Christian marriage.

In my opinion, it is erroneous to say flatly, "Marital intercourse *is* a renewal of the marriage covenant." Such talk fails to distinguish among the wide variety of sexual acts within marriage. On the one hand there is sex as it should be—affectionate and noncontraceptive. On the other, there are acts of marital rape, contraception and marital sodomy. Thus, in order to have realistic terminology, it is necessary to state what God intends sex to be and to avoid making "is" statements that cover a multitude of dissimilar acts.

10. *Simultaneous Norm and Ideal*

One of the most common errors of modern discourse about sexual matters is the treatment of the norm as an ideal. The context is inevitably that the ideal may be relevant for people far advanced in sanctity but not for the common man and woman. The notion that the doctrine of marital non-contraception reaffirmed by *Humanae Vitae* is a binding norm that applies to all is either denied or disregarded. Unfortunately, once this norm of marital chastity is treated as an idealistic dream, so are all of the other norms of chastity both within marriage and outside of it. And for good reason: it is certainly easier to practice the periodic abstinence required by natural family planning than the total abstinence required by the chaste single life whether heterosexual or homosexual.

Perhaps it may be easier to retain the norm as a norm if an ideal is presented simultaneously within the same concept. At any rate, that is what the covenant theology of sex does. The *norm* is that at a minimum the act of sexual intercourse must meet three conditions:

   1) The man and woman must be validly married to each other;

   2) The act must not be one of marital rape;

   3) The act must not be positively and intentionally closed to the transmission of life; i.e., it must be an act of non-contraceptive, nonsterilized, completed genital-genital intercourse.

The *ideal* goes beyond that and reminds each married couple that the act of marital coitus is really meant to be a renewal of the faith and caring love they pledged to each other at marriage, the more conscious and explicit this renewal, the better. The ideal sets the stage for an examination of conscience that can help each person grow in marital love. "If I'm anticipating 'making love' this evening, what is there about my day-to-day, hour-by-hour social intercourse with my spouse that reflects the caring love I pledged at marriage? Have I tried to be helpful, to lighten the burdens of my spouse? Have I done anything to make my spouse feel loved and esteemed?"

The challenge of the marriage covenant. To the extent that a married couple can answer such questions affirmatively, to that extent their acts of sexual intercourse can become more expressive of honest marital love.

Almost everyone will recognize his or her own failure in terms of the ideal, but such failures, depending upon their nature, are the matter of imperfections or venial sin and do not necessarily exclude one from the communion of the sexual embrace.

Such a theology of sex does not condemn marital coitus for the relief of sexual tension provided that it fulfills the minimum requirements of the norm. However, it is realistic and recognizes that such acts are a far cry from those acts which reflect much more explicitly the caring love of the original marriage covenant. In short, this theology of sex recognizes that it is the little things of daily and hourly social intercourse between husband and wife — taking out the garbage, cleaning up a mess, the kind word, the smile—that are the elements of "making love" in marriage; it recognizes that the act of marital coitus "makes love" pretty much in direct proportion to the effort put into the non-genital aspects of the marriage.

In my opinion, an especially beautiful attribute of the covenant theology of sex is that it provides a challenge to each married couple at every stage of their life together—young or old, fertile or infertile. The non-contraceptive aspects of the norm will pass into practical irrelevance after menopause, but the challenge of keeping their sexual intercourse a symbolic renewal of the love they pledged at marriage will pass away only when they do.

The belief that sexual intercourse is intended by God to be at least implicitly a renewal of the marriage covenant is rooted in Scripture and is based also on the personal commitment of the couple. It is a simple concept that is ecumenical and provides a key for explaining the evil of non-marital sex.

Finally, at one and the same time, it affirms the norm of marital non-contraception and provides an ideal, a never ending, marriage building challenge to each and every married couple regardless of age or fertility.

All of this leads me to hope that many will find the covenant theology of sex useful for helping couples improve their marriages as well as for defending the teaching of the Church reaffirmed by *Humanae Vitae.*

FURTHER READING

The predecessor to his most recent book was *Birth Control and the Marriage Covenant* (Collegeville, Minn.: Liturgical Press, 1976). See also "Holy Communion: Eucharistic and Marital", *Ave Maria* 105, no. 8 (February 1967): 9–12; "Continued Dissent: Is It Responsible Loyalty?" *Theological Studies* 32, no. 1 (March 1971): 48–65; "Catholic Sexual Ethics: The Continuing Debate on Birth Control", *Linacre Quarterly* 41, no. 1 (February 1974): 8–25; "Preaching about Natural Family Planning", *Homiletic and Pastoral Review* 83, no. 4 (January 1983): 56–61; "A Covenant Theology of Sex", *Homiletic and Pastoral Review* 83, no. 11 (August–September 1983): 22–33; with Sheila K. Kippley, *The Art of Natural Family Planning* (Cincinnati, Ohio: The Couple to Couple League, 1984). Kippley also has numerous pamphlets on related issues published by the Couple to Couple League.

12

THE IMPORTANCE OF THE CONCEPT OF *"MUNUS"* TO UNDERSTANDING *HUMANAE VITAE*

by
Janet E. Smith

In the modern age, raising children is often considered to be a burdensome chore. Many couples choose to limit their child-bearing to one boy and one girl. Few appreciate that having and raising children is a way that spouses can be coworkers with God in His redemptive work. That having children is a great gift from God and a great gift to God is a concept captured by the word *"munus"*, a word that has a distinguished history in church documents. Vatican II is shaped around the understanding that Christ has the threefold *munus* of priest, prophet, and king. All who are part of the kingdom of God share in these *munera* in some important fashion. Many of the documents of Vatican II attempt to explain the role that specified members of the Church have. Having and raising children is special *munus* of spouses. The following article attempts to explain this concept and to show how it is central to understanding the message of *Humanae Vitae*.

This article appeared in *Humanae Vitae: 20 Anni Dopo* (Milano: Edizioni Ares, 1989) 671–90. A fuller version of it appeared as "The *Munus* of Transmitting Human Life: A New Approach to *Humanae Vitae*," *The Thomist* 54:3 (July 1990) 395–427. Another version appeared in "The Importance of the concept of *Munus* to the Understanding of Humanae Vitae" in *Trust the Truth: A Symposium on the Twentieth Anniversary of the Encyclical Humanae Vitae* (The Pope John Center, 1991) 79–102.

THE IMPORTANCE OF THE CONCEPT
OF *"MUNUS"* TO UNDERSTANDING
HUMANAE VITAE

by
Janet E. Smith

The first line of *Humanae vitae* invokes a concept of marriage and the Christian life that is quite foreign to our current ways of thinking. The fourth word of the encyclical, the word *munus,* is one of particular interest to us here. It carries with it a number of ideas that provide a context to the whole of *Humanae vitae.* The first part of this chapter will provide an abbreviated philological account of the meaning of the word *munus* to suggest how important it is for spouses to live up to the challenges of their *munus.* The second portion will develop some analogies based on the concept of *munus* that I hope will ease resistance to *Humanae vitae's* condemnation of contraception. Finally, the third portion of the chapter will explore what may be called the "interiority" of *munus.* There the argument will be made that fulfilling the *munus* of transmitting human life, or of having children, is essential to the ultimate purpose of marriage, to the sanctification of the spouses and their children into the loving, generous, and self-sacrificing individuals all Christians are called to be.

Meaning of Munus

So what does this word *munus* mean and why is it important to *Humanae vitae?* The very first line of *Humanae vitae* in Latin reads *humanae vitae tradendae munus gravissimum.* This line is usually rendered "The most serious duty of transmitting human life. . . ." The translation "duty", however, does not fully convey the richness of the term *munus.* The chief problem with the translation "duty" for *munus* is that for many modern English-speaking people the word "duty" has a negative sense. A duty is often thought of as something that one ought to do and something that one is frequently reluctant to do. The word *munus,* though, truly seems to be without negative connotations; in fact, a *munus* is something that one is honored and, in a sense, privileged to have.

Munus means much more than duty. One who knows classical Latin would as readily translate *munus* as "gift", "wealth and riches", "honor", or "responsibility" as "duty". One common classical Latin use of the word would be in reference to the bestowal of a public office or responsibility on a citizen. Being selected for such an office or responsibility would be considered an honor; the selection would entail certain duties, but ones that the recipient willingly embraces. The word is also often used synonymously for "gift" or "reward": it is something freely given by the giver and often, but not always, with the connotation that the recipient has merited the gift in some sense; it is given as a means of honoring the recipient. In Scripture and in the writings of St. Thomas Aquinas the word *munus* is used to refer both to gifts that men consecrate to God and to gifts and graces that men receive from God. I would recommend that the first line of *Humanae vitae* be translated to read not "the most serious duty of transmitting human life" but "the extremely important mission of transmitting human life". Rather than being a burdensome duty, a *munus* is much closer to a being an assignment or mission that is conferred as an honor on one who can be trusted and who is chosen to share the responsibility of performing good and important work. The next lines of *Humanae vitae* reinforce this reading for they speak of the "spouses fulfilling this mission freely and deliberately and thereby offering a service to God the Creator", and later in section 8 of *Humanae vitae* we read:

> It is false, then, that marriage results from chance or from the blind course of natural forces; God the Creator wisely and providently established marriage with the intent that he might achieve his own designs of love through men. Therefore, through the mutual gift of self, which is proper and exclusive to them, the spouses seek a communion of persons, by which, in turn, they perfect themselves so that in the procreation and education of new lives, they might share a service with God.

A chief meaning of *munus,* then, is that it is a work that one does at the behest of God and as a service to God. This word has great currency in Church documents, especially the documents of Vatican II and commonly refers to the designated tasks which different individuals have in building up the Kingdom of God. Translations of Vatican II commonly render *munus* as "role", "task", "mission", "office", and "function". In these documents, *munus* is also closely linked with "vocation", "mission", "ministry", and "apostolate" and at times seems interchangeable with them. The general meaning of *munus,* like these words, carries the meaning of something that the Christian is called to do. While occasionally *munus* is translated simply as "task", it routinely refers to tasks that have the nature of a solemn "assignment". *Munus* quite regularly refers to a special assignment that is entrusted to one, the completion of which is vital for the successful institution of the Kingdom of God. Again, it is conferred as an honor, often empowers one, and entails serious responsibilities and obligations.

The documents of Vatican II regularly identify the *munus* of different individuals in the Church. One primary reference of the word is to the triple *munera* of Christ of being priest, prophet, and king (LG, 31). Christians, in their various callings, participate in these *munera;* they do so by fulfilling other *munera,* specifically entrusted to them. For instance, Mary's *munus* (role) is being the

Mother of God (LG, 53 and 56) which also confers on her a maternal *munus* (duty) towards all men (LG, 60). Christ gave Peter several *munera:* for instance Peter was given the *munus* (power) of binding and loosing and the *grande munus* (special duty) of spreading the Christian name—which was also granted to the apostles. The apostles were assigned the *munera* (great duties) of "giving witness to the gospel, to the ministration of the Holy Spirit and of justice for God's glory" (LG, 21). To help them fulfill these *munera* they were granted a special outpouring of the Holy Spirit (LG, 21). By virtue of his *munus* (office), the Roman Pontiff has "full, supreme, and universal power" in the Church (LG, 22) and also by virtue of his *munus* (office) he is endowed with infallibility (LG, 43). Bishops, by virtue of their episcopal consecration, have the *munus* (office) of preaching and teaching (LG, 21). The laity, too, sharing in the priestly, prophetic, and kingly *munus* of Christ, have their own mission [*missio*]; they are particularly called [*vocantur*] to the *munus* (proper function) of "working, like leaven, for the sanctification of the world from within, and especially so by the witness of their lives. By shining forth with faith, hope, and charity, they are to manifest Christ to others" (LG, 31). *Munera* are conferred by one superior in power upon another; it is important to note that Christ is routinely acknowledged as the source of the *munera* for each of the above-mentioned groups. *Munera* are not man-made but God-given.

Many Church documents use the word *munus* in their titles or subtitles. *Familiaris consortio,* for instance, is about the *munus* or role of the family in the modern world and the title of the document is routinely translated as such. The use of *munus* in the title of *Familiaris consortio* and in the first line of *Humanae vitae,* then, follows typical practice in ecclesial documents. And I think their appearance serves the purpose of linking these documents to each other and to the Vatican II document *Gaudium et spes.*

The section of *Gaudium et spes* that treats of marriage repeatedly makes reference to the *munus* of spouses, which is the *munus* of parenthood. One paragraph provides a summary statement: "Married couples should regard it as their proper mission [*missio*] to transmit human life and to educate their children; they should realize that they are thereby cooperating with the love of God the Creator and are, in a certain sense, its interpreters. This involves the fulfillment of their role [*munus*] with a sense of human and Christian responsibility ... " (GS, 50).[1]

Later in the same section, there is mention of "those among the married couples who thus fulfil their God-given mission [*munus*], special mention should be made of those who after prudent reflection and common decision courageously undertake the proper upbringing of a large number of children" (GS, 50).

So what does *Humanae vitae* mean when it speaks of the *munus* of transmitting human life? This *munus* is clearly a special task chosen by God for spouses. It is a responsibility that they have but a responsibility given to one as a kind of honor. To reject this *munus* is to reject what God has ordained for spouses. We hear modern couples speaking of "choosing" to have a family, but it would be a very odd for Christian spouses to speak in this way, for Christian marriage has as one of its purposes the bringing forth of children into the world and the raising them up to be worthy to be citizens of the kingdom of God. *Casti connubii* states this principle well:

> Christian parents should understand that they are destined not only to propagate and conserve the human race, nor even to educate just any worshippers of the true God, but to bring forth offspring for the Church of Christ, to procreate fellow citizens for the Saints and servants of God, so that the worshippers devoted to our God and Savior might daily increase (AAS 454).[2]

The closing of the section of *Gaudium et spes* on marriage reads:

"Let all be convinced that human life and its transmission are

---

[1] Translations for the documents of Vatican II are taken from *The Documents of Vatican II,* ed. by Austin Flannery, O.P. (Collegeville, Minn.: Liturgical Press, 1975 and 1984).

[2] The translation for *Casti connubii* is mine.

realities whose meaning is not limited by the horizons of this life only: their true evaluation and full meaning can only be understood in reference to man's eternal destiny" (GS 51).

Spouses should not underestimate the enormity of the responsibility bestowed upon them through the *munus* of transmitting life; nor should they underestimate the importance of the task entrusted to them. God is the creator of each and every human life. Indeed, it is through a special act of creation that each and every human soul comes into existence. And all souls are destined for eternal union for God, a union that God might be described as desperately desiring. Again, spouses do not create this life, God does. He *transmits* this life through the act of sexual intercourse. It is appropriate that this act be performed by spouses only for only spouses are able to imitate God's creative act properly. That is, God's act of creation is an act that is free, responsible, and loving; a spousal relationship is the only one that has the features of being free, responsible, and loving in a way appropriate to the bringing forth of new life. Indeed, couples—particularly those hoping to conceive a child—not infrequently feel that God is present in a special way during their love-making, and this feeling has a sound foundation in reality. The emotions that flow and the bonding that takes place during love-making are of a grand and mysterious—not to say sacred—nature. Again, this is understandable considering that God is the source of love and life and that he has privileged spouses with being the transmittors of life through an act of love. Those who do nothing to contravene the baby-making possibilities of sexual intercourse have, in a sense, left God space to perform his act of the creation of a new soul, if he so chooses.

Humanae vitae, then, relies upon an understanding of the nature of the *munus* of transmitting human life that acknowledges how elevated is the task of bringing forth new life. *Humanae vitae* has as its purpose clarifying certain facets of the *munus* of spouses, the *munus* of bringing forth children and of being responsible parents to them, with a view to guiding them to be worthy of eternal union with God.

Use of munus *to ease resistance to* Humanae vitae's *condemnation of contraception*

The above understanding of *munus* may offer some assistance in explaining how contraception violates God's intent for spousal intercourse. Here I will employ a few rather imaginative analogies to show how the use of contraception would be a reneging on one's *munus* of transmitting human life, to help explain why "each and every act of marital intercourse must remain ordered to procreation" and why the procreative and unitive meanings of marital intercourse are inseparable.

The first analogy requires that we imagine a good and generous king of a country who asked one of his worthy subjects to help him build his kingdom. The king needs a responsible individual to perform this *munus* since it is important, indeed essential, to the kingdom to keep contact with a distant borough. He chooses to honor his subject George with this *munus* of keeping contact with one of the outlying boroughs. In order for George to perform this service, he gives George the use of a fine horse and buggy that will enable him to travel to the distant borough. The king has business that he wants conducted in this borough whenever George visits it and makes it clear that George should never go to this borough unless he attends to the king's business while he is there. He has another motive in providing George with the horse and buggy for he also wishes George to prosper. The horse and buggy will enable George to attend to his own business when he travels to the distant borough. The king makes it clear to George that those who live in the borough and George himself will fare better if George uses the horse and buggy as designated, for the king desires both that the kingdom prosper and that George prosper—indeed, it is quite impossible for either to prosper without the other. So George achieves two ends by the use of the horse and buggy; he advances his own prosperity and that of the kingdom. The king also tells George that business is closed in the outlying borough one week of every month and during that week George may freely use the horse and buggy for his own purposes. Moreover, since the horse and buggy are handsome and efficient it is pleasurable for George to employ them, but pleasure is an added benefit to the use of the horse and buggy, not the purpose of the horse and buggy. The king more or less leaves it up to George how often and when he visits the borough when business is in session. He simply asks George to be generous and to use his own good judgment. Now, if George were to accept this *munus* and the horse and buggy that go with it but refused to drive to the outlying borough, then he would be reneging on the *munus* that he accepted. And if he were to go to the borough but refuse to attend to the king's business while there, he would again be failing to live up to the demands of his *munus*.

There are parallels here with the *munus* of transmitting human life. God has given this *munus* to spouses because he wishes to share the goods of his kingdom with more souls and he has chosen to call upon spouses to share with him the work of bringing new life into the world. This work is an honor and entrusted only to those willing to embrace the responsibilities of marriage. Those who perform the responsibilities of marriage in accord with God's will benefit both themselves and the rest of society. The spouses achieve the good of strengthening their relationship through sexual intercourse, i.e., the good of union, and they achieve the good of having children, i.e., the good of procreation. Both goods are goods that also benefit God's Kingdom for he wishes love between spouses to flourish and he desires more souls with whom to share the goods of his Kingdom. Thus, sexual intercourse is a part of the *munus* of transmitting human life, a *munus* that is intimately bound with other goods. Those who accept this *munus* need to respect the other goods that accompany it. Still, in the same way that the good king allowed George to use the horse and buggy even when business was not in session in the outlying borough, God has so designed human fertility and human sexuality, that humans are sometimes fertile and sometimes not. It is permissible for spouses to enjoy marital intercourse at any time, whether they are infertile or fertile. God seems to have designed the human system this way to foster greater union and happiness between spouses. But he has asked them to be receptive to new life, generously, and in accord with their best judgment, and not to misuse the *munus* that he has given them. To choose never to have children is like refusing to go to the outlying district ever. It is to renege on the *munus* that comes with marriage. To have contraceptive sex is like driving to the outlying borough and ignoring the king's business. The contracepting couple is repudiating the *munera* of their own fertility and altering the functioning of the body. They are pursuing pleasure while emphatically rejecting the good of procreation. They may not feel that they are engaging in an act of emphatic rejection of the good of procreation but in terms of their *munus,* that is exactly what they are doing. (It is also true that the good that they achieve, pleasure, is not the good of union, which can be achieved only if the procreative good is also respected. More will be said about this below.) But the good king allowed George to use the horse and buggy when business was not in session, and that is exactly what the couple is doing who are having sexual intercourse during the infertile period. They are pursuing one good, the good of union *when another is not available.* Again, the contracepting couple is repudiating a *munus* that they have accepted; the noncontracepting couple is cooperating with the complexity of the *munus* that God has entrusted to them.

Let us now use another analogy to attempt to further clarify why *Humanae vitae* makes the claim that it is impossible to separate the procreative meaning of spousal intercourse from the unitive meaning. Here we shall be daring and use the responsibilities entailed in presiding over the sacrament of the Eucharist. This analogy may seem far-fetched but we must remember that in being a sacrament marriage is more like the priesthood than is it like an appointment by a king.

What we need to focus on here is that vocations have a certain reality and make certain demands upon those embracing their vocation. *Humanae vitae* 10 speaks to this point:

The responsible parenthood of which we speak here has another dimension of utmost importance: it is rooted in the objective moral order established by God—and only an upright conscience can be a true interpreter of this order. For which reason, the mission [*munus*] of responsible parenthood depends upon the spouses recognizing their duties towards God, towards themselves, towards the family, and towards human society, as they maintain the right hierarchy of goods.

For this reason, in regard to the mission [*munus*] of transmitting human life, it is not right for spouses to act in accord with a private judgment, as if it were permissible for them to define subjectively and willfully what is right for them to do. On the contrary, they must accommodate their behavior to the plan of God the Creator, a plan made manifest both by the very nature of marriage and its acts and also by the constant teaching of the Church.[3]

By freely and deliberately accepting the calling of marriage, spouses also freely and deliberately accept the *munera* that go along with that calling in the same way that a priest in responding to the calling of the priesthood also accepts the *munera* of that "assignment". To be married but not to accept the *munus* of transmitting life, is like taking on an assignment but not taking on the full responsibilities of that assignment—and not realizing the full goods of that assignment both for one's self and for others. For instance, a man may wish to be a priest, but not wish to perform some of the sacraments; that would be a repudiation of his calling and the *munera* of his calling. The following elaboration of this parallel with the priesthood cannot be made exactly coordinate at all points, but if it is a correct parallel at some key points it should illuminate why it is wrong to attempt to separate the goods integrally united within a given act.

Participation in the Eucharist is parallel to the marital act in so far as it too conveys several goods, the good of sacramental grace, for instance, and the good of united community activity. It is possible that a priest may wish to pursue the good of united community activity without pursuing the good of sacramental

---

[3] The translations of passages from *Humanae vitae* are mine.

grace. He may be facing a community that includes both Catholics and non-Catholics and not wish to exclude any from receiving the Eucharist. Knowing that he should not distribute the Eucharist to non-Catholics, he may do something to invalidate the consecration—he may not say the proper formula or may use invalid matter for the eucharistic bread and may then distribute it to all present. (Admittedly it makes the example somewhat preposterous to speculate that a priest who would have qualms about serving the Eucharist to non-Catholics would choose to invalidate the sacrament, but let us suspend our disbelief for the sake of the analogy!) Thus he would gather the community together but not violate the norms for distribution of the Eucharist. But it should be clear that it amounts to a sort of deception or indeed a sacrilege to pretend that one is distributing the Eucharist, while having deliberately deprived the act of one of its essential—and sacral—dimensions. The intention of the priest may be good, but he could achieve the end of unifying the community by some other ceremony; he need not violate the meaning of the Eucharist to do so. Or, he could distribute the Eucharist only to the Catholics present and tolerate the "imperfection" of a not fully united community. But he ought not to seek the good of a united community at the expense of the good of the sacrament. The ultimate irony, of course, is that he is not truly achieving the good of union if he excludes the good of sacramental grace, for it is precisely the sharing in sacramental grace that effects the truly meaningful union of the assembly. Any other sort of union is superficial in comparison.

Spouses, too, may be tempted to pursue one good achievable through sexual intercourse and not another. Yet they are faced with the same reality as the priest; to pursue one good without the other is to fail to achieve either. As noted, the priest who distributes a non-consecrated "eucharist" achieves at best only a superficial uniting of the community for he fails to effect the sacramental grace that is the source of true unity achieved through reception of the Eucharist. Similarly, couples achieve only a superficial union through contracepted sexual intercourse; they do not achieve the union appropriate to spouses. As *Humanae vitae* states, the goods of union and procreation are inseparable; spouses cannot achieve one good without due ordination to the other. Certainly couples may believe that they are achieving the good of union through contracepted sexual intercourse, but their actions do not correspond to their intentions. The fact is that contracepted sexual intercourse yields neither the good of procreation nor the good of spousal union. To be sure, some sort of union takes place, for shared activity nearly always produces some sense of union among the participants. For instance, strangers viewing a sporting event together experience a sense of union with each other, but such is a fleeting and insubstantial union. Sexual intercourse, being by its nature a very intimate activity, undoubtedly creates bonds even when engaged in with strangers but these are not the bonds appropriate to spousal intercourse. (Indeed, sexual intercourse engaged in with strangers or with nonspouses is not only a source of union [albeit superficial] but it is also a source of alienation; for the sexual partners know that they do not intend the depth of union inherently promised by the act of sexual intercourse. Therefore, although they have achieved some kind of bond it is not an authentic, trustworthy or spousal bond.)

Nor does sexual intercourse robbed of its procreative meaning create the bond that is proper to spousal intercourse, for spousal union requires that the spouses give fully of themselves to one another. Theirs is to be a total self-giving. But by using contraception they are withholding their fertility and all that being open to child-bearing entails. Being open to child-bearing is an essential feature to spousal sexual intercourse. And "being open to child-bearing" does not mean the couple must intend to have a child with every act of sexual intercourse. Rather, it means that the couple has done nothing to deprive an act of sexual intercourse of its baby-making possibilities. Thus, those who are infertile whether through age or physical abnormality, or through the periodic infertility all women experience by nature, have not negated the procreative meaning of sexual intercourse. If engaging in sexual intercourse in a spousal way, they are still expressing the desire for a union appropriate for spouses—one that would accommodate children if children were a possibility. The meaning may be present in sexual intercourse only symbolically but it is there nonetheless.

Let us consider somewhat further the claim that being open to baby-making, at least symbolically, is essential to spousal intercourse. Consider the common description of contracepted sexual intercourse as "recreational" sex. It is sex that is engaged in for play. Now such sex obviously could be engaged in with a large number of individuals. That is, most individuals could easily find others with whom they would enjoy a romp in the hay. But when we start thinking of the baby-making possibilities of sex and start thinking of those with whom we are willing to share the responsibilities of child-rearing, the list of potential partners for such sexual activity becomes quite short. And this is because we know what kind of bond is appropriate for being parents—it is, in fact, the bond characteristic of spouses—i.e., one that is faithful and exclusive and committed to a lifetime union with another. Thus those responsibly engaging in non-contracepted sexual intercourse with another are engaging in an activity which expresses the kind of commitment or love that spouses should have for one another. Indeed, a sign that one loves another as a spouse is one's willingness to have and raise children with this individual, the willingness to interlock one's life together with another in the way that is appropriate for raising faithful Christians. Therefore, written into the desire for union characteristic of the spousal love of Christians is an ordination to having children. On the other hand, those who rob their sexual intercourse of its procreative meaning are also severely diminishing its unitive meaning; indeed it no longer expresses the kind of union that spouses are meant to desire with one another. Truly, spouses using contraception are desiring pleasure more than union for they have deliberately diminished the unitive meaning of their act.

And finally, let it be noted that just as a priest can pursue community union through other means as effectively as doing so with an invalid Eucharist (and truly more effectively when sacrilege is not present), so, too, there are many ways that spouses may express their love and foster union apart from intercourse. What is wrong is deliberately depriving a sexual act of the essential good of fertility all in the name of union—or again, more properly, all in the pursuit of pleasure. To do so is to use one's *munus* improperly; to be selective about the way that one will serve God through the gifts and responsibilities that he has entrusted to one.

The above analysis of *munus* has, I hope, shown that contraception is so very popular because spouses have such an imperfect understanding of the meaning of sexual intercourse. Were they to understand that the act of spousal intercourse is united with the *munus* of transmitting human life and that the ability to achieve meaningful spousal union is integrally united with the procreative meaning of sexual intercourse, they may not so easily tamper with the integrity of the sexual act. The fairly common view that sex is a superior form of recreation would permit few objections to contraception. But the view that sexual intercourse is part of the *munus* of transmitting human life, of performing a service for God, and of facilitating a unique human relationship and human union that is unachievable without a procreative meaning, suggests all sorts of reasons why contraception might be morally objectionable.

The Interiority of Munus

To this point the discussion of *munus* has focused largely upon the external dimensions of *munus,* upon its status as a task bestowed as an honor on man by God. What is needed now is a consideration of the kind of internal benefits gained by one who eagerly embraces and seeks to fulfill his or her vocation, mission, or *munus.* What we need to do is focus on the interior changes in the individual who lives his or her married commitment faithfully. And we wish to place particular emphasis on the role of children in fostering these interior changes. When *Humanae vitae* asserts that one of the defining characteristics of marriage is its fruitfulness, it states:

"[Conjugal] love is fruitful since the whole of the love is not contained in the communion of the spouses, but it also looks beyond itself and seeks to raise up new lives."

Humanae vitae cites further from *Gaudium et spes:*

"Marriage and conjugal love are ordained by their very nature to the procreating and educating of children. Offspring are clearly the supreme gift of marriage, a gift which contributes immensely to the good of the parents themselves."

This final portion of the paper will, very briefly, elaborate on this claim of *Gaudium et spes* and *Humanae vitae* that children contribute immensely to the good of the parents. The fundamental point is that having children and raising children is a source of great good for the parents, that having to meet the responsibilities entailed in the *munus* is their way of participating in the threefold *munera* of Christ of being priest, prophet and king.

Here we will be drawing upon the work of Pope John Paul II—in particular from observations made in *Sources of Renewal* and *Familiaris consortio*. In these works, the Pope puts a great deal of emphasis on man's internal life, on his need for transformation in Christ. The focus on interiority is characteristic of Pope John Paul II; it flows from his interest in personalist values, from his interest in the kind of self-transformation one works upon one's self through one's moral choices. He repeatedly depicts life as a continuous process of transformation. For instance, in *Familiaris consortio* he states:

What is needed is a continuous, permanent conversion which, while requiring an interior detachment from every evil and an adherence to good in its fullness, is brought about concretely in steps which lead us ever forward. Thus a dynamic process develops, one which advances gradually with the progressive integration of the gifts of God and the demands of His definitive and absolute love in the entire personal and social life of man (FC 9).[4]

In his book *Sources of Renewal* Karol Wojtyla placed great emphasis on the "attitude of participation" required from Christians in Christ's mission, which he calls the "central theme of the Conciliar doctrine concerning the People of God".[5] There he makes reference to Christ's threefold power or *munus* as priest, prophet, and king in which Christians must participate. He maintains that sharing in this power or *munus* is not simply a matter of sharing in certain tasks, rather it is more fundamentally a participation in certain attitudes. He tells us that man has the power or " 'task' or 'office' (Latin: *munus in tria munera Christi*) together with the ability to perform it." The claim that participating in a *munus* involves not just the power to act, nor simply the responsibility to complete an external act, but also requires an internal attitudinal change on the part of Christians adds another dimension to the complexity of this word. In *Sources of Renewal,* Karol Wojtyla outlines the different attitudinal changes required to be faithful participants in Christ's threefold *munus.* He identifies a certain attitude associated with each of the three *munera* or priesthood, prophet, or king.

It is possible to crystalize these attitudes in the following way. In conjunction with the *munus* of *priesthood* shared by the laity, the attitude needed is a sacrificial one, whereby "man commits himself and the world to God".[6] Sharing in the *prophetic munus* of Christ requires that spouses work to bring the truth of Christ to the world, through evangelization. And the *kingly munus* is best exercised by man not in rule over the world, but in rule over himself. Thus, to be a priest, one must be self-sacrificing, to be a prophet, one must evangelize, and to be a king, one must govern — and govern one's self above all.

---

[4] Translations for *Familiaris consortio* are from *The Role of the Christian Family in the Modern World* (Boston: St. Paul Editions, Boston, 1981).

[5] Karol Wojtyla, *Sources of Renewal,* translated by P. S. Falla, (San Francisco: Harper and Row, 1980), 219.

[6] Ibid., 223.

It is in *Familiaris consortio* that we find more detailed instruction on how spouses are to participate in the threefold *munus* of Christ, how they are to be priests, prophets, and kings, or how they are to be self-sacrificing, evangelical, and self-mastering. *Familiaris consortio* speaks specifically about the family's part in the threefold *munus* of Christ; it states:

> The Christian family also builds up the Kingdom of God in history through the everyday realities that concern and distinguish its *state of life*. It is thus in *the love between husband and wife and between the members of the family* — a love lived out in all its extraordinary richness of values and demands: totality, oneness, fidelity, and fruitfulness — that the Christian family's participation in the prophetic, priestly, and kingly mission of Jesus Christ and of his Church finds expression and realization. Therefore love and life constitute the nucleus of the saving mission of the Christian family in the Church and for the Church (FC 50).

In the remainder of *Familiaris consortio,* he explains how the family fulfill their participation in Christ's threefold *munus.* He identifies the *prophetic* office with the obligation of the family to evangelize, especially to its own members. The Pope rehearses the obligation of parents to be educators of their children, especially in matters of the faith. *Familiaris consortio* refers to the evangelization of children as an original and irreplaceable ministry (FC 53). For the family, the *priestly* office is fulfilled by engaging "in a dialogue with God through the sacraments, through the offering of one's life, and through prayer" (FC 55). And the *kingly* office is fulfilled when the family offers service to the large community, especially to the needy.

The family participates in the threefold *munus* of Christ by being true to its own *munus.* The family serves to build up the Kingdom of God insofar as it is a school of love; as the Pope puts it: "The essence and role of the *munus* of the family are in the final analysis specified by love" (FC 17). He goes on: "Hence the family has the mission to guard, reveal and communicate love." *Familiaris consortio* states:

All members of the family, each according to his or her own gift or *munus,* have the grace and responsibility of building, day by day, the communion of persons, making the family "a school of deeper humanity": this happens where there is care and love for the little ones, the sick, the aged; where there is mutual service every day; when there is a sharing of goods, of joys and of sorrows (FC 21).

Successfully adapting to family life fosters love and generosity, the ability to forgive, and a whole host of related virtues. Both the parents and the children and ultimately the whole of society stand to grow in these virtues as the family attempts to be true to its nature.

The *munus* of transmitting life, of educating children, of being parents, then, yields multiple goods. Creating a family where self-giving and all the virtues might begin to flourish is an activity that has multiple purposes. Certainly, it works towards achieving God's end of producing more souls to share with Him eternal bliss. Having children also helps parents mature and acquire many of the virtues they need to be fully human and fully Christian. Furthermore, building families is to the good of the whole of society for generosity and love should flow from the family to the larger community, especially to the poor and needy.

What is key here for our understanding of *Humanae vitae* is to recognize that to reject the procreative power of sexual intercourse, is not a simply rejection of some biological power—it is the rejection of a God-given *munus.* The resistance to the procreative power of sexual intercourse that accompanies the desire to use contraception predictably involves an underestimation of the value of the family—to God, to the spouses, and to the larger society. True Christian spouses know that to reject the *munus* of transmitting life, to limit the number of children they have, is to limit the number of gifts and blessings that God gives to them, it is to limit the gifts that they return to God, and it is to limit their opportunities and ability to grow as Christians.

PART FIVE

Specific Problems

13

HUMANAE VITAE AND
THE PRINCIPLE OF TOTALITY

by
Ralph McInerny

The most controversial line of *Humanae Vitae* states that "*each* conjugal act [must] remain ordained in itself [*per se destinatus*] to the procreating of human life" (*Humanae Vitae* 11; my emphasis). If the word "each" did not appear in this phrase, the document would be rendered relatively innocuous. Many accept the connection between sexual intercourse and procreation but fail to see why each act of sexual intercourse must remain ordained to procreation. Constructing an argument based on the "principle of totality", some theologians maintain that if the totality of one's marriage is open to children, each act need not be; they argue that it is morally permissible to sacrifice the good of a part for the good of the whole. This was one of the arguments advanced by the majority on the special commission that advised Pope Paul VI that the Church's condemnation of contraception could be changed; it was the only argument for contraception directly addressed in *Humanae Vitae*.

Ralph McInerny, one of the foremost Thomists of our age, defends the encyclical in its claim that the principle of totality cannot be properly applied to justify the use of contraception. He invokes the fundamental moral principal that one may never do evil so that good might come from it and proceeds to explain the proper mode of analyzing moral behavior that looks to the faithfulness of each of one's acts to the good.

This essay, originally entitled "*Humanae Vitae* and the Judgement of Conscience", appeared in *Humanae Vitae: 20 Anni Dopo* (Milan: Edizioni Ares, 1988), 199–209.

13

HUMANAE VITAE AND
THE PRINCIPLE OF TOTALITY

by
Ralph McInerny

> Men of our time, we think, are especially able to under-
> stand that this teaching is in accord with human reason (HV,
> no. 12).

Pope Paul VI's prediction in *Humanae vitae* that his contemporaries
were particularly well disposed to see that the inseparability of the
unitive and procreative meanings of the conjugal act precludes
contraception has not in the short term been borne out, at least if
one is guided by the amplified voices of dissenters. It is ironic
that a general confidence in people of our day should have had
so fragile a basis among some of the faithful themselves, even
those to whom the Church has entrusted the teaching of moral
theology. It was precisely to this inseparable connection between
the unitive and procreative meanings of the conjugal act that
Cardinal Ratzinger appealed in the *Instruction on Respect for Human
Life in Its Origins and on the Dignity of Procreation.* Many have
noted the symmetry between *Humanae vitae* and the *Instruction on
Respect for Life.* It is the same principle that forbids separating the
unitive from the procreative meanings in contraceptive sex and
the separating of the procreative from the unitive in homologous
artificial fertilization.

In this paper, after reflecting on that principle, I want to
consider the objection to it based on the so-called "principle of

329

totality", a symmetrical form of which has surfaced in reaction to the *Instruction on Respect for Life.*

I. UNITIVE AND PROCREATIVE MEANINGS

The second part of *Humanae vitae* running from n. 7 through 18 is called in one English translation Doctrinal Principles. The Holy Father urges a proper understanding of the nature of the conjugal act, on the one hand, and of responsible parenthood, on the other, since these have been appealed to on behalf of behavior traditionally regarded as immoral.

Quocirca per mutuam sui donationem, quae ipsorum propria est et exclusoria, coniuges illam persequuntur personarum communionem, qua se invicem perficiant, ut ad novorum viventium procreationem et educationem cum Deo operam sociant (HV, no. 8).	By means of the reciprocal personal gift which is proper and exclusive to them, husband and wife tend toward that communion of their beings whereby they help each other toward personal perfection in order to collaborate with God in the begetting and rearing of new lives (Calegari trans.).[1]

This understanding of the marriage act is taken to be that which all men should have on the basis of natural reason. Paul VI then added that for baptized persons marriage takes on the dignity of a sacramental sign of grace and represents the union of Christ and the Church.

The characteristics and demands of spousal love that the encyclical then develops are four. It is human, that is, a love both

---

[1] I am using the English translation of *Humanae vitae* made by Marc Calegari, S.J., and published by Ignatius Press, San Francisco, 1978. Sometimes the slightest of variations have been made but more for stylistic than doctrinal reasons. Of course no translation satisfies, which is why I put the original and the English side by side.

sensible and spiritual. As a human act, spousal love is an act of deliberative will bearing on the use of our bodies in such a way as to promote an enduring union between man and wife and their mutual attainment of human perfection. It is a total and mutual giving of self, faithful and exclusive until death, which by its very nature is fruitful, ordered to bring new lives into existence.

Clearly this is a description of this human act as it ought to be, but these demands are exigencies of the act itself; it is a moral ideal that can and should be realized; that is, it is the measure of each instance of such activity. The doctrine of the encyclical is sometimes described as an "ideal" that should be acknowledged, but apparently not as one that can and should be realized. This kind of acceptance of *Humanae vitae* as the expression of an unrealizable ideal that should nonetheless gain our assent, is of course a rejection of and dissent from it, to characterize practical advice as in effect impractical is a somewhat Pickwickian way to praise it let alone accept it.

Paul VI's remarks about responsible parenthood continue to develop a moral ideal on the basis of the nature of spousal love as human action. "Quoniam humana ratio in facultate vitae procreandae biologicas deprehendit leges, quae ad humanam personam pertinent: the intellect discovers in the power of giving life biological laws that are part of the human person" (no. 10). The reference here is to the *Summa theologiae,* IaIIae, q. 94, a. 2, where practical reason's judgments concerning the pursuit of the goods which are the object of natural inclinations are called the first principles of natural law. The biological laws are not themselves precepts of natural law, needless to say. Practical reason directs acts of deliberate will which bear on the ends of natural inclinations.

Porro ea, de qua loquimur, conscia paternitas praecipue aliam eamque intimam secum fert rationem, pertinentem ad ordinem moralem, quem obiectivum vocant, a Deoque statutum, cuius recta	Responsible parenthood also and above all implies a more profound relationship to the objective moral order established by God, and of which a right conscience is the

conscientia est vera interpres. Quapropter paternitatis consciae munus id postulat, ut coniuges sua officia erga Deum, erga seipsos, erga familiam, erga humanam societatem agnoscant, rerum bonorumque ordine recte servato (HV, no. 10 in fine).	faithful interpreter. The responsible exercise of parenthood implies, therefore, that spouses recognize fully their duties toward God, toward themselves, toward the family and society, in a correct hierarchy of values.

It is against this background that Paul VI says that the Church is calling men back to the observance of the norms of natural law when she says that each and every conjugal act must remain open to the transmission of life (HV, no. 11).

Humanly to engage in sexual activity is to respect the end and purpose of the activity engaged in and to relate it to the total good of the person, the marriage, the family, society, God. The conjugal act, sexual activity as engaged in by responsible human agents, both unites the partners and enables them to generate new life.

Quodsi utraque eiusmodi essentialis ratio, unitatis videlicet et procreationis, servatur, usus matrimonii sensum mutui verique amoris suumque ordinem ad celsissimum paternitatis munus omnino retinet, ad quod homo vocatur (HV, no. 12).	By safeguarding both these essential aspects, the unitive and the procreative, the conjugal act preserves in its fullness the sense of mutual love and its orientation to man's most high vocation to parenthood.

It is the profoundly reasonable and human character of this principle that, to return to my beginning, caused the Holy Father to think that men nowadays were particularly capable of confirming it. Why? Because of our readiness to see that for one spouse to force the conjugal act on the other without regard to particular circumstances and desires is no act of love and is in fact "a denial of the right moral order in the relations between spouses". A forced act of mutual giving meant to enhance personal union as well as transmit life is a contradiction of the act, not an instance of it. The Pope's assumption that this would be readily seen does not seem overly optimistic. So he goes on.

Pariter, si rem considerent, fateantur oportet, actum amoris mutui, qui facultati vitam propagandi detrimento sit, quam Deus omnium Creator secundum peculiares leges in ea insculpsit, refragari tum divino consilio, ad cuius normam coniugium constitutum est, tum voluntati primae vitae humanae Auctoris (HV, no. 13).	By parity of reasoning, one who reflects carefully must also recognize that an act of mutual love that prejudices the capacity to transmit life that God the Creator, according to particular laws, inserted therein is in contradiction with the design constitutive of marriage and with the will of the Author of life.

What is the argument? The unitive and procreative meanings of the conjugal act are inseparable from it. A forced conjugal act destroys the unitive meaning, contraception destroys the procreative meaning. Neither is an appropriate instance of the act; both are negations of the nature of the act. That is what Pope Paul VI thought men of our day are particularly ready to accept.

II. THE PRINCIPLE OF TOTALITY

When at the outset of *Humanae vitae* Paul VI lists some of the reasons why it was thought necessary to take a new look at the traditional Church teaching on marriage, reasons he states with fairness and sympathy, he identifies one putative basis for reconsideration as based on the principle of totality.

An praeterea, principio totalitatis, quod appellant, in hac re adhibito, non liceat arbitrari consilium fecunditatis	Or else, by extending to this field the application of the so called 'principle of totality', could one not admit

minus uberis, sed magis rationi consentaneae, posse actum, physice sterilitatem afferentem, in licitam providamque gignendae prolis moderationem vertere. An videlicet fas non sit opinari finem procreandae prolis potius ad totam coniugum vitam, quam ad singulos quosque eius actus pertinere (HV, no. 3).

that the intention or a less abundant but more rationally controlled fertility transforms a materially sterilizing intervention into a permissible and wise control of births? Could one not admit, in other words, that the procreative finality pertains to conjugal life taken as a whole, rather than to its single acts?

Not only does the encyclical cite this argument, it responds to it. Nonetheless, dissenters sometimes invoked it as if the Pope had overlooked it.[2] It underscores the symmetry of *Humanae vitae* and the *Instruction on Respect for Life,* that the principle of totality should be invoked in dissenting from the latter to suggest that a couple's having recourse to homologous artificial fertilization can be justified if attention is paid to the whole story of their life together.

"There is, I would say, good reason to consider contraception, IVF and AIH as capable of enhancing the natural course of a marital life in the same way that a caesarean section and bottle-feeding with special supplements do. There can be artifice and technology that enhance nature. But that needs to be evaluated within the full continuity and integrity of a couple's sexual life.

---

[2] Thus my colleague James T. Burtchaell, C.S.C., writing in the *National Catholic Reporter* on May 8, 1987 on the occasion of the appearance of *Respect for Life,* about to invoke the principle of totality against the teaching of the instruction, recalls his dissent from *Humanae vitae* on the same ground. "According to the ethical model followed by *Humanae vitae,* one must assign moral value to method of coitus, rather than the full sequence and story of love and childbearing throughout the course of a marriage. The pope parts company with his advisory commission, which reported, "The morality of sexual acts between married people takes its meaning first of all and specifically from the ordering of their actions in a fruitful married life, that is, one which is practiced with responsible, generous and prudent parenthood. It does not then depend on the direct fecundity of each and every particular act'" (p. 21).

The moral worth of technical intervention would derive from whether the union itself was generous between the spouses and toward offspring".[3]

Professor Oliver O'Donovan of Oxford objected that in *Humanae vitae,* "Chastity in marriage was analyzed into a series of particular acts of sexual union, a proceeding which carried with it an unwitting but unmistakable hint of the pornographic". Since Burtchaell cites O'Donovan at some length, it can be assumed that what the Oxonian has to say of *Humanae vitae* as well as of the *Instruction on Respect for Life* is considered a high example of the defense of the principle of totality.

"A married couple do not know each other in isolated moments or one-night stands. Their moments of sexual union are points of focus for a physical relationship which must properly be predicated of the whole extent of their life together. Thus, the virtue of chastity as openness to procreation cannot be accounted for in terms of a repeated sequence of chaste acts, each of which is open to procreation. The chastity of a couple is more than the chastity of their acts, though it is not irrespective of it either".[4]

---

[3] Ibid. With respect to the Instruction's arguing that (in Father Burtchaell's paraphrase) "sexual union is damaged when it involves a generative act that does not involve the marital embrace", Father Burtchaell writes, "Here, I suspect, some good principles might be getting a careless application. The generative act is being viewed as an isolated event, separate from the sequence of sexual union that the married couple have enacted all along. And we are not given a principle adequate to discern when technology is assisting and when it is intruding" (p. 21). With regard to that last specific point, since the technology could be carried on years after the spouses are dead it could not be said either to assist or intrude into their generative act. And the same is true of the present. It is not their act.

[4] O'Donovan as quoted by Burtchaell in the article cited. The application of this line of thinking to the problems of the Instruction is also made by O'Donovan. Speaking of IVF and AIH, O'Donovan writes, "There are *distinct* acts of choice, which may involve persons other than the couple, in any form of aided conception, including those forms of which [Catholic official opinion (sic)] approves. Whether they are *independent* acts of choice is precisely the question which requires moral insight. If they are indeed independent (and not subordinate to the couple's quest for fruitfulness in their sexual embrace), then

Burtchaell and O'Donovan provide us with fairly recent statements of the way the principle of totality is invoked to justify
what the Church condemns. I find a very curious theory of action
lurking behind their remarks and I think it will be useful to bring
it out into the open, the more so because it seems to me that the
principle the two men invoke provides a very feeble defense of
what they have set out to champion.[5]

How does *Humanae vitae* reply to the argument based on
the principle of totality? Reconsideration has led the Holy Father
to declare once again that "cum quis dono Dei utitur, tollens,
licet solum ex parte, significationem et finem doni ipsius, sive
viri sive mulieris naturae repugnant eorumque intimae necessitudini, ac propterea etiam Dei consilio sanctaeque eius volun-
tati obnititur: those who make use of this divine gift while
destroying, even if only partially, its significance and its finality,
act contrary to the nature of both man and woman and of their
most intimate relationship, and therefore contradict also the
plan of God and his will" (n. 13). Given this judgment, following
on the very nature of the conjugal act, the dismissal of the

---

they are certainly offensive. But that point cannot be settled simply by
asserting they are distinct. The question remains: Is there a moral unity which
holds together what happens in the hospital and what happens at home in bed?
Can these procedures be understood appropriately as the couple's search for
help within their sexual union (the total life-union of their bodies, that is, not a
single sexual act)? And I have to confess that I do not see why not."

[5] O'Donovan's curious suggestion that taking acts singly is somehow pornographic seems to invoke a principle used in legal quarrels over pornography.
Episodes in a story must be considered in the light of the role they play in the
whole. The novelist will of course write of immoral acts and as a rule his
treatment of them will be judged in terms of the role they play in the overall
story. Doubtless it is when sexual misbehavior, say, or simply sexual activity, is
so described as to appeal to the reader's prurience that the episode asserts itself
independently of the whole novel. That would be an artistic flaw. A form of
the principle of totality is involved in saying that such a novel can have
sufficient redeeming merit to save it from such civic condemnation as is still
possible. Of course the principle of totality in this second sense is very different
from that which would apply to the artistic unity of the novel.

argument for contraception based on the principle of totality is inevitable.

Neque vero, ad eos coniugales actus comprobandos ex industria fecunditate privatos, haec argumenta ut valida afferre licet: nempe, id malum elegendum esse, quod minus grave videatur; insuper eosdem actus in unum quoddam coalescere cum actibus fecundis iam antea positis vel postea ponendis, atque adeo horum unam atque parem moralem bonitatem participare. Verum enimvero, si malum morale tolerare, quod minus grave sit, interdum licet, ut aliquod maius vitetur malum vel aliquod praestantius bonum promoveatur, numquam tamen licet, ne ob gravissimas quidem causas, facere mala ut eveniant bona . . . (HV, no. 14)	And to justify conjugal acts made intentionally infertile one cannot invoke as valid reasons the lesser evil, or the fact that when taken together with the fertile acts already performed or to follow later, such acts would coalesce into a whole and hence would share in one and the same moral goodness. In truth, if it is sometimes permissible to tolerate a lesser moral evil in order to avoid a greater evil or to promote a greater good, it is not permissible, not even for the gravest reasons, to do evil so that good may follow therefrom.

Paul VI must of course view the argument drawn from totality as violating the principle that evil may not be done that good might come. A conjugal act so engaged in that it is directly rendered infertile is a denial of one of the very meanings of the act, its procreative signification. As such, contraceptive sex is morally wrong. To engage in contraceptive sex on the assumption that good things will thereby come about for the couple and their family is to do an evil that good may come.

Those who dispute this do not of course want to allow that the contraceptive act is immoral. To avoid this they suggest another way of appraising actions, not one at a time, but as elements in a moral unity which is the whole marriage. O'Donovan agrees that without subordination to the couple's quest for fruitfulness in their union homologous artificial fertilization would be an offensive act. By parity of reasoning, presumably, the contraceptive act would have to be subordinate to the couple's quest for union. Or perhaps in either case the subordination is to the couple's quest for union and fruitfulness. The point of the dissent in any case is that the act taken singly has no moral value.

This must be distinguished from the tack taken by Burtchaell in the passage quoted above where contraception, IVF, AIH, caesarean sections and bottlefeeding were lumped together as all involving artifice and technology. It is of course disingenuous to read the Instruction as expressive of a Luddite distrust for technology since it goes out of its way to make clear that is not the point.[6] Despite this lapse on Burtchaell's part as to what the principle of totality is taken to justify—surely the questions raised about contraception and homologous artificial fertilization are not raised about caesarean sections and bottle-feeding—his statement of the principle is helpful. "The moral worth of technical intervention would derive from whether the union itself was generous between the spouses and toward offspring."[7]

Kierkegaard contrasted what he called the aesthetic sphere, symbolized by the seducer, and the ethical sphere, symbolized by the husband. The former is episodic, the repetition of moments, the same damned thing over and over; this note of the aesthetic is captured by Leporello's aria in *Don Giovanni* citing his master's conquests—one thousand and three in Spain alone! The ethical, on the other hand, involves the acquiring of a history by surmounting the moment and developing a life. Those who invoke the principle of totality remind us that marriage is a pact meant to

---

[6] "Science and technology are valuable resources for man when placed at his service and when they promote his integral development for the benefit of all; but they cannot of themselves show the meaning of existence and of human progress" (Introduction, no. 2).

[7] Ibid., p. 21. Burtchaell goes on to invoke the Instruction's insistence that human sex is unlike animal sex "and its biological aspects must be viewed in the light of its human aspect".

last a lifetime, that the spouses enter into it with an eye to the long haul, pledging their love until death do them part. A marriage is thus a mutual effort to acquire a character, to do well a work that neither spouse can do alone. The marriage is somehow a whole that is greater than its parts and it is the whole which confers moral value on the parts, not the other way around.

The theory was not invented ad hoc to discuss marriage. It is a theory about the moral life as such seemingly reminiscent of Aristotle's, "One swallow does not make a spring." One good action does not give us a good character: and of course when virtue is had, a good character gained, it is a cause of further good acts, not simply their effect. The attractiveness of the appeal to totality, then, is that it calls attention to features of the moral life which have long been recognized. It seems clear that those who invoke it have in mind such home truths as that a human life does not consist of a single episode, that the moral life is a task over time in which a history is acquired and we become the kind of person we morally are.

Nonetheless, the principle of totality seems to me to be quite different from the tradition it apparently evokes, a sign of which is that neither a Kierkegaard nor an Aristotle would have accepted the theory of action thought to be implied by the principle of totality.[8] Kierkegaard's notion that the ethical life is the acquisition of a history never leads him to suggest that the acts making it up should be, on the average, good. No more does Aristotle, insofar as he distinguishes between a good action and a good character, think that actions taken one at a time cannot be morally appraised. Surely the goodness or badness of the moral life taken as a whole is essentially dependent on the goodness or badness of the acts which make it up. If this is so, it cannot be the case that the individual acts are what they are morally because they are compo-

[8] When Aristotle seeks to establish what makes a man good, he seeks the function the well performing of which makes a man good. The person is denominated good because he acts well; when acting well is grounded in character he will be called a good person in a more profound sense. He can be counted on to perform singular acts of a given moral kind.

nents of a good life. Surely when we say of someone that he has lived a good life we are speaking of the constituent acts of his life; the life is good because the acts which make it up are good, not the other way around.

The proponents of the principle of totality would not want to countenance an act of marital infidelity by saying that when absorbed into the marriage taken as a whole it loses its negative note. Yet they seem to invite such an appeal.[9] Say it is a single lapse. Our attitude toward the unfaithful partner would be a good deal different than it would be if such infidelity were frequent; the one time adulterer is not as bad as the married philanderer. True as that is, it in no way alters the fact that the act of adultery as such is morally wrong. One sin does not make a vicious person any more than one good act makes one virtuous. But it is single acts that are the primary carriers of moral quality and are good or bad. Perhaps what misleads here is confusing habits or character and acts. One must have a track record of a certain kind before we account him courageous or just. But he will acquire the desired character by means of acts of a certain moral kind.[10]

The conceptual question facing the proponents of the principle of totality, then, seems unanswerable. How can a plurality of acts have a moral character denied to each of them taken singly? To speak of single acts as episodes suggests that they can have no moral value as such. But if they cannot, neither can the life of which they form parts. The married life of a couple may indeed in the main be made up of morally good conjugal acts but this provides no basis for saying that this contraceptive conjugal act is not bad. To say that it is good because it is an episode in a good life will entail denying that the single act of adultery is wrong. We

[9] A candidate for the United States Senate from Maryland invoked the principle of totality (not by name) in just this fashion in an interview in the *Washington Post* on November 3, 1988. His antics at beach parties having come to the attention of the electorate, Mr. Robb said that he liked to have a little fun from time to time but he did not want voters to think his infidelity detracted from his love for his wife and daughters.

[10] In our previous meeting I developed this point further. See, "Fundamental Option", *Persona: Verità e Morale,* Città Nuova Editrice, Rome, 1987, pp. 427–34.

may have to wait years before we can confidently say that the spouses have a good married life, but in the meantime they must act and the deeds they do must meet presently applicable moral standards. On the basis of the dissenters' appeal to the principle of totality, "Make me chaste, Lord, but not yet", could become an exculpating principle of universal application.

Those who dissent from *Humanae vitae* on the basis of the principle of totality have in fact no basis for dissent. They admit that the life of the spouses will be morally good only if it is one of generosity toward one another and toward offspring, and this seems an acceptance of the unitive and procreative meanings as essential to married life taken as a whole. But if these two meanings can only be honored in singular acts, on which basis the married life taken as a whole is said derivatively to honor them, it is in singular acts that the moral significance of the spouses' life will lie. The principle of totality cannot ground the claim that singular acts which, taken as such are offensive, cease to be so when considered in the light of the moral life taken as a whole. The moral imperative is not that we should act well more often than not. Rather it is: Do good and avoid evil.

FURTHER READING

McInerny has published numerous books and articles, largely in the areas of metaphysics and more recently in ethics (rivaled in number by his mystery novels). Readers may find of particular interest his translation of Louis Bouyer's "*Humanae Vitae* Ten Years After: Toward a Positive Theology of Marriage", *The American Journal of Jurisprudence* 25 (1980): 133–45; "Marriage as a Sacrament", *Columbia* 61, no. 6 (June 1981): 4–7; *Ethica Thomistica* (Washington, D.C.: The Catholic University of America Press, 1982); "Eureka", *Crisis* 8, no. 5 (May 1990): 20–25; *A First Glance at St. Thomas Aquinas* (Washington, D.C.: The Catholic University of America Press, 1990); *Aquinas on Human Action: A Theory of Practice* (Washington, D.C.: The Catholic University of America Press, 1992).

14

CONTRACEPTION, INFALLIBILITY AND THE ORDINARY MAGISTERIUM

by
Russell Shaw

The debate about *Humanae Vitae* has been as much about ecclesiology, or about the nature and authority of the Church, as it has been about the principles of moral theology. Many argue that *Humanae Vitae* is not an infallible document, that it does not state an infallible teaching, and that thus Catholics may conscientiously dissent from the teaching.

Building upon the work of John C. Ford, S.J., and Germain Grisez, Russell Shaw argues that there is a strong case to be made that the teaching of *Humanae Vitae* has been infallibly proposed by the Ordinary Magisterium. He carefully sorts through different relevant texts of the documents of Vatican II and shows what it means to say that something is infallible by virtue of the Ordinary Magisterium. He looks closely at previous documents of the Church to place her teaching on infallibility into context. He responds to the arguments of John Noonan, who maintained that for the Church to abandon her teaching on contraception would be a legitimate development in the Church's teaching, that the Church had changed her teaching on moral issues in the past.

This article appeared in *Homiletic and Pastoral Review* 78 (1978): 9–19.

CONTRACEPTION, INFALLIBILITY AND THE ORDINARY MAGISTERIUM

by
Russell Shaw

Has the Church's teaching on contraception been proposed infallibly? In the ten years since *Humanae Vitae* was published, it has generally been assumed that the answer is no. A major article in the June 1978 issue of *Theological Studies* argues that the answer is yes. Entitled "Contraception and the Infallibility of the Ordinary Magisterium," the article seeks to show that the teaching on contraception meets the conditions for an infallible exercise of the ordinary magisterium set forth by Vatican II. The authors are the Rev. John C. Ford, S.J., Professor Emeritus of Moral Theology, Weston College, Weston, Massachusetts, and Dr. Germain Grisez, Professor of Philosophy, Campion College, University of Regina, Canada.

What follows is a summary of some major elements of the argument made by Ford and Grisez. Although they have reviewed this summary, the author takes sole responsibility for it. Readers interested in pursuing the argument in detail should consult the article in *Theological Studies,* which also discusses a number of matters impossible to touch on here.

The second Vatican Council identified specific conditions which must be met for the ordinary magisterium of the bishops throughout the world to be exercised infallibly. The teaching on contraception has been proposed in such a way as to meet these conditions. Obviously this has implications beyond the question of contraception; investigation might show, for example, that the same is true of certain other teachings on matters of faith and morals which have lately been called into question. The present discussion, however, is limited to the issue of contraception.

At the outset it is important to be quite clear about what is being argued. It is generally acknowledged that *Humanae Vitae* did not propose an *ex cathedra* definition. Many, however, have moved directly from the nondefinitive character of Pope Paul's pronouncement to the conclusion that infallibility is simply not at issue as far as the teaching on contraception is concerned. This overlooks the possibility that Paul VI's non-definitive pronouncement was in fact a reaffirmation of something *already* infallibly taught by the ordinary magisterium. Ford and Grisez argue that this is the case.

Criteria Are Stated

It is also important to be clear about what is *not* being argued in this discussion. Among the questions which are not being considered are whether the moral norm ruling out contraception is part of divine revelation and whether Pius XI proposed an *ex cathedra* definition in *Casti Connubii*. These questions are worth discussing, but they are not discussed here.

Finally, it is important to be clear about what is being assumed in this discussion. The major assumptions are, first, that the Catholic Church does enjoy the charism of infallibility in belief and teaching (though obviously not everything is infallibly believed and taught) and, second, that the ordinary magisterium is exercised infallibly when the conditions set forth by Vatican II are met.

The criteria for an infallible exercise of the ordinary magisterium of the bishops throughout the world are stated by Vatican II in *Lumen Gentium*, 25. The text reads:

Although the bishops individually do not enjoy the prerogative of infallibility, they nevertheless proclaim the teaching of Christ infallibly, even when they are dispersed throughout the world, provided that they remain in communion with each other and with the Successor of Peter and that in authoritatively teaching on a matter of faith and morals they agree in one judgment as that to be held definitively.[1]

An important footnote (no. 40) accompanying this statement cites four previous documents.

Two Things Not Said

An examination of the evolution—what one might call the legislative history—of this text within the conciliar process makes clear two things which the Council specifically is *not* saying here: first, that a strictly collegial act is necessary for an infallible exercise of the ordinary magisterium; second, that such an exercise of the ordinary magisterium can occur only when something divinely revealed is proposed for acceptance with the assent of divine faith. Had the Council said either or both things, it would have sharply limited the possibility of an infallible exercise of the ordinary magisterium of the bishops. In fact, it said neither.

To obtain a clear understanding of the conditions enunciated by Vatican II, it is necessary to look closely at the four documents cited in footnote 40.

The first is a passage from chapter 3 of Vatican I's *Dei Filius:*

Further, all those things are to be believed with divine and Catholic faith which are contained in the word of God, written or handed down, and which the Church either by a solemn

---

[1] The translations of this and all quoted documents whose originals are in Latin are by Ford and Grisez.

judgment or by her ordinary and universal magisterium proposes for belief as divinely revealed.[2]

Dei Filius treats of divine revelation; therefore this solemn teaching concerns matters which are proposed as divinely revealed, to be believed with divine faith. Nevertheless, the passage has a bearing on Vatican II's teaching concerning the infallibility of the ordinary magisterium. It states definitively that it is necessary to believe not only those things which have been defined but also certain things taught by the ordinary magisterium.

Bellarmine Is Cited

Next the note cites a passage added to Vatican I's first schema *De Ecclesia,* namely, a text drawn from Robert Bellarmine. Although the Vatican I document was never completed, the significance of the Bellarmine passage in this context arises from the fact that it is cited by Vatican II to illustrate its own teaching. Bellarmine, rejecting limitations on the Church's infallibility proposed by Protestant authors, wrote:

> Therefore, our view is that the Church *absolutely* cannot err, either in things absolutely necessary [for salvation] or in other matters which she proposes to us to be believed or done, whether expressly included in the Scriptures or not. And when we say, "The Church cannot err," we understand this to apply both to the faithful as a whole and to the bishops as a whole, so that the sense of the proposition, *The Church cannot err,* is this: that what all the faithful hold as of faith, necessarily is true and of faith, and similarly what all the bishops teach as pertaining to faith, necessarily is true and of faith.[3]

---

[2] H. Denzinger and A. Schönmetzer, S.J., *Enchiridion Symbolorum Definitionum et Declarationum de Rebus Fidei et Morum,* ed. 34 (Barcelona: Herder, 1967), 1792 (3011).

[3] J. D. Mansi et al., *Sacrorum Conciliorum Nova et Amplissima Collectio* (Arnhem and Leipzig: H. Welter, 1926), vol. 51, 579C.

Two things must be noted about this. First, Bellarmine refers both
to things which are to be *believed* and to things which are to be
done. Second, he does not limit infallibility to matters explicitly
contained in Scripture or to matters which are absolutely essential
for salvation.

The third document cited is Vatican I's revised schema for
Constitution II, *De Ecclesia Christi*, along with the commentary
by Joseph Kleutgen:

> And so we now define that this very high gift, by which
> *the Church of the living God is the pillar and bulwark of truth* (1
> Tim. 3:15), is placed in it so that neither the faithful as a
> whole in believing nor those who are appointed with the
> power of teaching the whole Church in exercising this office
> can fall into error. Therefore, all those points which in matters
> of faith and morals are everywhere held or handed down as
> undoubted under bishops in communion with the Apostolic
> See, as well as all those points which are defined, either by
> those same bishops together with the Roman Pontiff or by the
> Roman Pontiff speaking *ex cathedra,* are to be held as infallibly
> true.[4]

This is very close to the formulation finally adopted by Vatican II.
Where the schema of Vatican I says "held or handed down as
undoubted," the parallel expression of Vatican II is "to be held
definitively." Both support the view that the ordinary magisterium can infallibly teach things which are not divinely revealed
but which are necessary for the preservation and further understanding of what has been revealed. Kleutgen's commentary discusses
this point at length, arguing among other things that the Church
can infallibly teach truths of the moral order which are neither
explicitly nor implicitly contained in divine revelation.[5]

The fourth text to which footnote 40 refers is *Tuas Libenter* of
Pius IX.[6] In the passage cited Pius makes the point—later made

---

[4] Mansi, vol. 53, 313AB.
[5] Mansi, vol. 53, 324–31.
[6] Denzinger-Schönmetzer, 1683 (2879).

part of Vatican I's *Dei Filius* — that the act of divine faith is not restricted to defined dogmas.

The text of *Lumen Gentium* and the documents cited in the accompanying footnote make it clear that, as articulated by Vatican II, there are four conditions which must be met for an infallible exercise of the ordinary magisterium of the bishops throughout the world. These are: that the bishops be in communion with one another and with the pope; that they teach authoritatively on a matter of faith or morals; that they agree in one judgment; that they propose this as something to be held definitively. Each condition deserves separate consideration.

As the history of the conciliar text makes clear, the first condition — that the bishops be in communion with one another and with the pope — does not mean that they must act in a strictly collegial manner. It is necessary and sufficient that they remain bishops within the Catholic Church.

Bishops Act as Teachers

The second condition — authoritative episcopal teaching on a matter of faith or morals — requires that the bishops be acting in their official capacity as teachers, not merely expressing opinions as individual Catholics or as theologians. As for the subject matter of their teaching — "faith or morals" — the formula has a long history.[7] It is sufficient here to say that nothing in the pertinent documents limits "morals," in the sense intended by Vatican II, in such a way as to exclude specific moral norms, like that on contraception.

The third condition — that the bishops agree in one judgment — identifies universality as a requirement for an infallible exercise of the ordinary magisterium. What is necessary, however, is the moral unity of the body of bishops in union with the pope, not an absolute mathematical unanimity such as would be destroyed by

[7] See M. Bevenot, "Faith and Morals in Vatican I and in the Council of Trent", *Heythrop Journal*, 3 (1962): pp. 15–30.

even one dissenting voice.[8] Furthermore, if this condition has been met for a considerable period of time in the past, it would not be nullified by a future lack of consensus among bishops. To put it another way, the consensus of future bishops is not necessary for the ordinary magisterium to have taught something infallibly or for it to do so now. Otherwise one would be in the absurd position of saying that it is literally impossible that the conditions for an infallible exercise of the ordinary magisterium be met until the end of time: since at any moment in history the consensus of future bishops is an unknown. As for the evidence that this condition has been met, it would seem to lie essentially in this: that in different times, places and cultural circumstances, responding to different challenges, setting the teaching in different intellectual frameworks, and very likely offering different arguments to support it, bishops have repeatedly proposed the same judgment concerning a matter of faith or morals as one to be held definitively.

Faithful Corroborate

It bears noting that, corresponding to the infallibility of the ordinary magisterium in teaching, there is an infallibility of the body of the faithful in believing.[9] The faith and practice of members of the Church whose belief and behavior are in conformity with what is proposed by the ordinary magisterium provide a kind of corroboratory evidence of the universality of its teaching.

The fourth condition—that the bishops propose a judgment of faith or morals to be held definitively—means at least this: that the teaching is not proposed as something optional, either for the bishops or the faithful, but as something which bishops have an obligation to hand on and which Catholics have an obligation to accept. In the case of moral teaching, however, it is unlikely that those proposing the teaching will ordinarily present it as some-

[8] Mansi, vol. 51, 224–25.
[9] Cf. *Lumen Gentium*, 35; *Apostolicam Actuositatem*, 6.

thing to be held intellectually as true; it is more likely that they will propose it as a norm which followers of Christ will try to observe in their behavior.

Vatican II's teaching on the infallibility of the ordinary magisterium is not substantially new. Catholics have always believed the apostles and their successors to enjoy an unfailing charism of truth in proclaiming Christ's teaching. St. Vincent of Lerins as early as the fifth century sought to formulate the conditions for an infallible exercise of the ordinary magisterium.[10] In recent years, however, some have attempted to divide the sources of Catholic belief from the Church's assurance of the truth of what is believed. Thus attention is directed separately to Scripture, to apostolic preaching, to the contemporary magisterium, to philosophical argumentation; and, in each case separately, the question is asked whether the source is able to establish definitively the truth of the teaching in question. If not, the teaching is held to be questionable, perhaps untrue. Vatican II's teaching on the infallibility of the ordinary magisterium is an integrating remedy to the debilitating consequences of this strategy. The teaching of the ordinary magisterium of the past provides a firm ground for the teaching of the Church in the present.

Are Conditions Met?

For purposes of this discussion, however, the crucial question remains: Does the teaching on contraception meet the conditions identified by the Council for an infallible exercise of the ordinary magisterium of the bishops dispersed throughout the world? It does. The demonstration that this is so lies in showing, first, that at least up to 1962 the teaching was universally proposed by Catholic bishops and, second, that it was proposed as something to be held definitively.

[10] S. Vincentii Lirinensis, *Commonitorium Primum,* cc 2 et 23; J. P. Migne, ed., *Patrologiae cursus completus, series latina,* vol. 50, 639–40 and 667–69.

As to the first point, John T. Noonan, Jr., in his historical study of the Church's teaching on contraception, sums up the evidence this way:

> The propositions constituting a condemnation of contraception are, it will be seen, recurrent. Since the first clear mention of contraception by a Christian theologian, when a harsh third-century moralist accused a pope of encouraging it, the articulated argument has been the same. In the world of the late Empire known to St. Jerome and St. Augustine, in the Ostrogothic Arles of Bishop Caesarius and the Suevian Braga of Bishop Martin, in the Paris of St. Albert and St. Thomas, in the Renaissance Rome of Sixtus V and the Renaissance Milan of St. Charles Borromeo, in the Naples of St. Alphonsus Liguori and the Liège of Charles Billuart, in the Philadelphia of Bishop Kenrick, and in the Bombay of Cardinal Gracias, the teachers of the Church have taught without hesitation or variation that certain acts preventing procreation are gravely sinful. No Catholic theologian has ever taught, "Contraception is a good act." The teaching on contraception is clear and apparently fixed forever.[11]

Since Noonan's book was published in 1965, a great many scholars have dealt with this topic and examined the data. None has published evidence to contradict Noonan's point. On the contrary, the evidence shows that, at least until 1962, Catholic bishops dispersed throughout the world universally agreed in their judgment and teaching on the morality of contraception. A review of the writings of theologians officially recognized by the representatives of the magisterium points to the same conclusion: not that the theologians unanimously agree in their principles or their arguments (which no one would expect); rather, they agree that individual contraceptive acts are intrinsically wrong and constitute the matter of grave moral evil.

[11] John T. Noonan, Jr., *Contraception: A History of Its Treatment by the Catholic Theologians and Canonists* (Cambridge, Mass.: Harvard University Press, 1965), p. 6. The author immediately goes on to suggest, however, that the teaching is not in fact fixed forever.

If the teaching was universal, however, was it also proposed to Catholics as something to be held definitively? Several considerations show that it was.

The first consideration is a negative one. No evidence has come to light that anyone proposed this teaching as a private opinion, a probable judgment, or a lofty ideal which there was no blame in failing to achieve. It was proposed instead as an obligatory moral teaching.

What Was Intended?

Second, the teaching is that contraceptive acts are the matter of mortal sin. Third, when in modern times the teaching was challenged from outside the Church, it was repeated with insistence and emphasis. Fourth, the teaching was often proposed as a divinely revealed moral norm. This is not to say that it *is* divinely revealed (a question excluded from this discussion). In this context, rather, the point is significant for the light it sheds on the intention of those proposing the teaching. If, in doing so, they contended that the teaching was divinely revealed, this can only mean that they proposed it as something to be held definitively; they would hardly have done the contrary—i.e., at the same time maintained that the teaching was divinely revealed yet proposed it as something which need not be held definitively.

Having reached this point, it is useful briefly to examine the major statements on contraception by Pius XI, Pius XII and Paul VI and to do so in light of what has been said up to now.

In condemning contraception as a sin against nature, Pius XI appeals to Scripture, to Augustine's exegesis of Genesis 38:9–10, and to the constancy of the Church's tradition. He declares himself to be restating, on behalf of the Catholic Church, something willed by God and pertaining to salvation.[12] Pius XII, officially summarizing the teaching of his predecessor, says he solemnly

---

[12] *Casti Connubii, AAS,* 22 (1930), pp. 559–60.

proclaimed anew the fundamental law concerning the procreative act. He states the matter emphatically: "This teaching is as valid today as it was yesterday; and it will be the same tomorrow and always."[13] Paul VI is less emphatic but no less clear. He says among other things that it would be impossible to accept some conclusions of his Commission for the Study of Problems of Population, Family, and Birthrate because they are not compatible with "the moral doctrine on matrimony, proposed by the magisterium of the Church with constant firmness" (*Humanae Vitae*, 6). He speaks of "the constant teaching of the Church" (*ibid.*, 10 and 11), says the Church by its teaching on contraception "promulgates the divine law" (*ibid.*, 20), and declares the teaching on contraception to be part of the "saving teaching of Christ" (*ibid.*, 29).

Neither Pius XI, Pius XII, nor Paul VI says the teaching on contraception has been proposed infallibly by the ordinary magisterium; but that is not the point. What they do say is not only compatible with this view, but supplies evidence for it.

Thus, a review of the data establishes that the teaching on contraception has been proposed in a manner which meets Vatican II's criteria for an infallible exercise of the ordinary magisterium. The controversy of the last fifteen years does nothing to change this fact, nor, if one accepts the criteria, does it call into question the objectively certain truth of the teaching. It is not the teaching which needs to be rethought but the widely held supposition that the teaching is or could be false.

Noonan Chooses Development

A number of questions and objections will naturally be prompted by this argument. Here it is possible to touch on only a few.

This discussion does not consider the question of whether the Church's teaching on contraception is divinely revealed. Many of those who have handed on the teaching have said explicitly that it

---

[13] "Address to the Midwives," *AAS*, 43 (1951): p. 843.

is, and this fact cannot lightly be set aside. At the same time, for purposes of this discussion, it is conceded that the teaching might not be divinely revealed. Noonan, for example, argues that, in condemning contraception, the Fathers of the Church were not restating primitive teaching but were making a fresh initiative. Supposing for the sake of argument that this is so, this should be viewed as a case of an authentic development of earlier Christian moral doctrine rooted in revelation. Such a view is entirely compatible with the view that the teaching on contraception has been infallibly proposed by the ordinary magisterium.

However, this points to another question. If the Church's teaching is a product of doctrinal development, how can we be certain that we have not been witnessing a further process of development in the controversy over this teaching which has been underway in the Church since 1963? This is the position taken by those, like Noonan, who argue for a "development" by which the Church's teaching would continue to safeguard those human goods which the traditional teaching was meant to safeguard, while making allowance for particular contraceptive acts within a marriage basically oriented to responsible parenthood.

The question of development of doctrine is a large and complex one. There has been authentic development in the Church's teaching on a number of matters, including questions of marital morality. An authentic development of doctrine, however, cannot be one which contradicts what has previously been infallibly taught, understood in the sense in which it was taught. First to say 'A' and then to say 'not-A' does not constitute a development; it is to say contradictory, incompatible things.

It is true that the Church's teaching on contraception defends the values of procreation and the rectitude of marital intercourse while rejecting selfish and hedonistic motives for engaging in intercourse. This, however, is not the whole of the teaching proposed by the ordinary magisterium. Rather, the specific teaching has been that certain acts intended to prevent procreation are in themselves gravely sinful; and it has never been taught that any such acts are good, permissible, or even only venially sinful. It would be extremely difficult, perhaps impossible, to say what values the tradition has always sought to safeguard and what subjective attitudes it has always rejected; but it can be said with certainty that the tradition handed on by the ordinary magisterium condemns contraceptive acts as gravely wrong.

Noonan and others have used the analogy of the Church's teaching on usury to argue that the teaching on contraception can change. Taking interest was once severely condemned and is now permitted. The same sort of change, it is said, could occur in the case of contraception.[14] With respect to the argument advanced here, however, this amounts to begging the question—the question being whether the condemnation of the taking of interest was infallibly proposed by the ordinary magisterium. In fact, it was not.

Scripture and the Fathers of the Church as well as the decrees of councils and popes up to 1450 condemn the taking of interest on loans to the poor and the greed of usurers; but they say nothing about charging interest as such nor do they envisage modern economic conditions in which money markets determine moderate rates of interest.[15] Noonan himself makes the crucial point in discussing scholastic theories of usury:

> Nothing here meets the test of dogma except this assertion, that usury, the act of taking profit on a loan without a just title, is sinful . . . This dogmatic teaching remains unchanged. What is a just title, what is technically to be treated as a loan, are matters of debate, positive law, and changing evaluation. The develop-

[14] John T. Noonan, Jr., "Authority, Usury and Contraception", *Cross Currents,* 16 (Winter 1966): pp. 71–75.

[15] See A. Vermeersch, S.J., "Usury", *The Catholic Encyclopedia,* vol. 15 (New York: Appleton, 1912), pp. 235–38, and the works cited by him; Thomas F. Divine, S.J., *Interest: An Historical and Analytical Study in Economics and Modern Ethics* (Milwaukee: Marquette University Press, 1959), pp. 5–11, 24–35, and 45–64.

ment on these points is great. But the pure and narrow dogma today is the same today as in 1200.[16]

Other objections have been raised and no doubt will continue to be raised which draw analogies with other alleged changes in the moral teaching of the Church. In many cases, the thrust of these objections is either to deny or to limit drastically the infallibility of the Church. As noted at the outset, the charism of infallibility is assumed for purposes of this discussion. Nevertheless, it is helpful to sketch the strategy for responding to such objections.

In some cases it appears that a teaching infallibly proposed has later been changed. On further examination, however, this is seen not to be so, for the change authoritatively admitted by the Church does not contradict what was previously taught if it is understood in the precise sense intended. In other cases, a teaching was proposed by the ordinary magisterium and later contradicted; but it was not in fact proposed infallibly, since it was not solemnly defined nor was it taught by the ordinary magisterium in a manner that met the conditions identified by Vatican II (e.g., some members of the magisterium may have proposed the teaching as something to be held definitively, but this was not the universal teaching of bishops dispersed throughout the world; or all members of the magisterium might have joined in proposing a teaching, yet refrained from proposing it as something to be held definitively, as could well be the case in purely disciplinary or devotional matters).

Outsiders' Views Don't Count

Two final objections should be noted. First, during the controversy over *Humanae Vitae* the dissenting views of Christians outside the Catholic Church were often cited as evidence against the

[16]John T. Noonan, Jr., *The Scholastic Analysis of Usury* (Cambridge, Mass.: Harvard University Press, 1957), pp. 399–400.

teaching. Essentially, however, the views of those who are not in communion with the pope simply do not count with respect to the universality which is a criterion of infallible teaching. This is not to say that they do not share in God's revelation (much less his grace) or that their opinions have no value. It is only to say that their views are beside the point as far as what is at issue here is concerned.

The second, similar objection concerns the fact many Catholics believe contraception to be morally permissible. This is cited as evidence of the *sensus fidelium*. However, this subjective "sense" is not independent of revelation, tradition, and the magisterium, the objective means of communicating God's revelation in and through the Church. On the contrary, the subjective sense of the faithful must be judged for authenticity in reference to the objective teaching of the Church; the *sensus fidelium* is reflected, not in those who dissent from the received teaching of the Church, but in the witness of those who hold to that teaching.

Few Are Negative

At the time of the publication of *Humanae Vitae,* many statements about the encyclical were issued by individual bishops and national hierarchies. Of the statements by individual bishops, the overwhelming majority seem to have been supportive of the encyclical and its teaching. Only a very few were negative in character; fewer still contradicted the teaching of the encyclical. As for statements by episcopal conferences, their teaching also is overwhelmingly consonant with the encyclical, though each statement has its own special character.

> Two points need to be emphasized about the divergences between the bishops' statements. The first is that no hierarchy fails to accept the encyclical. All of them accept it and all of them commend it to their people's acceptance. The second is that such divergences as there are, exist within the broader context

of wholehearted acceptance of the main thrust of the encyclical's teaching on marriage.[17]

At the same time, it must be acknowledged that certain of the hierarchies introduce qualifications with respect to the teaching, in an effort to provide some pastoral mitigation. Most do so without contradicting the teaching. A few, however, go further and, if they do not implicitly contradict it, at least put forward the strange idea that something which is objectively the matter of grave moral evil may also be permissible or even obligatory for some persons. Had there always been such teaching by Catholic bishops, the universality identified by Vatican II as a criterion for the infallible exercise of the ordinary magisterium would not be verified in the case of the teaching on contraception. However, an implicit contradiction of the teaching by some bishops in 1968 takes nothing away from the fact that the conditions identified by Vatican II had already been met in the case of this teaching. It does nothing, in short, to remove the objective certitude of the teaching.

The Aim Is Pastoral

In summary, there is an extremely strong case for the view that the teaching on contraception has been infallibly proposed by the ordinary magisterium. If the issue were something less sensitive and controversial than contraception, there would be little or no doubt on the matter in the mind of anyone who believes the Church to possess the charism of infallibility and accepts the conditions identified by the Council as valid and true. This has extremely important implications for episcopal teaching, theological discussion and pastoral practice. The aim should be, not to impose a harsh new burden on Catholics, but to act in an authenti-

---

[17] Austin Flannery, O.P., "Commentary or Qualification?" in John Horgan, ed., *Humanae Vitae and the Bishops: The Encyclical and the Statements of the National Hierarchies* (Shannon: Irish University Press, 1972), p. 355.

cally pastoral manner to alleviate the confusion about the Church's teaching on contraception which for the past fifteen years has been for so many people an agonizing part of their lives as Catholics.

FURTHER READING

In this essay, Russell Shaw draws upon the work of Rev. John C. Ford, S.J., and Germain Grisez, "Contraception and the Infallibility of the Ordinary Magisterium", *Theological Studies* 39, no. 2 (June 1978): 258–312; this article has since been reprinted as a part of the book coauthored with Grisez, Joseph Boyle, and William E. May, *The Teaching of Humanae Vitae: A Defense* (San Francisco: Ignatius Press, 1988).

See also his *Choosing Well* (Notre Dame, Ind.: University of Notre Dame Press, 1982). Two books coauthored with Germain Grisez may be of interest: *Fulfillment in Christ: A Summary of Christian Moral Principles* (Notre Dame, Ind.: University of Notre Dame Press, 1991) and *Beyond the New Morality* (Notre Dame, Ind.: University of Notre Dame Press, 3rd ed., 1988).

The argument of Ford and Grisez has met with considerable scholarly response, to which Grisez has responded. See pages 155–60 and footnote 38 to chapter five of my *Humanae Vitae: A Generation Later* for a review of this debate and a list of the relevant bibliographical references.

15

CONSCIENCE FORMATION AND THE TEACHING OF THE CHURCH

by
William E. May

Few have done more than William E. May to defend, by explaining, the Church's condemnation of contraception. Perhaps his signing the protest against *Humanae Vitae* promoted by Father Charles Curran was a *felix culpa* for which we should be grateful; his repudiation of that deed seems to have galvanized him to become one of the foremost moral theologians of our times, one of the two laymen serving on the International Theological Commission. Noted for his lucid thought and style and his thorough scholarship, he has addressed nearly every facet of the issue.

Those who dissent from *Humanae Vitae* regularly claim that Catholics are free to dissent from and act contrary to *Humanae Vitae* if their consciences so dictate. In this essay, May demonstrates that this claim is based on a faulty view of conscience. He cites extensively from the documents of Vatican II to show that a Catholic who is acting in good conscience is obliged to obey the teaching of the Church on contraception. Such obedience would not be a violation of one's conscience but a proper use of the conscience as the faculty that leads one to choose correctly in moral matters. After all, the Church speaks for Christ, and Christ promised us that the Church would be a reliable guide in matters of faith and morals. To part company with the Church on the issue of contraception is to part with more than the Church and to dissent on more than this issue; for instance, one invents a new meaning for conscience, and one rejects the teaching of the Church about her own nature.

This article appeared in *Homiletic and Pastoral Review* 87, no. 1 (October 1986): 11–20.

15

CONSCIENCE FORMATION AND
THE TEACHING OF THE CHURCH

by
William E. May

In the final chapter of his massive and important work on fundamental moral theology[1] Germain Grisez calls attention to some significant remarks by Karl Rahner, made in a book published in English translation in 1963, on the subject of a "Catholic" conscience.[2] Because Rahner, in this passage, so ably summarized the received teaching on conscience formation and the teaching of the Church, it will be worth our while to set forth his thought on this subject in some detail.

Rahner began by noting that conscience is the proximate source of moral obligation, and as such must be followed even when it is mistaken. Nonetheless, one must form one's conscience rightly and avoid confusing it with mere subjective inclination. Thus, Rahner insisted,

> Man has a duty to do everything he can to conform his conscience to the objective moral law, to inform himself and let

[1] Germain G. Grisez, *The Way of Our Lord Jesus Christ*, vol. 1, *Christian Moral Principles* (Chicago: Franciscan Herald Press, 1984), p. 878.

[2] Karl Rahner, S.J., *Nature and Grace: Dilemmas in the Modern Church* (London: Sheed and Ward, 1963), pp. 49–69. The title of the relevant essay is "An Appeal to Conscience", and it is found in a part of the book subtitled, "Dangers to Catholicism Today".

himself be taught and make himself prepared to accept (how difficult this often is!) instruction from the word of God, the magisterium of the Church, and every just authority in its own sphere.[3]

Rahner continued by saying that moral maturity means keeping the commandments given to us by God and proclaimed by the Church. He insisted that

> the Church teaches these commandments with divine authority exactly as she teaches the other "truths of the faith," either through her "ordinary" magisterium or through an act of her "extraordinary" magisterium in ex cathedra definitions of the Pope or a general council. But also through her ordinary magisterium, that is, in the normal teaching of the faith to the faithful in schools, sermons, and all the other kinds of instruction. In the nature of the case this will be the normal way in which moral norms are taught, and definitions by Pope or general council the exception; but it is binding on the faithful in conscience just as the teaching through the extraordinary magisterium is. It is therefore quite untrue that only those moral norms for which there is a solemn definition . . . are binding in the faith on the Christian as revealed by God, and must be accepted by him as the rule for his own behavior. . . . When the whole Church in her everyday teaching does in fact teach a moral rule everywhere in the whole world as a commandment of God, she is preserved from error by the assistance of the Holy Ghost, and this rule is therefore really the will of God and is binding on the faithful in conscience, even before it has been expressly confirmed by a solemn definition.[4]

Although an individual conscience can err guiltlessly, one must never, Rahner held, appeal from a norm taught by the Church to one's personal conscience to make an exception for oneself. On this matter Rahner was quite eloquent and forceful, for he wrote:

[3] Ibid., p. 50.
[4] Ibid., pp. 51–53.

If we Christians, when faced with a moral decision, really realized that the world is under the Cross on which God himself hung nailed and pierced, that obedience to God's law also entails man's death, that we may not do evil in order that good may come of it, that it is an error and heresy of this eudaemonic modern age to hold that the morally right thing can never lead to a tragic situation from which in this world there is no way out; if we really realized that as Christians we must expect almost to take for granted that at some time in our life our Christianity will involve us in a situation in which we must either sacrifice everything or lose our soul . . . then there would indeed be fewer Christians who think that their situation requires a special ruling which is not so harsh as the laws proclaimed as God's laws by the Church, then there would be fewer confessors and spiritual advisors who, for fear of telling their penitent how strict is God's law, fail in their duty and tell him instead to follow his own conscience, as he had not asked.[5]

Rahner concluded his essay by observing that in a sinful world God's law seems unrealistic, but the trouble is not with God's law but with the sinful world. The requirements of God's law in no way diminish the freedom of God's children; nor are they in any way opposed to the movements of his Spirit, for one who lives by the Spirit fulfills the commandments in a surpassingly marvelous way and does not violate them. In short, God's commandments expressed in Jesus are still spoken to us today by the mouth of the Church, and our obedience is required whenever we are tempted to disobey.

Thus did Rahner write in an essay composed shortly before Vatican Council II. After the Council, in the aftermath of *Humanae Vitae* Rahner himself explicitly supported dissent from magisterial teaching on moral questions.[6] Again, after the Council, and

---

[5] Ibid., pp. 55–56.

[6] See for instance, Rahner's "Theology and the Magisterium", *Theology Digest* 29.3 (1981): p. 261. A perceptive essay on the "later" Rahner and the harm that dissenting theologians are doing and how to remedy the matter is that of Ralph McInerny, "Whither the Roman Catholic Theologians?" *Center Journal* 1.2 (1982): 85–102.

again after Pope Paul VI's encyclical on marriage and the proper regulation of conception, a group of American theologians asserted that "it is common teaching in the Church that Catholics may dissent from authoritative, noninfallible teachings of the magisterium when sufficient reasons for doing so exist."[7] In 1978 one of those theologians, Charles E. Curran, had formulated as a general thesis the proposition that dissent can be legitimate with respect to ANY specific moral teaching proposed by the magisterium, and among the specific issues on which dissent from "official teaching" is legitimate, he claimed, are contraception, abortion, sterilization, euthanasia, remarriage after divorce.[8]

Avoid Subjective Inclinations

It is accurate, in my opinion, to say that the thesis set forth by Curran in 1978 is shared by many contemporary Catholic moral theologians and laypersons. It is also accurate, in my opinion, to say that this thesis is irreconcilable with the position articulated by Rahner prior to Vatican Council II. Some may conclude that this simply shows that Rahner's earlier position—remember, he himself rejected it later—reflects a "pre-Vatican II mentality," and that Rahner's later view and Curran's thesis are rooted in the teaching of Vatican Council II. This conclusion, however, is far from being self evident; it is possible that it may be quite incorrect. To determine whether or not it can be supported by the teaching of Vatican Council II it is first necessary to examine relevant material from the Council documents.

Here I propose to examine the teaching of Vatican Council II

---

[7] Charles E. Curran, Robert E. Hunt, and the "Subject Professors", with John F. Hunt and Terrence E. Connelly, *Dissent in and for the Church: Theologians and Humanae Vitae* (New York: Sheed and Ward, 1969), p. 26.

[8] Charles E. Curran, "Ten Years Later", *Commonweal* 105 (July 7, 1978): 429. See also his *New Perspectives in Moral Theology* (Notre Dame, In.: University of Notre Dame Press, 1974), pp. 19–22, 41–42, 192–193, 211, 271–276.

on (1) the relationship between personal conscience and the natural law or objective morality, (2) the authority of the Church to teach on moral questions, (3) some very specific moral teachings firmly set forth by the Council, and (4) the insistence of Vatican Council II on the magisterium's authority to propose truths of both faith and morals infallibly and to bind the consciences of the faithful even when the teachings it proposes are not proposed infallibly.

I. CONSCIENCE, THE NATURAL LAW, AND OBJECTIVE MORALITY

The Council respected the dignity of human persons and of personal conscience. Emphasizing this dignity, it declared:

> In the depths of his conscience man detects a law which he does not impose upon himself but which holds him to obedience. Always summoning him to love good and avoid evil, the voice of this law can when necessary speak to his heart more specifically: do this, shun that. For man has in his heart a law written by God. To obey it is the very dignity of man: according to it he will be judged (*Gaudium et Spes,* no. 16).

The law mentioned here is called "natural law" in the Catholic tradition, and in another context the Council taught that the natural law is our participation as intelligent beings in God's divine, eternal law:

> The highest norm of human life is the divine law—eternal, objective, and universal—whereby God orders, directs, and governs the whole world and the ways of the human community according to a plan of his wisdom and love. God makes man a sharer in this his law so that, by divine providence's sweet disposing, man can recognize more and more the unchanging truth (*Dignitatis Humanae,* no. 3).

That the Council Fathers were here invoking the long Catholic tradition on the natural law is unmistakably clear, for at this point they provide a footnote to three texts of St. Thomas Aquinas,[9] including this: "The eternal law is unchanging truth; and everyone somehow knows the truth, at least the general principles of the natural law, even though in other matters some people share more and some less in the knowledge of truth."[10]

Thus there was nothing startling in the Council's teaching that human persons share in the eternal law, and it clearly made its own the Angelic Doctor's view that the natural law is "the participation of the eternal law in the rational creature", who is subject to divine providence in a more excellent way than other creatures insofar as the rational or intelligent creature provides for himself and others and thus shares in divine providence itself.[11]

It is this law that conscience discovers. Conscience is the witness to this law, and through the mediation of conscience, the Council taught, human persons come to know "the dictates of the divine law" and in this way deepen their participation in it.[12]

Continuing its exposition of conscience, Vatican Council II describes it metaphorically in a way earlier adopted by Pope Pius XII.[13] "Conscience is the most secret core and sanctuary of a man. There he is alone with God, whose voice echoes in his depths. In a wonderful way conscience reveals that law which is fulfilled by love of God and neighbor" (*Gaudium et Spes*, no. 16).

---

[9] The three texts of Aquinas to which reference is made are *Summa Theologiae*, 1-2, q. 91, a. 1; q. 93, a. 1; and q. 93, a. 2.

[10] *Summa Theologiae*, 1-2, q. 93, a. 2.

[11] See *Dignitatis Humanae*, no. 3, and *Summa Theologiae*, 1-2, q. 91, a. 2.

[12] For an excellent analysis of this entire subject see John M. Finnis, "The Natural Law, Objective Morality, and Vatican II", in *Principles of Catholic Moral Life*, ed. William E. May (Chicago: Franciscan Herald Press, 1981), pp. 113-50.

[13] Pius XII, radio message on rightly forming the Christian conscience in youth, March 23, 1952. AAS 44 (1952): 271.

Humans Participate

At this point, the Council refers to the precept of love found in the New Testament (cf. Mt. 22:37–40; Gal. 5:14). Implicit is the teaching that the law which Christian love fulfills and must fulfill is the natural law.

Since conscience expresses the natural law, which can be known, at least to some degree, by everyone, and since this law is objective, the Council Fathers affirmed that

> in fidelity to conscience Christians are joined with the rest of mankind in the search for truth, and for the genuine solution to the numerous problems which arise in the life of individuals and from social relationships. Hence the more that a correct conscience holds sway, the more persons and groups turn away from blind choice and strive to be guided by objective norms of morality. (*Gaudium et Spes,* no. 16).

Note that here the Council Fathers speak of a "correct" conscience. When correct, conscience demands that one be reasonable, not arbitrary; that one conform to objective or true norms, not to subjective opinions arbitrarily chosen. But conscience is not infallible. As the Council Fathers observed, "conscience frequently errs from invincible ignorance without losing its dignity". But, they continued, "the same cannot be said of a man who cares little for truth and goodness, or a conscience which by degrees grows practically sightless as a result of habitual sin" (*Gaudium et Spes,* no. 16).

Conscience Witnesses

From these texts it is evident that the Council respected the dignity of moral conscience. Yet it specified the nature of this dignity: the dignity of conscience consists in its capacity to disclose the objective truth about what is to be done, both in

particular assessments and in general norms. Through the mediation of conscience we can come to know objective moral norms
whose truth is a living image of the unchanging truth of God.
This teaching of the Council corresponds to and is indeed an
explicitation of an equally unwavering and even more frequently
repeated conciliar teaching, namely, that human dignity consists
in the capacity to understand, to some extent, what God expects
of us, and then to choose freely to shape our choices and actions
according to that understanding and thereby to relate ourselves to
God in faith, hope, and love.

2. THE AUTHORITY OF THE CHURCH
TO PROPOSE OBJECTIVE MORAL NORMS

It has already been noted that moral conscience, our capacity
to come to know what God requires of us, can be mistaken.
Thus it is necessary for us to instruct or form our conscience,
to seek the truth. In short, if we are to carry out responsibly
our obligation in conscience to seek the truth we have an obligation in conscience to look for the truth where we can reasonably expect to find it. And obviously, as Catholics, who believe
that the Catholic Church is the living body of Christ; we
regard the Church as the LUMEN GENTIUM, God's light to the
people of the world. Thus its teaching on moral questions is
obviously one major source where the Catholic will look in
order to shape and instruct his conscience. And Vatican Council II
was quite insistent and clear on this point, for it taught the
following:

> In forming their conscience the faithful will pay careful atten-
> tion to the sacred and certain teaching of the Church. For the
> Catholic Church is by will of Christ the teacher of truth. It is
> her duty to proclaim and teach with authority the truth which
> is Christ and, at the same time, to declare and confirm by her

authority the principles of the moral order which spring from human nature itself (*Dignitatis Humanae*, no. 14).

The Council, moreover, is very clear in specifying who has the authority, given by Christ, to teach in his name. It makes its own the doctrine firmly set forth at Vatican Council I[14] that the Roman Pontiff, by the institution of Jesus himself, is the successor to Peter as head of the Church (*Lumen Gentium*, no. 18), and it adds to this teaching by saying:

> Just as the role that the Lord gave individually to Peter, the first among the apostles, is permanent and was meant to be transmitted to his successors, so also the apostles' office of nurturing the Church is permanent, and was meant to be exercised without interruption by the sacred order of bishops. Therefore, this sacred Synod teaches that by divine institution bishops have succeeded to the place of the apostles as shepherds of the Church and that he who hears them hears Christ, while he who rejects them rejects Christ and him who sent Christ (*Lumen Gentium* no. 20).

There can then be no question who is authorized to speak in behalf of the whole Church. The authority of Christ himself has been vested in his vicar, the Roman Pontiff, and in the bishops throughout the world when they speak in union with and under the headship of the Pope.

More texts from Vatican Council II could be cited to support what has already been said in this section (cf. e.g., *Dei Verbum*, no. 10), but the passages already cited and referred to suffice to show how firmly Vatican Council II proposes as a doctrine of Catholic faith the truth that Jesus himself has entrusted to the Pope and to bishops in communion with him his own teaching authority, an authority to which the Catholic faithful, including theologians and bishops and popes as members of the Church, must in conscience defer in settling issues of faith and morals.

---

[14] *Enchiridion Symbolorum*, ed. Henricus Denzinger and Adolphus Schönmetzer (32d. ed. Barcelona: Herder, 1963), no. 3058.

3. SPECIFIC MORAL TEACHING OF VATICAN COUNCIL II

Moreover, it is evident from an examination of the texts of the Council that the authority of the Church on moral questions is not limited to the articulation of very general norms of the divine and natural laws—norms that people everywhere can grasp for themselves, such as that good is to be done and pursued and evil is to be avoided.[15] The authority of the Church, i.e., of its divinely instituted magisterium or teaching office, extends to specific questions of morality.

Binding Force of Natural Law

Thus, in speaking of the terrible problem of war, the Council Fathers found it necessary to specify the limits of what one can rightly choose to do in protecting human rights. The Council Fathers first called to the attention of all "the permanent binding force of universal natural law and its all-embracing principles. Man's conscience", the Fathers declared, "itself gives ever more emphatic voice to these principles" (*Gaudium et Spes,* no. 79). Here the Council called attention to general principles or norms of the natural law, principles known to all men through the mediation of conscience. But the Fathers then continued: "Therefore, actions which deliberately conflict with these same principles, as well as orders commanding such actions, are criminal" (ibid.). They then specified actions "deliberately opposed" to the universally binding norms of the natural law, namely, "those actions which by intention exterminate a whole people, nation, or ethnic minority" (ibid.) and "every warlike act which tends indiscriminately to the destruction of entire cities or of extensive areas along with their populations" (ibid., no. 80).

[15] See *Summa Theologiae,* 1–2, q. 94, a. 2.

Here the council Fathers are teaching that from the universally binding *principles* of the natural and divine law one can derive universally binding specific *norms* of morality, norms absolutely proscribing specifiable sorts of human choices and actions. The Council is here clearly teaching that the following specific norm is absolutely binding,[16] with no possible exceptions, namely, *one ought never intend to kill noncombatant populations, even in the waging of a war to defend human rights.*

Again, in a context dealing with the inestimable dignity of the human person and the absolutely inviolable rights of human persons (*Gaudium et Spes,* no. 26), the Council Fathers unequivocally declared:

> Whatever is opposed to life itself, such as any sort of homicide, genocide, abortion, euthanasia, and wilful suicide . . . all these and others of their like are indeed shameful. While they poison human civilization they degrade those who act more than those who suffer the injury (*Gaudium et Spes,* no. 27).

Here several moral absolutes, i.e., nondefeasible specific moral norms, are clearly proposed by the Council. In the judgment of the Council Fathers it is absolutely wrong and contrary to the divine and natural law to choose to kill unborn children, suffering individuals whether dying or nondying, and oneself.

From these texts we can see that the Fathers of Vatican Council II not only taught that there are general moral principles binding all persons but also very specific moral norms derived from these principles that are universally valid and binding on the consciences of all. Nor was this teaching of the Council regarded as surprising when it was given, for the Council Fathers were simply reaffirming longstanding Catholic tradition.

---

[16] Dissenting moral theologians, such as Curran, Richard McCormick, Philip Keane, Timothy O'Connell and others, hold that no specific concrete norms are absolutely true. At most they are "virtually exceptionless". For a critique of this view, see Grisez, *Christian Moral Principles,* chap. 6.

4. THE MAGISTERIUM'S AUTHORITY
TO PROPOSE MORAL TRUTHS INFALLIBLY
AND THE BINDING FORCE OF
NONINFALLIBLY PROPOSED MORAL NORMS

Here it is useful to recall that Rahner had insisted that the Church proposes moral norms infallibly through the "ordinary magisterium". He said that, with respect to moral norms, this would generally be the way in which such truths were taught. A central passage in *Lumen Gentium* makes the very same point, it seems to me. In fact, the passage is almost a paraphrase of the material from Rahner cited at the beginning of this essay. It reads as follows:

> Although the bishops, taken individually, do not enjoy the privilege of infallibility, they do, however, proclaim infallibly the doctrine of Christ on the following conditions: namely, when, even though dispersed throughout the world but preserving for all that amongst themselves and with Peter's successor the bond of communion, in their authoritative teaching concerning matters of faith and morals, they are in agreement that a particular teaching is to be held definitively and absolutely (*Lumen Gentium,* no. 25).

As this passage makes clear (and as Rahner had made clear earlier), it is not necessary for there to be a solemn definition on the part of the magisterium in order for its teachings on faith *and morals* to be infallibly proposed. So long as the teachings of the magisterium are proposed in such a way that they meet the criteria set forth in this passage, they are infallibly proposed.

If we examine specific moral teachings of the magisterium and apply to them these criteria we shall, I am convinced, discover that the substantive core of Catholic teaching on moral issues has been infallibly taught (e.g., the moral norms set forth in Decalogue, as this has been constantly understood by the Church, i.e., as holding as absolutely immoral the killing of the innocent, adultery [or sexual union by a married person with someone other than his or her spouse], fornication, perjury). In 1978 Germain G. Grisez and John Ford, S.J., provided massive evidence that the Church's teaching on the immorality of contraception (an immorality that Pope John Paul II has subsequently sought to show is intimately linked to divine revelation[17]) has been infallibly proposed.[18] Francis Sullivan, S.J., sought to call the analysis of Grisez and Ford into question in a work he authored on the magisterium of the Church,[19] but the weaknesses in Sullivan's presentation have been clearly exposed by Grisez in a patient and painstaking review of Sullivan's work.[20]

Solemn Definition Not Required

Moreover, it is instructive, in my judgment, to note what the American bishops said in their pastoral on peace and war, *The Challenge of Peace.* While noting that in some places (e.g., no first use of nuclear weapons) they were presenting their own considered prudential judgments from which Catholics might, in conscience, disagree, they insisted that in other places they were merely reaffirming the constant, firm teaching of the Church (e.g., the absolute immunity of noncombatants from direct attact, the absolute immorality of killing the innocent), and that such teaching was absolutely binding.[21] They evidently thought that on the issue of innocent human life they were reaffirming what is taught definitively and decisively, i.e., infallibly, by the

[17] Pope John Paul II, *Reflections on "Humanae Vitae"* (Boston: St. Paul Editions, 1984).

[18] Germain G. Grisez and John C. Ford, S.J., "Contraception and the Infallibility of the Ordinary Magisterium", *Theological Studies* 39 (1978): 258–312.

[19] Francis J. Sullivan, S.J., *Magisterium* (New York: Paulist Press, 1984).

[20] Germain G. Grisez, "Infallibility and Specific Moral Norms: A Review Discussion", *Thomist* 49 (1985): 248–87.

[21] *The Challenge of Peace,* A Pastoral Letter of the Bishops of the United States (Washington, D.C.: United States Catholic Conference, 1983), nos. 9, 104.

Church. They evidently concurred with Rahner's judgment that on this matter they were simply teaching what the Church "in her everyday teaching does in fact teach . . . as a commandment of God," and that the Church, by so teaching, is preserved from error by the assistance of the Holy Spirit.

Thus, in my judgment, a very strong case can be (and has been) made that the central core of the Church's teaching on moral questions has been infallibly proposed. Not only was it universally taught from the time of the *Didache* on that abortion, infanticide, adultery, and fornication were absolutely incompatible with Christian moral life, the teaching on the absolute inviolability of human life from direct attack, on the immorality of adultery, and on fornication was clearly set forth in *The Catechism of the Council of Trent,* a catechism prepared to help implement that Council's reform of Catholic life and one used either directly or as a source for catechetical instruction for over 400 years. Thus these moral norms were proposed, and proposed definitively in the "everyday" teaching of the Church throughout the world.

Moreover, Vatican Council II insisted that Catholics are to adhere to the teachings of their bishops on matters of faith and morals even when the teaching proposed by the bishops is not proposed infallibly. The council stressed that "this loyal submission of the will and intellect must be given, in a special way, to the authentic teaching authority of the Roman Pontiff, even when he does not speak ex cathedra" (*Lumen Gentium,* no. 25). Surely new questions of moral import do arise. For instance, today there is the question of artificial insemination by a husband and of in vitro fertilization. There is not, of course, a longstanding Catholic tradition on these issues. But the Roman Pontiffs, in particular Pope Pius XII, have provided clear teaching on these questions, judging that such modes of generating human life are not in conformity with God's intelligent plan for human existence. I believe that this teaching of the Roman Pontiffs can be shown to be true and I have tried to show why in several articles.[22] But

[22] For instance, in " 'Begotten, Not Made': Reflections on the Laboratory

perhaps this teaching has not been proposed in a way that meets the criteria for infallibly proposed teaching as these criteria are set forth in *Lumen Gentium*. Yet it is still authentic teaching of the magisterium of the Church and, as such, a teaching that ought to be given assent by Catholics. Still, it may be that this teaching is not clearly seen to be true in all cases by some. What, then, are they to do? According to approved authors (prior to the Council), individuals might provisionally withhold assent from such teachings when there are sufficient reasons to do so.[23] But withholding assent, while continuing to study the matter with a willingness to accept the magisterial teaching in question, is quite different from actively dissenting.

Authentic Teaching Authority

This paper began by citing extensively from an important essay by Karl Rahner on the formation of a Catholic conscience. His observations on the obligation of Catholics to form their consciences in accordance with the teaching of the Church were simply an exceptionally well articulated presentation of what was, at the time, "received teaching". It clearly recognized that the Church has infallibly proposed specific moral norms and that Catholics are bound, in faith, to accept these as true.

While some contemporary theologians assert that the position set forth by Rahner in a work written prior to the Council reflects a pre–Vatican II mentality and while some contemporary theologians assert that *no* specific teachings of the Church on moral questions have been infallibly proposed, no contemporary theolo-

---

Generation of Human Life", in *Pope John Paul II Lectures in Bioethics,* vol. I, *Perspectives in Bioethics,* ed. Francis J. Lescoe and David Q. Liptak (Cromwell, Ct.: Pope John Paul II Center, 1983), pp. 31–63.

[23] On this see Franciscus A. Sullivan, S.J., *De Ecclesia* (Rome: Gregorian University, 1963), p. 354; L. Salaverri, S.J. *De Ecclesia Christi,* in *Sacrae Theologiae Summa,* vol. I, *Theologia Fundamentalis,* ed. 5 (Matriti: Biblioteca de Autores Cristianos, 1952), p. 708, no. 669.

gians have been able to show that Vatican Council II repudiated the position taken by Rahner. I believe that I have shown that this Council, far from repudiating that position, made it its own.

In our struggle to come to know what we are to do if we are to be the beings God wills us to be we need help. God is our best and greatest friend and he has come to our help. For he has, through his Son, given to us the Church in which his Spirit dwells. It is the house of truth, the light to the nations, the guide for our consciences.

FURTHER READING

Professor May's contributions on this issue are legion: *Sex, Marriage, and Chastity: Reflections of a Catholic Layman, Spouse, and Parent* (Chicago: Franciscan Herald Press, 1981); "Church Teaching and the Immorality of Contraception", *Homiletic and Pastoral Review,* vol. 82, no. 4; (January 1982): 9–18; *Contraception and Catholicism,* Common Faith Tract no. 5 (Front Royal, Va.: Christendom Publications, 1983); "'Begotten, Not Made': Reflections on the Laboratory Generation of Human Life", in *Perspectives in Bioethics,* edited by Ronald D. Lawler and William E. May (New Britain, Conn.: Mariel Publications, 1983); *Contraception, "Humanae Vitae", and Catholic Moral Thought* (Chicago: Franciscan Herald Press, 1984); "Aquinas and Janssens on the Moral Meaning of Human Acts", *The Thomist* 48 (1984): 566–606; "'Begotten, Not Made': Further Reflections on the Laboratory Generation of Human Life", *International Review of Natural Family Planning* 10, no. 1 (Spring 1986): 1–22; "The Sanctity of Human Life, Marriage and the Family in the Thought of Pope John Paul II", *Annales Theologici* 2, no. 1 (1988): 83–97; "Catholic Moral Teaching on In Vitro Fertilization", in *Reproductive Technologies, Marriage and the Church* (Braintree, Mass.: The Pope John Center, 1988), 107–21; "The Moral Methodology of Vatican Council II and the Teaching of *Humanae Vitae* and *Persona Humana*", *Anthropotes* 5, no. 1 (1989): 29–45; *Moral Absolutes: Catholic Tradition, Current Trends, and the Truth* (Milwaukee, Wis.: Marquette University Press, 1989); "'Humanae Vitae', Natural Law and Catholic Moral Thought", *Linacre Quarterly* 56 (November 1989): 61–87; "The Natural Law and Objective Morality: A Thomistic Perspective", in *Principles of Catholic Moral Life,* edited by William E. May (Chicago: Franciscan Herald Press, 1980, 151–90; and with John C. Ford, S.J., Germain

Grisez, Joseph Boyle, Jr., and John Finnis, *The Teaching of Humanae Vitae: A Defense* (San Francisco: Ignatius Press, 1988). See the entry under John Finnis' essay for a listing of articles that contest some points of May's moral analysis.

There are a multitude of essays on *Humanae Vitae* and conscience. Two ecclesial documents may be of particular interest: "Statement on the Formation of Conscience", by the Canadian Bishops (Boston: Daughters of St. Paul, 1974), and "Conscience and Morality", by the Irish Episcopal Conference (Boston: Daughters of St. Paul, 1980).

16

THE PROLIFERATION OF POPULATION PROBLEMS

by
Herbert F. Smith

The fear of overpopulation is one of the most prominent justifications for contraception. To most, it is unthinkable and irresponsible to suggest that contraception is immoral, for without it they think we would soon deplete the world's resources. Some seem to think that overpopulation is such a great threat that it does not matter whether contraception is moral or not; on purely utilitarian grounds they think it is necessary to control population growth. The implications of this position escape some, for few would think that *any* means—moral or not—ought to be used to control population; one would hope that recommendations to kill everyone over a certain age or under a certain IQ rating would be met with horror. But if morality of means is of indifference, where do we draw the line in population control measures? China, after all, has a policy of forced abortions after the first child is born to a couple.

But perhaps the need for drastic population control measures is not as desperate as is generally believed. It is not widely known that many experts in population argue that there is no universal problem with overpopulation. They note that many industrialized nations are not reproducing themselves and face shortages of population in the very near future; some are already suffering from too few children fueling the economy. They also note that the world's resources can easily feed the existing and the projected population for years to come; they argue that most starvation, illness, and suffering attributed to overpopulation are more properly attributed to bad planning and poor distribution of available goods. Moreover, in some countries of Africa, death from AIDS is predicted to decimate the population to the point that population control measures are no longer desirable.

Herbert Smith handily reviews the arguments of the experts who challenge those who think there is a dangerous population explosion. He notes how methods of natural family planning have been ignored as suitable means for controlling the population.

This article appeared in *Homiletic and Pastoral Review* 87, no. 5 (February 1987): 11–23.

16

THE PROLIFERATION OF
POPULATION PROBLEMS

by
Herbert F. Smith

PART ONE: EVALUATING FACTS,
FICTIONS AND FUTURES

Is a population explosion in progress? Or massive famines looming? Why are we so often left by the media with the impression of mixed and confusing signals? The answer is that world population problems have splintered. They involve trends, the arresting of trends, and countertrends. The sea of people is awash in diverse currents not susceptible to facile reporting. To illustrate: Kenya's growth rate is 4.1 percent. By the year 2,000 its current population of 19.37 million is projected to very nearly double.[1] On the other hand, in many developed nations of the west, the population danger has inverted. A population implosion has begun. Germany's 1985 population of 61 million is projected to fall below 50 million in 35 years.[2]

This flurry of movement and change leaves theory and practice

[1] *Statistical Abstracts of the United States* 1985 (Washington, D.C., Department of Commerce, Bureau of the Census, 1985), pp. 840, 842.
[2] "World Population: Toward the Next Century" (Washington, D.C., Population Reference Bureau, 1985), p. 9.

and all but the most splintered elements of reporting lagging behind the complex population realities. Outdated theses and policies are still being propounded and still in charge. In the U.S., Zero Population Growth people remain active after years of less-than-replacement fertility rate[3] has raised the red flag of social and economic dangers down the line.

This report considers the historic changes that landed us on new shores. It quotes statistics, reports the hopeful new factors in the population equation, and cites the problems still to be resolved. Since the solution to the population problems hinges on methods of fertility control, an under-reported phenomenon in that sphere will be surveyed.

Though Clergyman-Professor Robert Thomas Malthus is commonly credited with originating the thesis that the population grows geometrically, that thesis predates him. Long before he did his work the idea that population progressed geometrically was propounded by Nichols, Scheucher, Wildeburg, Euler, Whiston, Hume, Wallace and others.[4] Malthus, in his Preface to the Second Edition, acknowledges drawing on Hume and Wallace.[5]

The ancients—Plato and Aristotle among them—were already worrying about the population explosion. Yet world population did not reach 300 million until about one A.D. Some 1600 years later, the population had less than doubled, tallying 510 million in 1650. If, since 1650, the population had doubled every 25 years, and progressed at the geometrical rate, by 1950 it would have been over 2,000 billion, instead of the actual 2.5 billion.[6]

---

[3] *Statistical Abstracts of the United States* 1985, p. 63, chart no. 84.

[4] "History of Population Theories," Population Division, United Nations, Ed: Charles B. Nam (New York, *Population and Society,* 1968), p. 69.

[5] Rev. Prof. Malthus, *An Essay on the Principle of Population and Its Effects on Human Happiness* (London, Ward, Locke, 1890), p. xxxv.

[6] *The World Almanac and Book of Facts* 1985 (New York, Newspaper Enterprise Association, 1985), p. 501.

A Premise Proved Simply Wrong

Neither Malthus nor his predecessors claimed that the population does in fact grow geometrically; they all recognized repressive factors. The sixteenth century Italian, Giovanni Botero, a true pre-Malthusian, erroneously held that already for three millennia or more the supply of food and the population had remained constant— presumably meaning that the population had risen to the point where it was held in check by the limited natural resources.[7]

The real Malthusian call-to-arms in the year 1798 was the alarming thesis that, while unchecked population growth proceeds at a geometrical rate, "the means of subsistence, under circumstances the most favorable to human industry, could not possibly be made to increase faster than in an arithmetical ratio."[8] Thus people would multiply at a rate 1, 2, 4, 8, 16, 32, while food only at the rate, 1, 2, 3, 4, 5, 6.

In this basic premise of his whole thesis, Malthus was simply wrong. World population rose from 1.6 billion in 1900 to 2.51 billion in 1950 to 3.8 billion in 1970 to 4.6 billion in 1982.[9] Yet the food supply has not only kept up with this near-geometrical increase; it has exceeded it.

One of the great ironies is that in 1848, exactly 50 years after Malthus published his shattering thesis that production could not keep pace with unrepressed population growth, Marx and Engels, in *The Communist Manifesto,* propounded a dramatically opposed specter of overproduction run riot: "Modern bourgeois society with its relations of production, exchange and property, a society that has conjured up such gigantic means of production and exchange, is like the sorcerer, who is no longer able to control the powers of the nether world whom he called up by his spells." The authors maintained that this bourgeois society could control

[7] *Population and Society,* p. 68.
[8] Malthus, *op. cit.,* p. 6.
[9] *The World Almanac and Book of Facts 1985,* p. 501.

the unloosed jinni of productivity only by "enforced destruction of a mass of productive forces . . . and by the conquest of new markets. . . . "[10]

According to U.N. statistics, world food production is growing about one percent faster than population, and the production of animal protein increases at twice that rate. Contrast this with the 1960s doomsday prediction of Erlich in *The Population Bomb,* that "In the 1970s and 1980s hundreds of millions will starve to death in spite of any crash programs embarked on now." (Erlich also makes the statement, "You see, Lake Erie is dead."[11] To the Buffalo-born author, this is a classic example of two premature burials!)

The malnutrition and outbreaks of starvation that exist today are written neither in the stars nor the limits of earth's resources. They result in wars, social injustices, and general political incompetence or malfeasance. The expansion of the Green Revolution to the globe, bringing even such former importing giants as China and India close to food self-sufficiency, has left the United States with bulging surpluses that have nowhere to go.[12]

Wrong in his thesis about the relation of population growth to productivity, Malthus propounded a second grave and damaging error. In his 1798 work, he maintained that, since only misery or vice would curb population growth (vice included contraception and abortion), attempting to ease the suffering of the poor by social programs merely led to a higher birth rate that redoubled human suffering. Today there is extensive evidence to the contrary: The poorer the family, the larger the number of children—its only form of "social security" in many countries.

On the basis of his theory, Clergyman Malthus opposed the socially beneficial "Poor Laws," and, according to the Encyclopedia Brittanica, "For a century his theory was used by economists

[10] *Essential Works of Marxism,* ed: Arthur P. Mendel (New York, Bantam Books, 1965), pp. 18–19.

[11] Dr. Paul R. Ehrlich, *The Population Bomb,* revised edition (New York, Ballantine Books, 1971), pp. xi, 39.

[12] "Exports of Grain Decline", *Philadelphia Inquirer* (Sept. 1, 1985).

and policy makers to justify laissez-faire and oppose efforts toward social or economic reform."[13]

A Problem Exists Only in Theory

What is the world population prognosis today? It is in considerable disarray. Population theories have been eclipsed by a flurry of new developments which require examination to manifest the tendentiousness of some theories, and the tentativeness of most. A world-wide population problem has never yet existed except in theory. In our time existing problems have splintered into pockets with contrary characteristics, as has been mentioned, and as statistics below will show. Family planning and world planning remain necessary, but within a different set of parameters than Malthus envisioned. It is necessary here to treat of those new parameters.

Several developments of this century have, on the one hand, multiplied the subsistence factor for the support of human population, and on the other introduced new population checks.

Under the category of "subsistence factor multiplication" must be listed the scientific, industrial, and agricultural revolution. Malthus' economic pessimism, in part a reaction to wooly-headed optimists like Rousseau, has been brushed aside by history. Even many of Malthus' early critics argued that, in the forseeable future, population growth would be matched by a proportionate *per capita* subsistence output.

This was an underestimate. With the advent of mechanization and automation, person-hours have fallen steadily in proportion to output. By the forties, in the U.S., non-productive workers exceeded productive workers, releasing a flood of people into research and human care occupations. This whole configuration attacked and reduced the human misery which Malthus held to be inevitable.

Most dramatically significant of all, perhaps, was the Green

[13] *Encyclopedia Brittanica,* 15th ed., vol. II, s.v. *Malthus.*

Revolution. High-yield seed, breeding techniques, chemical fertilizer, irrigation, and machine-intensive farm labor have shrunken the number of farmers even as population soared. None of the early demographic theoreticians seem to have envisioned this application of research and technology to the enhancement of food production. It is a cogent instance of the difficulty of predicting future global population limitations.

Green Revolution Debunks Theories

The eventual rise of social concern and labor unions in many western countries brought a more equitable distribution of what labor produced, again reducing rather than escalating the misery which the clergyman saw as inevitably accompanying growing population.

Now, a look at old and new population checks. To the two checks on population noted in his 1798 work (misery and vice), Malthus later added a third: self-restraint. Since, at that time, and until 1930, the Protestant ranks stood with the Catholics in considering contraception a vice, Malthus did not envision family planning, but did advocate late marriage, as was common in Ireland, to reduce family size and enable a man better to support his family. (Yet in Ireland late marriages did not yield small families.)

Since then, the contraceptive revolution has occurred. Nature's own arrangement to assure reproduction is widely being rendered sterile. The ultimate consequences are unforseeable. Already, in some countries, there is a birth dearth.

Everywhere that contraception has gone, abortion has followed. In ten years, world-wide abortions have mounted. In the U.S., there were 1.57 million legal abortions in 1982.[14] To see their true impact, one must remember that preventing or eliminating children by contraception/abortion eliminates also their children and their children's children.

[14] *Statistical Abstracts of the United States 1985*, p. 68.

A third element in this triad of population checks is the great influx of women into the labor force and the tandem feminist movement. Self-supporting, career-oriented women are slow to marry; when they marry they bear fewer children.

The sexual revolution has been attended and facilitated by the decline of moral authority. The decline advanced when government parted company with the morality of the people in such policies as the Supreme Court's 1973 Roe vs Wade decision legalizing abortion. It continued when many people parted company with their religious leaders on this and other moral issues. These developments are perhaps the most fluid and indeterminate elements in the current status of the population prognosis. No one has seen the last of either the abortion or the contraceptive controversies.

One other new factor should be mentioned here, though it will be treated below: the development of natural family planning (NFP). While it has not yet attracted vast numbers of users, the respected NFP-surveyor and researcher Dr. Hanna Klaus reports that it is the fastest-growing reversible method of family planning.

The preceding developments illuminate the problem of prognosticating the future of a world population that is splintering into pockets with contrary characteristics.

In its *Statistical Yearbook 1982,* the U.N. gives the annual rate of world population increase for the years 1975–80 as 1.7 percent.[15] This is a far-lower rate of increase than prevailed in the preceding thirty years, and the rate continues to drop. During the 1975–80 period, the U.S. rate of increase was only one percent. However, U.S. *Statistical Abstracts* 1984 reports that the fertility rate for 1975–80 dropped to the point where it is 6.3 percent below replacement level.[16] If this rate continues, the native-born U.S. population, as it ages, will eventually shrink at the rate of 6.3 percent per generation in a geometrical degression.

Already some years ago, Dr. Charles Westhoff of the Princeton

---

[15] *Statistical Yearbook* 1982 (New York, United Nations, 1985), p. 6.
[16] See n. 3, above.

Office of Population Research declared that the U.S. may have to pay people to maintain the population.[17] Commentator Ben Wattenberg pointed out the ominous effects of a shrinking population on the future of Social Security, and observed that "The primitives were right: The propagation of the species is our real Social Security."[18] Reversing the trend, however, is compounded by a new difficulty: surgical sterilization for contraceptive purposes of 38.9% of wives or husbands has raised to 47.3% the number of U.S. couples of childbearing age who cannot bear children.[19]

Propagation Is Social Security

This phenomenon of non-replacement fertility is not unique with the U.S. The March/April, 1981 issue of *Family Planning Perspectives* states that "fertility rates in Belgium, Denmark, France, Great Britain, Norway and the United States have dropped below replacement level."[20] Some have dropped far below. Today, in France, the government provides incentives to promote births. *U.S. News & World Report* (Dec. 6, 1982) heralded a steep decline in the Russian birth rate. The problem is further aggravated by the fact that only a high birth rate among the non-Russian minorities keeps the level from sinking lower. By 2,000 A.D. 40 percent of Russian eighteen-year olds will be Moslems.[21] The Russians too have invoked fertility incentives. In most of the developed western countries the population bomb is imploding.

Ben Wattenberg, in a 1982 article "In 'Suhtlam,' Population

---

[17] "U.S. Birth Subsidy Eyed in Future", *Philadelphia Inquirer,* (Dec. 23, 1982).

[18] "Social Security Solution: Children." *Philadelphia Inquirer,* (Dec. 23, 1982).

[19] *Statistical Abstracts Of The United States* 1985, p. 66, No. 98.

[20] *Family Planning Perspectives,* March/April, 1981, p. 94.

[21] "The Population Time Bomb That Kremlin Faces" *U.S. News And World Report* (Dec. 6, 1982), p. 28.

Declines" (Suhtlam is Malthus backwards) presents a geometrical progression in reverse. Using figures from demographer Carl Haub, he instances West Germany: if its present low birth rate should continue its current population of 62 million would shrink to under 40 million by the middle of the next century, to 9 million by the end of the twenty-first century, and to a quarter of a million by the 25th century.[22] Note that these are not predictions, but simple projections of what is presently going on.

This writer contacted demographer Haub, and learned that his projection of the German population was based on a fertility rate of 1.5. Since then, the fertility rate has dropped to 1.3. The German population degression is accelerating, despite the fact that pro-natalist measures are in place. Haub points out that this raises historic new questions. "Will there be massive population losses in developed countries?" he asks, "Or will a new era of unanticipated growth eventually begin?"[23]

France Will Be a Moslem Country

A release this year by Human Life International updates the German picture: With abortions nearing the number of children born, there were 5.7 percent fewer children in the schools in 1985 than 1984; of those, more than one-third, in the large German cities, are children of the five million Moslem foreigners.[24] France presents a similar picture. It has been calculated that before the middle of the twenty-first century, France will be a Moham-medan country.

The contrary picture is presented by a country like India. That

[22] "In 'Suhtlam', population declines", *Philadelphia Inquirer,* (Nov. 16, 1982).

[23] Carl Haub, "Beyond the Demographic Transition: The Case of West Germany" (Intercom, May/June, 1982), pp. 9–10.

[24] "Special Report No. 14" (Washington, D.C., Human Life International, undated, but issued in Spring, 1985), p. 3.

nation is launching an intense population control program. If goals are met, its population will reach nearly one billion by the year 2,000. If goals are not met, it could reach 1.3 billion by 2010, exceeding China.[25]

India and China, Africa and Latin America are the regions which suffer the greatest demographic pressures. Until the world's nations recognize the demographic problems of these areas as their problems, and see that the hope of a solution lies in the world as a whole, there will be no humane solution.

It is not enough to decry the forced sterilizations in India under Indira Gandhi, and the forced abortions current in China. Population pressures in these lands are so great that foreign protests will be futile without foreign aid.

The historic—and certainly archaic—underdevelopment of the common bond of humanity on the international political scene has allowed these problems to grow. In the Second Draft of the National Conference of Catholic Bishops' *Pastoral Letter on Catholic Social Teaching and the U.S. Economy,* there is reference to the "800 million people living in absolute poverty" on the world scene, and the "450 million malnourished or facing starvation" (p. 2).

Until nations learn the ethics of global obligation, and cooperate seriously to fulfill them, there will be, in many lands, vast pockets of human distress. That is both a present fact and a prognosis.

[25] "India Steps up Efforts to Curb Its Soaring Birthrate", *Philadelphia Inquirer* (Oct. 27, 1985), 11A.

PART TWO: KEY POPULATION QUESTIONS:
TOWARD SOLUTIONS

This report on the complex global population problems has lined up the basic data for facing the key question: what does the future hold? An intelligent prognosis, using U.N. and U.S. Government statistics and estimates, is presented in the The Population Reference Bureau's booklet, "World Population: Toward The Next Century." The mid-1985 world population of 4.85 billion is growing at an estimated rate of 1.7 percent per year, down from the peak of 2 percent in 1965, and still dropping.[26] The median U.N. prediction is that the world population could stabilize at 10.5 billion people in the year 2110 if present trends and policies continue. Even in most of the developing countries, fertility is already falling. *Statistical Abstracts Of The United States* 1985 projects a drop in world growth rate from 1.7 to 1.4 in the next 20 years.[27]

What of the problems of feeding, employing, housing and schooling this gigantic population? First, some general observations on the malady of scare tactics, and then some sober particulars. Dr. Paul Erlich's *The Population Bomb* cried terror in an irresponsible manner. His projection of a famine explosion was belatedly discredited by a statement from the U.N.'s World Food and Agricultural Organization (F.A.O.). That agency had itself made unsubstantiated claims that half the developing countries were malnourished. But in 1971, the F.A.O.'s Dr. Pawley declared it was time to desist from claiming that a supposed global inability to provide food was an argument for limiting population. Such claims, he conceded, were worse than erroneous. They were counterproductive, since experts like (agricultural economist) Colin Clark could readily show to the contrary. Dr. Pawley went on to say that the world food production "could easily be increased to

[26] Elaine M. Murphy, "World Population: Toward the Next Century" (Washington, D.C., The Population Reference Bureau, 1985), p. 1.

[27] *Statistical Abstracts of the United States* 1985, p. 838, no. 1474.

50 times its present level," which "would suffice to feed 36 billion people."[28]

Demographers like Colin Clark have forced a new honesty into the theorizing and debating by showing with cold facts that the impossibilities were in the minds of the theorists, not in the resources of the planet. What is required to nourish the projected population is the will and cooperation to do it.

Do those qualities exist? In the summer of 1984, the F.A.O. released a food study report briefly in the January, 1985 issue of *Population Today*. The study approaches the problem with realism by asking the right questions; not, can the world feed itself, but can the burgeoning-population countries feed themselves, singly and collectively? It finds that, even with low technology and investment, the less-developed countries can, as a whole, support their Year 2,000 projected populations, with a 50 percent margin to spare. But the F.A.O. stated that this finding depends on many factors, such as massive exchanges of food and laborers between the 117 countries tabulated. In general, trade and international cooperation would have to exceed by far what takes place today.[29]

Concretely the Issue Is Money

What is finally surfacing in the demographic debate is the will to name if not to face the tough issue, which is not in any near future time an inadequate globe but an inadequate use of human resources and international cooperation. Trade, development assistance, and global concern are all necessary. The alternative may well be starvation, turmoil and war.

In still more concrete terms, the issue is money. People will need food and other subsistence commodities. Will they have the

---

[28] Quoted from Colin Clark, *Population Growth: The Advantages* (Santa Monica, CA, Life Quality Paperback, 1975), pp. 35–36.

[29] "World Food News Report", Population Today, Jan., 1985, p. 2.

money to pay for them? To push the matter further, the issue is enterprise. The world resources, the need, and the potential wage earners and market will be there. Will businessmen hazard putting them together, and will governments triumph over the administrative ineptness and corruption that block the way?

Of special interest to us is the U.S. population projection. Fortunately, we now have, from the U.S. Department of Commerce, Bureau of Census, *Projections of the Population of the United States by Age, Sex, and Race: 1983 to 2080* (issued May, 1984). There are three estimates. The high estimate, which assumes a total fertility rate of 2.3 children per woman (much higher than the current 1.8), projects a 2080 population of 453.4 million. The middle estimate, which assumes a fertility rate of 1.9, projects 310.76 million. The low estimate, which assumes a fertility rate of 1.6 children per woman (lower than the current 1.8, but higher than Germany's 1.3), projects a 2080 population of 223.8 million, which is lower than our current population of 233.7 million.[30] The best guess is that the reality will fall somewhere between the low and middle estimate.

The hysteria over population growth has too long tabooed the discussion of one crucial factor in the population debate. Unhappily, the otherwise-commendable booklet mentioned above "World Population: Toward The Next Century", abides by the taboo. In answering the question, "What is the impact of rapid population growth?" the booklet catalogs only *disadvantages.* Yet human resources are the key to unlocking all resources. This populous century has afforded leaps into new realms by unlocking the power of the atom, the secrets of the living cell, the way to the Green Revolution, the power of the computer, and the path to the planets.

"Leisure is the basis of culture," and every worthwhile idea or invention of one person can—and often did—enrich all the earth's people present and future. In that sense, each of us has 4.8 billion

[30] *Projections of the Population of the United States by Age, Sex, and Race: 1983 to 2080* (Washington, D.C., U.S. Department of Commerce, Bureau of the Census, May 1984), p. 17.

servants at work. Yet the view of what a growing population means is commonly presented only as a nightmare. In the real world, the burgeoning population is fashioning the materials to build a dream. People flock to the cities because they sense this, and some experience it. Population growth is not only a problem and a threat but a promise. People like Teilhard de Chardin, Colin Clark and Robert L. Sassone had the vision to insist on that long ago.

One of the brightest comets to rise from the outburst of creativity in recent decades is natural family planning (NFP). Without the moral, monetary, psychological or "Suhtlam" expense of contraception, sterilization and abortion, it provides both family planning and population control. Requiring far less restraint than the Malthusian idea of late marriage, it effectively subserves the same end.

NFP Rises as the Brightest Comet

The heart of modern NFP is the Billings Ovulation Method. Where the old calendar-rhythm method was based on the theory that past menstrual cycles can predict the length of future ones, NFP "reads" the present cycle directly. The only "calendar" the woman needs is her own body. Three signs—changing mucus, temperature, and condition of the cervix—signal approaching fertility and, in several days, its cyclic eclipse. Thus the couple can harmonize the marital act with her cycle of fertility in such a way as to either avoid or achieve pregnancy. In each cycle, this method provides two non-fertile periods during which intercourse will not result in conception: one after menstruation and before ovulation; the other after ovulation and before menstruation.

Both method and user effectiveness are reported as higher than certain contraceptives. Planned Parenthood's prestigious biostatistician Christopher Tietze reported at a 1970 meeting that the temperature method of NFP was 99 percent reliable (higher than most contraceptives). One spokesman claims that Tietze has changed his mind, but a World Health Organization study, and a number of other studies tabulated by Dr. Hanna Klaus show comparable results.[31] However, as in other methods, effectiveness depends on proper use. Recurrent denials of NFP effectiveness have less to do with facts than with the warfare between the proponents of natural vs artificial methods.

Mother Teresa, Nobel Peace Prize winner for her work with the poor in Calcutta, reports that her NFP program in India prevented 1.1 million unwanted births in that country.[32]

Even the popes have stepped into the picture of family planning and population control. The urging of popes from Pius XII to John Paul II has inspired medics and researchers like the Doctors Billings to engage in the most thorough research of a woman's fertility cycle ever undertaken. They have achieved fertility control breakthroughs that will certainly prove to be one of the most significant and far-reaching discoveries of the twentieth century.

Pope John Paul II has repeatedly and insistently urged the development and teaching of NFP. In his Apostolic Exhortation on the Family, he writes that "authentic ecclesial pedagogy displays its realism and wisdom only by making a tenacious and courageous effort to create and uphold all the human conditions . . . indispensable for understanding and living the moral value and norm . . . But the necessary conditions also include knowledge of the bodily aspect and the body's rhythms of fertility. Accordingly, every effort must be made to render such knowledge accessible to all married people and also to young adults before marriage

[31] *Natural Family Planning: A Review* by Dr. Hanna Klaus, *Obstetrical and Gynecological Survey,* vol. 37, no. 2 (1982), pp. 126–50; the 1985 reprint includes a brief report on the WHO study; "Planned Parenthood Eyes the Future", *National Catholic Register,* Dec. 7, 1980.

[32] "The Billings Ovulation Method of Birth Regulation" (World Organization Ovulation Method Billings, undated flyer), p. 1.

through clear, timely and serious instruction and education given by married couples, doctors and experts."[33]

The seriousness of the Catholic Church's will to promote family planning is stressed by the 1981 Vatican complaint to the U.N. Population Commission that it too often overlooks or ignores NFP in its birth control projects.[34]

Both the U.N. and the U.S. government are lending support to NFP, for not only is it a method which all major religions hold to be moral, but even the financial aspect makes it attractive. One estimate is that world contraceptive costs could escalate to 30 billion dollars a year. John Kippley, in the Couple to Couple League Newsletter (Jan/Feb 1983) calculates that an average couple using NFP for thirty years would expend from $64 to $209; use of condoms would range from $1,426 to $4,320; of diaphragm and foam, $5,100.[35] The economy of NFP is of special importance in the third world.

NFP Beats Competitors

The advantages of NFP can be sorted into several categories. In terms of user effectiveness, it is more reliable than currently widely-used methods like the condom. In terms of health, it is free of the dangers associated with most other methods. In terms of low monetary costs, it has no equal. In terms of moral acceptability, it alone is approved by all major religions. Further, user couples tend to grow in respect for fertility and marriage and the role of parenthood. In terms of intercourse, it is both physically and psychologically pleasing because it does not interfere with the natural act. Finally, it is the one method which serves both to

[33] Pope John Paul II, *On the Family* (Washington, D.C., United States Catholic Conference, 1981), pp. 30–31.

[34] "Vatican Asks for More NFP", *National Catholic Register*, (Feb. 15, 1981).

[35] The Couple to Couple League Newsletter, Jan.–Feb., 1985, p. 1.

avoid and to plan—and in the case of low fertility, enhance the possibility of—conception.

Written large, NFP is natural population control. Its regrettably slow dissemination is due to two factors: bias and abstinence.

Bias exists in both the people and the media. Among the people it originates in equating NFP with the old rhythm method —an error in knowledge and judgment. The media have contributed to this ignorance, possibly because of their own, and probably also because of a lack of faith in, and consequent repression of news about, a method which is considered untrustworthy because its trust is lodged not in devices but people.

That the media are uncooperative is evidenced by their persistence in calling NFP "the rhythm method" more than a decade after the names has been changed. In no other field is such remissness shown in changing terminology to reflect new developments. These biases are an aggravating impediment to the thousand-plus NFP Centers in the U.S. As this author wrote to one paper that published a shoddy and inaccurate Associated Press article which equated NFP with the rhythm method and quoted a pseudo-pundit who called it a hoax: "The hoax is to talk about rhythm at all. No one is teaching it."

Abstinence is another matter. Some ten days of sexual abstinence is required during the fertile period. Sexually active couples not practiced in self-control can find the adjustment difficult. However, the rewards of a cyclic "week of honeymoon and week of marriage" have proved attractive to many married couples, and that, along with several advantages cited above, is propagating the method. NFP is gaining ground the hard, grass roots way, but like that "dumb ox," St. Thomas Aquinas, its voice will be heard round the world.

Is there a population problem? No, there are population problems. In some areas of the world, the fertility rate is too high to be sustained without great misery; in China, the inhuman effort to animal-farm the population is inflicting worse miseries than those of overpopulation. On the other hand, the case of China underscores the error of neglecting the issue too long. In still other cases, the Malthusian nightmare has yielded to the dismal phenomenon of prospective self-inflicted genocide.

Malthus and his theories have been badly mauled by the centuries. As already indicated, the thesis for which he is so often evoked, that population growth is geometrical, did not originate with him. His theory that geometrical population growth goes in tandem with arithmetic productivity growth has been toppled by history, along with his contention that population growth inescapably depresses the standard of living.

We Must Revise Alarming Solutions

His apparent fear that vice (contraception and abortion) would be employed to lower fertility rates is the most ignored and rejected—and most accurate—of his major theses. It may yet find an acceptable alternative in NFP.

There was a time to awaken to the potentially disastrous population problem. Malthus sounded the alarm, and gradually the world awoke. Now is the time to be alarmed by the nature of the "solutions."

Some day the global village may find there really is a worldwide population problem. For the present, the problem resides in individual nations and families, and it is well to observe the editorial remark of the Wall Street Journal that "population growth has fallen fastest where the economies have grown the fastest. And those countries are the ones that have allowed their people, including their poor people, the most economic freedom."[36] But if free economies have produced both abundance and birth control, they have also produced in some countries a population shrinkage which is not likely to be reversed without a strenuous effort to recover moral fibre. The impetus to family planning and population control needs to be preserved, the means and degrees examined and revised.

[36] "The People Peril" (*Wall Street Journal*, editorial of Jul. 20, 1984).

FURTHER READING

For debunking of the view that there is a universal population problem, see, for instance, Jacqueline Kasun, *The War Against Population: The Economics and Ideology of Population Control* (San Francisco: Ignatius Press, 1988); P. T. Bauer, *Equality, the Third World, and Economic Delusion* (Cambridge, Mass.: Harvard University Press, 1981); and the works of Julian Simon, *The Economics of Population Growth* (Princeton, N.J.: Princeton University Press, 1977); *The Ultimate Resource* (Princeton, N.J.: Princeton University Press, 1981); "Too Many Trees? Too Few People? A Non-Catholic Economist Says the Pope Has It Wrong", *Crisis* 9, no. 2 (February 1991): 19–22. For information about the population control policy of China, see Steven W. Mosher, *Broken Earth: The Rural Chinese* (New York: The Free Press, 1983).

PART SIX

Contraception and Natural Family Planning

17

CONTRACEPTION AND
NATURAL FAMILY PLANNING

by
Joseph M. Boyle

Since contraception and natural family planning both enable couples to plan their family size and to limit the number of children that they have, many think that there is no moral difference between them; they think if contraception is immoral, so, too, must be natural family planning; if natural family planning is moral, so, too, must be contraception. In this essay Joseph Boyle, a noted moral philosopher in the Catholic tradition, reviews what makes contraception immoral and shows that the antilife nature of contraception is not true of natural family planning. He shows that there is a great difference between engaging in an act of sexual intercourse and simultaneously trying to thwart the possibility that the act will result in new life and refraining from engaging in an act of sexual intercourse. He shows how the intent of couples using contraception differs entirely from the intent of those using natural family planning.

This article appeared in *International Review of Natural Family Planning* 44, no. 4 (Winter 1980): 309–15.

17

CONTRACEPTION AND
NATURAL FAMILY PLANNING

by
Joseph M. Boyle

Contraception, as the word itself suggests, is the attempt to prevent conception. There has been considerable discussion of the meaning of the word "prevention" in the recent controversies over the morality of contraception. Therefore, it is useful to begin with a clear definition of the acts to which moral judgments about contraception are ordinarily taken to apply. Acts of this type can be called "contraceptive intercourse", and contraceptive intercourse can be defined as a dual act—that is, as an act in which one chooses to engage in sexual intercourse and also chooses to try to prevent it from giving rise to a new human life.[1] In performing such acts, people are necessarily attempting to prevent a new human being from coming to be because they believe that otherwise their act of sexual intercourse would be open to new life, and they do not want it to remain open. Thus, the contraceptive act as such is by its very nature immediately directed toward one and only one goal: the prevention of the realization of this good.

[1] The focus of this definition is somewhat different from that of *Humanae Vitae* no. 14; nevertheless, it is essentially the same as Pope Paul's authoritative definition: "Likewise, any act must be excluded that, when the conjugal act is anticipated, or carried out, or leads to its natural consequences, intends, either as an end to be obtained or a way to be employed, that procreation be impeded."

Unless one wished to prevent its realization, one would not choose to contracept.

Contraceptive intercourse, therefore, is different in meaning from birth control or family planning. Plainly, there are other ways to control births and plan one's family than by engaging in contraceptive intercourse. One can control or prevent births by abortion. One can plan one's family by natural family planning (NFP).

In general, there is nothing wrong with preventing the realization of a state of affairs even when the state of affairs is humanly good. But a couple choosing to engage in contraceptive intercourse prevent the realization of the good of procreation by making a choice that is *contrary* to this good. Such a choice is morally wrong.

The American bishops suggest why it is wrong: The separation of the unitive and the procreative (life-giving) meanings of marital intercourse involves a rejection of the life-giving meaning, and "the wrongness of such an act lies in the rejection of this value".[2] The bishops obviously do not mean to say that in contraceptive intercourse the rejection of the procreative good is a denial that procreation has any human significance and value. The rejection is in the contraceptive choice—in the couple's willingness to act against this good for the sake of other goods—however much the couple may otherwise cherish children and procreation.

This argument against contraception has two essential premises: that procreation is a basic human good and that one must not choose against basic human goods.

There can be little doubt that the first of these premises is true. In a passage taken from the Second Vatican Council and used by Pope Paul in *Humanae Vitae*, the American bishops say: "Children are really the supreme gift of marriage who in turn substantially enrich the lives of their parents."[3] The recognition of the goodness

[2] National Conference of Catholic Bishops, *To Live in Christ Jesus: A Pastoral Reflection on the Moral Life* (Washington, D.C., 1976), p. 18.
[3] Ibid., p. 17.

of procreation does not, of course, depend *only* on the teaching of the Church. Again and again, Scripture itself either states or supposes that the passing on of human life is a great and wonderful thing. For example, chief among the blessings promised to Abraham was a great progeny. Our Lord himself pointed to the great joy that followed the travail of childbirth. And what Scripture witnesses is what almost everyone knows. All who are parents know it quite directly and immediately. Others see procreation as a desirable possibility—as a good thing they can do. Or if they cannot or should not do it, they recognize that as a deprivation—as something good taken from them or as a good they must sacrifice.

The basis of this recognition is that human life is good and its continuation is also good. As organisms we are naturally inclined to preserve our species; as rational organisms we are able to see this continuation of humanity as a good thing; as Christians we are able to see human reproduction as pro-creation—that is, as cooperation with God in his act of creating another image of himself, another member of his Kingdom, another adopted child of God.

Of course, there are some who will deny that procreation is a basic human good. They will hold that when procreation is good it is only because it is instrumentally valuable, that is, not sought for its own sake as an end to be cherished and enjoyed. Having children, however, is not this kind of end. It is a blessing and a joy, as Scripture tells us and common human experience makes clear. It is true that people sometimes have children for ulterior purposes, but it is also true that for many people these ulterior purposes do not exhaust their reasons for having children. Moreover, it is also true that people sometimes have children simply because they see that it is good for another human being to exist.

Thus, to deny the appearances that procreation is a basic human good, one must have a strong reason to think it cannot be such. One reason is the view that no bodily goods, such as life, health, or procreation, can be genuine human goods because—as bodily— they are below the conscious, intelligent sphere of properly personal activity. The body and its activities are thus set apart from the mind or consciousness, and the human person is identified with the latter. This is the doctrine called "dualism"—a doctrine that denies the experienced unity of the human individual.[4]

As for the second premise—that one must not choose against basic human goods—a number of points should be kept in mind. First, basic goods are perfections of persons; in realizing these goods and holding the proper attitudes toward them, human beings are fulfilled and perfected as persons. These goods make many moral demands, but the very minimum that each requires is a kind of respect incompatible with choices contrary to the good. This respect is required because each of the goods participates in God's infinite goodness in an irreducibly distinct way and because each of the goods is the perfection of a dimension of the human self. Whatever does not respect all the manifestations of God's goodness and all the aspects of the human person is irreligious and self-mutilating. Thus, choices contrary to human goods are morally wrong.[5] We have, therefore, an argument that shows why contraception is wrong; in a word, it is a turning against human life as it is passed on.

This argument explains a number of points that have been made in the contraception debate.

Those who defended the Church's teaching on contraception in the 1960s pointed out that if contraception were allowed, there would be no way to prevent the acceptance of other sexual abuses. This consequence was, of course, denied at that time by the defenders of contraception. It is now clear that those who defended the Church's position were right. To allow contraception one must deny either that procreation is a good or that one must never act directly against a basic human good. Either of these denials is

---

[4] For a fuller discussion of "dualism" and its bearing on the contraception issue, see Germain Grisez, "Dualism and the New Morality", *Atti del Congresso Internazionale: Tommaso D'Aquino Nel Suo Settimo Centenario,* vol. 5, L'Agir Morale (Naples: Edizioni Domenicane Italiane, 1977), pp. 323–30.

[5] For an accessible account of the theory of obligation used here, see Germain Grisez and Russell Shaw, *Beyond the New Morality* (Notre Dame, 1974), pp. 85–95, 128–36.

sufficient to justify masturbation, sodomy, and so on. If life is not a basic good, there is no moral barrier to using one's genital activity to organize one's self around the satisfaction of sexual desire. Moreover, if one can justify acting against a good for overriding reasons, then one can act against the integral goods of human sexuality (by masturbation, sodomy, and so forth) for overriding reasons. If contraception is approved, therefore, other unnatural acts must also be permitted.

Furthermore, this argument shows why the approval of contraception leads—though not in such a direct and logical way—to the acceptance of abortion. Contraception is an attempt to prevent the handing on of life, and one who turns against life as it is passed on is likely to remain against it if the unwanted new life begins. The resolve to prevent a child from coming to be is often sufficiently strong that one will eliminate the child whose conception was not prevented. This anti-life attitude is often regarded as a "responsible" stance; it often includes the denial that human life is a basic good and the determination that one can do whatever is necessary to execute one's resolve to prevent a person from coming to be.

There are several objections to the Church's teaching on contraception. One objection is that the prohibition of contraception involves "physicalism"—namely, that this prohibition gives undue priority to one of the goods of marriage at the expense of the others. However, to state that procreation is a basic human good is not to say it is the *only* good or the chief good. If it is a basic good, then one should never act directly against it. It is in this sense only that, like other finite goods, the good of procreation imposes an absolute obligation.

Another objection to the Church's teaching on contraception is based on the alleged lack of difference between periodic continence and contraception. The Church has stated that couples may morally regulate the size of their families by refraining from sexual intercourse during fertile times. This practice has been called rhythm, periodic continence, and, more recently, natural family planning. Great strides have been made in recent years in perfecting NFP. Thus, the anxieties about this method are being shown to be unfounded. It is effective; it is a genuine, practicable option; it avoids the harmful physical and moral effects of contraception; and it has many good effects of its own.

Nevertheless, NFP appears to many to differ from contraception in ways that are not morally significant. How can it be that NFP is morally justified while contraception is morally wrong?

Behind this question there often lies the supposition that since NFP and contraception have the same purpose—that is, the avoidance of having a child—they must be morally the same. This supposition involves a fallacy of elementary logic. Two acts—or an act and a deliberate omission—having the same purpose need not be morally the same. One can steal or work for money to feed one's family, and one can work well or shoddily for one's wages; surely these acts are not morally the same. (Examples could be multiplied indefinitely.) The purpose of one's acts and policies is not the only factor in determining their morality.

Formally, the fallacy is that one draws an affirmative conclusion from a figure II syllogism:

From	All A is B
And	All C is B
One cannot conclude validly	All C is A.

For example:

From	All crows are birds
And	All eagles are birds
It does not follow that	All eagles are crows.

Thus:

From	All contraceptive acts are for avoiding children
And	All use of NFP is for avoiding children[6]
One cannot conclude validly	All use of NFP is contraceptive.

[6] This premise is not strictly true, since NFP can be used to achieve

Of course, it is assumed that avoiding children is—at least when the reason for avoiding them is itself morally legitimate—a morally justifiable purpose for a married couple to act on. It is not, therefore, the same as the intent to prevent conception that is essential to the notion of contraceptive intercourse. The purpose of avoiding children can be achieved by contraceptive intercourse, but by other means as well.

It is clear, moreover, that NFP achieves its purpose in a way that is essentially different from contraceptive intercourse. In practicing NFP a couple adopt a policy to have sexual intercourse at infertile times and to avoid it at fertile times. This policy involves no intention to prevent an act of intercourse from being procreative.

Refraining from intercourse is not contraceptive intercourse, since it is not intercourse at all. Moreover, refraining from intercourse has a different intentional relation to the good of procreation than contraceptive intercourse has. In the latter case one does what one believes to be a potentially procreative act and also acts to insure that the procreative potential is not realized. That is acting against the procreative good. In NFP, however, one achieves one's intention to avoid children by foregoing the act that one believes would be procreative; one does not necessarily act against this or any other good by refraining from acting for it. Mary Joyce has developed an analogy that clarifies this point very well:

> Just as there are times when truth should not be spoken, there are times when children should not be conceived. But the act of refraining from speaking differs essentially from the act of internally separating speech from its power truthfully to express and generate judgments in the mind of another. Similarly, the act of refraining from coital activity differs essentially from the

---

pregnancy. The use of NFP at issue here, however, is that in which the couple seek to avoid pregnancy. The premise could be reformulated to focus on this use of NFP.

act of internally separating coital union from its generative power.[7]

Thus, the refraining from intercourse that is involved in NFP does not involve the anti-procreative intention of contraceptive intercourse. Neither do the acts of intercourse in which a couple engage during infertile periods have this intention. Since these acts are believed not to be fertile, nothing is done to any of them to render them infertile. The other goods of marriage are quite legitimately pursued in these acts.

It has been objected that because the *timing* of these acts functions so as to render them infertile, in reality they are acts of contraceptive intercourse. Perhaps this objection is based on simply ignoring the distinction between anti-procreative acts and non-procreative acts. But it may be based on the claim that the timing of intercourse is just another contraceptive measure, like withdrawal, for example, which puts space between sperm and ovum. This version of the objection also fails, because it does not analyze carefully enough how the timing of the act effects the agents' understanding and intention. If a couple choose to have intercourse at times when they are not fertile, they cannot be choosing to engage in procreative activity; they believe they are not capable of reproduction at that time. They cannot have an anti-procreative intention, nor can they have a procreative intention, given what they know about the timing of fertility. The procreative good is not, as it were, engaged or at issue in these acts. A couple cannot be acting against the procreative good when they are convinced that the act of intercourse cannot in this instance be procreative. Thus, they act for the other goods of marriage and not against the good of procreation.

In other words, the timing of the acts of intercourse on the part of a couple using NFP to avoid pregnancy is not something

[7] Mary R. Joyce, *The Meaning of Contraception* (Liturgical Press: Collegeville, Minn., 1970), p. 41. Elizabeth Anscombe, *Contraception and Chastity* (London: Catholic Truth Society, 1977), p. 20, develops a different analogy, which brings out other aspects of the difference.

chosen to render infertile what is essentially a fertile act. The use of NFP is based on the recognition that not all acts of marital intercourse are fertile and that in those that are not, the other goods of marriage may be pursued without prejudice to the good of procreation. There is no supposition in the use of NFP that all acts of marital intercourse are fertile and that some otherwise fertile acts are rendered infertile by their timing. That is perhaps how proponents of contraception view the matter, but it simply ignores the fact that to spouses using NFP the timing of intercourse is relevant not as a barrier or spermicide or anovulant or abortifacient but rather as a component of their self-knowledge that permits a true understanding of the meaning of their various acts of marital intercourse. This self-understanding allows responsible pursuit of certain goods of marriage without ever adopting the anti-procreative proposal that every act of contraceptive intercourse involves.

NFP, therefore, is not contraceptive. Moreover, NFP not only does not hinder but actually promotes the other goods of marriage. The sexual life of the couple using NFP is controlled by chastity. The efforts of self-control must be mutual; thus couples living by NFP are united in a common effort of will. This chaste union obviates the temptation for couples to treat one another as mere instruments for sexual gratification and allows their sexual expression to be an expression of human communication, of their marital covenant, and of the love of Christ for the Church.

FURTHER READING

Boyle coauthored with John C. Ford, S.J., Germain Grisez, John
Finnis, and William E. May, *The Teaching of Humanae Vitae: A
Defense* (San Francisco: Ignatius Press, 1988). With Germain Grisez
and Olaf Tollefsen he coauthored *Free Choice: A Self-Referential
Argument* (Notre Dame, Ind.: University of Notre Dame Press,
1976); with Ronald Lawler, O.F.M. Cap., and William E. May, he
coauthored *Catholic Sexual Ethics* (Huntington, Ind.: Our Sunday
Visitor Press, 1984). He engaged in an important debate with John
Noonan over contraception in his "Human Action, Natural
Rhythms, and Contraception: A Response to Noonan", *The American Journal of Jurisprudence* 26 (1981): 32–46; the article he was
responding to was John Noonan, "Natural Law, the Teaching of
the Church, and the Rhythm of Natural Fecundity", *The American Journal of Jurisprudence* 25 (1980): 16–37. He has several articles
on the principle of double effect that bear upon his reasoning
about natural family planning: "*Praeter Intentionen* in Aquinas",
The Thomist 42 (1978): 649–65; "Toward Understanding the Principle of Double Effect", *Ethics* 90 (1980): 527–38; "The Principle of
Double Effect: Good Actions Entangled in Evil", in *Moral Theology Today: Certitudes and Doubts* (St. Louis, Mo.: Pope John Center,
1985), 243–60.

    Humanae Vitae: A Generation Later treats of the differences
between contraception and natural family planning on 118–28.

18

NATURAL REGULATION OF
CONCEPTION AND CONTRACEPTION

by
Elżbieta Wójcik

Elżbieta Wójcik, a Polish physician, brings to bear a special perspective on the question of the differences between methods of natural family planning and contraception. After having shown the compatibility of contraception with the hedonistic mores of the modern age, she contrasts the attitudes spawned by a contraceptive mode of life with the attitudes that inform a life lived in accord with the laws of God and the nature of man. She argues that contraception constitutes a revolt against God and a degradation of married love; she testifies to the psychological responses of women and men to contraceptive sexual intercourse and argues that natural family planning protects against both divorce and abortion. She also reviews the physical dangers of contraception.

This article appeared in the *International Review of Natural Family Planning* 9, no. 4 (Winter 1985): 306–26.

18

NATURAL REGULATION OF
CONCEPTION AND CONTRACEPTION

by
Elżbieta Wójcik

INTRODUCTION

Two Different Approaches

For each young married couple, responsible parenthood is a serious task and, at the same time, a problem requiring deep reflection. In our times, this problem has assumed particular importance in view of a considerable fall in the mortality of newborns and infants. Nearly 50 years ago, two scientists, Ogino and Knaus, discovered (simultaneously) and described the natural rhythm of fertility in women, and thus began the development of the knowledge about natural methods of regulating conception. At the same time, however, the pharmaceutical industry developed a contraceptive technology, starting a mass production of ever new contraceptives which were widely publicized and made readily available and, consequently, have spread rapidly all over the world.

There is a great and essential difference between these two approaches to regulation of conception. It lies, in the first place, in an opposite ethical qualification of these approaches: The natural approach is good, contributing to the development of spouses and the strengthening of their marital bonds; the contraceptive approach is bad, causing harm to individuals and married couples and, as a remote consequence, leading to a degradation of humanity. Whether man's deeds are good or bad cannot be without significance since they exert a deep influence on the development of his personality, his family and society, and his relationship with God, Who, as the Creator of man, has laid the laws of human existence.

Living according to the principle of natural regulation of conceptions, the spouses respect the natural fertility rhythm recognizing in this way the Lord's wisdom and His love for us. He "saw that what He created was good." On the other hand, married couples who use contraception oppose the plan of the Lord and, destroying the inner order of marriage, act to the detriment of their mutual love and themselves.

Another difference between the natural regulation of conceptions and contraception is the essentially opposite influence each approach has on the psychological aspects of the spouses' personality—the neuroticizing influence of contraception—as well as the different effect each has on physical health. As a rule, contraceptive agents are harmful to health, while natural regulation of conception is also called the ecological method since, basing itself on the natural course of fertility rhythm in the female organism, it spares the health of the woman.

If an individual chooses married life as his vocation, he should live his life as perfectly as possible since this is his and his spouse's way to God. In view of this, it is of essential importance to think over the problem of family planning, since care must be taken not to suppress mutual love and not to drift away from God, the source of love and life, but to contribute to the strengthening and maturation of marital bonds.

Causes of Rapid Spread of Contraception

It is surprising that contraceptive methods have spread so widely throughout the world, used in all countries it seems, despite their harmfulness both in the physical and the psychological spheres. On the other hand, the knowledge of the natural methods of fertility control spreads much more slowly and with difficulties. The reasons for this are varied:

— Many people believed that contraception, especially hormonal (the Pill), introduced about 25 years ago, would make completely reliable regulation of conceptions possible and would solve the problem of pregnancy interruption. (Actually the situation is quite the opposite, as we shall see.)

— The state of satiety or even surfeit, which is a typical feature of highly civilized societies, leads many people to a morbid refinement and egoism reflected mainly in seeking pleasures and satisfying whims which may lead certain individuals to a loss of joy of life, to depression or pessimism. Both these extreme states of mind are connected with fear of parenthood, with unwillingness to have a child or to have more than one or two children. Contraception seems to many such people the simplest way for protecting themselves against unwanted children.

— Fascination with the development of technique and wealth along with a concomitant independence of nature has led many persons to excessive assertiveness. Man feels now that he is the master of nature and of the self, the nearly absolute legislator who governs the laws of life. The feeling of sanctity and mystery of God and the awareness of man's dependence on God have disappeared in many individuals and even in certain populations. The pragmatism of wealth and consumption has pushed aside the higher feelings reflecting the strivings of man, his real greatness and dignity.

— A deluge of news from the mass media and, probably, also a greater easiness of life have contributed to a deplorable decrease of reflective thinking which has been replaced by widely publicized opinions.

— Contraception meets the human tendency for avoiding inconvenience, relieves man from the effort of controlling himself, and opens new vistas of complete sexual freedom. This may be regarded as a consumptionist attitude towards sex.

— The production of contraceptive agents brings great gains to the pharmaceutical firms who are interested in intensive advertising and in financing further studies on new agents.

— Contrary to contraception, natural regulation of conceptions requires no agents which could raise money for pharmaceutical firms, and therefore investigations on it and publicizing it are not supported financially by any industry. Teaching and propagation of a natural method require, on the other hand, a deeply humanistic attitude, personal enthusiasm, and conviction that this way of life is good for married people.

— The use of natural methods of conception regulation in marital life is not a mechanical activity such as that required in contraceptive methods but it is a certain mode of life requiring a deep consideration of a hierarchy of values such as personal dignity, parenthood and new human life, and also some humility in accepting one's insufficiency and one's dependence on a Higher Being.

— Besides that, some effort is necessary for understanding the natural fertility cycle, systematic conduction of observations, and particularly self-control.

— Modern man has grown so accustomed to using technical gadgets that the dependence "only on nature" and one's self in such an important field of life seems to him something like going backward in civilization. It is frequently forgotten that culture is more important than technical civilization. This may explain the unwillingness of physicians to learn the natural methods of conception regulation, while they have gotten accustomed to using drugs and instruments and deciding themselves. Besides that, physicians are children of the present technical civilization of consumption.

Differences in Attitudes

The above suggests that the use of contraception is related, as a rule, to an attitude which is superficial, consumption-oriented, inconvenience-avoiding, and particularly not sufficiently aware of the problems of marital life and spousal responsibility. The decision to live according to the ethical and ascetical principles required by periodic abstinence calls for acceptance and recognition of the basic values of persons, marriage, and human life as well as a more developed awareness of responsibility for others and for one's own behavior, including self-restraint and self-control. Periodic abstinence requires more personal effort which, however, engenders greater maturity and a deeper, more exalted mutual love of the spouses as well as greater durability of marriage and family. Paul VI wrote:

> He who uses the gift of marital love with recognition of the right of procreation acknowledges that he is not the master of the source of life but rather a servant in the plan established by the Lord. (*Humanae Vitae*, 13)

Sexuality Is a Mode of Person Existence

The question arises whether sexuality is a sufficiently important aspect of human personality that, in the discussion of it, the general attitude of man towards higher values should be considered. Some people believe and contend that sexuality belongs only to the body, that conception regulation is a rather external, bio-medical problem which does not concern the personality and that every individual has the absolute right to choose this or any other attitude. However, after consideration, it must be acknowledged that sexuality is not only a biological function of the body, such as digestion, it is a matter of human existence. Every sexual stimulus, however slight, experienced by the body concerns the whole human being, inducing a state of psychic tension. It influences emotions, will and mind, and necessitates a decision: I will act or I will not act, and this, like all human decisions, is connected with responsibility.

The centers of sexual reactions are situated in the brain, in a part called the diencephalon. Man, in contrast to animals, has the possibility of governing his sexual behavior. Each sexual activity is thus a deed of a person, not only a biological function of the body. It is true that sometimes man yields to an overwhelming sexual desire which sweeps away his mind and will, and leads him to deplorable behavior. This is, however, felt as an influence that degrades human dignity and causes harm.

A human being expresses itself through its body, and sexual behavior may be called "the speech of the body," keeping in mind that it is the expression of the whole human person.

If we accept that sexual behavior depends on the person as a whole, we must admit that this field of life is subject to moral estimation, and responsibility must be borne for it; the way in which sexual behavior is experienced exerts an influence on the whole development and spiritual level of a person. Each free action of man has the property of either raising him and making his personality better and stronger or, conversely, degrading him and making his personality worse and weaker. Man is realized through his actions.

The Necessity of Reflection

Since conscious and responsible planning of conception is necessary in marriage, the impression suggests itself that contraception is a positive affair. However, the dignity of man, who is a reasonable and responsible creature, requires that his actions are based on more profound thinking and on striving towards truth. Jesus Christ said: "He who fulfills the requirements of truth approaches to light." (Jn 3:21)

The conjugal life in which two persons give themselves each to the other is a matter of such high importance that it would be below the dignity of a person to base conjugal behavior on the "first impression" or on a prevailing opinion not yet verified. Personal dignity as well as the importance of the problem require that man should seek and reach true recognition of and conviction about the very core of the problem. As already mentioned, however, an escape from personal deeper reflections and from philosophical thinking can be observed in favor of easy acceptance of generally accepted opinions. At the same time, a particular unwillingness is observed to accept teachings and authorities, often also the authority of the Church. It is easily forgotten that the Church does not create laws concerning the essential problems of human existence but only reads the laws either revealed by God or written by Him in nature, laws which convey true good and happiness, certainly in the domain of human love.

THE HARM OF CONTRACEPTION

The harm caused by contraception could be considered in the following ways:

Contraception as a Revolt against God

God, the Creator, could in His omnipotence solve the problem of marital union and the mode of procreation in other ways but: "God has established an indissoluble bond between the double significance contained in marital intercourse, between the idea of union and the idea of parenthood." (*HV,* 12) The correlation between the experience of deep union in love and the resulting possible parenthood is obvious in the nature of marital intercourse.

This truth lies in the pattern of intercourse, and reason cannot gainsay this.

In using contraceptive agents, man tries to separate artificially these two significant truths destroying the inner order and truth of marital intercourse. John Paul II wrote:

> The problem is that marital intercourse should denote what it is objectively. A married couple cannot fulfill marital intercourse and deprive it of its inner, objective truth.... If it is to be consumed in truth, it must be correlated in the consciousness and in the attitudes of the participants with the awareness of possible parenthood and also—which is particularly important—a certain readiness for parenthood (I may be father, I may be mother).[1]

In his actions, man should not separate what God has joined in His plans. The use of contraception is thus a revolt against God and His laws written into human nature; it is also a token of the absence of adoration and trust in the wisdom and love of the Lord who "saw what was good" when He finished His works.

God gave to man the honor of participation in the work of creation of new life, and man, not responding to this gift with gratitude and veneration, desecrates it and frequently despises it after savoring its pleasure. In this, man shows not only his meanness but also his exuberant pride. Using contraception, man shows his willingness to become master of the creating power and to usurp the final decision about the creation of new people.

This is not always fully understood by man; despite this, however, actions against God's laws, as a rule, cause a state of internal restlessness in man. For suppressing God's laws, people often react aggressively against the Church which is accused of excessive severity in outlining ethical directives to be observed in sexual behavior. In this connection, it is not considered that the Church transmits only God's laws for the sake of man, human love, and

[1] Karol Wojtyla: *Love and Responsibility* (San Francisco: Ignatius Press, 1993).

family. God's laws can be understood by the human intellect, but this requires reflection and good will.

Maintaining ethical principles while controlling their sexual behavior, the spouses remain in harmony with their own nature and with the laws of the Lord which gives them a feeling of inner peace and joy and facilitates living in the state of grace. The words of the prophet Isaiah are appropriate here:

> I am the Lord your God,
> the one who wants to teach you for your own good
> and direct you in the way you should go.
> If only you had listened to my commands!
> Then blessings would have flowed for you
> like a stream that never goes dry!
> Victory would have come to you
> like the waves that roll on the shore. (Is. 48:17–18)

Contraception Weakens and Degrades Marital Love

In the conciliar documents of Vatican II, marital intercourse is defined as "a personal act during which the spouses give themselves each to the other and receive themselves." (*Gaudium et Spes*, 48) This definition expresses the essential truth of the conjugal act, that is, that it takes place between persons and includes the mutual endowment of one's self. The inner order of marital intercourse should thus correspond to the dignity and value of persons involved and should include a true gift, which is the gift of a person for life.

What does it mean that marital intercourse must correspond to the dignity and value of the participants? Every human being, created to resemble God, is loved by God and has, from Him, an internal freedom that includes the ability to understand one's own consciousness and undertake decisions. All this is evidence of the high value and dignity of every human being and indicates that we deserve esteem and love and cannot be treated as an object of pleasure since God, Himself, endowed us with such a high dignity. Treatment of human beings without love and esteem is against the order God established.

Marital intercourse with contraception is devoid of true love, and the participants do not give themselves fully to each other, since fertility and potential parenthood, features of a mature person, are rejected in it: I want you but I do not want your fertility or your parenthood; I reject them although they are parts of your person. Love is owed to a whole person. If a part of this person is not accepted and not esteemed, or frequently even detested, then the truth of love is transparent and false since what comes to the foreground is not a full love of a person but the use of this person for pleasure. This love is not directed toward a whole person. "Contraception contains the risk of reducing this deep interpersonal act which is marital intercourse to the level of sexual use only."[2]

These considerations may seem, at a first glance, too theoretical but life confirms them only too frequently as evidenced by neuroses of spouses, culminating in unhappiness and divorce.

One of the conditions for the development of marital love is a full, mutual acceptance of both persons. If the married couple practices contraception, as described above, the mutual gift of persons and mutual acceptance are not complete. Contraception is against human dignity, even if not realized by those practicing it. In women, especially, who are more sensitive and usually more exposed to the risks connected with contraception, a feeling of being wronged develops together with the thought that the husband expects only pleasure from her while she wants to be loved as a person, as an individual. Disappointment and a feeling of humiliation grow in them gradually, leading frequently to reactions of aggression or depression, even to frigidity and repugnance of the husband. Wives do not feel, then, that they are truly loved by their husbands. If frank talks between spouses are lacking,

[2] From the speech of Cardinal Karol Wojtyla during the conference on "Special Aspects of the Problem of Contraception", Cracow, Feb. 7, 8, 1976.

the husband most frequently is not aware of the cause of his wife's behavior, and, frequently, even she is not aware of the source of her depression or aggressive feelings. This condition may lead to marital unfaithfulness and breakdown.

Yet another psychological mechanism may play a role in this situation. If a wife is regularly taking the Pill or wears an IUD, her husband may possibly feel obliged to have frequent intercourse with her. If sexual intercourse is very frequent, occurring even after slightest stimulation, it may become the only expression of love with a consequent reduction of the frequency of other expressions of communication and love. Very frequent intercourse is, as a rule, experienced rather superficially: The more frequently and more regularly a need is fulfilled, the more superficial the experience connected with it becomes and the lower is the concomitant joy. This may lead to the seeking of special refinements.

The practice of periodic abstinence in marriage requires self-control during periods of fertility if the conception of a child is not planned. However, periodic abstinence not only does no harm to marital love but, with mutual understanding and well-wishing, it enriches this love with new spiritual values, contributes to its deepening and maturation, and increases mutual esteem and the feeling of responsibility. Self-control also prevents the development of egoism and treating of the spouse (especially the wife) as an object of pleasure which may readily occur when contraception is practiced.

The periods of sexual abstinence arouse marital love, prevent boredom, and promote marriage durability, since time periods resembling betrothal phases alternate with marital phases. Divorces hardly occur at all among married couples practicing natural family planning.

Wanda Póltawska, M.D. (Poland), has described, from her own medical practice, married couples with severe psychopathological conflicts and neuroses developing as a result of contraception practices, leading not infrequently to marital breakdown.[3] Josef

---

[3] Wanda Póltawska: "Die Einstellung zur Empfängnisverhütung und ihre Folgen für die Ehe", *Theologisches,* no. 124 (1980), pp. 3777-3788.

Rötzer, M.D. (Austria), the author of a sympto-thermal method, who has studied these problems for 30 years, reported that he had files on approximately 1,400 married couples practicing natural regulation of conceptions, couples who have remained in close contact with him. There was no case of divorce or pregnancy interruption in this group. It is worth stressing that, according to statistics in large European cities, every third marriage ends in divorce.

The practice of periodic sexual abstinence requires an agreement of both spouses who must discuss pertinent problems—this promotes better communication between them. In marital life, this communication is very important since it occurs not infrequently that, in the hurry of everyday life, spouses have time only for perfunctory remarks concerning current business and neglect more extensive emotional talks about themselves. This may lead, imperceptibly, to the shallowing or even extinction of friendship and mutual emotions.

The good of practicing natural control of conceptions is that the married couple remain in a clear and simple relationship to God and Church. It is easier then to meet together in common prayers and to receive more frequently the holy sacraments, the sources of grace and help.

It is also worth mentioning here the importance of natural regulation of conceptions for the well-being of the woman. Knowing better the course of her fertility rhythm and the precise and purposeful action of hormones in her organism, the woman—living in harmony with her nature—better understands and values her womanhood. Usually she feels a deep gratitude towards her husband for his protective, generous, and noble attitude and responds with greater warmth and joy in living with him.

A mark of satisfaction of spouses with natural regulation of conceptions is that, as a rule, spouses instruct their children in this method, and parents will always bequeath to their children what they regard as best.

John Paul II said: "Only in this way—the natural regulation of birth—can a married couple remain in harmony with the values of their humanity, in harmony with the laws of the Lord and with the truth of marital love."[4]

In the conciliary document, *Gaudium et Spes,* we read: "The divine law shows the full significance of marital love, protects it and stimulates it to full human perfection." (*GS*, 50)

Contraception as an Expression of a Hostile Attitude towards the Value of Human Life

Many people consider that they use contraception out of esteem for fertility and the possibility of conceiving of a new life which is not wanted at a particular time. This is, however, an error due to insufficient thinking over of the whole problem. Or it may be simply self-deception which is more convenient, it seems, and falls in line with advertising and mass media propaganda. Can esteem be expressed by hostility for fertility and destruction of new human life, a destruction which occurs especially with such methods as the IUD or the hormonal pill?[5] In contraception, one's own fertility, as well as that of the partner's, is treated without esteem, not as a value but rather as a hostile force opposed by man who tries to violate and destroy it by technical, hormonal, chemical, surgical, and other methods. Moreover, contraception cannot remove the fear of the child. This fear, made possible by the

---

[4] From the speech of the Holy Father to the participants in the Congress on Philosophy and Theology of Responsible Parenthood, Rome, June 8, 1984.

[5] During IUD use, ovulation occurs normally and fertilization of the ovum by the spermatozoon may take place in the Fallopian tube practically every month. However, the developing embryo cannot effect nidation in the endometrium damaged by the IUD and is eliminated. An IUD is thus an early abortifacient agent.

In the case of the Pill, the hormonal dosages in presently used preparations have been, for health reasons, so reduced that ovulation takes place frequently and fertilization of the ovum occurs but nidation cannot be reached since the endometrium has been damaged by the hormones and the embryo is eliminated similarly as in the case of IUD use.

hostile attitude toward and the active counteracting or destroying of fertility, changes frequently into true hatred against the child to be born. And, if unexpected pregnancy occurs, which may take place even if contraception is practiced, this arouses amazement leading frequently to aggression and the decision to abort the fetus. The responsibility for abortion is laid on firms producing contraceptive agents. The Institut der Sexualforschung (Institute for Sexual Research) in Hamburg published the information that since 1961, that is, from the time of Pill introduction, the number of pregnancy interruptions has doubled in the Hamburg region.

The respect for a person can be expressed only by an attitude full of esteem, generosity, and admiration and by caring for the well-being of that individual. A married couple expresses this attitude towards fertility and the possibility of conceiving new life when practicing natural family planning. Abstinence out of generosity during possible fertility is tantamount to affirming the gift of fertility and parenthood, respecting the spouse and the life of a new human being, as well as esteeming, respecting, and loving God.

The attitude of respect for the value of fertility and life present in the purposeful practice of periodic sexual abstinence increases love to each child and facilitates the acceptance of each child, even the unplanned one. As shown by responses to inquiries, marital life, including the practice of NFP, usually increases the longing for a child so that parents often decide to have a second or third or even more children. Probably, this phenomenon is connected with the attitude of respect and love for God, for life, for the gifts of fertility and parenthood.

The life of every human being is derived from God and is, from its very beginning, sacred. Thus, the ability of transmitting life belongs also to the sphere of the sacred. This idea is not new. The Fathers of the Church stated emphatically that contraception was a profanation of the procreation act which is sacred in itself. Presently, in the era of fascination with technique, a decline in the awareness of mystery and sacredness is observed in favor of rationalism and a willingness to conquer nature completely and overcome its laws. We transmit life, but we do not create it. Where lies the sanctity of human life? Sanctity is an attribute of God, Himself. Sacred is all that which shares something divine, something from the nature of God. Every human being has, from its beginning, an immortal soul and is destined to participate in the life of God. This is the source of the value and dignity of human life since man is not able to create human life. The high value and dignity of the life of a human person—as a thinking and self-determining being capable of loving, bearing responsibility, and exceeding its limitations— are recognized also by people who do not believe in God, as evidenced by secular laws and acts protecting human life.

Contraception as an Obstacle in Personality Development

Development is important for all living beings, and, for man, it is not only a need but also a duty for which he bears responsibility and which leads him to his final goals, to inner maturity, to happiness, and to God. The way to ever greater inner maturity is also the way to sanctity, since man realizes himself most completely through assimilation with God and fulfilling God's will. In the acceptance of sexual abstinence for the natural control of conception, the importance lies not so much in self-control as in the recognition of a true hierarchy of values, making human sexuality subordinated to true love, that is, love and adoration for God, the spouse, the child to be possibly born, and also oneself. Life should be compatible with truth, and truth is connected with the development and inner freedom of man.

Contraception, on the other hand, opposes the divine order as demonstrated in preceding sections. Man follows in this path chosen by himself for the sake of the convenient life and an ill-understood freedom which could be called lawlessness, since egoism always underlies the practice of contraception. Many people using contraceptive methods take pains to develop and do good in other fields of their life but it is worth quoting here the words of the mystic Spanish writer Francisco de Osuna (from his book, *The*

Art of Praying): "Remember that one unguarded gate is sufficient that Satan finds his way to the castle of the human heart."

A human person should be an integrated whole, and the need for development and transcendence is one of a person's greatest needs. The contraceptive attitude means that a part of the personality is excluded consciously, egoistically, and immaturely from the pathway of development. If human development is disturbed and inhibited, the human ego revolts. This revolt may take the form of inner restlessness or various neurotic reactions such as apathy, aggression, etc. The human mind defends itself against this inner restlessness and tries to get rid of it by using various defense mechanisms such as repression, rationalization, regression, transference, etc. These unconscious reactions lead to neurosis development, depression, neurasthenia. According to H. Binder, neuroses are disturbances in the solving of internal conflicts. Neurotic symptoms indicate that the individual with these symptoms may have insufficiently recognized and unresolved internal conflicts leading to subconscious anxiety which disturbs and inhibits personality development. Conflicts are normal in human life and, if after thinking them over an individual chooses a solution agreeing with accepted values and with truth, they may aid in personality development. Man acts inconsequently when he uses contraception in marital life: He wants to act but at the same time he fears and rejects the natural effects of his action, trying to prevent them by artificial means. In this way an internal split or ambivalence appears which also contributes to neurosis development.

Intending to live according to the principles of ethics and responsibility, man must make an effort to understand the natural fertility rhythm and learn to recognize the phases of fertility and infertility. After mastering this, he controls his behavior by means of his reason and will in this important and beautiful field of marital life. This is the worth of human dignity and human subjectivity. On the other hand, contraceptive methods deprive man of the subjectivity in his activities and release him from responsibility. Abandoning self-determination in this crucial field, man delegates his personal responsibility to the pharmaceutical firms who produce and widely advertise contraceptive agents. In this way, man is manipulated. Contraception prevents the development of inner freedom, reflective thinking, and responsibility which determine personal maturity.

Sterilization is not a therapeutic procedure but an intervention against human health, depriving people of full health. It is a surgical procedure usually requiring general anaesthesia and, similar to other operations, it is connected with a certain risk of complications and even death. The tendency of the organism to repair damage is evidenced by the fact that in 1 to 2 cases out of 1,000 tubal ligations, fertility returns since the cut tube restores its continuity and potency. The American medical literature reports cases of auto-immune diseases in sterilized men. After a vasectomy, spermatozoa are resorbed into the circulation where they act as a foreign protein leading to the production of auto-antibodies against themselves. This excessive production of auto-antibodies may lead to injury to various organs.

Mary R. Joyce, writing on sterilization, states:

> Consciously carried out sterilization of an individual is not only an interruption of a biological process, as this is the case in animals, but it is an invasion into the whole being of this individual. People may say that their self-consciousness has not been impaired, however, to be an individual is not tantamount to be aware of one's self. The subconsciousness knows what an individual is doing against his being as an individual, even if the subconsciousness is "fortunately" blocked or consciously repressed by the mind.[6]

The practice of coitus interruptus is also a contraceptive method and may give rise to neurosis development in both spouses.

The attitude of self-control and self-sacrifice needed in practicing periodic sexual abstinence may be difficult for certain individuals, especially at the beginning. However, usually the beneficial effects of this way of life on the marital bond soon begins to be experienced, pride is felt as well as a feeling of personal value as God's child.

---

[6] M. R. Joyce: *Love Responds to Life* (Kenosha, Wisconsin, 1972), p. 95.

In their requirements, divine laws do not exceed the possibilities of human nature but show the direction in development and maturation that human nature, in its full participation in God's life, should go. Natural regulation of conception helps man to "be more" rather than to "have more," and aids in pursuing the way of inner freedom and true love which are closely interrelated. Inner freedom is the ability to choose such behaviors which agree with love and truth.

Effect of Contraception Extends over the Whole of Mankind

The harmful effect of contraception extends not only to married couples but also to young people all over the world. In the consciousness of a young individual not used to the elaboration of a proper attitude towards love and marriage, sexuality is reflected only in contacts with other individuals of the opposite sex or simply as a domain of pleasure seeking, quite free of responsibility since fertility can be excluded by means of readily available contraceptive agents. Many young people take over this attitude from adults through mass media and sometimes through instructive lessons on sex which provide them with only biological and technical knowledge without mentioning the personal value of individuals, love, and marriage. Such an attitude is being named "contraceptive mentality". This attitude leads easily to decisions to abort undesired children as their conception is not associated with the sexual intercourse of the parents but rather with the experienced failure of the applied contraceptive method.

Development of an adult attitude—recognizing sexuality as a gift and value in the service of true love and procreation—is made considerably difficult if contraception is accepted, since the practice of contraception is connected with falsification of truth about love and the inner order of sexual intercourse. Because of that, many young people begin their sexual life very early, often after first falling in love (which they usually regard as true love) or from curiosity or a willingness to come up to others—thus separating sex from procreation.

For many young people, contraception eliminates the phase of friendship since, already at puberty, couples are bypassing this developmental phase important for the social maturation of man. Young people, occupied by their own erotic sexual experiences, are usually less prone to brood over the sense of life, truth, and human scale of values and take less interest in self-development of their own character. Because of that, psychic and social maturation of these young people to a full, responsible life based on an accepted scale of values is delayed or may even stop. Since the maturity of society includes the maturity of individuals, concerns may be raised as to the level of maturity and responsibility of generations to come, if contraception will be dominant in their young years.

Acceptance of contraception contributes to the presently widespread habit of beginning sexual relations before marriage. This reduces the probability of achieving a deeper love during the period of betrothal and also decreases the probability of a deeper understanding since sexual intercourse becomes the main factor in mutual contacts. This sexual relationship before marriage is usually associated with fear and a negative attitude towards pregnancy as a possible outcome of this relationship. On the other hand, sexual restraint before marriage with a proper scale of values and responsibility favors the maturation of an ability to love and be responsible.

In the 5th century B.C., the Chinese philosopher Confucius wrote:

> When the heart is set right, then the personal life is cultivated; when the personal life is cultivated, then the family life is regulated; when the family life is regulated, then the national life is orderly; and when the national life is orderly, then there is peace in this world. From the emperor down to the common man, all must regard the cultivation of the personal life as the root or foundation. There is never an orderly upshoot or superstructure when the root or foundation is disorderly. There

is never yet a tree whose trunk is slim and slender and whose top branches are thick and heavy. This is called "to know the root or foundation of things."[7]

PHYSICAL HARMFULNESS OF CONTRACEPTION

The above discussion concentrated on the effects of contraception and NFP on the marital bonds and on the spouses themselves as well as on the attitudes and psycho-social development of young people. However, not without importance is also the harmful effect of contraceptive agents on health, especially women's health. Medicine has already demonstrated the physical harmfulness of contraception. We restrict our discussion below to only the *main* harmful effects of contraceptives.

The Pill is presently produced in many varieties. As a rule, it contains a combination of two synthetic sex hormones in doses that achieve the following results:

— inhibition of ovulation by artificial maintenance of the organism from the beginning of the menstrual cycle as if during pregnancy or as in the second phase of the cycle when the corpus luteum naturally produces gestagens (or progesterone).

— inhibition of cervical mucus production.

— inhibition of endometrial development to prevent the nidation of the embryo.

In the case of ovulation and fertilization occurring despite taking the Pill (which, presently, is not infrequent after reduction of the hormone dosage in the Pill), the embryo cannot develop in the damaged endometrium and is eliminated.

Many people believe that the hormones present in the Pill exert their influence only on the genitals, inhibiting genital

---

[7] *The Wisdom of Confucius,* edited and introduced by Lin Yutang (New York: The Modern Library, 1966), p. 139.

functions. However, the genital functions depend on special nerve centers in a part of the brain called the hypothalamus. From there impulses are sent to the hypophysis and from the hypophysis to the peripheral endocrine glands, including the ovaries. By taking the Pill, a woman introduces into her organism greater amounts of synthetic sex hormones inhibiting the secretory activity of the hypothalamus and hypophysis. This may lead to harmful effects on the health. The production of one's own natural sex hormones is inhibited and the natural physiological course of the menstrual cycle is disturbed. Manifestations of the menstrual cycle are induced artificially by the synthetic hormones in the Pill. In this way, the female organism is manipulated. After discontinuation of prolonged Pill use, menstruation fails to appear spontaneously in about two percent of women and must be induced artificially.[8]

The action of sex hormones in the female organism is an alternating one: In the first part of the menstrual cycle, estrogens prevail while the second part is characterized by the prevalence of gestagens. The Pill provides the female organism with gestagens already at the beginning of the cycle for inhibition of maturation of the ovum.

The excessive non-physiological level of synthetic sex hormones causes a number of harmful side effects, mainly in the cardiovascular system, in the blood-clotting system, and in metabolic processes. Strokes[9] were described in young women, together with myocardial infarctions, and hepatic function disturbances. Symptoms and signs, such as excessive body weight, hyperpigmented spots on the skin, psychic changes (a feeling of fatigue, anxiety, depression, irritability) are frequent, and they are most probably due to hormonal disequilibrium in the organism. The

[8] Wenderlein: Post-Pill-Amenorrhoe und Menarche, *Fortschr. Med.,* 1978, 96, pp. 2243–48.

[9] H. Reisner, "Zerebrale Insulte im Zusammenhang mit dem Gebrauch von Ovulationshemmern." In: Pro sanitate cerebri et animae hominis. Aus der Neurologischen Klinik der Universität Wien. Prof. H. Reisner. Festschrift anlässlich des 60-jährigen Bestandes des Neurologischen Krankenhauses (Rosenhügel 1972).

number of contraindications listed for the Pill is so great that this sufficiently evidences that the Pill is not easily tolerated by the organism.

The action of the intrauterine device (IUD) is based mainly on continuous damage to the delicate endometrium in which numerous haemorrhagic spots and microthrombi are found in the presence of the IUD. The damaged endometrium is unable to receive the fertilized ovum. Fertilization in cases of IUD use can occur normally, that is, usually in the Fallopian tube, practically every month. After fertilization, the developing embryo travels for 5–8 days along the tube to the uterus, but nidation cannot take place if an IUD is present in the uterine cavity. Thus the IUD is an abortifacient agent. Unfortunately, most women do not know that the IUD is the cause of death of many already conceived children in the embryonal phase of their development.

For women wearing IUDs, cases of ectopic pregnancy occur much more frequently than on the average. Ectopic pregnancy is a severe condition requiring a major operation. In the *Wiener Klinische Wochenschrift*, Feichtinger wrote: "Women using IUDs have, in the first place, major bleedings.... The cause of these bleedings are local injuries of the endometrium which appear in histological examination to be small haemorrhagic necrotic foci due to fluctuations in the progesterone level. In part, these foci are caused by traumas to which all women using IUDs are subject."[10]

According to Beck and Hoffelner: "The incidence of side effects after 12 months of IUD use in 678 women was 11.9%, including pregnancy in 1.4% of cases, IUD falling out in 2.7%, bleedings and/or pains in 5%, and symptoms related to the psychic attitude of the woman in 2.8%."[11]

Chemical agents such as pastes, jellies, and foam-producing preparations contain spermicidal substances. They must, of necessity, exert a toxic effect on the cells in the female organism even if their

---

[10] Feichtinger et al., "Vergleich der klinischen Wirksamkeit von Progestasert mit dem Kupfer-T 200." *Wien. Klin. Wschr.* 14 (1980).

[11] Hoffelner-Beck, "Zum Problem der Schwangerschaft—und Blutungsstörungen bei Frauen mit kupferhaltigen IUD." *Wien. Klin. Wschr.* 14 (1980).

resorption through the mucosa is low. Allergic local reactions and inflammatory processes develop in the female genital tract especially if these agents are used frequently.

Only natural methods of birth regulation have no harmful effects since they are based only on the observation of the fertility rhythm. These methods are, strictly speaking, diagnostic tests since they are based on a description of phenomena during the menstrual cycle, and they provide the possibility of recognizing successive phases of the cycle. The proper method of "birth control" is the self-control of the spouses.

FURTHER READING

For evidence that contraception contributes to marital difficulties, see the work of Robert T. Michael, "The Rise in Divorce Rates, 1960–1974: Age-Specific Components", *Demography* 15, no. 2 (May 1978): 177–82; "Determinants of Divorce", in *Sociological Economics,* ed. by Louis Levy-Garboua (London: SAGE Publications, 1979), 223–54; "Why Did the U.S. Divorce Rate Double within a Decade?" in *Research in Population Economics,* vol. 6 (Greenwich, Conn: Jai Press, 1988), 367–99.

For the dangers of contraception, see J. C. Espinosa, M.D., *Birth Control: Why Are They Lying to Women?* (New York: Vantage, 1980); Ellen Grant, M.D., *The Bitter Pill* (London: Corgi Books, 1985); Kevin Hume, "The Pill and Cancer", *Linacre Quarterly* (November 1985): 297–320; J. N. Santamaria, "The Social Effects of Contraception", *Linacre Quarterly* (May 1984): 114–27.

THE MORAL USE OF
NATURAL FAMILY PLANNING

by
Janet E. Smith

Humanae Vitae states that methods of natural family planning may be used only for serious reasons. This essay considers why the Church would allow use of NFP only for serious reasons and attempts to sketch out what would constitute serious reasons. It consults writings of various popes who have given some guidance on these issues. It also considers if there is a "proper" family size.

This is a previously unpublished essay.

THE MORAL USE OF
NATURAL FAMILY PLANNING

by
Janet E. Smith

Many Catholics who use methods of natural family planning (NFP) are confident that since NFP is approved by the Church, it can be used morally. They are not so confident, however, that they know what constitute moral reasons for using NFP. Some, for instance, think it should be used only if severe hardships would result from having a child or another child. This essay will attempt to sketch out the types of circumstances in which methods of NFP can be used morally; in the course of doing so it will suggest that the range of reasons is broader and perhaps more liberal than many think.[1] It will draw heavily upon Church documents and papal statements for two reasons. One, the Church has given some attention to this issue. Secondly, most of those interested in this issue are Catholics, though the principles invoked

---

[1] There is little written on this question. A classic treatment of the moral use of periodic continence can be found in John C. Ford, S.J., and Gerald Kelly, S.J., "Pius XII on Periodic Continence", *Contemporary Moral Theology,* vol. 2 (Westminster, Md.: The Newman Press, 1964), 396–430. I treated the differences between NFP and contraception in chap. 4 of my book *Humanae Vitae: A Generation Later* (Washington, D.C.: Catholic University Press of America, 1991). See also Anthony J. Zimmerman, S.V.D., "Natural Family Planning vs. Contraception", *Homiletic and Pastoral Review* (May 1989): 52–65. Chap. 4 of my book also treats at some length why it is moral to use NFP.

should be acceptable to any reasonable individual, especially to Christians.

Before beginning, however, we must take note of another group of individuals that have come to doubt whether it is ever moral to use methods of natural family planning. They tend to believe that procreation is such a great good that couples should simply accept all the children that God sends them; determining how many children to have or when to have children seems to them to demonstrate a lack of trust in God. They believe that in accepting the vocation of marriage they have also accepted the obligation to have as many children as they could possibly care for, or at least they have the obligation to have a large family. This essay will not provide a full-blown argument justifying that it is moral to use NFP; such has been done elsewhere.[2] Rather it will address the question of the obligation to have children and the question of trust in God, since in addressing these questions we will establish some important principles that will assist us in determining when it is moral to use NFP.

First let us clarify what it means to have an obligation. The word *obligation,* in its roots, refers to something that is binding upon one, something that one should do; not to do it would be to sin by omission. Or one could have an obligation *not* to do something, and to do it would be to sin. Most obligations that bind absolutely, that have no exceptions, are those that are expressed in what are known as negative precepts. For instance, we all have a moral obligation never to deliberately kill an innocent man. Positive precepts such as "give alms" are generally relative to one's circumstances. For instance, we all have an obligation to support our children, but if we fail to do so because of some circumstance not of our making, such as famine, we would not be doing moral wrong through our failure to meet our obligation. In a Christian context, we all have an obligation to give alms, but this is an

---

[2] See Janet E. Smith, *Humanae Vitae: A Generation Later,* and the essays by Joseph Boyle and Mary Rosera Joyce in this book.

obligation qualified by our means; we all need to give something, but that something is relative to our means.

Moreover, it should be noted that in our modern age, an age that seems obsessed with freedom, we chafe at anything that binds, since we sense that it limits our freedom. Obligations laid on us by God, however, serve more to liberate us than to enslave us; his demands on us are designed to advance us in perfecting our human nature. So it should ultimately be a joyful experience to fulfill the obligations that God gives us, if, at times, they share an element of the cross. While recognizing that childbearing brings its hardships, *Humanae Vitae* in its first line speaks of the mission (*munus*) of transmitting human life that God has entrusted to spouses. The word *mission* (*munus*) is weighted with meaning; it refers to a special task that God gives to those wish to serve him, who wish to build up the Kingdom of heaven here on earth. To give a brief sense of the meaning of this word, the documents of Vatican II tell us that Mary has the *munus* of being Mother of God, the Pope has the *munus* of infallibly proclaiming Church doctrine, bishops have the *munus* of ordaining priests, priests have the *munus* of consecrating the sacraments, and spouses have the *munus* of transmitting life.[3] Thus this "obligation", this mission, of having children is not one that should be dispensed with as an arduous and unpleasant chore or be done in a minimalistic way. Rather, spouses realize that having and raising children responsibly is one of the major contributions they can make to the Kingdom of God. It brings with it some burdens and considerable responsibilities, but these are burdens and responsibilities that ennoble us to fulfill; they do not enslave us.

If spouses have an obligation to have children, what would be

[3] I have written on the meaning of this word in "The *Munus* of Transmitting Human Life: A New Approach to *Humanae Vitae*", *The Thomist* 54, no. 3 (July 1990): 385–427; a shortened version of this paper appeared as "The Importance of the Concept of *Munus* to Understanding *Humanae Vitae*", in *Humanae Vitae: 20 Anni Dopo* (Milan: Edizioni Ares, 1989), 671–90 (published as Chapter 12 in this book); a shorter version of both treatments can be found in *Humanae Vitae: A Generation Later*, 136–48.

the nature or source of that obligation? Are there limits to that obligation? The Church has traditionally taught that marriage, as the proper arena for sexual intercourse, has as one of its ends or purposes or goods the bringing forth of new human life.[4] In this day and age, a fairly complicated argument may be required for such a claim, one that can only be sketched out here. Indeed, to most it seems odd to speak of acts and institutions having purposes or ends. The basis for the Church's teaching is that marriage has certain ends or purposes that those who marry are obliged to pursue and that these ends or purposes are the goods of marriage; that is, they are the goods that marriage is meant to help people achieve and enjoy. Perhaps it is sufficient to note here that, among other reasons, the Church teaches that marriage has procreation as an end because children, in order to prosper, need to be raised in a stable home environment and cared for by both their mother and father; marriage, then, is for the well-being of children as much as for the well-being of spouses. Thus, to refuse to have any children would be a violation of the nature and purpose of marriage; it would be to use marriage for something other than its natural end.

Furthermore, bringing forth new life is a great good, first for the good of the child conceived who has the potential of enjoying many other goods, secondly for the spouses who enjoy the meaningful lives made possible by children and the many joys that accompany parenthood,[5] and thirdly for society, which needs individuals to work for the common good. Since these goods are so great, spouses should be willing to foster such goods.

Such reasoning and argumentation seem nearly absurd to the modern way of thinking, which considers childbearing an "option" to the point where there are married couples who proudly and conspicuously proclaim their voluntary childless state—often for the reason that children would impede their pursuit of various

---

[4] See chap. 2 of *Humanae Vitae: A Generation Later* for a discussion of procreation as the primary purpose of marriage.

[5] Rev. Cormac Burke, "Children and Values", *International Review of Natural Family Planning* 12, no. 3 (Fall 1988): 181–92.

avenues of self-fulfillment.[6] The modern view, however, is an anomaly; people in nearly every age, culture, and religion have generally considered children to be a great good and something that spouses naturally want. Those who voluntarily remained childless have been considered peculiarities. But many moderns think it irresponsible to bring more children into the world, since the world is, in their view, such a "messed up" place. Some also think that there is a worldwide population problem that makes it immoral to have children, at least many children. Others think children are a burden and not a gift, that they are a drain on the parents' energies and resources. Finally, it is often argued that some individuals would not make good parents and thus ought not to become parents.

While most of the above reasons may often be thinly disguised rationalizations of those who do not want to exert the effort necessary to be parents, it seems plausible that some may choose not to have children for good reasons. Suppose, for instance, a couple were involved in some greatly needed charitable work in the community, say, work directed toward helping impoverished youngsters get the skills needed to escape their impoverished lives. If these couples refused to use contraception and relied upon a method of NFP (or upon complete abstinence), would they be failing to fulfill some obligation to have children? Certainly, it is curious that they seek to pursue goods that are not per se proper to their state in life while declining to pursue the goods that are per se proper to their lives. Nonetheless, it seems arguable (though not necessarily ultimately justifiable) that such lives may well merit an "exemption" from the obligation to have children—but only because the goods being sought are common goods that go beyond their personal needs.[7] The modern disinclination to

[6] For a critique of the modern view, see G. E. M. Anscombe, "Why Have Children", in *The Ethics of Having Children,* ed. by Lawrence P. Schrenk, *Proceedings of the American Philosophical Association* 63 (1990): 48–54.

[7] When I speak of the "common" good and "selfish" goods, I do not mean to suggest that the good of the individual is at odds with the common good. "Selfish" does not mean "individual". The true good of the individual embraces

have children, though, rarely derives from such lofty motives; moderns generally believe many activities, not just service activities or charitable activities, rate higher as goods than the good of having children.

Christians understand the good of having children to surpass nearly all other goods. Children are seen as an even greater good than they are in purely natural terms. As was stated earlier, Christians in having children understand themselves to be fulfilling a mission given to them by God. God wishes there to be new life with whom he may share the goods of his creation and has chosen to entrust the mission (*munus*) of transmitting of new human life to spouses. As John Paul II interprets the creation story in *Genesis,* God created man and woman and their sexuality to expand the opportunities for love in this world. The body, in John Paul II's view, has a "nuptial meaning", a meaning that entails total self-giving, and total self-giving entails being open to the further gift of children.[8]

Let us further note that in the Catholic Church, canon law holds that if spouses enter marriage with the intent never to have children, their "marriages" are invalid;[9] that is, they are not marriages at all. The Church bases this restriction not on some arbitrary fancy or on some Machiavellian scheme of filling the earth with Catholics but on the very nature of marriage. Exhortations about the blessing that children are and about the obligation that parents have to have children are commonplace in Church

---

the common good; "selfish" goods are precisely those goods that the individual perceives to be good for himself without reference to goods beyond his own desires.

[8] For a review of John Paul II's teaching, see chap. 8 of *Humanae Vitae: A Generation Later* and my article "Pope John Paul II and *Humanae Vitae*", *International Review of Natural Family Planning* 10, no. 2 (Summer 1986): 95–112. See also Rev. Richard Hogan, "A Theology of the Body", *The International Review of Natural Family Planning* 6, no. 3 (Fall 1982): 227–312.

[9] There are some reasons which allow a couple to practice methods of natural family planning throughout their marriages (see page 455 below), but spouses must still be open to children.

documents.[10] *Casti Connubii* (echoed by *Gaudium et Spes*, *Humanae Vitae*, and *Familiaris Consortio*)[11] speaks of the child being the first among the blessings of marriage.[12] After citing the admonition in *Genesis* to "increase and multiply", *Casti Connubii* states:

> How great a boon of God this [having children] is, and how great a blessing of matrimony is clear from a consideration of man's dignity and of his sublime end. For man surpasses all other visible creatures by the superiority of his rational nature alone. Besides, God wishes men to be born not only that they should live and fill the earth, but much more that they may be worshippers of God, that they may know Him and love Him and finally enjoy Him forever in heaven; and this end, since man is raised by God in a marvelous way to the supernatural order, surpasses all that eye hath seen, and ear heard, and all that hath entered into the heart of man. From which it is easily seen how great a gift of divine goodness and how remarkable a fruit of marriage are children born by the omnipotent power of God through the cooperation of those bound in wedlock.[13]

Pius XII speaks explicitly about the obligation to have children but teaches that the obligation is not absolute; that is, there may be moral reasons for the spouses to elect not to fulfill that obligation. Pius XII's instruction on the nature of the obligation to have children is lengthy but deserves to be cited in full because of its importance:

> If the act [of sexual intercourse] be limited to the sterile periods insofar as the mere use and not the right is concerned, there is no question about the validity of the marriage. Nevertheless, the moral licitness of such conduct on the part of the couple

---

[10] Ford and Kelly maintain that the "obligation" to procreate was first articulated by Pius XII, but I believe it to have been implicit in the description of the primary end of marriage as procreation. Chap. 2 of my book argues that the traditional understanding of the ranking of the ends of marriage is not incompatible with *Gaudium et Spes*.

[11] See *Gaudium et Spes* 50, *Humanae Vitae* 9, and *Familiaris Consortio* 14.

[12] *On Christian Marriage* (Boston: St. Paul Editions, 1930), 8.

[13] *On Christian Marriage*, 9.

would have to be approved or denied according as to whether or not the intention of observing those periods constantly was based on sufficient and secure moral grounds. The mere fact that the couple do not offend the nature of the act and are prepared to accept and bring up the child which in spite of their precautions came into the world would not be sufficient in itself to guarantee the rectitude of intention and the unobjectionable morality of the motives themselves.

The reason for this is that marriage obliges to a state of life which, while conferring certain rights also imposes the fulfillment of a positive work in regard to the married state itself. In such a case, one can apply the general principle that a positive fulfillment may be omitted when serious reasons [*gravi motivi*], independent from the good will of those obliged by it, show that a similar demand cannot reasonably be made of human nature.

The marriage contract which confers upon husband and wife the right to satisfy the inclinations of nature, sets them up in a certain state of life, the married state. But upon couples who perform the act peculiar to their state, nature and the Creator impose the function of helping the conservation of the human race. The characteristic activity which gives their state its value is the *bonum prolis*. The individual and society, the people and the state, the Church itself depend for their existence on the order established by God on fruitful marriage. Therefore, to embrace the married state, continuously to make use of the faculty proper to it and lawful in it alone, and on the other hand, to withdraw always and deliberately with no serious reason [*un grave motivo*] from its primary obligation, would be a sin against the very meaning of conjugal life.

There are serious motives [*seri motivi*], such as those often mentioned in the so-called medical, eugenic, economic, and social "indications", that can exempt for a long time, perhaps even the whole duration of the marriage, from the positive and obligatory carrying out of the act. From this it follows that observing the non-fertile periods alone can be lawful only under a moral aspect. Under the conditions mentioned it really is so. But if, according to a rational and just judgment [*secondo un giudizio ragionevole et equo*], there are no similar grave reasons [*gravi ragioni*] of a personal nature or deriving from external circumstances, then the determination to avoid habitually the fecundity of the union while at the same time to continue satisfying their sensuality, can be derived only from a false appreciation of life and from reasons having nothing to do with proper ethical laws.[14]

Pius XII teaches that unless some serious circumstances arise, spouses are obliged to have children. But he also makes it clear that it is moral for spouses to limit their family size or even to refrain from having children altogether if they have sufficiently serious reasons. We shall consider below what constitute just reasons for limiting family size or for not having any children. (We shall also comment upon the proper understanding of the force of such phrases as "grave reasons", "serious motives", and "rational and just judgments" that appear in the text cited above and reappear in *Humanae Vitae*.)

Gaudium et Spes 50 also speaks of the obligation of spouses to have children and speaks of it in specifically Christian terms:

Married couples should regard it as their proper mission to transmit human life and to educate their children; they should realize that they are thereby cooperating with the love of God the Creator and are, in a certain sense, its interpreters. This involves the fulfillment of their role with a sense of human and Christian responsibility and the formation of correct judgments through docile respect for God and common reflection and effort.[15]

---

[14] Pius XII, "Address to the Italian Catholic Union of Midwives" (Oct. 29, 1951), in AAS XLIII (1951): 835–54. Trans. by Vincent A. Yzermans, *The Major Address of Pope Pius XII,* vol. 1 (St. Paul, Minn.: Worth Central Publishing, 1961), 168–69.

[15] Translation from Austin Flannery, O.P., ed., *Vatican II: The Conciliar and Post Conciliar Documents* (Northport, N.Y.: Costello Publishing Co., 1975), 953.

The very first line of *Humanae Vitae* picks up on this description of the proper mission of spouses: "God has entrusted to spouses the extremely important mission of transmitting human life." *Familiaris Consortio* speaks at great length about children as a gift and lauds the essential role the family plays in advancing the goods of civilization and in the process of evangelization and sanctification. Perhaps one line best sums up the thrust of the document: "The future of humanity passes by way of the family."[16]

John Paul II in other speeches and writings has regularly added his voice to the chorus on these points. In a homily on the mall in Washington, D.C., he said,

> In order that Christian marriage may favor the total good and development of the married couple, it must be inspired by the Gospel, and thus be open to new life—new life to be given and accepted generously. The couple is also called to create a family atmosphere in which children can be happy and lead full and worthy human and Christian lives.
>
> To maintain a joyful family requires much from both the parents and the children. Each member of the family has to become, in a special way, the servant of the others and share their burdens (cf. Gal 6:2; Phil 2:2). Each one must show concern, not only for his or her own life, but also for the lives of the other members of the family: their needs, their hopes, their ideals. Decisions about the number of children and the sacrifices to be made for them must not be taken only with a view to adding to comfort and preserving a peaceful existence. Reflecting upon this matter before God, with the graces drawn from the sacrament, and guided by the teaching of the Church, parents will remind themselves that it is certainly less serious to deny their children certain comforts or material advantages than to deprive them of the presence of brothers and sisters, who could help them to grow in humanity and to realize the beauty of life at all its ages and in all its variety.
>
> If parents fully realize the demands and the opportunities that this great sacrament brings, they could not fail to join in

---

[16] *Familiaris Consortio* (Boston: St. Paul Editions, 1981), 86.

Mary's hymn to the Author of life—to God who has made them His chosen fellow workers.[17]

The Catholic Church, then, teaches that children are a great good and it teaches that all couples have a moral obligation to be open to having children. Nevertheless, it teaches that there may be good reasons for spouses not to pursue the good of children at a certain time. And, what is expected to be a very rare occurrence, there may be good reasons that exempt spouses for the duration of the marriage from fulfilling their obligation.

Before we turn to examining what reasons might be good reasons for not pursuing the good of children, let us dismiss one false misunderstanding of the basis for the obligation to have children. Since Christians believe that in having children they are bringing forth new souls to share an eternity with God, some think that spouses must have children and have as many children as they can care for, since by not having children they would be denying souls the opportunity to come into existence. This view seems to be based on the false view that souls preexist and are, in a sense, awaiting a landing place. But souls do not preexist an act of sexual intercourse, nor is the act of sexual intercourse at a fertile time sufficient to bring forth new life. Rather, Christians believe that God creates a new soul for each new life that comes into existence and is thus the immediate source for that new soul coming into existence.[18] Sexual intercourse provides God an opportunity to do his creative work.[19] There is no "preexisting"

---

[17] Pope John Paul II, "Let Us Celebrate Life" (homily, Oct. 7, 1979), in *U.S.A.: The Message of Justice, Peace and Love* (Boston: St. Paul Editions, 1979), 281–82.

[18] On this point, Thomas Aquinas states, "The rational soul is a subsistent form, as was explained [Q. 75, a. 2], and so it is competent to be and to be made. And since it cannot be made of pre-existing matter,—whether corporeal, which would render it a corporeal being,—or spiritual, which would involve the transmutation of one spiritual substance into another, we must conclude that it cannot come to be except by creation" (*Summa Theologiae*, I–II, q. 94, art. 2, in *Basic Writings of Saint Thomas Aquinas*, ed. Anton C. Pegis [New York: Random House, 1945] vol. I, 866).

[19] See chap. 4 of *Humanae Vitae: A Generation Later* for further discussion of this point.

new life that is being denied an earthly existence because spouses seek to avoid a pregnancy. If this were so, it would seem that everyone would have an obligation to bring new life into the world; celibates would be doing possible future generations a great disservice by pursuing a life of celibacy. But, again, the claim that by not having children one is denying life an opportunity to come into existence is not plausibly true, for one cannot deny something to something or someone that does not exist. Spouses may be doing each other, society, and God an injustice in not having children, they may be making themselves willful and selfish arbiters of when it is good for a new life to come into existence, but they are not doing an injustice to some "possible child".

Although bringing new life into existence is a great good, spouses are not, therefore, obligated to have as many children as they can. In the remainder of the essay (1) I shall maintain that spouses need not have as many children as they can biologically, financially, and psychologically sustain; (2) I shall sketch out what constitute moral reasons for limiting family size; (3) I shall speculate about whether there is any size of family that should be considered minimal and attempt to give guidelines for spouses in their attempt to determine the best family size for their particular situation; (4) and finally, I shall address a question sometimes raised by those wary of NFP: Will those who use NFP lose sight of the procreative meaning of sexual intercourse and give themselves over to sensuality?

The Limits to the Obligation to Have Children

It is never possible to define positive obligations completely, that is, obligations *to do* something, since the contingencies and variables of life are so great. Again, it is much easier to define negative prohibitions that forbid the doing of something. It is always hard to determine when one has met one's positive obligations. For instance, when has one given enough to charity? Although it may be difficult to determine, it is not impossible to determine the limits to what one must give to charity; they are determined by one's means and one's other obligations and are best discerned through reasonable and prayerful reflection.

As has been established, marriage brings with it the positive obligation to have children. It might be said that all vocations bring with them obligations; for instance, a priest has an obligation to perform the sacraments, doctors have the obligation to heal, and lawyers have the obligation to do legal work. Yet, "obligation" is used in a somewhat loose sense here. Certainly, it would be curious for one to gain the skills of a profession and be unwilling to exercise them at all; however, only specific circumstances would make it a positive moral obligation to exercise those skills. We can all conceive of instances where we would think circumstances oblige a priest to hear a confession, a doctor to heal the sick, a lawyer to defend the accused. No one, however, would argue that priests are obliged to attempt to perform as many sacraments as possible, or doctors to heal as many patients as possible, or lawyers to do as much legal work as possible, or even that they have an obligation to do any given amount of their respective tasks. The virtue of prudence is needed to specify obligations of this nature; each individual will have to use prudence to determine if fulfilling a certain obligation is necessary in light of the other moral demands on him. For instance, a doctor may have many children of his own that he must help care for and may not be able to take more patients, a lawyer may be caring for elderly parents and not be able to take more cases, and so on. If priests, doctors, and lawyers may limit the exercise of the tasks to some degree obligatory for those in their vocations, would this not also be true of those called to be parents?

Of course, there is not a complete parallel between a married person choosing for or against parenthood and a lawyer deciding whether or not to plead a case. The obligations of parents, certainly, seem to be more closely analogous to those of priests; the sacrament of ordination brings with it obligations to administer the sacraments, an obligation much stronger than that of a lawyer ever to plead a case. Becoming a doctor or lawyer does not effect the ontological change upon one that ordination to the priest-hood does or marriage does. Once a priest, always a priest; those married are married for life; parents are parents for a lifetime. Taking the vow to be a priest or to be married is taking a vow to perform certain services for God; it is not a simple, revisable career choice. One of the elements of the pledge of marriage is to accept children.

But, to continue the analogy, a priest does not have to adminis-ter the sacraments if certain circumstances or other obligations preclude his doing so. For instance, a priest who is the president of a college would not need to hear confessions regularly. Even as president, though, he would have the obligation to hear a dying man's confession, no matter how inconvenient it is to do so. Thus, these sacramental modes of life bring with them certain obliga-tions that must be met if certain conditions prevail.

Although most couples may face circumstances that require them to limit their family, having children is something that can reasonably be undertaken by most couples; that is, having chil-dren does not put an undue burden on the resources, financial, physical, psychological, or spiritual, of most couples. It is also certainly true that having children imposes an undue burden on some couples. An extreme instance would be if a couple were living in a regime where they would be killed if they were to bear a child; they would be justified in postponing childbearing indefinitely and perhaps in never having children at all. The teaching of Pope Pius XII cited above illuminates this question. He counsels that couples with known genetic defects or a woman whose life may be threatened by a pregnancy could enter a marriage intending to practice periodic abstinence for the whole of a marriage as long as the spouses would accept lovingly any child they may happen to conceive. They do not "intend" to have children in a positive and direct fashion, but if they refuse to use unnatural methods of birth control, they can also be said not to intend to thwart the natural end of marriage, since they never engage in any positive action against that end. For just reasons, they choose not to pursue this end actively. The obligation to have children, then, is one that is not absolute; circumstances may exempt some spouses from fulfilling this obligation to have children.

Reasons for Limiting Family Size

In passing, several reasons that would legitimate limiting family size have already been given. Can we formulate any general principles that characterize these reasons? First I would like to take a look at what the Church states about this matter. Five different phrases are used in *Humanae Vitae* in speaking to this question. HV 10 states:

> If we look further to physical, economic, psychological and social conditions, responsible parenthood is exercised by those who, guided by prudent consideration and generosity, elect to accept many children. Those are also to be considered responsible, who, for serious reasons [*seriis causis*] and with due respect for moral precepts, decide not to have another child either for a definite or an indefinite amount of time.

HV 16 states: "Certainly, there may be just reasons [*justae causae*] for spacing offspring; these may be based on the physical or psychological condition of the spouses, or may be based on external factors." Further on it states the spouses may have worthy and weighty justifications (*argumenta ... honesta et gravia*), defensible reasons (*probabiles rationes*), and just reasons (*iustae rationes*) for limiting their family size. It is my view that the common rendering of some of these phrases, such as "serious reasons" or "grave reasons", may suggest weightier reasons are required than is necessary. I believe the phrase "just reasons" to reflect more precisely what is meant. Trivial reasons will not do, but reasons less than life-threatening conditions will. What are these reasons that lie between what is trivial and what is life-threatening?

A passage from *Gaudium et Spes* 50 suggests what constitutes a good decision by the spouses; it "takes into consideration their own good and the good of their children already born or yet to come, an ability to read the signs of the times and of their own situation on the material and spiritual level, and finally, an estimation of the good of the family, of society, and of the Church".[20] It seems right to say, then, that the Church teaches that in planning their family size, spouses need to be just to all their obligations: those to God, to each other, to the family they already have, and to all their commitments. They need to have defensible reasons, ones that are not selfish but that are directed to a good beyond their own comfort and convenience. As *Humanae Vitae* 10 states, physical or psychological reasons for limiting family size, and external factor—here one supposes financial and political factors are meant—also may shape a couple's decision about the responsibility of having a child.

Moreover, it must be understood that Christians have many ways of advancing the goods of the Kingdom of God, of which having children is only one. Those who are married have the mission (*munus*) of having children, but it is not their sole mission. They may be involved in other work that is also conducive to building up the Kingdom. Indeed, spouses may need to limit their family size precisely for the good of the family that they already have. Couples may have very good reasons for wanting to avoid a pregnancy: the wife may be ill, and another pregnancy may put undue strain on her health; she may have a sickly child or relative to care for and not be able to attend to the needs of an infant. A spouse may have psychological problems that makes him or her unsuited to be a parent at a given time. And let us repeat that health reasons are not the only morally acceptable reasons for avoiding pregnancy; *Humanae Vitae* 16 notes that "external factors" as well as the physical and psychological condition of the spouses may make the spacing of children necessary. The family may be

[20] Translation from Flannery, *Vatican II: The Conciliar and Post Conciliar Documents,* 953.

experiencing severe financial difficulties or perhaps even job-
lessness. As in China, spouses may face a forced abortion if a
pregnancy occurs. If couples have the knowledge (as they do with
NFP) that would assist them in avoiding a pregnancy without
doing anything immoral, it is morally licit for them to use such
means.

In a word, spouses may have many good and moral reasons
for wishing to limit their family size. Some Christians, however, might ask: Are couples who use NFP demonstrating too
little faith in providence? Are they refusing to trust in God
to provide for them and their families while they fulfill their
vocational obligations to parenthood? Are they assuming that
they know more about their health and financial needs, for
instance, than does God? Shouldn't spouses have faith that if
God "sends" them another child, he will provide the means to
care for that child? Many spouses have tales to tell of being
"miraculously" rescued and provided for when another child
arrives; hence the adage "A child always arrives carrying a loaf of
bread."

While it is undoubtedly true that God can and does provide for
our needs, especially when we are struggling ardently to do his
will, it is also true that our ability to reason and plan is also a gift
from God, and one that he expects us to use. It is certainly true
that some couples may be physically able to have more children
than they can care for. Karol Wojtyla (now John Paul II) counsels
that it is a moral necessity for some couples to limit their family
size:

> There are, however, circumstances in which this disposition [to
> be a responsible parent] itself demands renunciation of pro-
> creation, and any further increase in the size of the family
> would be incompatible with parental duty. A man and a woman
> moved by true concern for the good of their family and a
> mutual sense of responsibility for the birth, maintenance, and
> upbringing of their children, will then limit intercourse and
> abstain from it in periods in which this might result in another

pregnancy undesirable in the particular conditions of their married life and family.[21]

The Church has always taught that man is to be responsible in his disposition of the gifts and goods that God has given him. Saving for the children's education, for retirement, or for possible emergencies does not exhibit a lack of trust in God. Planning one's family size is befitting a creature who is able to reason. Recall the passage from HV 10 cited earlier: "If we look further to physical, economic, psychological and social conditions, responsible parenthood is exercised by those who, guided by prudent consideration and generosity, elect to accept many children." *Gaudium et Spes* also states: "Among the married couples who thus fulfill their God-given mission special mention should be made of those who after prudent reflection and common decisions courageously undertake the proper upbringing of a large number of children(50)."[22] Having many children, then, is to be the result of "prudent reflection", not the spontaneous result of a refusal to plan. Some couples may be so well situated that they need not plan when to have children and how many to have, but for them the decision not to plan is itself a prudent decision, a kind of a plan.

Some might still ask: Is there room even for those who are not altogether well situated just to let the babies come and trust God's ability to provide? In our materialistic age it is easy to overestimate what resources are needed to raise children well, and most of us need more diligently to seek the Kingdom of God first and trust him to provide as we do. Nonetheless, it is irresponsible for couples not to use NFP if they have little expectation that they could care for another child. Yet, if a pregnancy occurs in spite of their use of NFP (a very rare occurrence), then they should have confidence that God will provide. The need for heroic sacrifice, however, is not so hard to come by; perhaps it is not an oxymoron

[21] Karol Wojtyla, *Love and Responsibility* (San Francisco: Ignatius Press, 1993), 243.

[22] Translation from Flannery, *Vatican II: The Conciliar and Post Conciliar Documents*.

to note that "heroic faith" is needed in the *ordinary* circumstances of raising children, to make the sacrifices necessary to care for them, to exhibit the patience they need to have a loving upbringing. Some may be called to more extraordinary heroic faith if they bear a handicapped or retarded child. God will surely honor our willingness to undertake hardships to be generous with him, but we must be responsible in doing so. Primarily what he asks of us is that we graciously embrace the hardships that come our way.

But what about couples who are able to care well for many children, for whom having another child would not present an undue burden? Do they have an obligation to have as many children as they are able to care for well?

Again, many would find this to be a nearly an absurd question; they would argue that having children is one of the many goods of this world, but surely not a good to which all other goods must be sacrificed. Christians, however, with their heightened sense of the value of human life, may think that having children is a good to be pursued at the expense of all other goods. There is, though, little evidence that this is the view even of the Church. *Gaudium et Spes* states that it is up to the couple to decide how many children they ought to have.[23] The passage from *Gaudium et Spes* 50 cited above suggests that having a large family would be a generous thing to do. Surely all Christians are called to be generous, but they are called to be generous in different ways. There is a note of the "supererogatory" here. This term refers to actions that are beyond what is obligatory; we must all do what is obligatory (again, with the proper qualifications). What is "supererogatory" may be asked of some of us but is not required of all of us. Thus, having a large family is the generous act that God asks of some spouses; he will ask other kinds of generous acts of other spouses. It is likely that those who are good and able parents and enjoy being parents and have the resources to enable them to take care of a large number of children should have large families; such talents and circumstances suggest that this is what God is calling them to.

[23] Flannery, 954.

Other couples may not be so inclined or so situated. They may also have other very pressing and worthy obligations—say, to elderly parents, or to public service or the like—obligations that would be neglected should they have more children. These seem also to constitute serious and just reasons for limiting family size. These also constitute ways of being generous with God.

Proper Family Size

Is it right to conclude, then, that couples must have as many children as they can care for well without neglecting other obligations? I can find nothing in Church documents that suggests this or that even suggests what size a family might be considered a kind of norm. Since in past ages spouses have had little control over their fertility, such guidance was largely unnecessary, but since in the modern age methods of natural family planning have allowed us to be able to have a great deal of control over family size, such guidance would be helpful to many. Karol Wojtyla (now John Paul II), in his book *Love and Responsibility*, speaks of "the morally correct" number of children, whereby he seems to mean a number that constitutes a full family:

> The family is an institution created by procreation within the framework of marriage. It is a natural community, directly dependent on the parents for its existence and functioning. The parents create the family as a complement to and extension of their love. To create a family means to create a community, since the family is a social unit or else it is not a family. To be a community it must have a certain size. This is most obvious in the context of education. For the family is an educational institution within the framework of which the personality of a new human being is formed. If it is to be correctly formed it is very important that this human being should not be alone, but surrounded by a natural community. We are sometimes told that it is easier to bring up several children together than an only child, and also that two children are not a community—

they are two only children. It is the role of the parents to direct their children's upbringing, but under their direction the children educate themselves because they develop within the framework of a community of children, a collective of siblings.[24]

This passage seems to suggest that only two children would not constitute a complete family. One of my friends, independently of the Pope's suggestion, upon the birth of his third child, said with a sigh of relief, "Now we have a family." (This man is now father of seven and still hopeful for more.) He explained that he thought three children was a "critical mass" for a family. That is, he thought when there were simply two children, they could too easily be two "only" children, pampered and spoiled by the parents and easily able to divide goods. He said three children made a social unit in which they needed to negotiate with more seriousness among each other; they really needed to share and could not each "have a parent".

Now let us hasten to say that no judgment is meant, of course, on those who are not able to have many children, nor is the suggestion made that smaller families cannot be "proper" families. But perhaps there is a family size most conducive to achieving the ends of a family for community living and all that comes with it and that this should be a goal for couples, insofar as possible. As several of the passages cited above suggest, large families are generally good at fostering generosity and selflessness in their members. This is not to say that small families cannot be successful at the same, but it suggests that some characteristics are more easily developed in large families. What has been said here about the importance of at least three children for a family is not to suggest that those who can must have at least three, or that once a couple has had three, they need have no more. Rather, these reflections have been offered to suggest the kind of factors that should be taken into account when couples are assessing the wisdom of having or not having more children.

It is my observation that couples do not often feel confident in

---

[24] Wojtyla, *Love and Responsibility*, 242–43.

their parenting skills until the third child. Up to that point, parenting can seem (and often is) overwhelming. By the time of the birth of the third child, however, couples (for the sake of survival if nothing else) have begun to acquire some significant parenting skills and tend to enjoy greatly the interaction between the children. The oldest one starts being of some help, and the youngest is generally greatly amused by the antics of his siblings and requires less full-time attention from the parents. Parents who deliberately stop at two children might find they enjoy parenting much more were they to have three. I have heard many mothers remark that after four, it does not make all that much difference if there is one more, and then one more, etc. The exponential leap of demands made on one's self with one baby or two is simply not repeated as the family grows.

Let us address the final concern here: Will those who use NFP lose sight of the procreative meaning of sexual intercourse and give themselves over to sensuality? Are couples who confine sexual intercourse to the infertile period, in attempting to avoid a pregnancy and to achieve union, guilty of giving themselves over to sensuality, to the selfish pursuit of sexual pleasure? Let us here understand sensuality to be the state of being out of control in regard to one's sexuality, the state of seeking sexual pleasure irrespective of the pursuit of other goods, or even in violation of other goods. We shall understand sensuality to be a state of luxuriating in the sexual delights of sexual intercourse *without* regard for the deeper meanings of the sexual act.

How does pleasure factor into the understanding of sexual intercourse as an action that has two purposes or meanings of an unbreakable connection, that of union and of procreation? Often union and the seeking of pleasure are thought to be identical. But the pleasurable effect of sexual intercourse is not the same as the unitive meaning. Pleasure is not one of the defining purposes of sexual intercourse, though it generally follows upon sexual intercourse and is almost always the motivating reason for sexual intercourse. Those who seek to have sexual intercourse solely for the purpose of experiencing pleasure and with no intention of achieving union or of accepting the children that may result are violating the purpose of sexual intercourse and are guilty of sensuality. But those who partake in sexual intercourse during the infertile period for the sake of pleasure are not necessarily guilty of sensuality. It is wrong to think that couples who have sexual intercourse during the infertile period in order to avoid pregnancy are thereby necessarily guilty of pursuing sensual pleasures selfishly. Some may be guilty of such, but this is not the necessary or even likely consequence of the method;[25] selfish sensuality is more likely a result of their inability to order their passions or a result of not understanding the purpose and nature of sexual intercourse.

Not all sexual intercourse pursued for the sake of pleasure is hedonistic or a wrongful pursuit of sensual pleasure. Pleasure, again, may be the motive for engaging in an act that by its nature leads to union (and procreation), and so long as one embraces the goods that follow from the act, pleasure is not a vicious motive for performing it. One cannot contradict the other goods of an act when performing it (as one does when contracepting), but to seek the pleasure an act affords, while respecting the goods of that act, is not immoral. Seeking pleasure is not in itself a sin; seeking pleasure *selfishly* is a sin, but pleasure can also be sought in an unselfish way and in a way that brings goods to others as well as to one's self. Parents often play with their children because it pleases them; the play is not therefore vitiated because it was initiated because of a desire for pleasure. The good of the child need not be uppermost in the mind of the parents, but the good of the child may not be incompatible with the pleasure the parents intend. As long as the good of the children is also sought, for parents to seek their own pleasure is good since it properly satisfies natural human desires.

Those who engage in sexual intercourse for purposes of pleasure need not be doing so selfishly. If the desire for sexual pleasure

---

[25] Pope John Paul II does allow that methods of NFP can be used improperly, if separated from the ethical dimension proper to it. See, for instance, *Reflections on Humanae Vitae* (Boston: St. Paul Editions, 1984), 45.

motivates one to seek to have sexual intercourse with one's spouse, and if one is striving to help one's spouse achieve what is good also, one is acting morally and bringing about what is good. For instance, one may succeed in making one's spouse feel loved, or the mutual pleasure may foster intimacy and bonding, or comfort may be given and received. Here we see the unitive meaning of sexual intercourse being preserved without the procreative meaning being violated.

John Paul II teaches that far from fostering sensuality, the proper practice of NFP will enhance the loving relationship of the spouses and make their acts of sexual intercourse ones more expressive of love and acts more authentically expressive of total self-giving. The use of NFP, far from bringing about a state of sensuality, is more likely to assist one in gaining control of one's sexual appetites, in appreciating the deeper meanings of sexual intercourse, and in being better able to express them. Throughout his writings, John Paul II speaks to this point. Consider this passage:

> If conjugal chastity (and chastity in general) is manifested at first as the capacity to resist the concupiscence of the flesh, it later gradually reveals itself as a singular capacity to perceive, love and practice those meanings of the "language of the body" which remain altogether unknown to concupiscence itself and which progressively enrich the marital dialogue of the couple, purifying it, deepening it, and at the same time simplifying it.
>
> Therefore, that asceticism of continence, of which the encyclical speaks (HV 12), does not impoverish "affective manifestations", but rather makes them spiritually more intense and enriches."[26]

Those who have the virtue of self-mastery are better able to ensure that their acts of sexual intercourse are more truly acts of love-making rather than acts designed merely to satisfy sexual urges.

John Paul II claims that self-mastery gives one some freedom

[26] *Reflections on Humanae Vitae,* 64.

from one's sensual impulses and observes, "This freedom presupposes such a capacity to direct the sensual and emotive reactions as to make possible the giving of self to the other 'I' on the grounds of the mature self-possession of one's own 'I' in its corporeal and emotive subjectivity."[27] In other words, the freedom gained through self-mastery enables one to refrain from sexual intercourse when it would not promote the good of the marriage and to engage in it when it does. This control over one's sexual desires makes one a more thoughtful and attentive lover, for one will be having sexual intercourse in the context of what is good for the marriage, not as the result of uncontrollable sexual desires. Thus, John Paul II, far from thinking that NFP leads to sensuality, thinks that it can be a cure for sensuality. He also seems to think that those who use NFP will have a better understanding of the meaning of sexual intercourse, and that those who have this better understanding will enjoy sexual intercourse more since it will engage them not only physically but psychologically and spiritually as well. So, in his view, the use of NFP protects against sensuality and increases pleasure.

The free and unfettered enjoyment of sexual intercourse by spouses is undoubtedly a source of much pleasure and many goods for spouses when the circumstances of their lives allow such. To be able to find every pregnancy a welcome event, those unplanned as well as planned, is surely a great blessing. But there are times when couples must limit their family size and must curtail their sexual activity. They should be confident that if their decision to limit their family size is well discerned, in using NFP they should be confident that they are acting morally and not mistrusting God or misusing their sexual powers.

[27] Ibid, 80.

20

SENSIBLE SEX

by
Ruth D. Lasseter

Ruth D. Lasseter tells the reader a lot about herself and her family in this article. The mother of six (within 7 years of one another), a convert to Catholicism, she tells a powerful story of how contraception damaged and nearly ruined her marriage. Dissenters often argue that the Church's teaching on contraception is generally promoted by priests, who in their celibacy, are unable to appreciate the demands of married life that make contraception necessary. Here, the clear voice of experience proclaims that had Mrs. Lasseter and many other couples been faithful to the Church and her celibate advocates, she and they would have been spared much anguish. She speaks eloquently of the subtle alienation that creeps into a contraceptive marriage, an alienation from spouse, Church, and God, and speaks equally eloquent of the joy and mutual respect that are present in marriages in which God's laws are respected. Any who think contraception is no offense or a minor offense against God and marriage should reflectively read Ruth D. Lasseter's testimony.

This article appeared in *Homiletic and Pastoral Review* vol. 92, no. 11 (Aug–Sept. 1992), 19–31.

20

SENSIBLE SEX

by
Ruth D. Lasseter

Three old friends, middle-aged mothers all, are having lunch together. Nancy is a Methodist minister; the other, Mary Ann, is Catholic and a pro-life executive; the third is myself, a convert to Catholicism and freelance writer. The subject of contraception comes up.

"Why can't you Catholics just do it the *sensible* way," says Nancy in a good-natured crack.

"It may *look* sensible to you, Nancy, but you know the facts as well as I do: the society that accepts contraception inevitably comes to accept abortion, too," states Mary Ann.

As for me, like the tar baby, I ain't sayin' nuthin'. I listen to my two friends argue, their kind faces rigid and defensive now, and I am silent because I feel the "tar" of my own sins. I once thought, like Nancy, that artificial contraception was sensible. But Mary Ann is right; a contracepting society becomes a society that sanctions abortion and euthanasia, as experience and research have shown. My friends are deadlocked within these two irreconcilable attitudes toward unnatural contraception: Is it sensible? Or is it a preliminary to genocide, or at least infanticide? The Catholic Church recognizes that there can be no resolution and no compromise between the two attitudes, as incompatible as oil and water.

475

... the difference, both anthropological and moral, between contraception and recourse to the rhythm of the cycle ... is a difference which is much wider and deeper than is usually thought, one which involves in the final analysis two irreconcilable concepts of the human person and of human sexuality.

(*Familiaris Consortio,* section 32, p. 30)

Nancy, Mary Ann, and I are pro-life and pro-family Christian women; we are educated, responsible, and experienced. We have a host of subjects to discuss and many things in common. Yet we cannot discuss contraceptives. It isn't just that birth control is a tacky and taboo subject. Like all proper women have always done, we might (and do) freely talk about other equally tacky and private matters—labor and childbirth and nursing, childrearing (up to puberty, at least), piles and constipation, indigestion and canker sores, crime and pornography. But not contraception. It divides friends and ruins lunches. To Nancy, the method of Natural Family Planning seems so *un*sensible, so *un*necessary; it seems like the Amish using candlelight instead of electricity. To Mary Ann, the means are everything, since as she says, "they may lead to other ends than those intended or desired."

What's going on here? There's more than personal preference for an archaic technology, more than candlelight and electricity, that causes friends to fall silent and defensive. We don't talk about, don't ask about, don't discuss contraception. Easier just to swallow a pill, have our husbands put on sheaths, or have ourselves "fixed."

I Am Going to Break Silence. I Have a Story to Tell.

Why can't we talk about it? Are we too ashamed and hurt to do so? Too tarred? We women have submitted our female sexuality's cyclic nature to the constant male sex drive of our husbands. Are we *ashamed* to have made ourselves *always* available to our spouses, from the very beginning of marriage beyond our menopause? Ashamed to admit that we sophisticated and independent women have followed the Old Wive's Tale that a woman MUST be available for her man? Why do we not ask ourselves, if not other women, why we should feel ashamed and exploited in having done so? Are we afraid that the answer just *might* be another Old Wives Tale: that a man will leave her for another, more accommodating woman, if she doesn't "turn on the heat." Or that he might find her boring if they have to *talk* only and not work out their tensions in the bedroom. Most self-respecting women won't admit to themselves or anyone else that they, too, share petty jealousy, suspicion, resentment and even secret sympathy with the radical feminists, whose politics and tactics are deplorable. Yet, we should talk, for the answer is none of these phantoms. It is true that women who contracept do feel exploited by their husbands; husbands who resort to condoms feel resentment towards their wives' fertility. Here is another social rift; husbands and wives don't talk about contraceptives, either. As our own beloved children grow into puberty, we who are using unnatural contraceptives cannot talk to them about sexual chastity and self-control, even in the face of AIDS and STDs and every sort of promiscuously born disease of soul and body. Even while we are told that we are free at last, we know that we are helpless; we give our children condoms and are silent about chastity; we feel heartbroken, not knowing why. The tar is on us all.

I am going to "break silence." I have a story to tell. I want to tell this story so that other married couples may have the courage to know themselves and to begin talking again about their marriage and their love, and so come to find between them a truly Christian theology of the body. My perspective is unusual, but hardly unique; I am Protestant in heritage, Catholic by conversion. Having been connected since birth with a science and medicine-friendly family, I am quite familiar with the marvels of modern medical technology, including the whole hog of contraceptive devices, which are hardly conducive to health and well-being.

Since a story is a story, it cannot be a rational argument. However, story may be useful as example for the arguments put forth by others who have the gift of apologetics, as I do not. Janet

E. Smith's fine book *Humanae Vitae: A Generation Later,* has just been published by the Catholic University of America Press; its 425 pages contain a very complete and convincing rational argument in defense of the Catholic Church's unbroken teaching on unnatural contraception. In addition to its offering a new translation of the encyclical *Humanae Vitae,* it is a very sensible book.

I grew up with the two great Protestant imperatives: first, the importance of the individual's responsibility in forming a great love bond with his Creator (achieved through reading and meditating on Scripture, through personal prayer, through charitable acts); second, the realization of the good of passionate, romantic love between man and woman. It would take a book to discuss the particulars of these two Protestant pillars and how they have been pulled down by the permissiveness of our age—a modern God-hating Samson. While the pillars remain standing for the Evangelical Protestants, who strongly oppose abortion, they may yet topple because of these sects' general acceptance of contraception, a silent destroyer of just that married love and mutual respect which Protestants have so long recognized and properly praised. Yet, there are indications that at least some Evangelical Protestants are beginning to rethink this issue; the January, 1992, issue of the journal *First Things* had a feature on this new trend.

The Catholic view is that contracepted sex is inherently sinful, an offense against God's will for the purpose of human sexuality, and divisive of the two aspects of sacred marriage—the unitive and generative. Despite widespread civil laws (the Comstock Laws, enacted by Protestant legislatures, which were in effect until the 1930s in this country) which banned contraceptive devices, modern Protestants cannot understand all the fuss; they think it's mere ecclesiastical and legalistic hairsplitting. An impassioned Anglican friend said to us recently, "It isn't these silly rules over contraception that we should be quibbling about! The affirmation of LOVE is what is so needed today and you Catholics don't seem to realize this!"

Of course, it is true that the rules, and the quibble over rules, can lead away from love and from the vision of love. However, it is not a neat set of *rules* that is at stake. The sacredness of marital sexuality and its place in a greater divine order is what is at stake and under attack, and divorced from that order, the loss of love, indeed.

Under the guise of helping love, artificial contraception cunningly establishes a tyrant in the marriage: the sex act declines from a reaffirming of the whole marriage covenant, true love-making, to joint seeking of mutual satisfaction. A subtle shift, but a decisive one, away from God and the covenant of marriage.

The well-documented symptoms attending this shift are the grist of many marriage and sexual therapy manuals; yet, the authors of such books, many of them Christian, never consider that the contraceptive devices could be *causing* the familiar problems. The nuptial exchange between man and woman is replaced by a woman's sense, vague and miniscule at first, that she must be "available" to her husband; anxiety develops about "performance" and sensual attractiveness; she may begin to feel used by her spouse. The husband, in an equally subtle way, ceases to delight in his bride and begins to think of her as an object to arouse and satisfy passion. He has a vague sense that something is wrong; he feels restless and unsatisfied. If they try to talk about "what's wrong with us?" it often draws up petty resentments. They suspect, vaguely, that "something sexual" is wrong. They may just as often conclude that "something spiritual" is wrong. A vast and foggy field, in either case. They just don't seem able to come to an understanding over their difficulties. This couple may in every other way be moral and exemplary Christians; it has never occurred to them that artificial contraception could be destroying their marriage covenant and their love.

They may seek help for what they perceive is a sexual problem; they are encouraged, and sincerely try, to be more loving, considerate, and attentive to one another. They may pray together, but as the secrets of their innermost hearts have already been shut to each other and to God, the Lord and Giver of life, their prayer is blocked; they may develop a distaste for religion in all forms. Over all, there is a secret resentment against the other for his/her lack of . . . whatever it was that used to make life so good. The husband thinks: "If only she would stop this complaining and snap out of it! I'm doing the best that I can to show her that I love her, but it's not good enough for her." The wife thinks: "He doesn't love me anymore. He says that he does, but he doesn't really mean it. What can I do?" When there are children present, there is usually enough shared love for these children to keep the husband and wife in charity, but there is no doubt that *eros* (and *caritas,* reverence, and respect) between the couple is lessened or nonexistent. The last thing that such a couple will do is consider jettisoning the contraceptive device. They are likely to heed popular remedies: develop more sex appeal or get more involved in the community, or even do more things together as a family.

If a woman should have a surprise pregnancy at such a crisis as this, she is very likely to consider a secret abortion in a desperate attempt to save her husband's love. She may seek among women (often of charismatic or even feminist or New Age persuasion) the emotional contact and spiritual fellowship which is ebbing away from the marriage. She is likely to develop a distaste for "maleness"; her own vile thoughts may shock and disgust her. For his part, the husband may begin to wonder if a little innocent flirtation with another woman could really be so harmful. He may begin to treat his wife disrespectfully (in ways other than having contraceptive sex with her). His own behavior may disturb him, so that, in order to avoid his wife, he begins to spend more time away from home. He may turn more energetically to his work and to companionship with other males. He may begin to keep an eye out for the opportunity for a sexual misadventure. At no point is either aware that the communion of their marriage is betrayed by that lie, which began as such a tiny thing, accepted with such good intentions.

This tiny thing is so very subtle and slow in its tyrannical effect and usurpation; the small denials that anything is wrong (the unspoken concerns about damage inflicted on bodily health by the contraceptive device, the increased tension in conversation and in everyday life, the uneasy sense of future trouble, the steady growth of mistrust, the general boredom with family life in general and spousal sex in particular, the secret fantasies and desires) all go unnoticed until their cumulative effect has destroyed trust and made impossible the very love that the contracepting couple so fervently hoped to preserve. Yet, for most Protestants and a majority of Catholics, artificial birth control continues to be accepted and promoted as an unquestioned good.

On June 24, 1967, Rollin and I celebrated our wedding with a traditional Anglican marriage rite and nuptial mass. The church organ was amazingly pure, and there was a professional choir to sing three J. S. Bach hymns and the beautiful music of the Anglican liturgy. Our wedding took place at the Trinity Episcopal Church, Indianapolis, which is a perfect replica of a 13th Century English church, complete with rood screen, painted roof, lych gate, and cloistered garden. On June 23, I was confirmed at that same church; only five people were present at this ceremony, Bishop Grey (a tall, elderly man, radiating the odor of Anglican sanctity), Fr. Lynch (who had given me instruction and who presided at our wedding), Rollin (who was my sponsor), and his elderly mother. The Bishop gently urged me to fight "manfully" for Christ and to give my life entirely into God's care; he confirmed me with a light slap on my cheek. In memory, that tap, symbolic of the suffering that a Christian must endure, has become a stunning blow.

It is significant that my vow of obedience to Christ came the day before our vows of fidelity to our marriage in Christ. The vow of unconditional love and fidelity from Christ, for Christ, was immediately followed by our vows of unconditional love and fidelity for one another. Because of the immediate proximity of these rites to one another, the symbolic blow of Christian suffering and the symbolic kiss of unconditional love have flowed over the years, especially at times of crisis, from one into the other until they have become one. Suffering and sweetness are indivisible; both are essential. The adventure of faith, lived out in sacramental marriage, is one, great, mysterious union of suffering and unconditional love.

As we began our preparation for marriage, we talked with

everyone we knew who could help us make a good start. One Catholic couple, very dear to us, talked of the importance of family life and warned us about the dangers of contraception; they called it "psychological infanticide." Theirs was the only voice we heard that spoke of unnatural contraception as an evil; the encyclical *Humanae Vitae* was still a year away from publication. Everyone else with whom we talked looked on artificial contraception as a great medical breakthrough, a positive good, about which there could be no possible objection.

Aside from the Great New Reproductive Technology, talking about sexual matters twenty-five years ago, even with a clergyman or a doctor, was a very difficult thing to do; other than "among the girls," people did not discuss such private matters. Nevertheless, the sexual deviations were beginning to erupt on a vast scale and we needed to know how to establish our marriage in a Christian framework; there were few resources available. We asked Fr. Lynch, the venerable clergyman who married us, to help us with this matter of artificial contraception in our upcoming marriage. He replied that artificial contraception was warranted in some cases. He went on to state, mistakenly, that Catholicism had limited the purpose of sex to procreation only, and that the Anglican tradition held that while marriage must be open to procreation "in general," it need not be open to procreation in every act. That sounded convincing to untried postulants; we did not spot the logical flaw until years later. We know it well now. By the same formula of totality, extended into marital fidelity, need *every* act of sexual union necessarily be with one's spouse? Couldn't one affirm, by the principle of totality, that if one affirmed marriage *most* of the time, did one have to be faithful to marriage *all* of the time, every single time? The wide-spread infidelity which followed closely behind the argument for totality in matters of contraception is no accident; in fact, contraception made concupiscence and its justification possible.

Although we did not foresee these unintended consequences in society, we were afraid of the consequences of choosing wrongly in our own marriage. We wanted to be faithful to God, to our love, and to the family we hoped to have. We were not sure what to do, and we were too shy about such matters to talk freely yet with one another. My doctor, parents, and friends (all well-meaning) urged various methods and devices upon us; dire warnings were whispered about what would happen to our love if I were to get pregnant too soon. This was disheartening and very scary; Rollin was told similar well-intended lies.

In the end, we decided to listen to our Catholic friends who had warned us about the inherent evil of contraception. We decided that we would begin by giving ourselves to the will of God. We strengthened one another in faith; we reassured each other that our high and holy love would endure. We also assured ourselves that we could accept and provide for children, if they came early in our marriage. Besides all this, it was highly repugnant to us, as to any romantic couple, to carefully plan out and buy "life insurance" for every risk of life. This was an adventure!

No Life Insurance for the Marriage Adventure

We were certain of the high quest and vocation of marriage. We told each other that we could not give allegiance to Christ and at the time dictate the extent and terms of his grace in our lives. So, we galloped off together with very high spirits and a bit too much self-congratulation on our great undertaking.

During the first summer after our marriage, we conceived a baby, but I had a miscarriage in the first few weeks of pregnancy. The same thing happened again in the Fall, and again in the winter. My OB–GYN told us that, for one reason or another, we would probably never be able to have children. This was both disappointing and confusing; had we not eagerly given ourselves to the Lord of Life? Why were these tiny lives not carried to term? Didn't God care about them and us as we thought? Things weren't going our way.

Of course, we hadn't really surrendered to the will of God. We were eager to do so, but did not know about suffering, yet; we were young and looked only for the sweetness of God's gifts of love. We reviewed our first year of marriage, how much it meant to us and how we had come to find both love and holiness which we never imagined possible. Finally, we came to the certainty that we were wrong to demand that God give us children. Shortly after this, we became pregnant again, and our infant son, John, was born at full-term in December, 1968.

When John was born, we were blessed with a profound and awe-full experience of the holiness of life. Here was a child, a unique human being with a particular destiny in history. Where had he come from? How marvelous to have been chosen to be his parents! This wonder, this awe, at the fact of a new life and at the certainty of his God-given origins has never lessened with ensuing births: Will, Katie, Austin, Ben, and Helen. They are all "wonderfully and mysteriously made."

About the time of John's birth, the contraceptive controversy was in full fury. Six months previously, *Humanae Vitae* had been issued and everyone was talking about it, Protestants and Catholics, alike. The document was, above all, incomprehensible. No one could believe that the "men of Rome" could be so backward, so insensitive, so benighted as to deny this "help" to married couples. Those crazy clerics ridiculously predicted that contraception would open a Pandora's box of more dire ills: rogue male behavior, breakup of families, irreverence for women, cheapening of sex, increased violence and rape, abortion, child abuse, and euthanasia. Grim to realize how fast these evils did rush into society, just as the "stupid" encyclical warned that they would.

One of the "help for new mothers" booklets that was given me at the hospital contained an advertisement for spermicidal foam. It featured a picture of a sweet young mother holding a tiny infant to her breast; the caption beneath read: "You gave him life. Now, give him yourself." The serpent at his most eloquent! Foam was a fairly new product. Unlike the pill, it did not cause bloodclots and high blood pressure; it did not interfere with the spontaneity of the sex act; it purported to prevent conception. Like Eve and her apple, I showed it to Adam and bade him eat.

When we discovered that we were pregnant and would have another baby within a year of the first, we quarrelled seriously and viciously for the first time in our marriage. I had hated using the foam; it made me feel cheap. Rollin, taken unprepared, was annoyed at the prospect of another baby; he felt tricked by me.

The bitterness of this first quarrel *should* have alerted us to the effects of contraception on married love and trust. We did resolve, once again, to avoid using unnatural contraceptives, but were still unconvinced that *Humanae Vitae* was right as a universal statement for all Christians and all marriages.

A half-educated, partially committed effort at the calendar rhythm method was, most happily, unsuccessful in avoiding new pregnancies. A year and a half after our second son, William, was born, our Katie came to us. One year later, our twins, Austin and Ben, were born. Then two years later, Helen came. A great multiplication of Love!

It is a recognized trend that the older parents grow, the less they remember of unpleasantness and trials in their young families. We are no exception. Our memory of that time is of mad-cap joy, knee-deep in babies and toddlers, six of them, age five and under! That we were sometimes so dead tired that we could barely push through the day is remembered only vaguely.

In truth, I don't think we slept more than a few hours any night for at least seven years, and we were always worried about how we were going to support our family. We were filled with trust in one another and with a sense of purpose, and we drew strength from it; it kept us from being overwhelmed by anxiety and fatigue. There was a sense of divine protection and mystery behind everything that happened in those years.

Because we had chosen obedience to the will of God and had entrusted our fertility, as well as our souls, to one another, we knew the gift of unconditional love. This was a shared secret between us, given us by Christ, whose presence was constantly felt as a "third" in our marriage. This secret, pondered deeply in my heart and cherished in Rollin's, took the form of enormous confidence about what we were doing. This was not pride, though pride is ever a threat in every human being, but rather a certainty born of deep reverence for an awareness of the presence of Christ's holiness in our marriage. During this time, we thought a great deal about the revealed mysteries of Christianity; I said the rosary regularly and meditated often on Mary. Sometimes my thoughts would flow out to the Mother of God in silent, loving exchange; these meditative thoughts, really prayerthoughts, concerning the developing child in my womb. Every event, every new life, was embraced as a prayer answered, was known to be willed, under the mercy of God.

Our faith and our confidence came under very heavy siege, however, as the universities began to crumble, the judicial system to capitulate, and the Episcopal Church to succumb to radical feminism and homosexual politics. Unknown to ourselves, we were becoming desperate; we were too much alone and we were afraid of the changing world's condition and our children's maturation into it. Everywhere, every day we met relentless hammering against our faith and hostility against us for our choices. Despair! Despair! Despair pounded against our over-tired minds, weakening our resolve and eroding our sense of purpose.

In 1974, the year that Helen was born, Rollin sacrificed his tenured university position to begin studying for the ministry in the Episcopal church. The reasons for my opposition to Rollin's decision to do this would serve as a strong warning against married clergy in the Roman Catholic Church. Briefly, I did not see how we were to continue our soul-to-soul intimacy of marriage when he, necessarily, could not confide to me concerns heard by him in the confessional and elsewhere. More important, there was no way that our domestic church could remain as important to him as the parish church was bound to become, and, sooner or later, this would surely cause great problems for me and for our children.

At this time, Rollin and I decided that six children were all we could manage for awhile. Not being able to accept any known form of birth control as moral and consistent with God's will, and knowing the unreliability of "rhythm," we would observe total abstinence, we decided.

At the recommendation of some Catholic friends, we sought the help of their beloved monsignor. We told our story and our intention and asked his help, advice, and prayers. He replied that abstinence was "too heroic," and, as we were not Catholics, he did not understand why we did not just use contraception. ("Do it the sensible way," I hear my friend Nancy echo.) We tried to explain that we were seeking to be obedient to God's will in both the procreative and unitive aspects of our marriage, but we failed to convince him or to receive any support. We observed total abstinence for many months. Then, I made a radical decision and had a sterilization operation.

What made me change my mind, our minds? Two catalysts and a single cause. First, Rollin strongly and openly opposed the Episcopal Church's trend toward the ordination of women, the endorsement of various sexual aberrations, and the acceptance of abortion. The Episcopal bishop, a liberal fellow, would not accept him as a candidate. The bishop's rejection was devastating to him, and I determined that he didn't need to feel rejected by his wife, as well. This well-intentioned wifely solicitude was as much tainted by the serpent's pride as was the contraceptive advertisement for spermicidal foam that I'd bought into so many years before; it was just another variation of "You gave him life, now give him yourself." The second catalyst was the growing influence of Jungian psychology and Jungian devotees in our life. Like the contraceptive mentality, Jungianism exhibits a definite cultishness in its proud rejection of revealed Christian truth and moral authority. Behind both catalysts was a single cause: loss of faith. Under severe pressure from calamity both within and without, we abandoned our faith and trust in God and in each other.

The After-effects

Rollin was opposed to the ligation, but I had the so-called "band-aid" operation, anyway. ("It's my body and my decision," I had parroted.) No one else opposed this surgery at all, quite the opposite, in fact. The very first effect of this, as in an abortion, was relief. That relief didn't last long. Ensuing hormonal imbalance caused a deep, prolonged depression. In fact, as I later learned, my estrogen level dropped to a menopausal level, literally, overnight. I gained a lot of weight in a very short time, another common side effect. My mind was confused; and I was filled with irrational resentment. There was abdominal pain for months after the surgery, probably caused by the nitrous oxide gas that was used to inflate my abdomen for surgery. Periods became so heavy that twice I was hospitalized for excessive hemorrhaging, another common but seldom publicized side-effect. At the age of thirty, I was forced by deteriorating health to have a hysterectomy.

Until the hysterectomy, I had secret thoughts that the tubal ligation could be reversed, if we wanted more children. (N.B.: if *we* wanted more children; no longer *Thy Will Be Done.*) After this second, more radical, operation, however, it was impossible to have any more children.

Thereafter, Rollin and I seldom talked about the operation or what had led up to it. We seldom talked at all. We became very touchy about "slights"; we were impatient and sometimes rude to each other; we were often filled with self-pity. Despite a steady and comfortable income, we quarrelled constantly about money. We became stressed and tense. Our fears for the children's safety became exaggerated to the point of panic; we were terrified that we would lose one of these precious, irreplaceable lives. We lost our sense of humor and seemed to bicker over everything. He began to lose respect for me and I for him. Aversion to intimacy began to develop. Life became a horrid burden to us both, each secretly resenting and blaming the other.

While we were still firmly opposed to abortion, we were no

longer "pro-life" in any greater sense. Dark and cynical, we had become anti-life at a very basic level.

The After-effects Continued

When we talked about sexual matters, it was with a rather wry, sometimes bawdy, humor; it was no longer approached with reverence and awe. We seldom talked about anything else but our children, the one remaining source of delight to us both. It grieved me that I'd taken this veterinary approach, done this self-mutilation, to my body; quite irrationally, I blamed and hated Rollin for it. However, everyone who knew of it praised us to the skies: clergyman, relatives, doctors, and psychologist; we had finally joined the contraceptive cult. Women who have had abortions must surely feel like this, too. Everyone else — other women, medical personnel, their lover or husband, their family, their minister (or even some priests) — will try to "be compassionate and sensitive to the needs of women" and to tell the aborted woman that what she did was okay, but she knows it was not okay. Yet, she isn't allowed by these "sensitive" friends and family to grieve or even mention it, not ever again. Who will listen to the "silent scream" within the agonized soul of such women? There was no one there for me, for us, and this was not even an abortion.

At this time, we heard from the Catholic couple, who had talked so strongly to us before we were married about the dangers of contraception; they were not getting along and were thinking about divorce. This stunned us! Here was another couple with seven children. What had gone wrong? We snapped out of our own self-pity to try and turn them away from separation and divorce.

Our friends told us that they had decided that the whole Church was wrong, that it was just a power institution imposing rules on "little people" to spoil their sexual freedom. They renounced their former convictions about the evils of unnatural contraception;

they ridiculed themselves for ever having held such convictions. We were embarrassed by their rude jokes; they were insulting to each other; their language had become coarse and vulgar. Both had come to support abortion. They encouraged their children to use contraception themselves. They talked about sex as if they were talking about a tennis match. The final severance came when a newly-launched affair with a female graduate student became public scandal.

We were really horrified by this; the same shoals lay dead ahead of us. The fact was that this couple had given up their faith. So had we. Like our friends, we had stopped going to church ourselves, but we had not gone so far as both to hate the church and to reject the sacraments. We had not quite despaired. We were very near despair, really in much greater danger than either of us knew at the time. We did know, however, that we had reached such a point of desolation in love that there were no more resources left to us and that we would soon be as lost as our lost friends.

One night, while driving alone to the grocery, incongruously, I prayed a desperate prayer, asking God's help and promising to do whatever I was told to do. God spoke to me then! He made it known to me that we could go no further until we ended our isolation and committed ourselves again to Christ's Church.

The Hound of Heaven Had Barked Once Again

I considered this revelation and finally came to the conclusion that, although we would be rejected and shunned by family and friends, the Roman Catholic Church (progressive and trendy as it seemed then) was what I had to choose. I told Rollin that very night that I intended to become a Catholic. He did not seem surprised and by the next morning revealed to me that this was what he, too, wanted to do.

On the day that we were formally received, I said to Rollin that it felt like we had just gotten married, again. There was no trained choir for this nuptial; the organ was preempted by a guitarist who throbbed the strings with heavy hand; the church building was ugly, a yellow brick, auditorium-like affair; the priest's holiness was less than exemplary. It didn't matter at all. What mattered was our surrender to Christ and to his Church; through this surrender the restoration of our marriage could begin.

Our conversion to Catholicism brought great joy, but also great sorrow. We could hardly bear to see the American Catholic Church chasing after the very trendiness and politics that we had just left behind. Why would Catholics no longer want to say the Rosary? Why would they want to have the Stations of the Cross, and other images, removed? Why did they hate the Holy Father and the Church's teaching authority? How could they ever endorse abortion—or contraception? Why did so many Catholics seem to mistrust their own beautiful heritage?

We began to think about these questions again. We were a long way from unconditional love or trust; that had been too badly shattered to be rebuilt in a week or even years. It was being rebuilt for us, however, by him who had always been faithful, even when we were faithless.

We admitted that we were WRONG to have done what we did in ever using artificial contraception and, above all, in having a sterilization operation; we were also WRONG to have given so much allegiance to cultish thought, to Jungianism. The former violated the unity of our marriage; the latter denied and trivialized moral absolutes. This dual admission of guilt did not make it possible to reverse a surgical procedure which had removed my womb. It did make it possible to return to holiness, to find forgiveness, and to receive healing within our souls and marriage.

Until we came to this admission of error, we had gotten in the habit of denying that anything was wrong or, at most, justifying our actions, or casting blame on other people and each other. The most difficult act of all was admitting that we were wrong. We were wrong; we had sinned; we repented of that wrong and WE WERE FORGIVEN. We could, of course, have gone on living with no such admission of guilt; how heavy and sorrowful our lives, had we chosen self-pity and perpetual justification! Once such justification and blame begin, there is no end to it or the self-pity it generates. Yet, had we not sinned, there would have been no forgiveness, no grace—*O Felix Culpa!* Thanks be to God!

Unconditional love and trust has been given back to us, but it did not happen right away. We agreed that it wasn't enough to admit our faults to ourselves and to each other; we needed absolution. On our wedding anniversary, together we sought the sacrament of confession.

We remember these former betrayals of love as mistakes, not to be repeated. Nothing can undo the *fact* that these things did happen. Yet, the memory is without bitterness and without recrimination, though not without regret. We are terribly sorry to have ever been apart from God and from each other. The most dreadful experience, the most absolute evil, imaginable is to be totally cut off from the unconditional love of God and from its vessel, the love of our spouse. We regret its having happened because we never wanted nor intended to hurt one another, nor to despair of God's presence in our lives. On the other hand, our experience has made us acutely aware of the power of unnatural contraceptives and of cult-like thought to effect just this horror in the lives of loving spouses.

Some will no doubt say that had we lost our faith, we would not have resorted to contraception and would not have been tempted toward any cult; no doubt this is accurate. Others may think that we were only looking for something upon which to pin the woes of an already troubled marriage and chose contraception as the goat. This is not accurate; we know the facts and have presented them faithfully. From the beginning, we were given a great love; we unintentionally betrayed that love through the deliberate choosing of an inherently evil act. It matters not that our original intentions were sincere and benevolent. Sincerity does not undo reality. Through consciously choosing unnatural contraception and through buying into Jungianism as a substitute for religion, we abandoned our faith and ushered in the unhappy consequences that followed. Those consequences are not to be underestimated, for nothing less than eternal salvation, our family's permanence, and unconditional love is at stake.

Christian newly-weds are not faced with the same isolation that we were at the time of our marriage. Nor do they have to rely on calendar rhythm. Thanks to doctors John and Elizabeth Billings, to John and Sheila Kippley, and to the research of others, the symptoms of a woman's fertility are known and easy to determine now, as they were not twenty-five years ago. The Couple to Couple League (P.O. Box 111184, Cincinnati, Ohio, 45211) is reliable in teaching couples how to use Natural Family Planning, which is in complete accord with the doctrines of the church and which violates no aspect of marriage, neither the unitive nor the procreative. Through fertility awareness and a few days per month of abstinence, couples can be sensible in their family planning, spontaneous in their sexual union, and true to the will of God. That will is to offer every act of marriage thoughtfully, responsibly, and prayerfully to God who sustains us and our love.

> The choice of the natural rhythms involves accepting the cycle of the ... woman, and thereby accepting dialogue, reciprocal respect, shared responsibility and self-control. To accept the cycle and to enter into dialogue means to recognize both the spiritual and corporal character of conjugal communion and to live personal love with its requirement of fidelity.
>
> (*Familiaris Consortio,* section 32)

It is not, as our ignorant brethren assume, that a woman should have as many babies as she possibly can, no matter what her health or the family's finances. It is that we should seek, first, the kingdom of heaven and to do no harm to others, to violate no life, no love.

We are rational creatures and are expected to use RIGHTLY our reason and our free will when approaching the holy ground of our sexuality. These brief periods of abstinence, of shared sacrifice, become times of love-making of another sort, of thanksgiving for God's gift of each to the other, each other's love, and the miracle of being loved.

> In this context the couple comes to experience how conjugal communion is enriched with those values of tenderness and affection which constitute the inner soul of human sexuality in its physical dimension also. In this way sexuality is respected and promoted in its truly and fully human dimension and is never "used" as an "object" that, by breaking the personal unity of soul and body, strikes at God's creation itself at the level of the deepest interaction of nature and person.

> (*Familiaris Consortio,* section 32)

The spousal union remains one of unconditional love between the spouses, and each carries the grace of Christ in sexuality, a grace found in a thousand daily acts of intimacy and of love to the beloved other.

> God does not ask the impossible, but by His commands, instructs you to do what you are able, to pray for what you are not able that He may help you.

> (*Casti Connubii,* section IV, p. 31)

In his boundless Mercy, he also forgives those who have not been able to "preserve in wedlock their chastity unspotted." Blessedly, there can be granted a second spring, a second virginity within marriage. Through God's forgiveness, chastity between spouses can be restored to its divine purity, its unconditional love.

We women have always held the sexual standards of society and had the responsibility for our children's moral education. Now, we have the knowledge of our own fertility. Is it unreasonable to ask our husbands to respect this, to center relations around *female* sexuality instead of the male sexual drive? In doing so, would it not then be easier to teach our children to save sex for marriage and to uphold standards of chastity for them? Would not widespread knowledge and endorsement of Natural Family Planning restore respect for women and the family to its rightful place in society? Would it not strongly censure or forbid pornographic material as the vile exploitation that it is?

This "tar baby" has seen the consequences of contraceptives in her own life and marriage. I'd gladly endure the briar-patch, once again, to find the freedom and sanctity of married love that has been restored to us through familiarity with NFP. It really is the only truly sensible way of family planning.

FURTHER READING

Ruth D. Lasseter has just begun her writing career and has several works in progress. This essay is a portion of a book, *Paradise Retained,* to be published by Ignatius Press.

For further testimony from couples who have found that the use of methods of natural family planning has enhanced their marriage life and who have found contraceptives destructive to their marriage, see Nona Aquilar, *No-Pill, No-Risk Birth Control,* 2nd ed. (New York: Rawson, Wade Publishers, 1986) and John and Sheila K. Kippley, *The Art of Natural Family Planning* (Cincinnati, Oh.: The Couple to Couple League, 1984).

PART SEVEN

A Generation Later

21 and 22

HUMANAE VITAE AT TWENTY
AND
PAUL VI AS PROPHET

by
Janet E. Smith

These two essays were written during the twentieth-year anniversary of *Humanae Vitae*. The first briefly reviews the history of the encyclical and sketches the status of the debate about the issue. The second attempts to show that the predictions made by Pope Paul VI about the bad consequences that would ensue when contraception became widely available have become true beyond his wildest nightmares. Little has changed in the last five years. Few can see the connection between the use of contraception and the multitude of other evils decimating our society. The Church has shown us how to steer a wiser course that leads to greater human happiness. We should rejoice in this wisdom, attempt to live by it, and then live in the hope that many other good things will come our way.

" '*Humanae Vitae*' at Twenty", appeared in *Crisis* 6, no. 6 (June 1988): 14–20. "Paul VI as Prophet" appeared in *Respect Life,* the annual Respect Life publication for the US Bishops; reprinted in *Crisis* 6, no. 8 (Sept. 1988): 30–35.

21

HUMANAE VITAE AT TWENTY

New Insights into an Old Debate

by
Janet E. Smith

In certain respects 20 years is a long time. While it's not quite a generation, there exists a whole cohort of adult Catholics who were not alive during the sixties or who were too young to be aware of the tumult the issuance of *Humanae Vitae* engendered. Catholics of this generation are an assorted lot. Some have grown up with the awareness that although the current Pope has regularly reiterated the Church's condemnation of contraception, most adult Catholics live quite comfortably in opposition to it. They have heard of *Humanae Vitae,* but few have read it or feel in the least bit compelled to live by it. Many have been through marriage preparation courses that have encouraged them to become aware of all birth control options. They have done so and have decided to use one of the usual forms of contraception.

Other young adult Catholics have come to accept the validity of the Church's teaching on contraception and cannot understand how a doctrine they think to be fully plausible and elevating of the dignity of marriage should have come to be so widely denigrated and ignored. They think natural family planning is an eminently sensible and workable means of responsible parenthood and cannot understand the resistance of so many Catholics to the Church's teaching on contraception.

The Catholics most perplexed by the present situation are converts who have had good instruction. They joined the Church in part because of its more distinctive and challenging doctrines and practices, such as the sacraments and the saints, and the teachings on marriage. They find it curious that so few priests and parishes provide good instruction on morality in marriage. Indeed, it is not easy to find such instruction. Recently a student group at a major Catholic university in the midwest wanted a speaker to explain the Church's teaching on contraception. They were most astonished to find that in a theology department of over thirty, not one professor could be found who was willing to give a public lecture explaining and defending the Church's teaching on contraception. What do we know about *Humanae Vitae* twenty years later that would explain these reactions of young Catholics, that would explain this reality on Catholic campuses?

There has been an interesting reversal in strategy by both those for and against contraception. Prior to *Humanae Vitae,* those who advocated change in the Church's teaching found fault with natural law reasoning and suggested that a greater awareness of personalist values supported the use of contraception. Those who maintained that the Church could not change its teaching relied largely upon natural law principles. But in recent years, those who advocate a revision in traditional Catholic moral theology concentrate largely on making some crucial changes in natural law reasoning and rarely provide extended explanations of personalist values and their bearing on contraception. Those who defend the teaching of *Humanae Vitae* have not abandoned natural law defenses and, indeed, have labored to dispel false interpretations of natural law theory. The interesting switch is that many opponents of contraception have worked hard to show that personalist values, far from justifying the use of contraception, serve to provide additional reasons why contraception is immoral. Most distinguished for work in this regard is Pope John Paul II.

But before we show how Pope John Paul II's work is situated in the modern debate, let us get a sense of the situation surrounding the issuance of *Humanae Vitae*. Many young people are surprised to learn that the Church's teaching against contraception has *not* been a controversial teaching throughout Church history. Indeed, all of Christendom was quite united on the immorality of contraception until 1930, when the Anglican Church approved the use of contraception in marriage. In 1931, Pope Pius XI wrote his famous encyclical *Casti Connubii*. Pius XII, in the forties and fifties, occasionally referred to contraception in his addresses to various learned societies, but he was not defending a teaching under attack. Indeed, there was virtually no movement within the Catholic Church advocating change. Society at large seemed to share to a large extent the Church's opposition to contraception: until the early sixties, the sale and use of contraceptives was illegal in several states, by virtue of laws written largely by Protestant legislators.

The first slight indications that a change in Church teaching might be warranted occurred in the late fifties at about the time when the contraceptive pill began to be considered safe and effective. Not until 1963 did a few influential articles appear in serious theological journals advocating a change in Church teaching. With the opening of the Second Vatican Council Pope John XXIII convened a small commission to advise him on these questions. After John's death, Pope Paul VI greatly expanded what was called the Commission for the Study of Problems of Population, Family, and Birthrate, until eventually it grew to approximately 60 members, including three married couples. This commission was at the heart of the tumult over contraception in the sixties. Karol Wojtyla (now Pope John Paul II) was a member of this commission but was unable to attend the meetings. He did contribute to a response by several Polish theologians and bishops to the reports coming out of the commission, which may have influenced the writing of *Humanae Vitae*. In his biography of Pope John Paul II, Paul Johnson reports that Paul VI was reading Karol Wojtyla's *Love and Responsibility* at the time he wrote *Humanae Vitae*. This may account in part for the Pope's remarkable insights into *Humanae Vitae* — his own ideas may have been a source for some of the claims of the encyclical.

The original mandate of the papal commission seemed to be limited to discerning the morality of the Pill, for it was a form of contraception that did not obviously interfere with the integrity of the marital act. But the commission quickly began to conceive its purpose as being a reconsideration of the Church's condemnation of contraception. Events surrounding the commission were dramatic. Private documents of the commission were leaked to the press, individuals abandoned life-long support of the Church's teaching on contraception, and, in general, the existence and momentum of the commission led many to believe that Paul VI would come to find some forms of contraception compatible with the Catholic view of marriage. Robert Kaiser's book, *The Politics of Sex and Religion,* though disgruntled and even polemical, nonetheless makes for fascinating reading about the dynamics of the commission. George A. Kelly, disgruntled for opposite reasons, also provides an account in his book, *The Battle for the American Church.*

The commission met during the Second Vatican Council. There was much debate about whether it was appropriate for the Vatican Council to speak directly to the issue of contraception. The writing of the relevant portions of *Gaudium et Spes* in itself provides an intriguing mini-drama. To make a complicated story short, Paul VI intervened in the writing of the document and had inserted into it the famous footnote 14. This footnote cites the very passages of *Casti Connubii* that condemn contraception, but at the same time notes that Paul VI was reserving final judgment for himself until the work of the commission was done. This further flamed speculation that a change in Church teaching was possible. John Noonan, a consultant to the commission, provided historical background to the Church's teaching on contraception, which he later published in his book *Contraception* (1965). While he observed in his book that the history of Church teaching on contraception shows that "the teaching on contraception is clear and apparently fixed forever," he gave the clear impression that the Church could change its teaching on contraception, a suggestion buttressed by an article he wrote about usury and contraception. Noonan argued that a change in the Church's teaching on contraception would be little different from its changing its teaching on usury.

That there was a growing expectation that the Church would change its teaching is manifested by the number of books and articles appearing at that time advocating change. For instance, we find books entitled *Contraception and Holiness,* by Archbishop Roberts and *The Experience of Marriage,* edited by Michael Novak. Novak's book is a compilation of essays by married laypeople who reported the damage that too many children or that the use of the rhythm method had on their marriages. Few attempted to defend the Church's teaching. Most notable was the pioneering work of Germain Grisez, *Contraception and the Natural Law.* Still, few strictly theological explorations were written on either "side."

The best place to find the state of the theological arguments at the time is in the documents of the Papal Commission. These were published in both the *National Catholic Reporter* and the *Tablet* in the spring of 1966. The majority on the commission had voted in favor of a change in Church teaching. They wrote two reports, known as the Majority Report and the Majority Rebuttal. (I shall conflate them and speak of both as the Majority Report.) The Minority Report arguing that a change in Church teaching was impossible reportedly carried the signatures of only three theologians. It seems unlikely that these documents were ever meant to be made public, but they were leaked to the press, evidently with the purpose of forcing the Pope's hand in issuing the encyclical.

The Majority Report asserted that the natural law arguments against contraception given in *Casti Connubii* were "vague," "imprecise," and "unpersuasive." It argued that God has given man greater dominion over nature than has previously been acknowledged. It claimed that humans have the obligation to regularize their fertility and that to do so it is morally permissible to make use of technology. The key argument was that it is not necessary for each marital act to remain open to procreation so long as the "totality" of the acts are so open. The Report also asserted that "Infertile conjugal acts constitute a totality with fertile acts and have a single moral specification." Although many theologians since have concurred with this position, it is important to note that the Majority Report really gave no thorough argumentation for its position. Several theologians, dissenters among them, have noted that theological arguments made in the Majority Report were not of the quality to warrant overturning centuries of Church opposition to contraception.

The Minority Report, on the other hand, stressed the constancy of Church teaching on contraception and argued that a change would be disastrous for Church authority. It gave several reasons why the Church teaches that contraception is a serious moral wrong. These reasons are based primarily on an understanding of the human act of sexual intercourse as the mode whereby human life, given special status by God, is generated. And the Minority Report insisted that a change in the teaching on contraception would warrant a change in other teachings about sexuality, such as masturbation. These arguments were not fully developed in the Report, but remain crucial concerns for those testing the justifiability of dissent on this issue.

Humanae Vitae does not examine the arguments pro and con on contraception; it does not weigh the arguments of the Majority and Minority Reports. Indeed, many have argued that this encyclical does not provide sufficient argumentation for the claims it advances. But it was not intended to offer such argumentation; it was intended to *clarify* Church teaching, not provide an extended defense of that teaching. It relies upon a whole history of moral analysis developed over the centuries, and indicates what use it makes of this tradition by citations in the footnotes. Anyone who wishes to understand thoroughly the encyclical should read closely the material cited in the footnotes.

The encyclical does pay rather special attention to one argument which is still popular—that the principle of totality justifies the use of contraception. This argument agrees that marriage is ordained to children and that it is therefore essential for a marriage to be open to children. But the argument goes on to claim that *every* marital act need not be open to procreation *if* the totality of the acts of marriage are open to procreation.

In response to this argument, *Humanae Vitae* cites (in a footnote) two speeches by Pope Pius XII directed to the medical community. At the time some were using the principle of totality to justify removing vital organs from dying humans in order to transplant them into those who had a chance for survival. These persons argued that the good of the part (the dying man) could legitimately be sacrificed for the good of the whole (the human community or another member of the community). Pius XII replied with the important distinction between an organic whole and a moral whole. The body, he notes, is an organic whole, and therefore it is permissible to amputate limbs for the sake of the whole organism. The state or human community, however, is not an organic whole; human beings do not exist for the sake of such a whole, but each has his own intrinsic worth and cannot be sacrificed for the sake of the whole.

To apply this to contraception, one must ask, if one alleges the permissibility of sacrificing the nature of single acts of intercourse for the whole, what whole would this be? Does not each act have its own intrinsic worth? Consider the claim that acts of intercourse must be with one's spouse only. If it is necessary only that the totality of one's acts, and not every act, be with one's spouse, then by this reasoning adultery would be permitted.

Few of those who were arguing for a change in Church teaching in the sixties thought they were arguing for a complete revolution in moral theology and ecclesiology. Most believed themselves to be arguing in accord with principles of traditional Catholic moral theology and believed their request for change to be for only a slight change. Many opponents of change, however, saw at the time that approval of contraception, even in limited cases, would not be any slight change. Ten years after *Humanae Vitae* Father Charles Curran admitted:

One must honestly recognize that "the conservatives" saw much more clearly than "the liberals" of the day that a change in the teaching on artificial contraception had to recognize that the previous teaching was wrong.

Opponents of contraception also argued that a change on this issue would justify change in all of the Church's teaching on sexuality, if not in its whole teaching on morality. Few now argue that these were idle worries. Again, Father Curran is most candid in admitting that theologians have thrown into question the major teachings of the Church:

Catholic theologians frequently deny the existing teaching of the hierarchical magisterium on such issues as contraception, sterilization, artificial insemination, masturbation, the generic gravity of sexual sins. Newer approaches have recently been taken to the question of homosexuality. . . . All these questions in the area of medical and sexual morality are being questioned today.

Still, many theologians at the time were arguing that a change in Church teaching on contraception would be simply a justified historical development. All eagerly awaited the Pope's decision. After having set up another commission to advise him on how to handle the report of the first commission, Paul VI waited nearly two years after the publication of the commission reports before he issued *Humanae Vitae*. In the interim, of course, the expectation that a change would occur only grew greater. When *Humanae Vitae* appeared with its total condemnation of contraception, the cries of protest were immediate and aggressive. Never before had a papal statement met with such a reception. The response of Charles Curran was, perhaps, most notable for its promptness and public dimensions. In a press conference called within 24 hours of the release of *Humanae Vitae,* he announced that he had the names of 87 theologians who disagreed with the encyclical. This list, reportedly, eventually grew to over 600. The support for *Humanae Vitae* was not visible or vocal. There were a few heroic supporters, such as Msgr. Austin Vaughan, president of the American Theological Society, who stated:

> I don't think it is possible that what has been laid down in this document could be anything else than what the Holy Spirit, who guides our use of our resources with his providence, wants and expects of us as Catholics, at this moment in the plan of salvation, apart from what the direction the course of that plan might take in the future. If it were, the guidance of the Holy Spirit, promised to the magisterium, according to the *Constitution on the Church* would be an illusion.

Cardinal Patrick O'Boyle in Washington, D.C., made a noble attempt to discipline renegade priests who refused to teach or counsel in accord with *Humanae Vitae,* but he received little support from the rest of the American hierarchy. Most of the bishops' conferences throughout the world, including that of the U.S., issued statements in support of *Humanae Vitae*—though some, notably the French and Canadian bishops, issued statements that certainly fell short of full support.

The tumult has certainly not died down. *Humanae Vitae* has been called many things: a "watershed," an "albatross around the Church's neck," "a prophetic statement," a "litmus test," and "that damn encyclical." The Church's teaching against contraception seems to be the Church teaching most difficult for laypeople to accept and the one theologians are most reluctant to defend.

Does the widespread rejection of *Humanae Vitae* by laypeople and by theologians indicate that compelling arguments have been offered for the morality of contraception? Does it indicate that the Church is for some perverse reason refusing to yield to the dictates of logic and reason? Have those who have defended the document failed to supply valid and convincing counterarguments to the dissenters? Although these questions can be answered with a confident "no," we are still very much at the beginning or, at best, at the middle of this debate. It is a debate that has extended far beyond the Church's teaching on contraception.

Although nearly all admit that *Humanae Vitae* is at the center of much of the dispute among moral theologians today, and maybe even the source of much of the dispute, relatively little scholarly criticism has been directed towards it. Articles offering full and thorough defenses of Church teaching are much easier to find than articles criticizing it. This is not, of course, because defenders vastly outnumber the critics. Rather, it is because the critics generally ignore *Humanae Vitae,* or dismiss it in passing.

How can the neglect of *Humanae Vitae* be explained? Right after it was issued, many theologians were quick to register their dissent, but few explained where they found the teaching defective. Most were concerned to establish that they had a "right" to dissent, and wrote on problems of authority and dissent, on questions of ecclesiology, and on conscience. Such concerns remain a part of the debate today. One of the most important points of controversy has been whether or not the document advances a teaching that is infallible. In 1978 John Ford and Germain Grisez published an article arguing that the teaching has been proclaimed so constantly throughout Church history that it must be an infallible teaching. A recent book in Italian by Father Ermenegildo Lio argues that *Humanae Vitae* uses language that meets the criteria established by the Church as suitable for an infallible pronouncement. The dissenters, of course, emphatically reject the suggestion that *Humanae Vitae* is infallible teaching. Yet John Paul II recently referred to the Church's condemnation of contraception as part of the "permanent patrimony" of the Church.

Charles Curran and Bernard Haering were among the few who engaged in any kind of sustained critique of the arguments of *Humanae Vitae.* Curran's arguments are truly a wholesale attack on traditional natural law theory. In brief, he claims that natural law theory is based on a static view of nature and does not exhibit the historical consciousness developed in the modern age; that natural law is "physicalistic"; and that natural law reasoning is "a priori" and deductive rather than "a posteriori" and inductive. He does a close analysis of *Humanae Vitae* to show how all of these deficiencies in natural law theory are present there. Most modern theologians have not abandoned this basic critique of traditional natural law, though their arguments for the legitimacy of each of these charges now differ considerably. And it is well that they have, for any natural law theorist who reads Father Curran's portrayal of the theory will find how little he is able to recognize the portrayal as accurate.

Traditional natural law theorists find Curran's portrayal of natural law to be a caricature. They point out that since they certainly consider human intentions in their analysis of moral acts, theirs is not a physicalistic analysis. They add that since they think each man must undergo a transformation of his "nature" in order to be moral, theirs is not a static view of nature. Finally, they deny that theirs is an "a priori" morality since natural law morality draws constantly upon experience and can be altered by circumstances.

Father Curran has repeated his charges against natural law many times and has not abandoned his approval of contraception. If anything he has expanded his approval; in a recent essay, he entertains the startling possibility that on occasion society may have to *mandate* the use of contra eption.

After the initial rejection of *Humanae Vitae,* most theologians broadened their critique to the very principles of moral analysis upon which *Humanae Vitae* is based. Following *Casti Connubii, Humanae Vitae* taught that contraception is an intrinsic wrong, that there are no circumstances that permit the intention to thwart the reproductive powers. Traditional moral theology has always argued that some acts, apart from circumstances and intentions, are morally indifferent. (A famous example is picking up a leaf.) If the agent's intention or the circumstances of the act are unknown, one cannot determine if such an action is moral or immoral. But traditional moral theology has also maintained that some actions can be defined precisely enough that the moral determination is clear; some actions are the *kind* of actions a human being ought never choose to do, no matter what good may come of them. Rape, adultery, and direct killing of the innocent are considered to be such actions. The use of contraception is another. These are intrinsically disordered, hence immoral, acts.

Humanae Vitae sustains this analysis of contraception and insisted on the fundamental principle of Catholic moral thought: "that it is never licit, even for the gravest reasons, to do evil so that good might come from it" (no. 14). Revisionist theologians, as the dissenters now call themselves, deny that they have rejected this principle, but claim they have redefined the proper characterization of certain actions. They reject the term and concept "intrinsic evil" and prefer instead such terms as "premoral," "ontic," or "physical evils." Most would consider masturbation, contraception, killing and sleeping with one who is not one's spouse to be as kinds of acts, premoral or ontic evils. They argue that the *moral* evil of such actions can be determined only when one knows the circumstances of the action.

Whether or not the rejection of the concept "intrinsic evil" constitutes a radical break with the tradition is a matter of some dispute. As mentioned earlier, when *Humanae Vitae* was issued dissenters did not necessarily understand themselves to be advocating a radical break with traditional Catholic moral theology. Even today, many of the dissenters or revisionists maintain that they are modifying the Catholic moral tradition only slightly. The fact remains that some theologians have been attempting to effect a revolution in Catholic moral theology. Germain Grisez, in response to an article written in 1972 by Peter Knauer, charged that Knauer was "carrying through a revolution in principle while pretending only a clarification of traditional ideas." Father Richard McCormick at the time agreed with Grisez, and stated, "I believe this is true—and Knauer explicitly admits it in this study. The only question, then, is the following: Is the revolution justified? Is it solidly grounded?"

Many who hold views once deemed "revolutionary" by friend and foe alike now state they are not waging a revolution, but are simply engaging in dialogue with the tradition. Whereas the tradition, the dissenters observe, has taught that all abortions, all use of contraception, all homosexual intercourse, and all masturbation is wrong, the new way of thinking would allow some abortions, some use of contraception, some acts of homosexual intercourse, some instances of masturbation. But it is not the *degree* of difference that constitutes a revolution in theology, but the *reasons* for the difference.

It is not easy to give a quick description of the position of revisionists, also known as "consequentialists," "proportionalists," "teleologists," and "situation ethicists." I shall offer a sketch of one version of the revisionist position and indicate how a refutation of this position might proceed. I do so knowing that there are many versions of the revisionist position, and consequently a number of appropriate responses as well.

As we have noted, much of the justification for the revisionist mode of reasoning derives from a rejection of natural law. Revisionist theologians typically echo the charge of Father Curran that traditional natural law theory is "physicalistic," i.e., condemns acts such as adultery, contraception, and masturbation because they violate in some way the nature of a physical action. These theologians claim that it is inappropriate to draw moral conclusions from physical natures. They do not think physical natures should have *no* bearing on the moral evaluation of an action, but they do argue that these natures should not be determinative of the morality of an action. They allow (with the exception of Father Curran) that there is some evil in contraception and masturbation, for instance, but that this evil does not render them the *kind* of actions which should never be done. The evils are not intrinsic moral evils.

The heart of this argument is that contraception and masturbation can bring about goods which outweigh the evil in these actions. Such goods might be harmony in a marriage or the testing of fertility. Thus, the circumstances, motives, or intentions for an action need to be known before the act can be assessed morally.

Germain Grisez, John Finnis, Joseph Boyle, William May and others have challenged the revisionist theologians. They focus largely on showing that the "consequentialism" or "proportionalism" of the revisionist is not consistent with the Catholic moral tradition and that it is not a tenable mode of moral reasoning. One major claim in their refutation of proportionalism is that it advises making moral decisions by balancing various goods against one another, goods which are rarely commensurable; that is, it is not possible to weigh how much good or evil is being sacrificed for other goods, since these goods are not of the same kind.

When faced with a situation where one must sacrifice some goods, it is obvious that he should try to protect the greater good *when the goods are of the same kind.* For instance, if one must unavoidably, but legitimately (i.e., morally), kill either one person or ten, he ought clearly to choose the action which kills one rather than ten. As Germain Grisez has argued so well, this is an uncontroversial, morally sound "balancing" of goods. But not all decisions can be made in this way, since not all goods are commensurate. If one can buy only enough food to feed one's family of three, he must use his money to feed his family, rather than send it to a foreign country where it can feed thirty. Feeding thirty might seem to be better than feeding three, but more than a mere balancing and simple calculation of goods must enter into moral decision making. It would not be moral to sacrifice the lives of the three for whom one is directly responsible for the sake of thirty for whom one is not directly responsible. One may attempt to do both without sacrificing the good of his immediate responsibilities, but he should not decide by assigning values to all the goods involved and mechanically choose the good of "greater" value.

Reasoning about the goods of marriage resembles the second situation more than the first. The choice to use contraception is not a matter of balancing commensurable goods. What value, for instance, does one give to the harmony in a marriage which would outweigh the good of remaining open to procreation? Both are goods, and rather than sacrificing one to the other, a means must be found to protect both.

The revisionist position is subject to many other kinds of critique. The claim that the natural law tradition thought actions were morally evil simply because of their physical nature, for example, is manifestly a misreading of this tradition. This error can be demonstrated by showing how differently natural law tradition responds to physically identical actions when performed by or on animals and when performed by or on human beings. Traditional moralists do not object to sterilizing animals, or to the fact that animals may masturbate or be unfaithful to their mates. Why not? These actions seem to involve the same physical evil which is involved in human sterilization, masturbation, and infidelity.

But isn't it clear that the condemnation of such actions for humans is not based solely on their physical nature? Rather, they are considered to be immoral only when they are a matter of a person's choice, of one who is capable of realizing that basic human goods are being sacrificed when humans perform these actions. It is not just that the sperm and egg are not following their natural courses that constitutes the objection to contraception (for certainly some forms of medication are permitted which have the same effect). The objection is that the *deliberate obstruction* of sperm meeting egg constitutes the kind of choice which undermines fundamental human goods. Central to the opposition to contraception is an understanding which sees every human life as the result of a special act of creation by God. It is the life-creating dimensions of the sexual act, whereby spouses become co-creators with God, that completely remove condemnation of contraception from a focus solely on the "physical" nature of the sexual act.

A third kind of argument against the revisionist position objects to its claim that the effort to protect "personalist values" justifies the choice to contracept. Revisionist theologians regularly chide the tradition for not heeding personalist values, which are rooted in the ability to make free choices, to take responsibility for these choices, and to make choices which enhance the freedom of the person. They claim that the natural law tradition has been "deontological," based upon morality as lawabidingness, rather than viewing morality as based on freedom and responsibility. They also claim that their moral reasoning has much greater scriptural basis than traditional natural theory, which is a child of Greek and Roman philosophical thought.

While those who oppose contraception have relied greatly on natural law arguments, they have not neglected arguments based upon personalist values or arguments rooted in scripture. Even prior to *Humanae Vitae,* several pioneering articles explained how contraception is contrary to "self-giving" in marriage and invalidates the body's "language of love." *Gaudium et Spes* in particular laid great emphasis on the value of self-giving in marriage and required that

> ... when there is a question of harmonizing conjugal love with the responsible transmission of life, the moral aspect of any procedure does not depend solely on sincere intentions or on an evaluation of motives. It must be determined by objective standards. These, based on the nature of the human person and his acts, preserve the full sense of mutual self-giving and human procreation in the context of true love. Such a goal cannot be achieved unless the virtue of conjugal chastity is sincerely practiced [no. 51].

Pope John Paul II has drawn deeply from the well of *Gaudium et Spes* in his writings on marriage, the family, and *Humanae Vitae.* One of his first extended explanations of the importance of self-giving in marriage appeared in *Familiaris Consortio;* he spoke of contraception as a "lie," a violation of the language of love spoken by the body. He also issued a "pressing invitation" to theologians "to unite their efforts in order to collaborate with the hierarchical magisterium and to commit themselves to the task of illustrating ever more clearly the biblical foundations, the ethical grounds, and the personalistic reasons behind this doctrine [on the proper regulation of family size; no. 31]."

Pope John Paul II has also drawn our attention to a few key texts in scripture which reveal the importance of the procreative power of sex in defining the proper relationship between the sexes. Of central importance is the necessity for men and women to gain self-mastery in order to achieve fully loving relationships with each other. John Paul argues that contraception impedes this full giving of spouses to each other, for it withholds the gift of one's fertility from one's spouse. Lovers wish to give themselves fully to each other, and to receive each other fully in return; the body intends to express this love through intercourse. Contraception, however, obstructs the full giving of spouses to one another.

John Paul has developed this argument through a fascinating exegesis of passages in Genesis about human creation and of the passages in the Gospel about divorce. He discovers in these scriptural texts a complete theology of the body and an understanding of the relationship of the sexes which is based upon the most fundamental Christian truths. Surely, in time his views will be acknowledged as a major contribution to protecting the procreative power of sexual intercourse. People will likewise come to see that he has shown how contraception violates the unitive, no less than the procreative, meaning of sexual intercourse.

Some have cautioned that it is divisive to stress the Church's teaching on contraception. The divisions, however, already exist. We must work to heal the divisions by patiently teaching the doctrine of the Church in season and out. G.K. Chesterton's remark that Christianity has not been tried and found wanting, it has been found difficult and not tried, could be applied to *Humanae Vitae:* it has not been studied and taught and been rejected, it has not been studied and taught. When more start teaching *Humanae Vitae,* more will start living by *Humanae Vitae,* and more will experience the peace and joy that come with doing God's will.

See Further Reading for Article 21.

22

PAUL VI AS PROPHET

Humanae Vitae Made Some Bold Prophecies
Two Decades Ago. Did They Come to Pass?

by
Janet E. Smith

Prophecy is a tricky business. If a prophet predicts that something
will happen and it does not, the prophet is discredited. But what if
he predicts truly? Doesn't the truth of his prediction give credence
to the prophet's insight, authority, reasoning—to whatever is the
source of his ability to prophesy? Would we not be inclined to
trust the one proven to be a true prophet?

Humanae Vitae 20 years ago "prophesied" that marriages and
society would suffer if the use of contraception became widespread.
Now the vast majority of spouses, as well as those who are
unmarried, use some form of contraception. It seems a good time
to evaluate the legitimacy of *Humanae Vitae*'s prophetic voice. For
if the "prophecies" are true, if contraception has been responsible
at least in part for many of the troubles we have today, the
widespread neglect of this encyclical has been foolish, to say the
least.

To be sure, the encyclical was not written to be a prophetic
document. Rather, it was written to be a clarifying document,
meant to present what the Church teaches about contraception.

The encyclical does present this teaching clearly but has been little heeded in the last 20 years. Statistics show that few Catholics live by this teaching, and it seems safe to suppose that few Catholics have read *Humanae Vitae* or reflected upon it. Most simply accept the common view that using a contraceptive differs little from taking an aspirin. Furthermore, many theologians call into question the truth of the teaching and work to establish that Catholics have a "right" to dissent from it.

Indeed, when *Humanae Vitae* was issued, many were furious with the Church for continuing to maintain the retrograde view that sexual intercourse can be engaged in morally only when its procreative meaning is maintained. Many thought the Church was standing in the way of progress and human happiness. They "prophesied" that contraception would solve, or at least reduce, social problems such as overpopulation and pregnancy out of wedlock. Perhaps even more ardently, they believed that contraception would enhance married life by reducing sexual strain caused by the fear of pregnancy. As mentioned, *Humanae Vitae* "prophesied" quite the contrary. Whose prophecies were true? Has contraception had a good or bad effect on marriages and society?

Before we review the prophecies of *Humanae Vitae,* we must bear in mind that Pope Paul VI did *not* base his condemnation of contraception on predictions that its use would have bad consequences. Rather, he situated the Church's teaching in the Christian view of the dignity of the human person and the meaning of marriage, and argued that contraception violates both. Christians understand marriage to be an elevated calling whereby God enlists spouses in the all-important enterprise of bringing forth new human life. The Church teaches that to use contraception is to reject God and his life-giving ways. The Church teaches not that contraception is wrong because it has bad consequences, but that because contraception is wrong, it will have bad consequences.

Paul VI made four rather general "prophecies" about what would happen were the Church's teaching on contraception to be ignored (see *Humanae Vitae,* section 17). No one would be sadder than he to learn how true his predictions were.

First Prophecy

The Pope first noted that the widespread use of contraception would "lead to conjugal infidelity and the general lowering of morality." That there has been a widespread decline in morality, especially sexual morality, in the last 20 years is very difficult to deny. The increase in the number of divorces, abortions, out-of-wedlock pregnancies, and venereal diseases should convince any skeptic that sexual morality is not the strong suit of our age. It would be wrong to say that contraception is the single cause of this decline, but it would also be unthinkable not to count contraception among the contributing factors.

Consider the phenomenon of teenage pregnancy as one instance of a source of misery caused by contraception. By age 19, eight of every 10 males and seven of every 10 females has had sexual intercourse. Four of 10 teenagers have had at least one pregnancy. One of every four black babies is born to a teenage mother; nearly a third of black teenage mothers have a second baby before they are 20. Nearly a million and a half abortions occur each year and nearly a third of these (almost 400,000) are obtained by teenagers. More than one in seven teenagers has had at least one abortion.

These figures are chilling; so too is their meaning. It is disturbing that they seem to be self-perpetuating; consider that roughly 80 percent of girls who are mothers at age 15 are daughters of women who had babies when they were teenagers. Two-thirds of all teenagers who have children before they turn 19 drop out of school. Many young women who get pregnant out-of-wedlock regularly end up welfare mothers; their children grow up with no father at home, with an immature mother, and with all the handicaps of poverty. More than half of the women who receive

Aid to Families with Dependent Children were teenagers when they had their first child.

The long-term consequences for these young women, their children, and society are incalculable. We have hardly begun to realize the cost of sexuality run wild, the cost of single-parent households and broken homes. It is not speculation to think that much drug-dependency, crime, and sexual maladjustments can be traced to ailing family life. Children who do not have mature and loving parents have a hard time meeting the demands of life while resisting the call to easier pleasures and other modes of escape. And who can calculate the cost of the insecurity, the low self-image, and other psychological problems experienced by those who do not enjoy a secure childhood? These problems may not cripple one, but they certainly make life a good deal more difficult than it otherwise would be.

There is no question that contraception is behind a lot of this trouble. Contraception has made sexual activity a much more popular option than it was when fear of pregnancy deterred a great number of young men and women from engaging in premarital sexual intercourse. The availability of contraception has led them to believe that they can engage in premarital sexual activity "responsibly." But teenagers are about as responsible in their use of contraception as they are in all other phases of their lives—such as making their beds, cleaning their rooms, and getting homework done on time.

Studies show that over 80 percent of young women who have had abortions are contraceptively experienced. They know all about contraception but choose not to use it for a variety of reasons: for instance, they do not like the side effects or they do not like to think of themselves as "prepared for sex." Or they intentionally get pregnant to force the young man to declare his intentions. That ready access to contraception should reduce teenage pregnancy has been a standard argument for a long time; but in fact, contraception definitely seems to have exacerbated the problem. Indeed, studies show that in places where efforts to provide teens with contraceptives have intensified, there has been no clear decrease in teenage pregnancy, and in some cases there have been increases.

Teenage pregnancy is a major problem in our society, abortion an even worse problem. What is the connection between contraception and abortion? In the early days of the prolife movement most prolifers argued that abortion and contraception were quite distinct issues. This argument seemed to have considerable plausibility since abortion is the taking of a human life already begun, whereas contraception (which is truly contraceptive and not abortifacient) prevents life from beginning. Indeed, all will agree that the magnitude of moral wrong in abortion is much greater than that in contraception, but many now recognize that widespread use of contraception has paved the way for more abortions.

Most abortions are the result of unwanted pregnancies, most unwanted pregnancies are the result of sexual relationships outside of marriage, and most sexual relationships outside of marriage are facilitated by the availability of contraception. To turn this "progression" around; contraception leads to more extra-marital sexual intercourse; more extra-marital sexual intercourse leads to more unwanted pregnancies; more unwanted pregnancies lead to more abortions. Not many women intend to use abortion as a "back-up" to failed contraception, but it is undeniable that it is often so used.

Nor must we fail to consider how many abortions are the result of contraceptives working properly. There is much evidence to show that not all contraceptive pills work by stopping ovulation. With many forms of the Pill a woman may still be ovulating and thus may be conceiving. If she conceives when on the Pill, she will most likely self-abort. Since the contraceptive has made the uterine wall hostile to a fertilized egg, the fertilized ovum, the new young life, does not implant and dies an early death. The IUD, it is believed, nearly always works this way. Thus, IUDs and some forms of the Pill not only contribute to abortion, they in fact *cause* abortions; they are abortifacients. Is it not clear, then, that contraception is a leading cause of abortions?

Second Prophecy

Paul VI also argued that "the man" will lose respect for "the woman" and "no longer (care) for her physical and psychological equilibrium" and will come to "the point of considering her as a mere instrument of selfish enjoyment, and no longer as his respected and beloved companion." This concern reflects what has come to be known as a "personalist" understanding of morality: Paul VI is not just concerned that couples will be breaking some divine law when they use contraception (though this seems to be a fair concern for those who understand that they are showing their love for God by respecting His laws, which, after all, are for our benefit). The personalist understanding of wrongdoing is based upon respect for the dignity of the human person. The Pope realizes that the Church's teaching on contraception is designed to protect the good of conjugal love. When spouses violate this good, they do not act in accord with their innate dignity and thus they endanger their own happiness. Treating their bodies as mechanical instruments to be manipulated for their own purposes, they risk treating each other as objects of pleasure.

Contraceptors do not even treat their bodies very respectfully as instruments. It seems truly prophetic that Paul VI should mention the dangers of contraception to a woman's "physical and psychological equilibrium" at a time when these dangers were not well-known. They are still not fully known, but are becoming more widely recognized. The IUD has been taken off the market because of so many lawsuits stemming from harm done to women using them. The contraceptive pill has a list of "contra-indications" so long it's a rare woman who does not experience some of these. Indeed, some doctors who have studied the effects of the contraceptive pill state that they would never put their wives or one of their daughters on it. The disturbing increase in infertility among women is likely caused, at least in part, by the use of contraception, since contraception alters a woman's delicate hormonal balance for many years. Another major source of infertility is the increase in the frequency of sexually transmitted diseases, an increase linked to greater promiscuous sexuality—which in turn is facilitated by the widespread acceptability of contraception.

Feminists, too, are beginning to warn women about the dangers of the Pill. Germaine Greer, a prominent feminist, has written a lengthy tome, *Sex and Destiny,* which rebukes women for their careless use of the Pill. I heard her speak some 10 years ago at a feminist conference where she chastised the women in the audience for taking the Pill, the effects of which were not known. She ridiculed women for taking massive doses of chemicals daily to counteract an event—fertility—that occurs only a few days a month, and very predictable days at that. She was even more angry that contraception was being pushed on women in the Third World who did not have the education required to know the dangers of the "medication" being forced upon them.

What are the dangers to the "psychological" equilibrium of women who use contraception? Certainly, one of the side-effects of the Pill is depression, but I think more is involved than that. Paul VI warned of "the man" losing respect for "the woman." He saw that the use of contraception encourages "the man" to look upon "the woman" not as a special woman with her own needs and desires, not as a female with a marvelous procreative faculty, but as an object. He can easily come to look upon her as one from whom he can derive sexual pleasure without risking the personal bonding that comes through participating in sexual intercourse open to procreation.

The bond created by sexual intercourse open to procreation needs to be more fully understood. Young girls often have a preference for "unprotected" intercourse for they feel they are thereby giving themselves more fully, are showing their love more completely, to their boyfriends. There is something fundamentally right about that "feeling." Few (surrogate mothers notwithstanding) are willing to have "procreative" sex with someone whom they do not love, with whom they are not willing to share a lifetime of responsibilities. "Recreational" sex admits a large number of partners for they are partners only for momentary sexual pleasure, not for sharing in a lifetime project. The possibility of procreation obviously points to child-bearing, which in turn points to lifelong responsibilities. Thus, engaging in "procreative" sex bespeaks a commitment much more profound than engaging in sex that is closed to procreation. In procreative sexual intercourse the man and woman are potentially engaging in a lifetime project with each other and are expressing a willingness to effect such a lifetime bond.

There is rarely "mutuality" in the use of contraception. Most often the woman bears the responsibility for it and she must suffer most of the unpleasant "side-effects" of its use. Natural family planning (NFP), on the other hand, needs the cooperation of both spouses to succeed. Whereas men who engage in contracepted sexual intercourse often come to view women as objects and desire to have them always at their disposal, men using natural family planning learn self-mastery and begin to appreciate the woman and her cycles and needs. Natural family planning is based on respect for both female and male fertility and requires a loving and respectful relationship for successful use. More will be said about the differences between natural family planning and contraception momentarily, but this difference of mutual responsibility based upon respect is in itself indication of a profound difference between the two. Disenchanted former users of contraception and converts to natural family planning are often the most avid and eloquent defenders of the difference between them.

Interestingly, the incidence of divorce among couples who use NFP is almost negligible. Certainly, these couples have a commitment to the indissolubility of marriage that other couples may lack, but surely most couples when they marry hope never to divorce. Yet nearly 50 percent of marriages end in divorce. That the increase in the number of divorces coincides with the increased use of contraception makes one suspect a causal connection of some kind. Surely, contraception makes infidelity easier, and infidelity leads to divorce. Lowering the barriers to infidelity may not, though, be the chief reason for the incredibly higher rate of divorce among contraceptors. The above analysis suggests that couples using NFP communicate better and experience much stronger bonds with each other. Contraception, then, rather than being a source of happiness in a marriage may be assisting in its breakdown.

Third Prophecy

Paul VI also observed that the widespread acceptance of contraception would place a "dangerous weapon ... in the hands of those public authorities who take no heed of moral exigencies." The history of the family planning programs in the Third World is a sobering testimony to this reality. In Third World countries many undergo sterilization unaware of what is being done to them. The forced abortion program in China shows the stark extreme to which governments will take population control programs. Moreover, few are willing to face the increasing evidence that many parts of the world now face not a problem of overpopulation but of underpopulation. It will take some time to reverse the "anti-baby" legislation and attitudes now entrenched in many societies. France and West Germany, for example, have tried without much success to pass legislation making child-bearing more attractive to their citizens.

Fourth Prophecy

The final warning Paul VI gave about contraception is that it would lead man to think that he had limitless dominion over his own body. Again, the Pope did not specify what he had in mind, but his worry seems well-grounded. For instance, sterilization is now the most widely used form of contraception in the U.S.; individuals think it so appropriate that they have control over their own body that they are not hesitant to alter its very make-up.

Again, we have not begun to realize the long-term physical and psychological ramifications of widespread sterilization. We are tampering unthinkingly with one of the chief sources of human pleasure and happiness: the ability to have children.

The desire to have unlimited dominion over one's body extends beyond contraception. We see it in many areas of life. The making of babies in test tubes is another indication of a refusal to accept the limitations of the body, as is euthanasia and the use of organs for transplantation from the nearly dead. We want to adjust the body to our needs and desires and timetables rather than adjusting ourselves to its needs and timetables.

For each of these problems there are undoubtedly a host of contributing factors, but I think it is not unfair to say that the use of contraception is one of the contributing factors. Ironically, contraception was predicted to help solve some of these problems.

Positive Prophecies

In *Humanae Vitae* Pope Paul VI made positive as well as negative prophecies. He sketched out the good that comes from abiding by the Church's teaching on contraception. He acknowledged that spouses may have difficulty in acquiring the self-discipline needed to practice methods of family planning that require periodic abstinence. But he thought this was possible, especially with the help of sacramental graces. In section 21, he remarked that

> the discipline which is proper to the purity of married couples, far from harming conjugal love, rather confers on it a higher human value. It demands continual effort yet, thanks to its beneficent influence, husband and wife fully develop their personalities, being enriched with spiritual values. Such discipline bestows upon family life fruits of serenity and peace, and facilitates the solution of other problems; it favors attention for one's partner, helps both parties to drive out selfishness, the enemy of true love; and deepens their sense of responsibility.

> By its means, parents acquire the capacity of having a deeper
> and more efficacious influence in the education of their offspring;
> little children and youths grow up with a just appraisal of
> human values, and in the serene and harmonious development
> of their spiritual and sensitive faculties.

This passage of *Humanae Vitae* is rarely studied. John Paul II,
however, is one commentator who recognizes its deep wisdom. It
plays the central role in his reflections on *Humanae Vitae*. He
focuses on the importance of "self-mastery" for the proper use of
sexuality, and explains the meaning of the human body and the
human person as these bear upon our sexuality.

Fundamental to his understanding of man is the distinction
between what he calls man's "original condition" and his "historic"
condition. In his commentaries on *Genesis,* the Pope explains that
man and woman were created to be a loving community with
each other. In this original condition man and woman did not
experience lust or any disorder in their passions. Thus they were
able to love each other authentically without the troublesome
emotions and disordered passions men and women now experience.

After the fall, however, a great deal of selfishness entered into
human relationships; individuals easily exploit one another in the
realm of sex, as well as in every other realm. For man and woman
to regain the authentic loving relationship for which their hearts
yearn, they must learn to control their disordered passions. If they
do not do so, they will be expressing lust rather than love in their
sexual relationships. Rather than giving themselves as gifts and
receiving the other as a gift, they will be imposing themselves on
each other and using one another. But if they learn the self-
mastery spoken of in *Humanae Vitae* they will find tremendous
fruits for their own conjugal relationship and for the other relationships of their lives, especially those within the family.

The passage cited earlier from *Humanae Vitae* indicates what some
of these "fruits" are. It claims that spouses will develop especially
the spiritual dimensions of their personalities. It speaks of the

"serenity and peace" that come with discipline, a discipline that flows over to other areas of one's life. Perhaps most important, spouses become unselfish; they begin to be concerned more about the well-being of their spouses rather than of themselves. Not to be underestimated is the value of the witness they give their children and other young people.

One practitioner of NFP told me what a great witness his commitment was to the young males at his workplace, to whom he was trying to counsel restraint in sexual behavior. They were impressed with his argument, that if he could sleep in the same bed with the woman he loved and control his sexual desire, they could control their sexual desire for the women they were dating. Young people sense the attitudes about sex held by adults; if their parents have a reverence for the meaning of sex, if their parents have learned how to exercise self-control, they are more likely to be responsible about their own sexuality.

Some think there is little difference between the use of NFP and contraception since both contraceptors and practitioners of NFP want to have control over their fertility. But users of NFP gain this control by self-mastery, by attaining internal control over themselves; contraceptors seek this control by technological mastery of their bodies. Indeed, users of contraception and users of NFP agree that there is a great difference between the two; neither switch easily or readily to the other. Contraceptors are generally reluctant to try NFP because they fear that they will lose control over a very important part of their lives, that they will be casting their fate to the winds—or to their fertility, as it were. They do not take a lot of comfort in the reassurances that NFP is every bit as effective a form of family planning as the most effective form of contraception. One senses, however, that what they don't trust is not the method, but themselves and the strength of their marriage. Even though they may have had to abstain many times in their marriage for reasons of illness or prolonged separation, they do not think it is wise deliberately to plan to abstain.

Practitioners of NFP, on the other hand, are repulsed by the thought of using contraception. Although they may experience powerful sexual desires during the periods of abstinence, the thought of purchasing and using a contraceptive is repugnant to them. For them, contraception understood as something that violates human dignity is not some elevated abstract phrase, but is nearly a physical feeling. Certainly, most of them have struggled with NFP and with their sexual desires. Those who have been chaste before marriage and have never contracepted have an easier time of it. But many struggle with the irritability abstinence may cause; they struggle with trying to live with their frustration without taking it out on their spouses. Eventually, they learn to communicate better with their spouses about their sexual feelings, in fact about all of their feelings. They begin to gain the virtue of self-mastery. Once progress is made, they assure others that self-restraint enhances rather than harms one's love life; that it improves rather than harms one's relationship with one's spouse.

John Paul II recently spoke of the Church's teaching on contraception as part of the "permanent patrimony" of the Church. Twenty years of neglecting *Humanae Vitae* have produced enough unpleasant consequences to enable us to recognize how foolish and dangerous it is to waste this patrimony. The successful marriages and happiness of couples who use NFP suggest that once we reclaim this patrimony, we shall begin to experience joys and benefits we have nearly forgotten. Paul VI in *Humanae Vitae* implored priests, doctors, educators, and spouses to promote the teaching of the encyclical. John Paul II has reiterated this plea. It is time we all do what we can to answer it, for the benefits will be ours and will be great.

FURTHER READING

A thorough study of *Humanae Vitae* is available in Smith's *Humanae Vitae: A Generation Later* (Washington, D.C.: Catholic University of America Press, 1991). See also "Natural Law: Does It Evaluate Choices or Acts?" *American Journal of Jurisprudence* 36 (1991), 171–201; "*Humanae Vitae:* A Hidden Treasure", *The Family* (Nov. 1988): 28–30; "Pope John Paul II and *Humanae Vitae*", *International Review of Natural Family Planning* 10, no. 2 (Summer 1986): 95–112 (reprinted in this volume), and "The Connection between Contraception and Abortion", *Homiletic and Pastoral Review* vol. 93, no. 7 (April, 1993): 10–18.

APPENDIX

TRANSLATION OF *HUMANAE VITAE*

TRANSLATOR'S INTRODUCTION

The currently available English texts of *Humanae Vitae* are based extensively, if not primarily, on the Italian version of the encyclical.[a]

[a] The claim that *Humanae Vitae* was written in Italian and French is made by Lucio Brunelli, "The Pill That Divided the Church," *Thirty Days* 4 (July–August 1988), p. 66. A comparison of some of the Italian phrases with the Latin can be found in Innocentius Parisella, "Latinae Quaedam Voces Locutionesque in Encyclicis Litteris *Humanae Vitae* Occurrentes cum Sermone Italico Comparatae," *Ephemerides Iuris Canonici* 24 (1968) 265–270, and reprinted in *Latinitas* 17 (1969) 115–120.

In preparation for this translation reference was made to six English translations. The most commonly available is that first published in the English edition of the *L'Osservatore Romano* when *Humanae Vitae* was released and made widely available in this country through the Daughters of Saint Paul (hereafter referred to as the "usual translation" and designated by DSP). Popular, too, is the translation by Marc Calegari, S.J., *Humanae Vitae* (San Francisco: Ignatius Press, 1978) (hereafter IP). The Catholic Truth Society sponsored a translation, by Rev. Alan C. Clark and Rev. Geoffrey Crawfurd (London: Catholic Truth Society, 1968) (hereafter CTS), with a revised edition in 1970 (hereafter CTS2); a revised version of the CTS translation is also to be found in *The Pope Speaks* 13:4 (1969) 329–46 (hereafter CTS3). (It is difficult to determine the extent of the revisions, but they seem not very significant, except for the crucial last line of *Humanae Vitae* 11; see the comment on this section in the following notes.) A

Reprinted from *Humanae Vitae: A Generation Later* by Janet E. Smith (Washington, D.C.: Catholic University of America Press, 1991). This translation, with an introductory essay, has been published as a separate pamphlet, "*Humanae Vitae*: A Challenge to Love" (New Hope Kentucky; Catholics United For Life, 1993).

Since the encyclical was originally composed in Italian and French, this is understandable. Nonetheless, Latin remains the official language of the Church and thus the Latin version of *Humanae Vitae* is the official text. The following translation of *Humanae Vitae* is based on the Latin text.

For the most part the Italian and Latin texts do not differ substantially, though there are several important differences in tone and in some key phrases. Moreover, the Latin has important correspondences with earlier Church writings and serves better to show the continuity and development of certain arguments. For instance, the fourth word in the Italian text is *dovere,* which is properly translated "duty" in English. In Latin, one would have expected to have found *officium* (duty). But one finds *munus,* meaning "reward," "honor," "gift," "responsibility," "task," "office," "function," and so on; this choice is not surprising because it is a word that, as Chapter 5 seeks to substantiate, has a distinguished history in Church documents. My studies have led me to believe that "mission" captures best the word's many connotations. Since *munus* is so central to my interpretation of *Humanae Vitae,* all occurrences of the word have been noted by the insertion of the Latin in the translation.

Even more significant is a difference in the crucial passage in section 11 usually translated "Each and every marriage act must remain open to procreation." The Italian reads "Che qualsiasi atto matrimoniale deve rimanere aperto alla trasmissione della vita."

---

text that seems to be identical to CTS2 is published in *Vatican Council II* vol. 2, ed. by Austin Flannery, O.P. (Northport, N.Y.: Costello Publishing Co., 1982), 397–416, though the claim is made that the translation was done by the Vatican Press Office (p. 414). Although the CTS translation is accompanied by the notice that it was made on the basis of the Latin text it seems to this reader to be truer to the Italian, except in a few crucial passages. The only translation that used the Latin as the primary base is that by A. Durand, " 'The Encyclical' – A Fresh Translation," *Homiletic and Pastoral Review* 69:11 (Aug. 1969) 851–864 (hereafter HPR), which seems to this reader to be quite a free translation. I am indebted to these translators for felicity of phrasing that I have "borrowed" on occasion. The translation published here is based on the Latin, though on a few occasions, when the Latin seemed irrecoverably obscure, recourse was made to the Italian.

The Latin substitutes the words *per se destinatus* ("in itself destined") for the Italian *aperto* ("open"), though the Latin *apertus* ("open") would easily have worked here. As the commentary in Chapter 3 argues, the phrase *per se destinatus* is philosophically more precise and more in keeping with the context.

The Latin of the document has no identifiable source of reliable decipherment; it is a kind of "modern" or "Church" Latin, which is an odd combination of classical Latin and the language the Church has developed over the centuries. The method of translation employed here has involved consultation of classical and medieval dictionaries, reference to arguably representative classical and medieval authors, tracing of the word being considered through the documents of Vatican II, consideration of the appearance of a word in other Church documents, cross-reference to other uses of a word within *Humanae Vitae* itself, reference to the Italian "original," and reference to other translations. I have included Latin words or phrases when I thought the reader with a little Latin might like to know how the Latin reads.

As any who have attempted to translate Latin know, it is a language that loves long and intricate sentences. The form of these sentences is not easily or wisely transported into English. Consequently, I have customarily broken down long sentences into at least three English sentences. Certainly, this translation attempts to follow the Latin closely, but some slight liberties were taken when necessary for respecting English idiom. Some stiltedness and convolutedness inevitably remain. I have also taken the liberty of breaking some of the paragraphs into smaller units in the hopes that this will enable the reader to see the structure of the argument more easily.

Subtitles are given periodically throughout the Italian text. These do not appear in the Latin text. But since they are accurate and useful, I have decided to employ them here.

The numbered notes are to the documents that are cited by the encyclical. The lettered notes are explanatory of my reasons for preferring certain translations.

And, as is the practice throughout the body of this book, when *Man* is capitalized it is to be understood to be the generic use of the word *man,* that is, inclusive of both males and females.

HUMANAE VITAE

An encyclical letter on the proper regulation
of the propagation of offspring [addressed]
To the Venerable Patriarchs, Archbishops, Bishops
and to all the local Ordinaries,
Who are in peace and communion with the Apostolic See
to the Clergy and the Christian Faithful of the
whole Catholic realm [*totius Catholici Orbis*]
and to all Men of goodwill.
Pope Paul VI
To Our venerable brothers and beloved sons,
Greetings and [Our] apostolic blessing

THE TRANSMISSION OF LIFE

1 . God has entrusted spouses with the extremely important
[*gravissimum*] mission [*munus*][b] of transmitting human life. In
fulfilling this mission spouses freely and deliberately [*consciam*]
render [*tribuunt*] a service [*opera*] to God, the Creator.[c] This

[b] See Chapter 5 for a discussion of the word *munus*.

[c] This second line has been translated "for which married persons are the
free and responsible collaborators of God the Creator." The Italian word for
"collaborators" appears in the Italian and may be an echo of *Gaudium et Spes*
50.2, which refers to the duty of transmitting and educating human life (*in
officio humanam vitam transmittendi atque educandi*) and speaks of spouses as
cooperators and interpreters of God's love in this duty (*cooperatores . . . amoris
Dei Creatoris*). But in Latin the phrase is *tribuunt operam. Operam* is from *opera*,
not *opus;* the Lewis and Short Latin dictionary notes, "*Opus* is used mostly of

service has always been a source of great joy, although the joys are, at times, accompanied by not a few difficulties and sufferings.

Fulfilling this mission [*munus*] has always raised some difficult questions [*quaestiones*]d for the consciences of married couples. Furthermore, in recent times, the evolution of human society has brought with it changes that raise new questions. The Church cannot ignore these questions, for they concern matters intimately connected with human life and happiness.

---

the mechanical activity of work, as that of animals, slaves, and soldiers; *opera* supposes a free will and desire to serve." *Opera* is more properly translated as "service." *Tribuunt* has very much the sense of "pay back" or "render"; "transmitting life" is, indeed, something that the spouses do *with* God, but the way it is stated here puts some emphasis on the fact that in doing so, they perform a service or give a return to God for the *munus* He has entrusted to them. This interpretation coincides with the meaning of *munus* as a task that God delegates to Man, and, in a sense, needs him to do, so that He may advance His kingdom.

Consciam is the word that later in the document is allied with *paternitas* (paternity or parenthood) and with it is translated as "responsible parenthood." Humans, when engaging in sexual intercourse, are capable of knowing that a result of this intercourse may be the conception of a child. To engage in sexual intercourse responsibly they must be prepared to be good parents to a child. More is said about responsible parenthood in section 10, but the presence of the word *consciam* here indicates that "transmitting human life" involves more than simple reproduction.

d This first sentence of the second paragraph has been translated: "At all times the fulfillment of this duty has posed grave problems. . . . " This translation again follows the Italian rather than the Latin. "Problems" is the English cognate of the Italian *problemi,* but it is not perhaps the best translation even of the Italian. In Italian the word is closer in meaning to the English "questions" (a cognate of the Latin used here), which means a query that one might raise about something; it is more neutral than "problems," which connotes that one has some difficulty with something. Indeed, there is the suggestion here that it is not always easy for spouses to understand the *munus* that is theirs and that at times it can be difficult for them to accept it, but it is important not to stress the acknowledgment that a *munus* may involve difficulties without, at the same time, stressing what an honor it is.

PART I. NEW ASPECTS OF THE QUESTION
AND THE COMPETENCE OF THE MAGISTERIUM

2. The various changes that have taken place [in modern times] are truly of great importance. In the first place, there has been a rapid increase in population, an increase that causes many to fear that the population of the earth will grow faster than its available life-sustaining resources. This [disparity] could result in even greater hardships for many families and for many developing nations. Public authorities may easily be tempted to fight the danger by rather severe methods. Moreover, contemporary conditions of work and housing, as well as increased expenses involved in providing for, raising, and educating children, often make it burdensome to support a large family adequately.

It must also be noted that there have been changes in how we view the person of woman and how we view her role [*munere*] in society; indeed there have even been changes in the value we place on conjugal love and on how we understand the meaning of acts of sexual intercourse [*actibus coniugum*]ᵉ in light of this love.

Finally, and above all, it must be noted that because Man has made such remarkable progress in controlling [*moderandis*] the forces of nature and in rationally organizing them, he also strives to extend this control [*moderationem*] to the whole of his life: that is, to his body, to the powers of his mind [*ad sui animi vires*], to his social life, and even to the laws that regulate the propagation of life.

3. This state of affairs gives rise to new questions. [Some ask:] Given the conditions of life today and given the importance of marital intercourse for marital harmony and fidelity, is it not appropriate to reconsider [*recognoscere*]ᶠ the moral norms that

---

ᵉ *Actibus coniugum* is variously translated as "conjugal acts" (DSP, IP, CTS3) and "intimate married life" (CTS1 and CTS2). Conceivably "conjugal acts" could refer to activity in married life other than sexual intercourse, but it does not seem to be too presumptuous to assume that such is its meaning here.

ᶠ The Italian here refers to a need for a *revisione* of the norm. Both DSP

have obtained up to now? Is not a reconsideration especially appropriate if it is believed that these norms cannot be observed without serious sacrifices [*gravia incommoda*], sometimes heroic sacrifices?g

Or, is it not possible to apply the so-called principle of totality to this problem? Would it not be possible to use this principle to justify using one's reason to reduce one's fertility? Would not an act that causes sterility become a licit and prudent way to limit one's family size? That is, would it not clearly be right to consider the goal [*finem*] of having children to pertain more to the whole of married life than to each and every act [of sexual intercourse]? And, again, given the fact that moderns have an increased sense of their responsibilities, [they ask] whether it is not right for them to entrust the mission [*munus*] of transmitting life more to their reason and will, than to the biological rhythms [*certis... vicibus*] of their bodies?

Competence of the Magisterium

4. Certainly, questions of this kind require that the Magisterium of the Church give new and deeper consideration to the principles of the moral teaching concerning marriage, a teaching that is

---

and IP translate *recognoscere* as "revise," which, although a cognate of the Italian, perhaps in English suggests a greater change than the text intends to suggest. CTS uses "review," which I believe is closer to the Latin. "Revise" is certainly what many wanted the Church to do; "review" or "reconsider" is what in fact the Church did.

g The translation for *incommoda* as "sacrifices" has been adopted from DSP and IP, which are following the Italian *sacrifici*. The Latin *incommoda* has the connotation more of "inconvenience" than of "sacrifice"; "difficulties" would perhaps be a more precise translation. A literal English translation would read: "serious difficulties which are sometimes a worthy [challenge] for the strongest men and women [*fortissimis viris digna*]." But, since it does not work in English to say "heroic difficulties," I have stayed with the more idiomatic "heroic sacrifices." The question of the morality of asking spouses to make heroic sacrifices was part of the concern of the Schema.

rooted in natural law, illuminated and made richer by divine revelation.

Let no one of the faithful deny that the Magisterium of the Church is competent to interpret the natural moral law. For it is indisputable—as Our predecessors have often declared[1]—that when Jesus Christ imparted His divine authority [*potestatis*] to Peter and the other apostles and sent them to all nations to teach His Commandments,[2] He established those very men as authentic guardians and interpreters of the whole moral law, that is, not only of the law of the Gospel, but also of natural law. For natural law [as well as revealed law] declares the will of God; [thus] faithful compliance [*fidelis obtemperatio*][h] with natural law is necessary for eternal salvation.[3]

Moreover, the Church has always been faithful in fulfilling this command. In recent times, she has more amply provided an integrated teaching [*congrua documenta*][i] on the nature of marriage, on the moral use of conjugal rights, and on the duties of the spouses.[4]

---

[1] Pius IX, encyclical *Qui Pluribus*, Nov. 9, 1846, in Pii IX *P. M. Acta*, I, 9–10; St. Pius X, encyclical *Singulari Quadam*, Sept. 24, 1912, in AAS 4 (1912) 658; Pius XI, encyclical *Casti Connubii*, Dec. 31, 1930, in AAS 22 (1930), 579–81; Pius XII, "Address to the Episcopate of the Catholic World," Nov. 2, 1954, in AAS 46 (1954) 671–72; John XXIII, encyclical, *Mater et Magistra*, May 15, 1961, in AAS 53 (1961), 457.

[2] Cf. Matt. 28:18–19.

[3] Cf. Matt. 7:21.

[4] Cf. *Catechismus Romanus Concilii Tridentini*, part II, ch. 8; Leo XIII, encyclical, *Arcanum*, Feb. 19, 1880, in *Acta Leonis* XIII, II (1880) 26–29; Pius XI,

---

[h] CTS translates *obtemperatio* as "observance"; DSP uses "fulfillment"; I have chosen "compliance" since I believe that "observance" seems somewhat weak and vague. "Obedience" would not be wrong, but since modern Americans, at least, seem to think all obedience is servile, I have selected "compliance" since this seems to capture both the sense of necessary adherence and the notion of voluntary cooperation.

[i] There is quite a variation on the translation of the phrase *congrua documenta*: DSP reads "has provided a coherent teaching on"; IP reads "has provided an integrated teaching on" and CTS1 and CTS2, "has always provided consistent teaching"; CTS3, "has always issued appropriate documents."

Special Studies

5. Conscious of Our responsibility [*muneris*] in this regard, We
approved and enlarged the commission established by Our venerable predecessor John XXIII in March of 1963. In addition to
many experts in the relevant disciplines, the commission also
included married couples. The commission was to consider opinions and views concerning married life and, in particular, [it was
to reflect upon] the legitimate means of controlling family size
[*rectem progignendae prolis temperationem*].ʲ It was to report the
results in due time to the Magisterium so that it could provide a
fitting response to the faithful and to people worldwide who were
awaiting an answer.⁵

---

encyclical *Divini Illius Magistri,* Dec. 31, 1929, in AAS 22 (1930), 58–61; Pius XI,
encyclical *Casti Connubii* in AAS 22 (1930) 545–46; Pius XII, "Address to the
Italian Medico-Biological Union of St. Luke," Nov. 12, 1944 in *Discorsi e
Radiomessaggi di S.S. Pio XII* 6, 191–92; Pius XII, "Address to the Italian
Catholic Union of Midwives," Oct. 29, 1951, in AAS 43 (1951) 835–54; Pius
XII, "Address to the Congress of the Family Front and of the Association of
Large Families," Nov. 28, 1951, in AAS 43 (1951) 857–59; Pius XII, "Address to
the Seventh Congress of the International Society of Hematology," Sept. 12,
1958, in AAS 50 (1958) 734–35; John XXIII, encyclical *Mater et Magistra* in AAS
53 (1961) 446–47; Second Vatican Council, Pastoral Constitution, *Gaudium et
Spes,* Dec. 7, 1965, nos. 47–52, in AAS 58 (1966) 1067–74; *Code of Canon Law
1917,* Canons 1067, 1068.1, 1076.1–2.
⁵ Paul VI, "Address to the Sacred College of Cardinals," June 23, 1964, in

ʲ All the translations use "birth regulation" or "regulation of births,"
which is true to the Italian. The Latin *rectem progignendae prolis temperationem,*
which strictly translated reads "the correct regulation of having offspring,"
may be equivalent to "birth regulation." Neither "birth regulation" nor "birth
control" is equivalent to "contraception," since they both refer to any methods
that spouses might use to regulate the number of children that they are to have
and therefore could include natural methods. Yet this phrase "birth regulation"
may be the cause of some confusion since in English it is too easily equated
with birth control, which, in turn, is too easily identified with contraception.
"Contraception" refers to devices or drugs that actively work *against* conception
and, therefore, does not include natural methods of family planning.

The investigation of the experts and the opinions and advice from Our confrères in the Episcopate—some spontaneously offered and some solicited by Us—enabled Us to consider very thoroughly all aspects of this complex subject. For which reason We offer Our most sincere thanks to all.

The Response of the Magisterium

6 . We could not, however, consider the conclusions of the commission in themselves as carrying the force of a certain and definite judgment; nor could their judgment relieve Us of Our duty [*officium*] of deciding a question of such great importance through Our own consideration. There were several reasons why this was necessary. First, there was no full consensus within the commission concerning what moral norms ought to be proposed. And even more importantly, certain methods and criteria [*viae rationesque*] were used in answering the question that departed [*discedentes*] from the firm and constant teaching of the Magisterium on what is moral within marriage.

We have carefully evaluated the findings sent to Us and most thoroughly considered this matter. Now, after assiduous prayer, We think it right, through the power given to Us by Christ, to give an answer to these weighty questions.

AAS 56 (1964) 588; Paul VI, "Address to the Commission for the Study of Population, the Family and Birth Regulation," Mar. 27, 1965, in AAS 57 (1965) 388; Paul VI, "Address to the National Congress of the Italian Society of Obstetrics and Gynecology," Oct. 29, 1966, in AAS 58 (1966) 1168.

PART 2. DOCTRINAL PRINCIPLES

A Total Vision of Man

7. The question of having children,[k] like other questions regarding human life, cannot be addressed adequately by examining it in a piecemeal way, that is, by looking at it through the perspectives of biology, psychology, demography, and sociology. Rather, [the question] must be addressed in such a way that the whole Man and the whole mission [*munus*] to which he has been called will be taken into account, for this [mission] pertains not only to his natural and earthly existence but also to his supernatural and eternal existence.

Many who attempt to defend artificial ways of limiting the number of children[l] give as their reason the demands of conjugal love or their duty to responsible parenthood [*paternitatis sui officii consciae*]. [Therefore] it is necessary to provide a precise definition and explanation of these two important [*gravia*] elements of married life. As We undertake to do this, We will keep foremost

---

[k] The translation of the first clause of this section is problematic. The Latin reads: *De propaganda prole questio.* The Italian reads: *Il problema della natalità.* It is translated variously; DSP has "the problem of birth"; IP, "the problem of birth regulation"; CTS1 and CTS2, "the question of the birth of children"; CTS3, "the question of human procreation." I have chosen "the question of having children," since I think the question being addressed here is larger than the question of *limiting* how many children one has: it touches on, for instance, why one should have children and the responsibilities of having children.

[l] This phrase differs considerably in the Latin and the Italian. The Latin phrase *artificiosas vias . . . quibus liberorum numerus coerceatur* corresponds to the Italian phrase *i metodi artificiali di controllo delle nascite;* the usual translation is "artificial methods of birth control." But the Latin is more concrete in speaking of the "artificial ways by which the number of children is limited." I think this concreteness, that it is children who are being "limited" rather than the more abstract "birth," is important.

in Our minds what was taught about this matter with the highest authority in *The Church in the Modern World* [*Gaudium et Spes*], the pastoral constitution recently issued by the Second Vatican Council.

Conjugal Love

8. Truly, conjugal love most clearly manifests to us its true nature and nobility when we recognize that it has its origin in the highest source, as it were, in God, Who "is Love"[6] and Who is the Father, "from whom all parenthood [*paternitas*] in heaven and earth receives its name."[7]

It is false to think, then, that marriage results from chance or from the blind course [*cursu*] of natural forces. Rather, God the Creator wisely and providently established marriage with the intent that He might achieve His own design of love through Men. Therefore, through mutual self-giving, which is unique [*propriam*] and exclusive to them, spouses seek a communion of persons [*personarum communionem*]. Through this communion, the spouses perfect each other so that they might share with God the task [*operam socient*][m] of procreating and educating new living beings.

Moreover, for the baptized, matrimony is endowed with such dignity that it is a sacramental sign of grace representing the union of Christ and His Church.

[6] Cf. 1 Jn. 4:8.
[7] Eph. 3:15.

[m] The phrase *cum Deo operam socient* is a bit peculiar. The Italian text speaks of the spouses being collaborators with God, as do several of the translations; others note that spouses "cooperate" with God. Again, I thought it important to note that *operam* is not the word for "work" but for "service." *Socient* means that there is a sharing of the service. This notion, again, is at the root of the word *munus* (mission), which refers to a task that God entrusts to others, needs them to do, and will help them to achieve.

Characteristics of Conjugal Love

9. When these matters are placed in the proper light, we can clearly see the characteristic marks and requirements of conjugal love. It is of the greatest importance to have an exact understanding of these.

First of all, [this] love is *human* and therefore both of the senses and of the spirit. For which reason, it is a product not only of natural instinct and inclinations [*affectuum*]; it also and primarily involves an act of free will. Through this act of free will [the spouses resolve] that their love will not only persevere through daily joys and sorrows but also increase. Therefore it is especially important that they become one in heart and soul, and that they obtain together their human perfection.

Next, this love is *total* [*pleno*]; that is, it is a very special form of personal friendship whereby the spouses generously share everything with each other without undue reservations and without concern for their selfish convenience. One who truly loves his spouse not only loves her for what he receives from her but also for her own sake. This he does joyfully, as he enriches [his beloved] with the gift of himself.[n]

Furthermore, conjugal love is both *faithful and exclusive* to the end of life. Such, in fact, do the bride and groom conceive it to be on the day of their marriage, when they freely and consciously [*planeque conscii*] unite themselves by means of the marital bond [*matrimoniali se vinculo devinxerunt*]. Even if fidelity at times presents difficulties, let no one deny that it is possible; [rather] fidelity is always noble and of much merit. The example of many spouses throughout the ages has proved that fidelity is in accord with the very nature of marriage; even more, it has proved

[n] The final sentence presents difficulties to the modern translator who works in an atmosphere where all masculine pronouns are taken to refer to the male. This is especially awkward when speaking of marriage, which clearly involves the reciprocal responsibilities of both sexes. The Latin easily includes the obligations of both sexes to each other, whereas it is impossible to convey this in modern-day English.

that intimate and lasting happiness flows from fidelity, just as from a fountain.

And finally, this love is *fruitful,* since the whole of the love is not contained in the communion of the spouses; it also looks beyond itself and seeks to raise up new lives. "Marriage and conjugal love are ordained [*ordinantur*] by their very nature [*indole sua*] to the procreating and educating of children. Offspring are clearly the supreme gift [*donum*] of marriage, a gift that contributes immensely to the good of the parents themselves."[8]

Responsible Parenthood

10. For the above reasons, conjugal love requires that spouses be fully aware of their mission [*munus*] of responsible parenthood [*paternitatem consciam*]. Today's society justly calls for responsible parenthood; thus it is important that it be rightly understood. Consequently, we must consider the various legitimate and interconnected dimensions [*rationibus*] of parenthood.

If we consider biological processes first, responsible parenthood [*paternitas conscia*] means that one knows and honors [*observantiam*] the responsibilities [*munerum*] involved in these processes.[o] Human reason has discovered that there are biological laws in the power of procreating life that pertain to the human person.[9]

If then we look to the innate impulses and inclinations of the

---

[8] Second Vatican Council, Pastoral Constitution, *Gaudium et Spes,* no. 50, in AAS 58 (1966) 1070–72.

[9] Cf. St. Thomas, *Summa Theologiae,* I–II, q. 94, a. 2.

[o] The phrase *munerum ad eos* [*biologicos processus*] *attinentium* is difficult to capture. *Munerum* is translated by DSP and IP and all the CTS versions as "functions," which seems to reflect the Italian *funzioni.* Durand (translating from the Latin) renders it "obligations associated with these [biological processes]." See also *Humanae Vitae* 17 for two other instances of forms of *munus* used in reference to physical processes.

soul, responsible parenthood asserts that it is necessary that reason and will exercise mastery over these impulses and inclinations of the soul.

If we look further to physical, economic, psychological, and social conditions, responsible parenthood is exercised by those who, guided by prudent consideration and generosity, elect to accept many children. Those are also to be considered responsible who, for serious reasons [*seriis causis*] and with due respect for moral precepts, decide not to have another child for either a definite or an indefinite amount of time.

The responsible parenthood of which we speak here has another intrinsic foundation [*intimam rationem*]P of utmost importance: it is rooted in the objective moral order established by God—and only an upright conscience can be a true interpreter of this order. For which reason, the mission [*munus*] of responsible parenthood requires that spouses recognize their duties [*officia*] toward God, toward themselves, toward the family, and toward human society, as they maintain a correct set of priorities.q

For this reason, in regard to the mission [*munere*] of transmitting human life, it is not right for spouses to act in accord with their own arbitrary judgment [*arbitratu suo*], as if it were permissible for them to define altogether subjectively and willfully [*modo ominino proprio ac libero*] what is right for them to do. On the contrary, they must accommodate their behavior to the plan of God the Creator, a plan made manifest both by the very nature of

---

P It is difficult to determine a literal reading of *intimam rationem* (it is used again in HV 12); perhaps "most profound justification" would serve; *ratio* has many legitimate translations. Following the Italian *un più profondo rapporto;* DSP and IP have "a more profound relationship." CTS1 and CST2 have "a further and deeper significance of paramount importance"; CTS3 has "one further essential aspect of paramount importance." Durand has "is chiefly characterized by another and intimate quality."

q This last phrase is translated a bit loosely. The Latin is *rerum bonorumque ordine recte servato,* which literally means "with the order of affairs and goods having been kept rightly." DSP and IP, following the Italian *in una giusta gerarchia dei valori,* have "in a correct hierarchy of values." All CTS versions have "keeping a right order of priorities," and Durand has "all in due order."

marriage and its acts and also by the constant teaching of the Church.[10]

Respect for the Nature and Finality of the Conjugal Act

11. The conjugal acts by which spouses intimately and chastely unite [*copulantur*], and by which human life is transmitted, are, as the recent council reiterated, "good and worthy of human dignity."[11] Conjugal acts do not cease being legitimate if the spouses are aware that they are infertile for reasons not voluntarily caused by them; these acts remain ordained [*destinatio*] to expressing and strengthening the union of the spouses. Indeed, as experience shows, new life does not arise from every act of conjugal union. God has wisely arranged the natural laws and times of fertility so that successive births are naturally spaced. But the Church, which interprets natural law through its unchanging doctrine, reminds men and women that the teachings based on natural law must be obeyed [*observandis*] and teaches that it is necessary that each conjugal act [*matrimonii usus*] remain ordained in itself [*per se destinatus*] to the procreating of human life.[12r]

[10] Cf. Second Vatican Council, Pastoral Constitution, *Gaudium et Spes*, nos. 50–51, in AAS 58 (1966) 1070–73.

[11] Cf. ibid., no. 49, in AAS 58 (1966) 1070.

[12] Cf. Pius XI, encyclical *Casti Connubii*, in AAS 22 (1930) 560; Pius XII, "Address to the Congress of the Italian Catholic Association of Midwives," in AAS 43 (1951) 843.

[r] There is little doubt that the last sentence of this section has caused translators the most difficulty. See Chapter 3 for a discussion of this sentence. The DSP translation reads, "[The Church] teaches that each and every marriage act must remain open to the transmission of life." The IP translation is identical to the DSP translation. CTS1 reads, "[The Church] teaches as absolutely required that *any use whatever of marriage* must retain its natural potential to procreate human life." CTS2 reads, "[The Church] teaches as absolutely required that *in any use whatever of marriage* there must be no impairment of its natural capacity to procreate human life." CTS3 reads, "[The Church] teaches that each and every marital act must of necessity retain its intrinsic relationship

Two Inseparable Aspects: Union and Procreation

12. The doctrine that the Magisterium of the Church has often explained is this: there is an unbreakable connection [*nexu indissolubili*] between the unitive meaning and the procreative meaning [of the conjugal act], and both are inherent in the conjugal act. This connection was established by God, and Man is not permitted to break it through his own volition.

Therefore, because of its intrinsic nature [*intimam rationem*][5] the conjugal act, which unites husband and wife with the closest of bonds, also makes them capable of bringing forth new life according to the laws written into their very natures as male and female. And if both essential meanings [*ratio*] are preserved, that of union and procreation, the conjugal act fully maintains its capacity for [fostering] true mutual love and its ordination to the highest mission [*munus*] of parenthood, to which Man is called. Men of our time, we think, are especially able to understand that this teaching is in accord with human reason.

Faithfulness to the Design of God

13. People rightly understand that a conjugal act imposed on a spouse, with no consideration given to the condition of the spouse or to the legitimate desires of the spouse, is not a true act of love. They understand that such an act opposes what the moral order rightly requires from spouses. To be consistent, then, if they reflect further, they should acknowledge that it is necessarily true that an act of mutual love that impairs the capacity of bringing

---

to the procreation of human life." And the Durand translation reads, "[The Church] teaches the following necessary principle: every single act of marriage must retain all of its natural potential to generate human life."

[5] In paragraph two of this section *intimam rationem* remains problematic. DSP and IP, following the Italian *intima struttura,* have "intimate structure." CTS1 and CTS2 have "fundamental structure," and CTS3 has "fundamental nature." Durand has "inherent structure."

forth life contradicts both the divine plan that established the nature [*normam*] of the conjugal bond and also the will of the first Author of human life. For this capacity of bringing forth life was designed by God, the Creator of All, according to [His] specific laws.

Thus, anyone who uses God's gift [of conjugal love] and cancels, if only in part, the significance and the purpose [*finem*] of this gift is rebelling [*repugnat*] against either the male or female nature and against the most intimate relationship [*intimae necessitudini*]; for this reason, then, he is defying the plan and holy will of God. On the other hand, the one who uses the gift of conjugal love in accord with the laws of generation acknowledges that he is not the lord of the sources of life but rather the minister [*ministerium*] of a plan initiated by the Creator.

In fact, Man does not have unlimited power over his own body in general. So, too, for good reason, he clearly does not have power over his generative faculties as such [*genitalium virium*], for they by their very nature are directed to bringing forth human life, and God is the source of human life. Indeed, "Human life must be recognized as sacred by all Men" as Our Predecessor John XXIII declared; "Indeed, from its very beginning it requires the creative action of God."[13]

Morally Impermissible Methods of Regulating Birth

14. Thus, relying on these first principles of human and Christian doctrine concerning marriage,[t] we must again insist [*edicere*]

---

[13] John XXIII, encyclical *Mater et Magistra* in AAS 53 (1961) 447.

[t] The Latin here reads *primariis hisce principiis*, or "first principles." The Italian reads *con questi capisaldi*, or "with this foundation stone." The English translations are disparate: DSP reads "landmarks," CTS2 uses "first principles," and IP uses "fundamental elements." "First principles" should be the preferred translation since it captures the technical philosophical sense of *principiis*. A proper inquiry must proceed from first principles; without agreement on these

that the direct interruption of the generative process already begun must be totally rejected as a legitimate means of regulating [*temperandi*] the number of children. Especially to be rejected is direct abortion—even if done for reasons of health.[14]

Furthermore, as the Magisterium of the Church has taught repeatedly, direct sterilization of the male or female, whether permanent or temporary, is equally to be condemned.[15]

Similarly there must be a rejection of all acts that attempt to impede procreation,[u] both those chosen as means to an end and those chosen as ends. This includes acts that precede intercourse, acts that accompany intercourse, and acts that are directed to the natural consequences of intercourse.[16]

Nor is it possible to justify deliberately depriving conjugal acts of their fertility by claiming that one is choosing the lesser evil. It

[14] Cf. *Catechismus Romanus Concilii Tridentini,* part 2, chap. 8; Pius XI, encyclical *Casti Connubii,* in AAS 22 (1930) 562–64; Pius XII, "Address to the Italian Medico-Biological Union of St. Luke," Nov. 12, 1944, in *Discorsi e Radiomessaggi di S.S. Pio XII,* 6, 191–92; Pius XII, "Address to the Italian Catholic Union of Midwives," in AAS 43 (1951) 842–43; Pius XII, "Address to the Congress of the Family Front and of the Association of Large Families," in AAS 43 (1951) 857–59; John XXIII, encyclical *Pacem in Terris,* Apr. 11, 1963, in AAS 55 (1963) 259–60; Second Vatican Council, Pastoral Constitution, *Gaudium et Spes,* 50, in AAS 58 (1966) 1072.

[15] Cf. Pius XI, encyclical *Casti Connubii,* in AAS 22 (1930) 565; Pius XII, Decree of the Holy Office, Feb. 22, 1940, in AAS 32 (1940) 73; Pius XII, "Address to the Italian Catholic Union of Midwives," in AAS 43 (1951) 843–44; Pius XII, "Address to the Seventh Congress of the International Society of Hematology," in AAS 50 (1958) 734–35.

[16] Cf. *Catechismus Romanus Concilii Tridentini,* pt. 2, chap. 8; Pius XI, *Casti Connubii,* in AAS 22 (1930) 559–61; Pius XII, "Address to the Italian Catholic Union of Midwives," in AAS 43 (1951) 843; Pius XII, "Address to the Seventh Congress of the International Society of Hematology," in AAS 50 (1958) 734–35; John XXIII, encyclical, *Mater et Magistra,* in AAS 53 (1961) 447.

---

principles, no progress can be made in reasoning about the matters which the principles undergird.

[u] For the phrase translated here as actions that attempt "to impede procreation," the Latin is *ut procreatio impediatur;* the Italian is *di rendere impossibile la procreazione.*

cannot be claimed that these acts deprived of fertility should be considered together as a whole with past and future fertile acts and thus that they [should be judged to] share in one and the same moral goodness of the fertile acts [of marriage]. Certainly, it is sometimes permissible to tolerate moral evil—when it is the lesser evil and when one does so in order that one might avoid a greater evil, or so that one might promote a greater good.[17] It is never permissible, however, to do evil so that good might result,[18] not even for the most serious reasons. That is, one should never willingly choose to do an act that by its very nature violates the moral order [*ex propria natura moralem ordinem transgrediatur*], for such acts are unworthy of Man for this very reason. This is so even if one has acted with the intent to defend and advance some good either for individuals or for families or for society. Thus, it is a serious error to think that a conjugal act, deprived deliberately [*ex industria*] of its fertility, and which consequently is intrinsically wrong [*intrinsece inhonestum*], can be justified by being grouped together with the fertile acts of the whole of the marriage.

Morally Permissible Therapeutic Means

15. The Church, moreover, does allow the use of medical treatment necessary for curing diseases of the body although this treatment may thwart one's ability to procreate. Such treatment is permissible even if the reduction of fertility is foreseen, as long as the infertility is not directly intended for any reason whatsoever.[19][v]

[17] Cf. Pius XII, "Address to the Fifth National Congress of Italian Catholic Jurists," Dec. 6, 1953, in AAS 45 (1953) 798–99.

[18] Cf. Rom. 3:8.

[19] Cf. Pope Pius XII, "Address to the Congress of the Italian Association of Urology," Oct. 8, 1953, in AAS 45 (1953) 674–75; Pius XII, "Address to the

[v] This is a short but important paragraph. I decided to cast the principle here in the positive rather than the negative. It may also be important to note that whereas most translators prefer "licit" and "illicit," which are cognates of the Latin, I have chosen to use "morally permissible" and "morally wrong."

The Morality of Recourse to the Infertile Period

16. Nevertheless, there are some in our times who oppose the teaching of the Church concerning conjugal morality, as we noted above (HV 3). [They claim] that it is the right and function [*munus*] of human reason to restrain the irrational forces of nature and to direct them to achieving ends that are beneficial to Man. Now some may ask: in the present day, is it not reasonable to use artificial birth control in many circumstances? Suppose family peace and harmony might better be achieved and better provisions might be made for educating the children already born? This question deserves a clear answer: the Church, of course, is the first to praise and commend the use of the human intellect in an endeavor that allies Man, rational creature that he is, so closely with his Creator. But the Church affirms that this must be done in accord with the order of reality [*rerum ordine*] established by God.

Certainly, there may be serious reasons [*iustae causae*] for spacing offspring[w]; these may be based on the physical or psychological condition of the spouses or on external factors. The Church teaches that [in such cases] it is morally permissible [for spouses] to calculate [their fertility by observing the] natural rhythms inherent in the generative faculties and to reserve marital intercourse for infertile times. Thus spouses are able to plan their families without violating the moral teachings set forth above.[20]

The Church is not inconsistent when it teaches both that it is morally permissible for spouses to have recourse to infertile periods

---

Seventh Congress of the International Society of Hematology," in AAS 50 (1958) 734–35.

[20] Pius XII, "Address to the Italian Catholic Union of Midwives," in AAS 43 (1951) 846.

[w] The Italian speaks of *seri motivi* for spacing children, whereas the Latin speaks of *iustae causae;* the translations that have been given for this are "serious motives," "well-grounded reasons," and "reasonable grounds." (See Chapter 4 for a discussion of the morality of the use of natural family planning.) For the most part the Italian for this passage is much more translatable than the Latin.

and also that all directly contraceptive practices are morally wrong, even if spouses seem to have good and serious reasons [*argumenta...honesta et gravia*] for using these. These two situations are essentially different. In the first, the spouses legitimately use a faculty that is given by nature; in the second case, the spouses impede the order of generation [*ordo generationis*] from completing its own natural processes.[x]

It cannot be denied that the spouses in each case have, for defensible reasons [*probabiles rationes*], made a mutual and firm decision to avoid having a child; and [it cannot be denied that] each of them is attempting to ensure that a child will not be born. Nevertheless, it must also be acknowledged that only in the first case are the spouses strong enough to abstain from sexual intercourse during the fertile times, when, for good reasons [*iustae rationes*], offspring are not desired. And then, when the time is not apt for conception, they make use of intercourse for the sake of manifesting their mutual love and for the sake of maintaining their promised fidelity. Clearly when they do this, they offer a witness to truly and completely upright [*recti*] love.

Serious Consequences of the Use of Artificial Methods of Birth Control

17. Responsible individuals will quickly see the truth of the Church's teaching [about contraception], if they consider what consequences will follow from the methods of contraception and the reasons given [*vias rationesque*] for the use of contraception.[y] They

[x] There are some interesting discrepancies between the Italian and the Latin in this paragraph. One choice of Latin seems to be inappropriate; where the Italian states, "the two cases are essentially different" ("Tra i due casi esiste una differenza essenziale"), the Latin reads, "these two causes differ exceedingly" ("hae duae causae inter se maxime discrepant"). The meaning of *causae* (reasons, motives, purposes, sources) does not seem appropriate here; it seems that *casus* (cases) is what is needed, and "essentially" seems somewhat more precise than "exceedingly."

[y] The second portion of this first sentence is translated variously. The Latin is *quae secutura sunt vias rationesque, ad natorum incrementa artificio coercenda*

should first consider how easy it will be [for many] to justify behavior leading to marital infidelity or to a gradual weakening in the discipline of morals.[z] Not much experience is needed to understand human weakness and to comprehend that human beings, especially the young, are so susceptible to temptation that they need to be encouraged to keep the moral law. It is wrong to make it easy for them to violate this law. Indeed, it is to be feared that husbands who become accustomed to contraceptive practices will lose respect for their wives. They may come to disregard their wives' psychological and physical equilibrium and use their wives as instruments for serving their own desires. Consequently, they will no longer view their wives as companions who should be treated with attentiveness and love.

And then [let reasonable individuals] also carefully consider that a dangerous power will be put into the hands of rulers who care little about the moral law. Would anyone blame those in the highest offices of the state for employing a solution [contraception] considered morally permissible for spouses seeking to solve a family difficulty, when they strive to solve certain difficulties affecting the whole nation? Who will prevent public authorities from favoring what they believe to be the most effective contraceptive methods and from mandating that everyone must use them, whenever they consider it necessary? And clearly it will come about that Men who desire to avoid the difficulties that are part of the divine law, difficulties that individuals, families, or

---

adhibitas. CTS1 and CTS2 have "the consequences of methods and plans for the artificial restriction of increases in the birth rate"; the other (IP), based on the Italian text (*alle conseguenze dei metodi di regolazione artificiale delle natalità*) is "consequences of the use of methods of artificial birth control." Although abortion may also be intended to be included here, it seems that contraception is the issue at hand and it would be the most succinct and accurate translation.

[z] The translation of this sentence has generally relied on the Italian (*allo abbassamento generale della moralità*). Most translations render this "a general lowering of morality." The Latin is, *ad morum disciplinam passim enervandam,* which literally means "to a little by little weakening of the discipline of habits."

society may experience, will hand over to the will of the public authorities the power of interfering in the most exclusive and intimate mission [*munus*] of spouses.

Therefore, if we do not want the mission [*officium*] of procreating human life to be conceded to the arbitrary decisions of Men, we need to recognize that there are some limits to the power of Man over his own body and over the natural operations [*munera*] of the body, which ought not to be transgressed. No one, neither a private individual nor a public authority, ought to violate these limits. For these limits are derived from the reverence owed to the whole human body and its natural operations [*naturalibus muneribus*], according to the principles acknowledged above and according to a proper understanding of the so-called principle of totality, as explained by Our Predecessor, Pius XII.[21]

The Church, the Guarantor of Authentic Human Values

18. It is possible to predict that perhaps not everyone will be able to accept a teaching of this sort easily. After all, there are so many critical voices—broadcast widely by modern means of communication—that are contrary to the voice of the Church. Therefore, it is not surprising that the Church finds herself a *sign of contradiction*[22]—just as was [Christ,] her Founder. But this is no reason for the Church to abandon the duty entrusted to her of preaching the whole moral law firmly and humbly, both the natural law and the law of the Gospel.

Since the Church did not make either of these laws, she cannot change them. She can only be their guardian and interpreter; thus it would never be right for her to declare as morally permissible

---

[21] Cf. Pius XII, "Address to the Congress of the Italian Association of Urology," in AAS 45 (1953) 674–75; Pius XII, "Address to the Directors and Members of the Italian Association of Cornea Donors and of the Italian Association of the Blind," May 14, 1956, in AAS 48 (1956) 461–62.

[22] Lk. 2:34.

that which is truly not so. For what is immoral is by its very nature always opposed to the true good of Man.

By preserving the whole moral law of marriage, the Church knows that she is supporting the growth of a true civilization among Men. She encourages Man not to abdicate human duties by overreliance on technology. In this way, she safeguards the dignity of spouses. Devoted to the example and teaching of the Divine Savior, the Church shows her sincere and generous love for Men as she strives to help them, even during their earthly pilgrimage, "to share, as sons [and daughters], the life of the living God, the Father of all Men."[23]

PART 3. PASTORAL DIRECTIVES

The Church as Mother and Teacher

19. We would hardly be adequately expressing the thoughts and solicitude of the Church, the Mother and Teacher of all nations, if after encouraging Men to keep and respect the law[s] of God concerning marriage, We did not also offer them support in morally permissible methods of regulating their family size; [after all,] ours is a time when families and nations face harsh conditions. But the Church can only conduct herself as did the Divine Redeemer; she knows mankind's weakness; she has compassion on the multitude, and she forgives their sins. She cannot, however, do otherwise than to teach the law that is proper to human life restored to its original truth and guided by the Spirit of God.[24]

[23] Paul VI, encyclical *Populorum Progressio,* Mar. 26, 1967, no. 21, in AAS 59 (1967) 268.
[24] Cf. Rom. 8.

The Possibility of Observing the Divine Law

20. The teaching of the Church about the proper spacing of children is a promulgation of the divine law itself. No doubt many will think this teaching difficult, if not impossible, to keep. And truly, just as with all good things outstanding for their nobility and utility, [keeping] this law requires strong motivation and much effort from individual Men, from families, and from society. Indeed, this law is not able to be kept without the abundant grace of God, on which the good moral choices [*bona voluntas*] of Men depend and from which they get their strength. Moreover, those who consider this matter thoroughly will see that [their] efforts [to keep God's law] increase human dignity and confer benefits on human society.

Self-Mastery

21. Moral family planning requires that spouses recognize and value the true goods of life and the family and also that they acquire the habit of complete mastery of themselves and their desires [*motibus*]. In order to control the drives of nature, the spouses need to become self-denying [*asceseos*] through using their reason and free will. Only then will the manifestations of love appropriate for married couples be what they ought to be. Self-mastery is especially necessary for those who practice periodic abstention.

Truly, discipline of this sort—from which conjugal chastity shines forth—cannot be an obstacle to love. Rather, discipline imbues love with a deeper human meaning. Although [such control] requires continuous effort, it also helps the spouses become strong in virtue and makes them rich with spiritual goods. And this [virtue] fosters the fruits of tranquility and peace in the home and helps in the solving of difficulties of other kinds. It aids spouses in becoming more tender with each other and more attentive to each other. It assists them in dispelling that inordinate self-love that is opposed to true charity. It strengthens in them an awareness of their responsibilities [*munerum exsequendorum*]. And finally it provides parents with a sure and efficacious authority for educating their children. As [their] children advance through life they will come to a correct appreciation of the true goods of Man and employ peacefully and properly the powers of their mind and senses.

Creating an Atmosphere Favorable to Chastity

22. We would like to take this opportunity to advise educators and all others whose right and duty it is to be concerned about the common good. They need to work to create conditions favorable to the cultivation of chastity, so that the norms of the moral order might be kept and true freedom might prevail over license.

Therefore, all those who are concerned with improving civilization and all who wish to protect the most important human goods should condemn with one voice all the forms of entertainment in today's modern society that arouse Man's [base] passions and that foster dissolute morals, such as obscene literature and corrupt theatrical and film productions. It would be perverse if anyone were to attempt to defend depravity of this kind by appealing to the needs of art or learning[25] or by appealing to arguments of "freedom of expression" concerning what authorities may permit in the public arena.

Appeal to Public Authorities

23. And We must also address the rulers of nations, since they have chief responsibility for the common good and are able to work toward safeguarding good morals. [We say to them:] Do not

[25] Cf. Second Vatican Council, Decree *Inter Mirifica,* Dec. 4, 1963, nos. 6–7, in AAS 56 (1964) 147.

allow the worthy morals of your own people to be corrupted; do not allow the law to be used to introduce into the family—that primary unit of the state—practices opposed to the natural and divine law. For surely civil authority can find and ought to use other means to resolve the problem of the increase of population: namely, they should legislate laws protective of the family and they should wisely educate the populace to safeguard both the moral law and the [true] liberty of the citizens.

Indeed We know well what a source of great difficulty [overpopulation is] for leaders of a state, especially in the developing nations. Indeed, We had these justifiable concerns in mind when We issued the encyclical letter *Populorum Progressio*. But here let Us reiterate the words of Our Predecessor, John XXIII: "It is necessary to solve these problems in such a way that Man does not use methods and means opposed to the dignity of Man. [State authorities] ought not to fear rejecting [the views] of those who hold that Man himself and his life are in every respect only material realities. We think this problem ought to be resolved only through economic and social progress that both respects each and every individual and the whole of society and that also increases goods deserving of the name."[26] Truly it would be a grave injustice to attribute to Divine Providence what seems, on the contrary, to be the result of unwise government policies, or of a rather weak sense of social justice, or of a hoarding of goods for one's selfish use, or finally of a careless negligence in undertaking the labors and tasks by which every people and all their offspring achieve a better standard of living.[27] Certainly some authorities have already begun to renew impressive efforts in regard to these matters; all authorities should energetically join these efforts. All members of the great human family should increase their zeal for coming to one another's assistance; [indeed] We think the opportunity for involvement by international aid organizations is nearly unbounded.

[26] John XXIII, encyclical *Mater et Magistra,* in AAS 53 (1961), 447.

[27] Paul VI, encyclical *Populorum Progressio,* Mar. 26, 1967, no. 21, in AAS 59 (1967) 281–84.

Appeal to Men of Science

24. Let Us also encourage scientists, who "are able to do much for the good of marriage and family and are able to assist peace of conscience if with their united efforts they attempt to clarify the conditions which favor a moral ordering of human procreation."[28] This ought especially to be hoped for—a request made earlier by Pius XII—that medical science, through the observation of natural cycles [of fertility], strive to establish a satisfactorily clear basis for the moral regulation of offspring.[29] In this way scientists— and especially those who proudly claim to be Catholic—will make it clear through their own work that, as the Church teaches, "No true contradiction exists between the divine laws for transmitting life and those for fostering true conjugal love."[30]

Appeal to Christian Spouses

25. Now Our attention must be directed in a particular way to Our sons and daughters and especially to those whom God calls to serve Him in the state of matrimony. For the Church, who teaches the inviolable conditions of the divine law, also proclaims salvation and through the sacraments unlocks the sources of grace. [For it is by these means that] Man is made a new creature who responds with charity and true liberty to the heavenly plan of his Creator and Savior and who finds the yoke of Christ to be sweet.[31]

Therefore, let Christian spouses humbly obey the voice of the

[28] Second Vatican Council, Pastoral Constitution, *Gaudium et Spes,* no. 52, in AAS 58 (1966) 1074.

[29] Cf. Pius XII, "Address to the Congress of the Family Front and of the Association of Large Families," in AAS 43 (1951) 859.

[30] Second Vatican Council, Pastoral Constitution, *Gaudium et Spes,* no. 51, in AAS 58 (1966) 1072.

[31] Cf. Mt. 11:30.

Church and remember that their proper vocation [*vocationem*] in the Christian life began with baptism and was more fully specified and confirmed anew with the sacrament of marriage. For by the sacrament of marriage spouses are strengthened and, as it were, consecrated so that they might faithfully fulfill their duties [*munia*], so that they might bring their vocation [*vocationem*] to its perfect end and so that, as befits them, they might openly offer the world a Christian witness.[32] To them the Lord entrusts [*committit*] the mission [*munus*] of making manifest to Men the holiness and indeed sweetness of the law that unites their mutual love and generous service [*adiutrice opera*] closely to the love of God, the author of human life.

Certainly We do not wish to ignore the difficulties, the sometimes serious difficulties, that Christian spouses might encounter, since for them, as for everyone, "the gate is narrow, and the way is difficult that leads to life."[33] Nevertheless their way will be illuminated by the hope of this life, just as by the clearest light, as long as they strive courageously "to live wisely and justly and piously in this world,"[34] knowing that "the form of this world passes away."[35]

Therefore, let spouses willingly take up the labors that have been assigned [*destinatos*] to them, strengthened both by faith and by hope, which "do not disappoint: because the charity of God is poured into our hearts through the Holy Spirit who is given to us."[36] Let them constantly pray for divine assistance. And let them especially drink of grace and charity from the eternal font of the Eucharist. If, however, they are hampered by their sins, let them not lose heart, but let them humbly and constantly flee to the mercy of God, which the sacrament of penance abundantly

[32] Cf. Second Vatican Council, Pastoral Constitution, *Gaudium et Spes*, no. 48, in AAS 58 (1966) 1067–69; Dogmatic Constitution *Lumen Gentium*, no. 35, in AAS 57 (1965) 40–41.

[33] Mt. 7:14; cf. Heb. 12:11.

[34] Cf. Tit. 2:12.

[35] Cf. 1 Cor. 7:31.

[36] Rom. 5:5.

provides. It is by this way of life that spouses will be able to advance toward perfection in their married life, which the Apostle explains in these words: "Husbands love your wives, just as Christ loved the Church. . . . Therefore also husbands ought to love their wives as their own bodies. For he who loves his wife, loves himself. Indeed, no one is able to hate his own flesh; but he nourishes it and cares for it, as Christ does for the Church. . . . And this is true for each and every one of you: let everyone love his wife as he loves himself; and let wives respect their husbands."[37]

Apostolate of Spouses

26. Moreover, great fruits are to be expected when the divine law is kept by a devout soul. The most outstanding of these fruits results from the frequent desire of spouses to share their experience with other spouses. Thus it happens that a new and especially worthy kind of apostolate is added to the already ample vocation of the laity: like will minister to like. That is, spouses fulfill their apostolic mission [munus] in behalf of other spouses by becoming guides for them. Among all the forms of Christian apostolate this apostolate seems most suitable today.[38]

To Doctors and Health Care Professionals

27. Let Us express Our highest admiration for doctors and those health professionals who, in performing their mission [munus], desire to safeguard what is compatible with their Christian voca-

---

[37] Eph. 5:25, 28–29, 32–33.

[38] Cf. Second Vatican Council, Dogmatic Constitution *Lumen Gentium*, Nov. 21, 1964, no. 35, 41, in AAS 57 (1965) 40–45. [Father Calegari persuasively argues that AAS pages for *Lumen Gentium* should be 40–41 and 45–47.] Pastoral Constitution *Gaudium et Spes*, 48–49, in AAS 58 (1966) 1067–70; Decree, *Apostolicam Actuositatem*, Nov. 18, 1965, no. 11, in AAS 58 (1966) 847–49.

tion rather than what corresponds to some human advantage [*utilitatem*]. Therefore let them constantly pursue only those solutions that are in accord with faith and right reason. And let them strive to gain the agreement and the compliance [*observationem*] of their colleagues in this matter. Moreover, let them consider it their special mission [*munus*] to acquire all necessary learning in this difficult area. Thereby they may be able to give good advice to spouses seeking their counsel and to direct them along the right path. Spouses rightly seek such direction from them.

To Priests

28. With complete confidence We call upon you priests, Our beloved sons, you who are the advisers and spiritual guides of individuals and families. For it is your great and manifest mission [*munere*] —and We address especially those of you who are moral theologians—to promote completely and clearly the teaching of the Church concerning marriage. In performing your ministry you must be an example of the sincere obedience [*obsequii*] that must be given both inwardly and outwardly to the Magisterium of the Church. For truly, you know that you are bound to such obedience [*obsequio*] not only for the reasons given [in behalf of a teaching] but also on account of the light of the Holy Spirit, whose guidance the Fathers of the Church particularly enjoy when setting forth the truth.[39] Nor let it escape you that it is of the utmost importance for safeguarding the peace of souls and the unity of the Christian people, that in moral as in dogmatic matters, all should obey the Magisterium of the Church and should speak with one voice. Wherefore, adopting the anxious words of the great Apostle Paul, We call upon you again with Our whole heart: "I beg . . . you brothers through the name of our Lord Jesus Christ: that you might all speak as one and that there might be no

[39] Cf. Second Vatican Council, Dogmatic Constitution *Lumen Gentium*, no. 25, in AAS 57 (1965) 29–31.

division among you: that you may be united in the same mind and the same judgment."[40]

29. Refusal to compromise anything concerning the saving doctrine of Christ is an outstanding act of charity to souls; yet at the same time it is necessary always to combine this with tolerance and charity. When He spoke and associated with Men, the Redeemer Himself exemplified this truth. Coming not to judge the world but to save it, He was severe against sin but patient and merciful to sinners.[41]

Therefore, let spouses in their times of trouble find in the speech and hearts of their priests the image of the voice and love of our Redeemer.

So Beloved Sons, preach with full confidence and be certain that the Holy Spirit of God, who guides the Magisterium in its teaching, will illuminate the hearts of the faithful and invite them to give their assent. Teach spouses the indispensability of prayer; instruct them properly so that they may come regularly and with great faith to the sacraments of the Eucharist and of penance and that they may never become discouraged because of their weakness.

To Bishops

30. Now, at the conclusion of this encyclical letter, Our mind reverently and lovingly turns to you [Bishops], beloved and venerable Brothers in the episcopal mission [munus]; with you We share very closely the care of the spiritual good of the people of God. We make this urgent request of you: We ask all of you to take the lead with the priests who assist your sacred ministry and all your faithful. With complete zeal and no delay, devote yourselves to keeping marriage safe and holy, so that the life of married couples may draw more closely to its proper human and Christian perfection. Truly consider this as the greatest responsibility [opus]

[40] I Cor. 1:10.
[41] Cf. Jn. 3:17.

of your mission [*munus*] and the greatest work [*onus*] committed to you at the present time. As you well know, [your] mission [*munus*] requires a certain coordination of pastoral ministry in all areas of human activity, including economic, social, and cultural matters. If progress is gained on all these fronts at the same time, then not only will family life of parents and children be more tolerable, it will be easier and happier. Once the plan God conceived for the world is faithfully kept, fellowship in society will be richer in fraternal charity and more safely grounded in a true peace.

FINAL APPEAL

31. Venerable Brothers, most beloved sons, and all men and women of goodwill, We now call you to the splendid work of education and growth in charity. Relying on the unshakable [*firmissima*] teaching of the Church, We, as the successor to Peter together with the whole Brotherhood of Bishops, faithfully guard and interpret it. Truly this is a great work, for it affects the good of the world and the Church. None can achieve true happiness, the happiness that they desire with the strength of their whole soul, unless they observe the laws inscribed on their nature by the Most High God. To be happy Man must prudently and lovingly cultivate these laws. Therefore, on this important work and on all of you and most especially on married couples, We invoke a wealth of supernatural graces given by our most holy and merciful God. As a pledge of these graces, We freely give you Our Apostolic blessing.

Given at Rome, from St. Peter's on the twenty-fifth day of July, on the feast of James the Apostle, in the year 1968, the sixth year of Our Pontificate.

Pope Paul VI

INDEX

Blessed Are the Pure of Heart,
196n, 233
body, 233, 239, 507, *see also*
language of the body
depersonalization, 258–59
dominion over, 527–28
dualism of person, 216–24,
411–12
nuptial meaning, 216–24,
452
theology of, 234–37
Boethius, 22n, 200, 208
Botero, Giovanni, 387
Boyle, Joseph, 513–14
Brunner, August, 30–31n, 33n
Burtchaell, James T., 334–35n,
336, 338

Caffarel, Henri, 86, 97n, 102–3
Calegari, Marc, 85, 330n
Calvin, John, 295
Canticle of Canticles, 49–51,
60
Canticle of Leibowitz, 11
Casti connubii, 47, 346, 503–5,
511
*Catechism of the Council of
Trent, The,* 378
"Catholic Teaching on Con-
traception and Sterilization",
26n
celibacy, 31, 125, 145, *see also*
chastity
Cervantes, Lucius F., 28n, 31–
32n
Challenge of Peace, The, 377

chastity, 124–25
in marriage, 31, 43, 99, 417,
470
Christian standards,
141–46
and contraception, 125–
32
as ideal, 301–2, 494
Chesterton, G. K., 517
China, 383, 388, 394, 401, 463,
527
Christian Moral Principles, 375n
Church, 96, 146, 19 8-99, *see
also* magisterium
accusations,
biologism, 155, 160, 253
physicalism, 18, 253, 413,
510–11
artificial fertilization, 167–
69
authority, 363–80, 427
Christian morality, 11–12,
121–25, 133–39
conscience formation,
363–80
contraception teachings,
42–43
breach of chastity, 125–
32
historical background,
503–13, 519–20
infallibility, 343–61
moral evil, 12, 132–39
Scripture, 20–21
infallibility, charism of, 346,
358, 360